Briefs of Leading Cases in Law Enforcement

Briefs of Leading Cases in Law Enforcement, Tenth Edition, offers extensive updates on the leading Supreme Court cases impacting law enforcement in the United States, creating a must-have reference for police officers to stay up-to-date and have a strong understanding of the law and their function within it. All cases are briefed in a common format to allow for comparisons among cases and include facts, relevant issues, and the Court's decision and reasoning. The significance of each case is also explained, making clear its impact on citizens and law enforcement. The book provides students and practitioners with historical and social context for their role in criminal justice and the legal guidelines that should be followed in day-to-day policing activities.

Rolando V. del Carmen retired in May 2011 as Distinguished Professor of Criminal Justice (Law) in the College of Criminal Justice, Sam Houston State University. He has authored numerous books and articles in various areas of law related to criminal justice. He has won all three major awards given by the Academy of Criminal Justice Sciences, has taught numerous graduate and undergraduate classes in law, and has been a mentor and friend to many of his students. And he is terribly missed by all who knew him.

Jeffery T. Walker is a professor and Chair of the Department of Criminal Justice at the University of Alabama, Birmingham. Dr. Walker has written 10 books and almost 100 journal articles and book chapters. He has obtained over $15 million in grants from the Department of Justice, National Institute of Drug Abuse, National Science Foundation, Center for Disease Control, and others. His areas of interest are social/environmental factors of neighborhoods, legal issues of policing, and crime mapping/crime analysis. He is a past President of the Academy of Criminal Justice Sciences. Editorial experience includes service as Editor of the *Journal of Criminal Justice Education*. Previous publications include articles in *Justice Quarterly*, and *Journal of Quantitative Criminology*, and the books *Legal Guide for Police* (Eleventh Edition) and *Foundations of Crime Analysis*. Walker also served as a Special Agent with the Air Force Office of

Special Investigations (AFOSI), conducting major felony crime investigations. In September 2001 he was mobilized to provide counterintelligence, protective services, and force protection support to military personnel in the US and overseas locations. His final assignment was Superintendent of Counterintelligence Investigations at Headquarters/AFOSI in Washington, DC.

Briefs of Leading Cases in Law Enforcement

Tenth Edition

Rolando V. del Carmen

Jeffery T. Walker

Routledge
Taylor & Francis Group

NEW YORK AND LONDON

Tenth edition published 2020
by Routledge
52 Vanderbilt Avenue, New York, NY 10017

and by Routledge
2 Park Square, Milton Park, Abingdon, Oxon, OX14 4RN

Routledge is an imprint of the Taylor & Francis Group, an informa business

First edition published by Anderson Publishing Co. 2001
Ninth edition published by Routledge 2015

Library of Congress Cataloging-in-Publication Data
Names: Del Carmen, Rolando V., author. | Walker, Jeffery T.,
author.
Title: Briefs of leading cases in law enforcement / Rolando V. del
Carmen & Jeffery T. Walker.
Description: Tenth edition. | Milton Park, Abingdon, Oxon ;
New York, NY : Routledge, 2020. | Includes index.
Identifiers: LCCN 2019015169 (print) | LCCN 2019018277 (ebook) |
ISBN 9780429053139 (Ebook) | ISBN 9780367146900 (hardback) |
ISBN 9780367146924 (pbk.) | ISBN 9780429053139 (ebk)
Subjects: LCSH: Criminal procedure–United States–Digests. |
Law enforcement–United States–Digests. | Searches and seizures–
United States–Digests.
Classification: LCC KF9610.3 (ebook) | LCC KF9610.3 .D45 2020
(print) | DDC 345.73/05–dc23
LC record available at https://lccn.loc.gov/2019015169

ISBN: 978-0-367-14690-0 (hbk)
ISBN: 978-0-367-14692-4 (pbk)
ISBN: 978-0-429-05313-9 (ebk)

Typeset in Times New Roman
by Swales & Willis, Exeter, Devon, UK
Printed by CPI Group (UK) Ltd, Croydon CR0 4YY

Visit the eResources: www.routledge.com/9780367146924

This edition—and all editions of this book past and future—are dedicated to Dr. Rolando del Carmen. Here, I want to say a few words about what he meant to me. When I finally figured out what I wanted to do with my life, Dr. del Carmen went to bat for me to get me into the PhD program at Sam Houston. He also got me a top fellowship, which I desperately needed. Most importantly, he adopted me as his graduate assistant. One day in the spring of my first year of the program, he came to me and said "we are going to write a book." WE! What? I am just a first-year doctoral student. You want me to co-author a book? Most of the people in the program were begging to get fourth author on an article. There were people in the program with law degrees. Why would he want me to co-author a book with him? But that was Rolando (it took me years after I graduated to not call him Dr. del Carmen). That was this book. I learned more from him about the intricacies of criminal law while writing the book than most people do in top law schools (proven multiple times). Of course, I was head strong. We argued for weeks about whether Brewer v. Williams *was a Fifth Amendment or Sixth Amendment case. In the end, we compromised and put it in two places in the book. And I am only one of many students who had the privilege of being mentored by Rolando. He was a one of a kind. If I can be half the mentor he was, I will consider myself a success regardless of what else I accomplish. That was nine editions ago. Over the years, Rolando let me do more of the book writing without his input. But this is the first edition I have had to do by myself. It is sobering and humbling. I just hope I can do Dr. del Carmen proud.*

This edition is for you Dr. del Carmen.

Contents

Preface to the Tenth Edition

This Tenth Edition of the book contains additions of cases and has undergone some rearranging (moving the chapter on What Constitutes Interrogation for *Miranda* Purposes before the other *Miranda* chapters). Following on the extensive revisions of cases in the two last editions, this edition has more minor revisions of adding important cases and making sure the book stays on topic for police officers in their everyday actions. As with all versions of the book, this edition adds the significant cases that were decided by the Supreme Court since the last printing. The cutoff date for this edition is June 15, 2018. Cases decided after that date will be included in the next edition.

Eight new cases were added to this edition. Classified according to the chapters, these cases are:

- In Chapter 3, covering Stop and Frisk: *Utah v. Strieff*
- In Chapter 5, covering Seizures of Things: *Birchfield v. North Dakota*
- In Chapter 9, covering Vehicle Stops and Searches: *Byrd v. U.S.*
- In Chapter 14, covering Searches by Dogs: *Rodriguez v. U.S.*
- In Chapter 15, covering Computer and Cell Phone Searches: *Carpenter v. U.S.*, *Packingham v. U.S.*
- In Chapter 16, covering Use of Force: *County of Los Angeles, California, et al. v. Mendez, et al.*
- In Chapter 18, covering Confessions and Admissions: Cases Affirming *Miranda*: *Montejo v. Louisiana*.

The original decisions of the United States Supreme Court in these cases are readily available in various ways, particularly on the Internet. To find these cases, go to the Supreme Court's Web site at www.supremecourtus.gov and click on "Opinions," then the year of the decision. If more research is desired on a case, use the LexisNexis Web site or conduct Internet searches for the desired cases. Any in-depth research should also include examining articles and comments from law review journals.

As in the past, the authors welcome suggestions and comments for improvement.

Rolando V. del Carmen
Distinguished Professor of Criminal Justice
Sam Houston State University, Huntsville

Jeffery T. Walker
Professor of Criminal Justice
University of Alabama, Birmingham

List of Top 10 Cases in Day-to-Day Policing

There are so many cases in policing, the question often arises regarding which are the most important. If a person could only choose 10 cases to examine, which would those be? Included in this edition is a list of what we consider to be the top 10 cases most influencing day-to-day policing in the United States. They are listed in reverse order, along with their holding.

10. *Brewer v. Williams*, 430 U.S. 387 (1977)
    Under the *Miranda* rule, interrogations can be "actual" (as when questions are asked) or the "functional equivalent" thereof.
9. *Illinois v. Gates*, 462 U.S. 213 (1983)
    The two-pronged test for probable cause established in previous cases is abandoned in favor of the "totality of circumstances" test.
8. *United States v. Ross*, 456 U.S. 798 (1982)
    When making a valid search of a car, the police may search the entire car and open the trunk and any packages or luggage found therein that could reasonably contain the items for which they have probable cause to search.
7. *Riley v. California*, 573 U.S. 373 (2014)
    "The police generally may not, without a warrant, search digital information on a cell phone seized from an individual who has been arrested."
6. *Tennessee v. Garner*, 471 U.S. 1 (1985)
    The police may not use deadly force to prevent the escape of a suspect unless it is necessary and the officer has probable cause to believe that the suspect poses a significant threat of death or serious physical injury to the officer or to others.
5. *Chimel v. California*, 395 U.S. 752 (1969)
    After an arrest, police may search the area within a person's immediate control.
4. *Carroll v. United States*, 267 U.S. 132 (1925)
    The warrantless search of an automobile is valid if probable cause is present.
3. *Terry v. Ohio*, 392 U.S. 1 (1968)
    A stop and frisk based on reasonable suspicion is valid.
2. *Mapp v. Ohio*, 367 U.S. 643 (1961)
    The exclusionary rule applies to all state criminal proceedings.
1. *Miranda v. Arizona*, 384 U.S. 436 (1966)
    Evidence obtained by the police during custodial interrogation of a suspect is not admissible in court to prove guilt unless the suspect was given the *Miranda* warnings and there is a valid waiver.

List of Cases with Principle (Capsule) of Law

Chapter 1: Probable Cause

Draper v. United States, 358 U.S. 307 (1959) **2**
  Information from an informant that is corroborated by an officer may be sufficient to provide probable cause for an arrest even if such information is hearsay.

Illinois v. Gates, 462 U.S. 213 (1983) **3**
  The two-pronged test for probable cause established in previous cases is abandoned in favor of the "totality of circumstances" test.

United States v. Sokolow, 490 U.S. 1 (1989) **4**
  The totality of circumstances can establish a reasonable suspicion, sufficient for officers to make an investigative stop without a warrant.

Devenpeck v. Alford, 543 U.S. 146 (2004) **5**
  The Fourth Amendment does not require the offense establishing probable cause for an arrest to be "closely related" to and based on the same conduct as the offense identified by the officer during the initial encounter.

Chapter 2: The Exclusionary Rule

Weeks v. United States, 232 U.S. 383 (1914) **10**
  Evidence seized by federal law enforcement officers in violation of the Fourth Amendment is not admissible in a federal criminal prosecution.

Rochin v. California, 342 U.S. 165 (1952) **11**
  Some searches are so "shocking to the conscience" that they require exclusion of the evidence seized based on due process.

Mapp v. Ohio, 367 U.S. 643 (1961) **11**
  The exclusionary rule applies to all state criminal proceedings.

Wong Sun v. United States, 371 U.S. 471 (1963) **12**
  Evidence obtained as a result of illegal acts by the police must be excluded. In addition, the "fruit of the poisonous tree" of that illegal act must also be excluded. Evidence that has been purged of the primary taint, however, is admissible.

United States v. Hensley, 469 U.S. 221 (1985) **30**
Reasonable suspicion based on a "wanted poster" is sufficient for a valid stop.

United States v. Sharpe, 470 U.S. 675 (1985) **31**
There is no rigid time limit for the length of an investigatory stop; instead, specific circumstances should be taken into account.

Alabama v. White, 496 U.S. 325 (1990) **32**
Reasonable suspicion is a less demanding standard than probable cause, and can be based on an anonymous tip corroborated by independent police work.

Minnesota v. Dickerson, 508 U.S. 366 (1993) **34**
A frisk that goes beyond that allowed in *Terry* is invalid.

Illinois v. Wardlow, 528 U.S. 119 (2000) **35**
Presence in a high-crime area, combined with unprovoked flight upon observing police officers, gives officers sufficient grounds to investigate further to determine if criminal activity is about to take place.

Florida v. J.L., 529 U.S. 266 (2000) **36**
"An anonymous tip that a person is carrying a gun is not, without more, sufficient to justify a police officer's stop and frisk of that person."

United States v. Arvizu, 534 U.S. 266 (2001) **38**
"In making reasonable-suspicion determinations, reviewing courts must look at the totality of the circumstances of each case to see whether the detaining officer has a particularized and objective basis for suspecting legal wrongdoing."

Hiibel v. Sixth Judicial District Court of Nevada et al., 542 U.S. 177 (2004) **40**
The Fourth Amendment allows officers, pursuant to a stop and frisk, to require a person to provide his or her name. The person may be arrested for refusing to comply.

Arizona v. Johnson, 555 U.S. 323 (2009) **42**
Officers may order passengers out of a lawfully stopped vehicle and pat them down if there is reasonable suspicion they may be armed and dangerous.

Utah v. Strieff, 579 U.S. ___, No. 14-1373 (2016) **43**
The discovery of a valid arrest warrant is a sufficient intervening event to break the causal chain between an unlawful stop and the discovery of evidence incident to an arrest.

Illinois v. McArthur, 531 U.S. 326 (2001) **59**
Under exigent circumstances, and where police need to preserve evidence until a warrant can be obtained, they may temporarily restrain a person's movements (thus temporarily seizing a person) without violating his or her Fourth Amendment right.

Atwater v. City of Lago Vista, 532 U.S. 318 (2001) **61**
"The Fourth Amendment does not forbid a warrantless arrest for a minor criminal offense, such as a misdemeanor seatbelt violation, punishable only by a fine."

Muehler v. Mena, 544 U.S. 93 (2004) **62**
Detaining occupants of the premises in handcuffs for a certain period of time while executing a search warrant does not by itself violate the Fourth Amendment prohibition against unreasonable searches and seizures.

Bailey v. United States, 568 U.S. 186 (2013) **64**
Detentions incident to the execution of a search warrant must be limited to the immediate vicinity of the premises to be searched.

Chapter 5: Seizures of Things

Schmerber v. California, 384 U.S. 757 (1966) **68**
Drawing blood from a suspect without his or her consent is not a violation of any constitutional right, as long as it is done by medical personnel using accepted medical methods.

Cupp v. Murphy, 412 U.S. 291 (1973) **69**
The police may make a warrantless seizure of evidence that is likely to disappear before a warrant can be obtained.

Winston v. Lee, 470 U.S. 753 (1985) **70**
Surgery requiring a general anesthetic to remove a bullet from a suspect for use as evidence constitutes an intrusion into the suspect's privacy and security that violates the Fourth Amendment. It cannot be allowed unless the government demonstrates a compelling need for it.

City of West Covina v. Perkins, 525 U.S. 234 (1999) **72**
The due process clause does not require the police to provide the owner of property seized with notice of remedies specified by state law for the property's return and the information necessary to use those procedures.

Groh v. Ramirez et al., 540 U.S. 551 (2004) **73**
A search warrant that does not comply with the requirement that the warrant particularly describe the person or things to be seized is unconstitutional. The fact that the application for the warrant (but not the warrant itself) adequately described the things to be seized does not make the warrant valid.

Schneckloth v. Bustamonte, 412 U.S. 218 (1973) **120**
Voluntariness of consent to search is determined from the totality of circumstances, of which knowledge of the right to refuse consent is a factor but not a requirement.

Florida v. Royer, 460 U.S. 491 (1983) **121**
More serious intrusion of personal liberty than is allowable on mere suspicion of criminal activity taints the consent and makes the search illegal.

Illinois v. Rodriguez, 497 U.S. 177 (1990) **122**
Searches in which the person giving consent has "apparent authority" are valid.

Florida v. Jimeno, 499 U.S. 934 (1991) **123**
Consent justifies the warrantless search of a container in a car if it is objectively reasonable for the police to believe that the scope of the suspect's consent permitted them to open that container.

Georgia v. Randolph, 547 U.S. 103 (2006) **125**
"[A] warrantless search of a shared dwelling for evidence over the express refusal of consent by a physically present resident cannot be justified as reasonable as to him on the basis of consent given to the police by another resident."

Fernandez v. California, 571 U.S. 292 (2014) **127**
The lawful occupant of a house or apartment may consent to a search, even over the potential objection of another lawful occupant, if the other occupant is not present or was removed on objectively reasonable grounds.

Chapter 9: Vehicle Stops and Searches

Carroll v. United States, 267 U.S. 132 (1925) **132**
The warrantless search of an automobile is valid if there exists probable cause to believe it contains contraband.

Chambers v. Maroney, 399 U.S. 42 (1969) **133**
If probable cause exists that an automobile contains contraband, a warrantless search is valid even if the automobile is first moved to a police station.

United States v. Chadwick, 433 U.S. 1 (1977) **134**
The warrantless search of a movable container found in a motor vehicle is invalid in the absence of exigent circumstances.

Delaware v. Prouse, 440 U.S. 648 (1979) **135**
Stopping an automobile at random and without probable cause is unreasonable under the Fourth Amendment.

Bond v. United States, 529 U.S. 334 (2000) **149**
A traveler's luggage is an "effect" and is under the protection of the Fourth Amendment. Officers may not physically manipulate (squeeze) the luggage to inspect it without a warrant or probable cause.

Maryland v. Pringle, 540 U.S. 366 (2003) **151**
An officer may arrest a passenger of a vehicle based on probable cause that a crime has been committed (or is being committed) in the vehicle and it is not clear who committed it, as long as there is a reasonable inference from the circumstances that the person arrested could have committed the crime.

Thornton v. United States, 541 U.S. 615 (2004) **153**
Officers may search the passenger compartment of a vehicle after a lawful arrest even if the suspect was not in the vehicle when arrested.

Arizona v. Gant, 556 U.S. 332 (2009) **154**
"Police may search a vehicle incident to a recent occupant's arrest only if the arrestee is within reaching distance of the passenger compartment at the time of the search or it is reasonable to believe the vehicle contains evidence of the offense of arrest."

Navarette v. California, 572 U.S. 393 (2014) **156**
An anonymous 911 call is sufficient to establish reasonable suspicion for an investigative stop if it contains enough information to enable officers to corroborate its veracity and reliability.

Byrd v. United States, 584 U.S. ___ (2018) **157**
The fact that a driver in lawful possession or control of a rental car is not listed on the rental agreement does not defeat his otherwise reasonable expectation of privacy.

Chapter 10: Searches of People in Vehicles

Florida v. Bostick, 501 U.S. 429 (1991) **160**
The test to determine whether a police–citizen encounter on a bus is a seizure is whether, taking into account all the circumstances, a reasonable passenger would feel free to decline the officers' requests or otherwise terminate the encounter.

Whren v. United States, 517 U.S. 806 (1996) **161**
The temporary detention of a motorist upon probable cause to believe that he has violated the traffic laws does not violate the Fourth Amendment's prohibition against unreasonable seizures, even if a reasonable officer would not have stopped the motorist absent some additional law enforcement objective.

Graham v. Connor, 490 U.S. 396 (1989) **217**
Police officers may be held liable under the Constitution for using excessive force. The test for liability is "objective reasonableness" rather than "substantive due process."

Scott v. Harris, 550 U.S 372 (2007) **218**
"A police officer's attempt to terminate a dangerous high-speed car chase that threatens the lives of innocent bystanders does not violate the Fourth Amendment, even when it places the fleeing motorist at risk of serious injury or death."

Plumhoff v. Rickard, 572 U.S. 765 (2014) **221**
The Fourth Amendment does not prohibit officers from using deadly force to terminate a dangerous car chase, and the officers were entitled to qualified immunity for their conduct because they violated no clearly established law.

County of Los Angeles, California, et al. v. Mendez, et al., 581 U.S. ___ (2017) **222**
The standard for use of force claims is set out in *Graham* as the totality of the circumstances. "An earlier Fourth Amendment violation cannot transform a later, reasonable use of force into an unreasonable seizure."

Chapter 17: What Constitutes Interrogation for *Miranda* Purposes?

Brewer v. Williams, 430 U.S. 387 (1977) **226**
Under the *Miranda* rule, interrogations can be "actual" (as when questions are asked) or the "functional equivalent" thereof.

Rhode Island v. Innis, 446 U.S. 291 (1980) **227**
The conversation in this case was merely a dialogue between police officers and did not constitute the "functional equivalent" of an interrogation, hence no *Miranda* warnings were needed.

Arizona v. Mauro, 481 U.S. 520 (1987) **229**
A conversation between a suspect and his wife, which was recorded in the presence of an officer, did not constitute the "functional equivalent" of an interrogation.

Chavez v. Martinez, 538 U.S. 760 (2004) **230**
"Statements compelled by police interrogation may not be used against a defendant in a criminal case, but it is not until such use that the Self-Incrimination Clause is violated."

Davis v. Washington, 547 U.S. 813 (2006) **232**
"Statements are nontestimonial [and therefore admissible in court] when made in the course of police interrogation under circumstances objectively indicating that the primary purpose of interrogation is to enable police assistance to meet an ongoing emergency."

Chapter 19: Confessions and Admissions: Cases Weakening *Miranda*

Table of Cases

Probable Cause

INTRODUCTION

"Probable cause" is the most important and most often used phrase in law enforcement. It is defined by the United States Supreme Court as more than bare suspicion; it exists when "the facts and circumstances within the officers' knowledge and of which they had reasonably trustworthy information are sufficient in themselves to warrant a man of reasonable caution in the belief that an offense has been or is being committed." *Brinegar v. United States*, 338 U.S. 160 (1949).

For purposes of day-to-day policing, probable cause is present if an officer has trustworthy evidence or information sufficient to make a "reasonable person" believe it is more likely than not that the proposed arrest or search is justified. Although never specifically stated in Supreme Court cases, in mathematical terms, probable cause exists if there is more than 50 percent certainty that the suspect has committed an offense or that the items sought can be found in a certain place.

Probable cause is used in four situations: arrests with a warrant, arrests without a warrant, searches of items with a warrant, and searches of items without a warrant. The definition of probable cause is the same in all four situations. The difference is the point at which an officer must justify the probable cause to the court (or judge). For arrests and searches with a warrant, a police officer has to prove probable cause before the warrant is issued. For arrests and searches without a warrant, the police officer has the burden of establishing probable cause in court if the validity of the arrest or search is later challenged.

Essentially, every case in this book has to do with probable cause. The cases in this chapter have a somewhat greater focus on probable cause itself rather than the arrest or search, and they contribute to an understanding of the meaning of probable cause. In reality, probable cause is subjective because its precise meaning may vary from one person to another. Probable cause is likely to be strengthened by quantity, in addition to quality, meaning that the more articulable reasons an officer has, the greater the likelihood that probable cause will be found by the courts. Police officers are therefore advised to articulate as many specific facts and circumstances as they can to justify the arrest or search.

The leading cases briefed in this chapter on probable cause are *Draper v. United States* and *Illinois v. Gates*. A more recent case is *Devenpeck v. Alford*, which held that there is no requirement in the Fourth Amendment for the offense establishing probable cause for an arrest to be "closely related" to and based on the same conduct as the offense identified by the officer.

DRAPER V. UNITED STATES
358 U.S. 307 (1959)

CAPSULE: Information from an informant that is corroborated by an officer may be sufficient to provide probable cause for an arrest even if such information is hearsay.

FACTS: A narcotics agent received information from an informant who had previously proven himself reliable that Draper had gone to Chicago to bring three ounces of heroin back to Denver by train on the morning of either September 8 or 9. The informant also gave a detailed physical description of Draper, the clothes he would be wearing, and that he habitually "walked real fast." Based on this information, police officers set up surveillance of all trains coming from Chicago. The morning of September 8 produced no one fitting the informant's description. On the morning of September 9, officers observed an individual, who matched the exact description the informant had supplied, get off of a train from Chicago and begin to walk quickly toward the exit. Officers overtook the suspect and arrested him. Heroin and a syringe were seized in a search incident to the arrest. The informant died prior to the trial and was therefore unable to testify. Draper was convicted of knowingly concealing and transporting drugs.

ISSUE: Can information provided by an informant, which is subsequently corroborated by an officer, provide probable cause for an arrest without a warrant? YES.

SUPREME COURT DECISION: Information received from an informant, which is corroborated by an officer may be sufficient to provide probable cause for an arrest even though such information, if presented at trial, would be hearsay and would not otherwise be admissible in a criminal trial.

REASON: The informant who provided information to the agent had provided reliable information in the past. When the agent personally verified each element of the informant's detailed description, except the part involving the possession of drugs, he developed probable cause to believe that the rest of the informant's description was true.

CASE SIGNIFICANCE: The evidence from the informant in this case could be considered hearsay, which ordinarily is inadmissible in a criminal trial. The Court held, however, that it could be used to show probable cause for purposes of a search; thus, evidence that may not be admissible in a trial may be used by the police to establish probable cause. This is important because all information from an informant is considered hearsay as the basis for police action, but the police can act on such information as long as it is good enough to establish probable cause. The Court held that there was probable cause in this case because the information came from "one employed for that purpose and whose information had always been found accurate and reliable." The Court added that "it is clear that [the police officer] would have been derelict in his duties had he not pursued it."

ILLINOIS V. GATES
462 U.S. 213 (1983)

CAPSULE: The two-pronged test for probable cause established in previous cases is superseded in favor of the "totality of circumstances" test.

FACTS: On May 3, 1978, the Bloomingdale, Illinois, police department received an anonymous letter stating that Gates and his wife were engaged in selling drugs, that the wife would drive her car to Florida on May 3 to be loaded with drugs, that Gates would fly to Florida and drive the car back to Illinois, that the trunk would be loaded with drugs, and that Gates had more than $100,000 worth of drugs in his basement. Acting on the tip, a police officer obtained Gates' address and learned that he had made reservations for a May 5 flight to Florida. Arrangements for surveillance of the flight were made with an agent of the Drug Enforcement Administration. The surveillance disclosed that Gates took the flight, stayed overnight in a hotel room registered in his wife's name, and left the following morning with a woman in a car bearing an Illinois license plate, heading north. A search warrant for Gates' house and automobile was obtained on the basis of the officer's affidavit setting forth the foregoing facts and a copy of the anonymous letter. When Gates arrived at his home, the police were waiting. A search of the house and car revealed marijuana and other contraband. Gates was charged with violating state drug laws and was convicted.

ISSUE: Did the anonymous letter, partially corroborated by the officer, provide sufficient facts to establish probable cause for the issuance of a warrant? YES.

SUPREME COURT DECISION: The two-pronged test established under *Aguilar v. Texas* and *Spinelli v. United States* is superseded in favor of a "totality of circumstances" approach. The task of an issuing magistrate is to make a practical decision whether, given all the circumstances, there is a fair probability that the evidence of a crime will be found in a particular place.

REASON: "Unlike a totality of circumstances analysis, which permits a balanced assessment of the relative weights of all the various indicia of reliability (and unreliability) attending an informant's tip, the 'two-pronged test' has encouraged an excessively technical dissection of informants' tips, with undue attention being focused on isolated issues that cannot sensibly be divorced from the other facts presented to the magistrate."

CASE SIGNIFICANCE: The two-pronged test for establishing probable cause in cases in which information is given by an informant is modified and superseded by the "totality of circumstances" test, making it easier for police officers to establish probable cause for the issuance of a warrant. Under the two-pronged test as enunciated in *Aguilar v. Texas*, 378 U.S. 108 (1964), probable cause based on information obtained from an informant could be established only if the following were present: (1) reliability of the informant and (2) reliability of the informant's information. Both conditions must have been satisfied before probable cause could be established. In contrast, under the "totality of circumstances" test, probable cause may be established if, based on all the circumstances (including hearsay), there is a fair probability that contraband or evidence of crime will be found in a particular place. The *Gates* case still preserves the two-pronged test established in *Aguilar*, but it does not treat the two aspects separately and independently. Instead, the "totality of circumstances" approach is used, meaning that whatever deficiencies there may be in one prong can be supplemented or overcome by the other, together with other available evidence.

UNITED STATES V. SOKOLOW
490 U.S. 1 (1989)

CAPSULE: The totality of circumstances can establish a reasonable suspicion, sufficient for officers to make an investigative stop without a warrant.

FACTS: Sokolow purchased two round-trip tickets for a flight from Honolulu to Miami under an assumed name. He paid for the tickets from a roll of $20 bills that appeared to contain about $4,000. He appeared nervous during the transaction. Neither he nor his companion checked any luggage. Additional investigation revealed that Sokolow had scheduled a return flight for three days later. Based on these facts, which fit a "drug courier profile" developed by the Drug Enforcement Administration (DEA), officers stopped the pair and took them to the DEA office at the airport where their luggage was examined by a drug detection dog. The examination indicated the presence of narcotics in one of Sokolow's bags. Sokolow was arrested and a search warrant was obtained for the bag. No narcotics were found in the bag, but documents indicating involvement in drug trafficking were discovered. Upon a second search with the drug detection dog, narcotics were detected in another of Sokolow's bags. Sokolow was released until a search warrant was obtained the next morning. A search of the bag revealed 1,063 grams of cocaine. Sokolow was again arrested and charged with possession with intent to distribute cocaine.

ISSUE: Were the factors matching Sokolow to a "drug courier profile" sufficient to justify his stop and temporary detention, which preceded the search without a warrant? YES.

SUPREME COURT DECISION: Taken together, the circumstances in this case establish a reasonable suspicion that the suspect was transporting illegal drugs, and therefore the investigative stop without warrant was valid under the Fourth Amendment.

REASON: Under the decisions in *Terry v. Ohio*, 392 U.S. 1 (1968) and *United States v. Cortez*, 449 U.S. 411 (1981), the totality of circumstances must be evaluated to determine reasonable suspicion for an investigative stop. Police officers may stop and briefly detain an individual to determine whether the person is involved in a criminal activity if the officer has reasonable suspicion, supported by articulable facts, that such activity is occurring.

CASE SIGNIFICANCE: This case addresses the issue of whether the use of "drug courier profiles" is valid under the Fourth Amendment. The Court said that there is nothing wrong with such use in this case because the facts, taken in totality, amounted to reasonable suspicion that criminal conduct was taking place. The Court indicated that whether the facts in this case fit a "profile" was less significant than the fact that, taken together, they establish a reasonable suspicion. In sum, the case appears to indicate that while a drug courier profile might be helpful, the totality of the circumstances is more important in establishing the legality of the stop and temporary detention that leads to a subsequent search.

DEVENPECK V. ALFORD
543 U.S. 146 (2004)

CAPSULE: The Fourth Amendment does not require the offense establishing probable cause for an arrest to be "closely related" to and based on the same conduct as the offense identified by the officer during the initial encounter.

FACTS: Alford pulled behind a disabled vehicle, activating wig-wag headlights. A patrol car passing in the opposite direction turned around to assist. When the officer arrived on the scene, Alford hurriedly returned to his vehicle and drove away. The officer radioed his supervisor that he was concerned Alford was a police impersonator. The officer pursued Alford's vehicle and pulled it over. Upon approaching Alford's vehicle, the officer observed that Alford was listening to a police scanner and had handcuffs in the car. When the supervisor arrived, he questioned Alford and received evasive answers. He then noticed a tape recorder in the seat with the record button activated. Alford was removed from the vehicle and officers confirmed Alford was recording the conversations. Based on a conversation between the supervisor and the prosecutor, the officers arrested Alford for violating the Washington State Privacy Act instead of impersonating a police officer. Alford filed a Section 1983 suit against the officers for unlawful arrest and imprisonment.

ISSUE: Is an arrest "lawful under the Fourth Amendment when the criminal offense for which there is probable cause to arrest is not 'closely related' to the offense stated by the arresting officer at the time of the arrest"? YES.

SUPREME COURT DECISION: For an arrest to be constitutional, there is no requirement in the Fourth Amendment for the offense establishing probable cause for an arrest to be "closely related" to and based on the same conduct as the offense initially identified by the officer.

REASON: The Court based the finding in this case on three principles. First, given the complexity of the law governing what constitutes a particular crime, officers are not required to know exactly what law matches the behavior for which an arrest is made. They may arrest under one provision of the law, then, upon further investigation by the officer or prosecutor, it may be determined that the actions actually are more appropriate for a different offense. Second, the Court, relying on previous cases (specifically *Whren v. United States*) reiterated the precedent that the officer's state of mind is not a factor in establishing probable cause. The Court held that the "closely related rule" violated this precedent because it would make the arrest rely on the motivation of the officer. Finally, while the Court recognized that it is "generally good practice to inform a person of the reason for his arrest at the time he is taken into custody," that is not a requirement of law.

CASE SIGNIFICANCE: This case gives officers some flexibility in determining the offense to be charged after an arrest. In this case, had the first officer arrested Alford based on the initial encounter, it would have been for impersonating an officer. After the supervisor arrived, the situation changed and Alford was arrested for violating the Washington State Privacy Act. The Court ruled that the officers were justified in making the arrest because probable cause was present (although for the different offense of impersonating an officer) at the time of the initial encounter. The fact that the law under which the suspect was finally charged did not closely resemble the initial suspicion of the police did not make the arrest unconstitutional because the police had probable cause to make the arrest, although for a different crime. This case was filed against the officers by Alford for civil liability (42 U.S.C. § 1983), alleging a violation of his constitutional right against unreasonable search and seizure. In these types of cases, an officer is not liable unless the constitutional right was "clearly established" at the time of the violation. The Court ruled that the "closely related offense" doctrine was not clearly established at the time of the officer's arrest of Alford because lower courts differed on its application. As a result, the officers were not civilly liable under federal law.

The Exclusionary Rule

2

INTRODUCTION

The exclusionary rule provides that any evidence obtained by the government in violation of the Fourth Amendment right against unreasonable searches and seizures is not admissible in a court of law. It is a judge-made rule, applied to the states through the Fourteenth Amendment, whose purpose is to deter police misconduct. The assumption is that, if evidence obtained by the police in violation of the Fourth Amendment cannot be used in court, police misconduct will be minimized.

The exclusionary rule applies only in cases involving violations of the prohibition against unreasonable searches and seizures under the Fourth Amendment. Evidence obtained by the police in violation of other rights under the Bill of Rights (such as the privilege against self-incrimination under the Fifth Amendment, or the right to counsel under the Sixth Amendment) is not admissible in court either, but that exclusion does not come under the exclusionary rule; rather, the evidence is excluded based on a violation of the constitutional right to due process.

The first exclusionary rule case decided by the United States Supreme Court was *Boyd v. United States*, 116 U.S. 616 (1886). In that case, the Court held that the forced disclosure of papers amounting to evidence of a crime violated the Fourth Amendment right of the suspect and, therefore, the evidence could not be used in court. In *Weeks v. United States*, 232 U.S. 383 (1914), the Court held that evidence illegally obtained by federal officers could not be used in federal criminal prosecutions. *Mapp v. Ohio*, 367 U.S. 643 (1961) is the leading and best-known case on the exclusionary rule. In *Mapp*, the Court held that the exclusionary rule also applied to state criminal prosecutions, thus extending the exclusionary rule to state criminal proceedings.

Although originally controversial, the exclusionary rule has been accepted and applied by the courts and is now an accepted part of policing. The United States Supreme Court continues to define exceptions, and there are many who say the exclusionary rule will be essentially abolished in the near future. Until then, however, the exclusionary rule remains as a form of protection against violations by the police of the public's right against unreasonable searches and seizures.

The leading cases briefed in this chapter on the exclusionary rule are *Mapp v. Ohio* and *Weeks v. United States*.

WEEKS V. UNITED STATES
232 U.S. 383 (1914)

CAPSULE: Evidence seized by federal law enforcement officers in violation of the Fourth Amendment is not admissible in a federal criminal prosecution.

FACTS: Weeks was arrested for using the mail to transport tickets for a lottery. Officers searched Weeks' home without a warrant and seized various articles and papers that were then turned over to the United States Marshals Service. Later in the day, police officers returned with a Marshal and again searched Weeks' home without a warrant and seized letters and other articles. Weeks was convicted of unlawful use of the mail.

ISSUE: Is evidence illegally obtained by federal law enforcement officers admissible in court? NO.

SUPREME COURT DECISION: Evidence illegally seized by federal law enforcement officers is not admissible in federal criminal prosecutions.

REASON: The Fourth Amendment freedom from unreasonable searches and seizures applies "to all invasions on the part of the government and its employees of the sanctity of a man's home and the privacies of life. It is not the breaking of his doors and the rummaging of his drawers that constitutes the essence of the offense; but it is the invasion of his indefeasible right of personal security, personal liberty and private property."

CASE SIGNIFICANCE: This decision excluded illegally obtained evidence from use in federal prosecutions. This rule was extended to state criminal prosecutions in 1961 in *Mapp v. Ohio*, 367 U.S. 643 (1961), making illegally obtained evidence inadmissible in both state and federal courts. It is interesting to note that from 1914 to 1960, federal courts admitted evidence of a federal crime if it was obtained illegally by state officers, as long as there was no connivance with federal officers. This questionable practice was known as the "silver platter doctrine." In 1960, the Court rejected the "silver platter doctrine" (*Elkins v. United States*, 364 U.S. 206), holding that the Fourth Amendment prohibited the use of illegally obtained evidence in federal prosecutions whether it was obtained by federal or state officers. The Court followed the year after with *Mapp*, holding that illegally obtained evidence was inadmissible, no matter who collected it or in what court it was presented.

ROCHIN V. CALIFORNIA
342 U.S. 165 (1952)

CAPSULE: Some searches are so "shocking to the conscience" that they require exclusion of the evidence seized based on due process.

FACTS: Having information that Rochin was selling narcotics, police officers entered his home and forced their way into the bedroom. When asked about two capsules lying beside the bed, Rochin put them in his mouth. After an unsuccessful attempt to recover them by force, the officers took Rochin to the hospital where his stomach was pumped. Two capsules containing morphine were recovered. A motion to suppress this evidence was denied and Rochin was convicted of possession of morphine.

ISSUE: Were the capsules recovered as a result of pumping Rochin's stomach admissible as evidence in court? NO.

SUPREME COURT DECISION: Although (at that time) searches by state law enforcement officers were not governed by the exclusionary rule, some searches are so "shocking to the conscience" as to require exclusion of the evidence seized based on the due process (fundamental fairness) clause of the Constitution.

REASON: "[T]he proceedings by which this conviction was obtained do more than offend some fastidious squeamishness or private sentimentalism about combating crime too energetically. This is conduct that shocks the conscience. Illegally breaking into the privacy of the petitioner, the struggle to open his mouth and remove what was there, the forcible extraction of his stomach's contents—this course of proceeding by agents of the government to obtain evidence is bound to offend even hardened sensibilities. They are methods too close to the rack and screw to permit of constitutional differentiation."

CASE SIGNIFICANCE: This case was decided prior to the extension of the exclusionary rule to the states in 1961. In this state prosecution, however, the Court decided that the evidence obtained could not be used in court, not because of the exclusionary rule, but because of the shocking conduct of the police officers, which violated Rochin's right to due process guaranteed by the Fourteenth Amendment. If the case were to be decided today, the evidence would be excluded under the exclusionary rule, not under the due process clause.

MAPP V. OHIO
367 U.S. 643 (1961)

CAPSULE: The exclusionary rule applies to all state criminal proceedings.

FACTS: Mapp was convicted of possession of lewd and lascivious books, pictures, and photographs. Three police officers went to Mapp's residence based on information that a person who was wanted in connection with a recent bombing was hiding out in her home. The officers knocked on the door and demanded entrance, but Mapp, telephoning her attorney, refused to admit them without a warrant. The officers again sought entrance three hours later, after the arrival of more police. When Mapp did not respond, the officers broke the door open. Mapp's attorney arrived but was denied access to his client. Mapp demanded to see the search warrant the police claimed to possess. When a paper supposed to be the warrant was held up by one of the officers, Mapp grabbed the paper and placed it in her bosom. A struggle ensued and the paper was recovered after Mapp was handcuffed for being belligerent. A search of the house produced a trunk that contained obscene materials. The materials were admitted into evidence at trial and Mapp was convicted of possession of obscene materials.

ISSUE: Is evidence obtained in violation of the Fourth Amendment protection from unreasonable searches and seizures admissible in state criminal prosecutions? NO.

SUPREME COURT DECISION: The exclusionary rule, applicable in federal cases, which prohibits the use of evidence obtained as a result of unreasonable searches and seizures, also applies to state criminal proceedings.

REASON: "Since the Fourth Amendment's right of privacy has been declared enforceable against the States through the Due Process Clause of the Fourteenth [Amendment], it is enforceable against them by the same sanction of exclusion as is used against the Federal Government. Were it otherwise, then just as without the *Weeks* rule the assurance against unreasonable searches and seizures would be 'a form of words,' valueless and undeserving of mention in a perpetual charter of inestimable human liberties, so too, without that rule the freedom from state invasions of privacy would be … ephemeral …."

CASE SIGNIFICANCE: *Mapp* is significant because the Court held that the exclusionary rule was thereafter to be applied to the states, thus forbidding both state and federal courts from accepting evidence obtained in violation of the constitutional protection against unreasonable searches and seizures. In the mind of the Court, the facts in *Mapp* illustrate what can happen if police conduct is not restricted. *Mapp* was therefore an ideal case for the Court to use in settling an issue that had to be addressed: whether the exclusionary rule should apply to state criminal proceedings. The Court answered with a definite yes.

WONG SUN V. UNITED STATES
371 U.S. 471 (1963)

CAPSULE: Evidence obtained as a result of illegal acts by the police must be excluded. In addition, the "fruit of the poisonous tree" of that illegal act must also be excluded. Evidence that has been purged of the primary taint, however, is admissible.

FACTS: Federal narcotics agents arrested Hom Way and found heroin in his possession. Although Way had not been an informant before, the agents went to "Oye's Laundry" based upon his statement that he had bought the heroin from "Blackie Toy," who owned the laundry. At the laundry, agent Wong got James Wah Toy to open the door by telling him that he was calling for dry cleaning. When Wong announced that he was a federal agent, Toy slammed the door and started running. The agents then broke open the door and began to chase Toy. Toy was placed under arrest in his bedroom. A search of the premises uncovered no drugs. There was nothing to link Toy to "Blackie Toy." Upon interrogation, he stated that he had not been selling narcotics but knew that an individual named Johnny had. He told the officers where Johnny lived, and described the bedroom where the heroin was kept and where he had smoked some of the heroin the night before. Based on this information, the agents went to the home of Johnny Yee and found him in possession of an ounce of heroin. Upon interrogation, Yee stated that he had bought the heroin from Toy and an individual named "Sea Dog." Further questioning of Toy revealed that "Sea Dog's" name was Wong Sun. Toy then took the agents to a multifamily dwelling where Wong Sun lived. After identifying himself, agent Wong was admitted by Wong Sun's wife who said he was in the back, asleep. Wong Sun was arrested by the agents. A search pursuant to the arrest found no narcotics. Each of the offenders was arraigned and released on his own recognizance. A few days later, Toy, Yee, and Wong Sun were interrogated again and written statements were made. Neither Toy nor Wong Sun signed their statements, but Wong Sun admitted to the accuracy of his statement. At the trial, the government's evidence consisted of: (1) the statements made by Toy at the time of his arrest, (2) the heroin taken from Yee, (3) Toy's pretrial statement, and (4) Wong Sun's pretrial statement. Wong Sun and Toy were convicted of transportation and concealment of heroin.

ISSUES: There were a number of issues in this case, but the important issues related to the exclusionary rule are:

1. Were the statements made by Toy after an unlawful arrest admissible? NO.
2. Were the narcotics taken from Yee after an unlawful arrest admissible? NO.
3. Was Wong Sun's statement admissible? YES.

SUPREME COURT DECISION: Statements or evidence obtained indirectly as a result of an unlawful arrest or search are not admissible in court because they are "tainted fruit of the poisonous tree." A suspect's intervening act of free will, however, breaks the chain of illegality, purges the evidence of the taint, and makes the evidence admissible.

REASON: The exclusionary rule has traditionally barred from trial physical, tangible materials obtained either during or as a direct result of an unlawful invasion. "Thus, verbal evidence which derives so immediately from an unlawful entry and an unauthorized arrest as the officers' action in the present case is no less the 'fruit' of official illegality than the more common tangible fruits of the unwarranted intrusion ...."

"We turn now to the case of ... Wong Sun. We have no occasion to disagree with the finding of the Court of Appeals that his arrest, also, was without probable cause or reasonable grounds. For Wong Sun's unsigned confession was not the fruit of that arrest, and was therefore properly admitted at trial. On the evidence that Wong Sun had been released on his own recognizance after a lawful arraignment, and had returned voluntarily several days later to make the statement, we hold that the connection between the arrest and the statement had 'become so attenuated as to dissipate the taint.'"

CASE SIGNIFICANCE: This case addresses the "fruit of the poisonous tree" aspect of the exclusionary rule. The exclusionary rule provides that evidence obtained in violation of the Fourth Amendment prohibition against unreasonable searches and seizures is not admissible in a court of law. This rule goes beyond that, however, and also says that any other evidence obtained directly or indirectly as a result of the illegal behavior is not admissible either. Hence, once an illegal act has been proved, any evidence obtained either directly or indirectly cannot be admitted in court either under the concept of the original illegality or as the "tainted fruit."

This case also carves out an exception to the exclusionary rule: the "purged taint" exception. What it says is that, despite the initial illegality, the evidence may nonetheless be admissible if it has been purged of the initial taint. An example is this case, in which the statement of Wong Sun, which initially was the product of unlawful behavior by the agents, was nonetheless admitted because of subsequent events. What happened was that after Wong Sun was released on his own recognizance and after lawful arraignment, he returned several days later and made a statement that was then admitted by the trial court. The Court said that the voluntary return by Wong Sun purged the evidence of the initial taint and therefore made the statement admissible.

NIX V. WILLIAMS
467 U.S. 431 (1984)

CAPSULE: Illegally obtained evidence may be admissible if the police can prove that they would have discovered the evidence anyway through lawful means.

FACTS: A 10-year-old girl disappeared from a YMCA building in Des Moines, Iowa. A short time later, Williams was seen leaving the YMCA with a large bundle wrapped in a blanket. A 14-year-old boy who helped him carry the bundle reported he had seen "two legs in it and they were skinny and white." Williams' car was found the next day, 160 miles east of Des Moines. Items of clothing belonging to the missing child and a blanket like the one used to wrap the bundle were found at a rest stop between the YMCA in Des Moines and where the car was found. Assuming the girl's body could be found between the YMCA and the car, an extensive search was conducted. Meanwhile, Williams was arrested by police in a town near where the car was found and was arraigned. Williams' counsel was informed that Williams would be returned to Des Moines without being interrogated. During the trip, an officer began a conversation with Williams in which he said the girl should be given a Christian burial before a snowstorm, which might prevent the body from being found. As Williams and the officer neared the town where the body was hidden, Williams agreed to take the officer to the child's body. The body was found about two miles from one of the search teams. At the trial, a motion to suppress the evidence was denied and Williams was convicted of first-degree murder. On appeal, the court ruled that the evidence had been wrongly admitted at Williams' trial. At his second trial, the prosecutor did not offer Williams' statements into evidence and did not seek to show that Williams had led the police to the body. The trial court ruled that the state had proved that, even if Williams had not led the police to the body, it would have been found by the searchers anyway. Williams was again convicted of murder.

ISSUE: Was the evidence (the body) admissible in court on the theory that the body would ultimately have been discovered anyway because of the ongoing search? YES.

SUPREME COURT DECISION: Evidence obtained illegally may be admissible if the police can prove that they would have discovered the evidence anyway through lawful means.

REASON: "The independent source doctrine teaches us that the interest of society in deterring unlawful police conduct and the public interest in having juries receive all probative evidence of a crime are properly balanced by putting the police in the same, not a worse, position than they would have been in if no police error or misconduct had occurred."

CASE SIGNIFICANCE: This case illustrates the "inevitable discovery" exception to the exclusionary rule. "Fruit of the poisonous tree" is evidence obtained as a result of illegal police behavior (in this case an illegal interrogation that led to the body). This evidence is usually inadmissible due to the illegality of police actions. The exception set out in this case states that evidence that is the "fruit of the poisonous tree" is admissible if the police can prove they would inevitably have discovered the evidence anyway by lawful means. In this case, the evidence was properly excluded during the first trial because no *Miranda* warnings were given to the suspect before he confessed. The Court stated that the evidence was properly admitted at the second trial because the evidence would have been discovered anyway as a result of the continued search.

UNITED STATES V. LEON
468 U.S. 897 (1984)

CAPSULE: The "good faith" exception to the exclusionary rule allows the use of evidence obtained by officers who are acting in reasonable reliance on a search warrant that is later declared invalid.

FACTS: Acting on the basis of information from a confidential informant, officers initiated a drug trafficking investigation. Based on an affidavit summarizing the police officer's observation, a search warrant was prepared. The warrant was reviewed by three deputy district attorneys and issued by a state court judge. Ensuing searches produced large quantities of drugs. Leon was indicted on drug charges. Motions to suppress the evidence were granted in part because the affidavit was insufficient to establish probable cause. The court rejected the argument of good faith of the officers in relying on the magistrate's issuance of the warrant and acquitted the defendant.

ISSUE: Is evidence obtained as the result of a search conducted pursuant to a warrant that was issued by a neutral and detached magistrate admissible in court if the warrant is ultimately found invalid through no fault of the police officer? YES.

SUPREME COURT DECISION: The "good faith" exception to the Fourth Amendment's exclusionary rule allows the use of evidence obtained by officers acting in reasonable reliance on a search warrant issued by a neutral and detached magistrate that is ultimately found to be invalid.

REASON: "In the ordinary case, an officer cannot be expected to question the magistrate's probable cause determination or his judgment that the form of the warrant is technically sufficient. '[O]nce the warrant issues, there is literally nothing more the policeman can do in seeking to comply with the law.' Penalizing the officer for the magistrate's error, rather than his own, cannot logically contribute to the deterrence of Fourth Amendment violations."

CASE SIGNIFICANCE: This case, together with *Massachusetts v. Sheppard*, 468 U.S. 981 (1984), are arguably the most important cases decided on the exclusionary rule since *Mapp v. Ohio*, 367 U.S. 643 (1961). They represent a significant, although narrow, exception to that rule. In these two cases, the Court held there were objectively reasonable grounds for the officers' mistaken belief that the warrants authorized the searches. The officers took every step that could reasonably have been taken to ensure that the warrants were valid. The *Leon* and *Sheppard* cases differ in one substantial way. In *Sheppard*, the issue was improper use of a search warrant form (it was one used in another district to search for controlled substances), which the judge said he would change where necessary, but mistakenly failed to do so. In *Leon*, the issue was the use of a questionable informant and stale information (failing to constitute probable cause), which the judge mistakenly approved. The cases are similar, however, in that the mistakes were made by the judges, not the police. The Court held that the evidence in both cases was admissible because the judge, not the police, erred and the exclusionary rule is designed to control the conduct of the police, not the conduct of judges.

Note, however, that this is a narrow "good faith" exception. Although the police acted "in good faith" in these cases, it cannot be said that evidence is admissible every time the police act "in good faith." For example, if the police acted illegally in obtaining evidence, they cannot later claim to have acted in good faith in arguing for the admissibility of the evidence obtained, even if they actually did act in good faith and can prove it. This is because the error was committed by the police, not a third person.

MURRAY V. UNITED STATES
487 U.S. 533 (1988)

CAPSULE: The "independent source" exception to the exclusionary rule allows the use of evidence obtained by officers who act in reasonable reliance on a search warrant that is based on information that was not obtained illegally.

FACTS: Suspecting illegal drug activities, federal agents followed Murray and several co-conspirators. At one point, Murray drove a truck and another person drove a camper into a warehouse. Twenty minutes later, when the two emerged from the warehouse, law enforcement agents could see a tractor-trailer bearing a long, dark container. The truck and camper were later turned over to other drivers who were arrested and found in possession of marijuana.

Upon receiving this information, the law enforcement agents returned to the warehouse, without a warrant, and forced entry. The warehouse was unoccupied but the agents observed, in plain view, several burlap-wrapped bales of marijuana. The law enforcement agents left the warehouse without disturbing the bales and did not reenter until they had a valid search warrant. In applying for the warrant, the agents did not mention the forced entry into the warehouse and did not rely on any information obtained during that search. After obtaining the warrant, law enforcement agents returned to the warehouse and seized numerous bales of marijuana and a notebook listing the destinations of the bales. Murray was arrested and convicted of conspiracy to possess and distribute illegal drugs.

ISSUE: Is evidence first observed in an illegal entry by officers but subsequently seized through a valid, independent search warrant admissible in court? YES.

SUPREME COURT DECISION: Even if the police illegally enter private property, evidence initially discovered during that illegal entry may be admissible in court if it is later discovered during a valid search that is wholly unrelated to the illegal entry.

REASON: The Court reasoned that the evidence ought not to have been excluded just because of unrelated illegal conduct by the police. If probable cause for a search warrant can be established apart from any illegal activity by the police, the evidence obtained in the subsequent search should be admissible.

CASE SIGNIFICANCE: This case illustrates the "independent source" exception to the exclusionary rule. In this case, the police illegally entered the warehouse and discovered bales of marijuana. The Court ruled that the marijuana was admissible because the officers later searched the warehouse pursuant to a valid warrant that was issued without being based on information that was obtained during the illegal entry. An initial illegal search, therefore, does not automatically exclude the evidence if the evidence is not seized at the time of the illegal entry, but pursuant to a valid warrant that is later obtained without relying on information obtained during the illegal entry.

MINNESOTA V. OLSON
495 U.S. 91 (1989)

CAPSULE: A warrantless, nonconsensual entry of a residence by police to arrest an overnight guest violates the Fourth Amendment.

FACTS: The police suspected Olson of being the driver of the getaway car involved in a robbery-murder. Based on an anonymous tip, the police surrounded the home of two women with whom they believed Olson had been staying as a guest. A detective then telephoned the home and told one of the women that Olson should come outside, whereupon he heard a male voice saying, "Tell them I left." When the woman told the detective this, he ordered the police to enter. Without permission or a search warrant, and with their weapons drawn, the police entered the house and arrested Olson, who was hiding in a closet. Based on an incriminating statement made by Olson, he was convicted of murder, armed robbery, and assault.

ISSUE: Is the Fourth Amendment violated when the police make a warrantless, nonconsensual entry and arrest without exigent (emergency) circumstances? YES.

SUPREME COURT DECISION: The warrantless nonconsensual entry by the police of a residence to arrest an overnight guest violates the Fourth Amendment, unless justified by exigent circumstances.

REASON: "[W]e think that society recognizes that a houseguest has a legitimate expectation of privacy in his host's home." An overnight guest "seeks shelter in another's home precisely because it provides him with privacy, a place where he and his possessions will not be disturbed by anyone except his host and those his host allows inside. ... The houseguest is there with the permission of his host, who is willing to share his house and his privacy with the guest. ... The host may admit or exclude from the house as he prefers, but it is unlikely that he will admit someone who wants to see or meet with the guest over the objection of the guest." Hosts, therefore, "will more likely than not respect the privacy interests of their guests, who are entitled to a legitimate expectation of privacy despite the fact that they have no legal interest in the premises and do not have the legal authority to determine who may or may not enter the household." Because Olson's "expectation of privacy in the host's home was rooted in 'understandings that are recognized and permitted by society,' it was legitimate, and [Olson] can claim the protection of the Fourth Amendment."

CASE SIGNIFICANCE: This case establishes the principle that the arrest of a suspect in another person's home requires a search warrant for entry into the home (an arrest warrant is not sufficient), except: (1) if exigent circumstances are present or (2) if consent is given by the owner of the house. In this case, suspect Olson was an overnight guest in the home. There was no reason to believe that he would flee the premises, hence exigent circumstances were not deemed present. The Court ruled that the police should have obtained a search warrant to enable them to enter the third person's house legally. An overnight guest has an expectation of privacy that society is prepared to recognize as reasonable, hence a warrant should have been obtained. The statement made after his arrest was not admissible in court.

ARIZONA V. EVANS
514 U.S. 1 (1995)

CAPSULE: The "good faith exception" to the exclusionary rule does not require suppression of evidence seized in violation of the Fourth Amendment where the erroneous information resulted from clerical errors of court employees.

FACTS: Police officers saw Evans going the wrong way on a one-way street in front of the police station. When Evans was stopped, officers determined that his driver's license had been suspended. When Evans' name was entered into a computer data terminal in the officer's patrol car, it indicated that there was an outstanding misdemeanor warrant for Evans' arrest. While being handcuffed, Evans dropped a hand-rolled cigarette that turned out to be marijuana. A search of Evans' car revealed more marijuana under the passenger's seat. At trial, Evans moved to suppress the evidence as fruit of an unlawful arrest because the arrest warrant for the misdemeanor had been quashed 17 days prior to his arrest but was not entered into the computer due to a clerical error of a court employee. Evans also argued that the good faith exception to the exclusionary rule was inapplicable in this case. These motions were denied and Evans was convicted.

ISSUE: Does the exclusionary rule require suppression of evidence that is seized by an officer acting in reliance on erroneous information resulting from clerical errors of court employees? NO.

SUPREME COURT DECISION: "The exclusionary rule does not require suppression of evidence seized in violation of the Fourth Amendment where the erroneous information resulted from clerical errors of court employees."

REASON: "The exclusionary rule operates as a judicially created remedy designed to safeguard against future violations [by police officers] of Fourth Amendment rights through the rule's deterrent effect." The application of the exclusionary rule was for police officers rather than court employees (see *United States v. Leon*, 468 U.S. 897 [1984]). In this case, the Court found "no sound reason to apply the exclusionary rule as a means of deterring misconduct on the part of judicial officers" because application of the exclusionary rule to court personnel could not be expected to alter the behavior of the arresting officer. Furthermore, "[t]here [was] no indication that the arresting officer was not acting objectively reasonably when he relied upon the police computer record. Application of the *Leon* framework supports a categorical exception to the exclusionary rule for clerical errors of court employees."

CASE SIGNIFICANCE: This case extends an exception of the exclusionary rule when an error is committed by court employees rather than the police. The exclusionary rule was fashioned to deter police misconduct; hence the Court refused to apply it to cases in which the error was not made by the police. Previous cases have held that, if the error is made by a magistrate (as in *Massachusetts v. Sheppard* and *United States v. Leon*— see above) or by the legislature (as in *Illinois v. Krull*, 480 U.S. 340 [1987]), the exclusionary rule does not apply. The theme in these cases is that if the error is not committed by the police, then the exclusionary rule should not apply because it was meant to control the behavior of the police. *Evans*, therefore, is consistent with the Court's holdings in previous cases and came as no surprise. The unanswered question is whether error by any public officer other than the police would be an addition to this rule. The dissent in *Evans* argued that the Fourth Amendment prohibition against unreasonable searches and seizures applies to the conduct of all government officers, not just the police. The majority in *Evans* disagreed, preferring instead to focus on the original purpose of the exclusionary rule, which is to control police conduct.

BRIGHAM CITY, UTAH V. STUART ET AL.
547 U.S. 47 (2006)

CAPSULE: "Police may enter a home without a warrant when they have an objectively reasonable basis for believing that an occupant is seriously injured or imminently threatened with such injury."

FACTS: Officers responded to a call regarding a loud party at a residence. Upon arriving at the house, they heard shouting from inside. They also observed two juveniles drinking beer in the backyard. They entered the backyard and saw through a screen door and windows a fight taking place in the kitchen of the home involving four adults and a juvenile. After observing several people being punched, the officers then opened the screen door and announced their presence with no response from the occupants. The officers entered the kitchen and again announced their presence, at which time the fight then ceased. The officers arrested the adults and charged them with contributing to the delinquency of a minor, disorderly conduct, and intoxication.

ISSUE: May the police enter a home without a warrant when they have an objectively reasonable belief that an occupant is seriously injured or imminently threatened with injury? YES.

SUPREME COURT DECISION: "Police may enter a home without a warrant when they have an objectively reasonable basis for believing that an occupant is seriously injured or imminently threatened with such injury."

REASON: "It is a 'basic principle of Fourth Amendment law that searches and seizures inside a home without a warrant are presumptively unreasonable.'" (Internal citations omitted.) "One exigency obviating the requirement of a warrant is the need to assist persons who are seriously injured or threatened with such injury." "Accordingly, law enforcement officers may enter a home without a warrant to render emergency assistance to an injured occupant or to protect an occupant from imminent injury."

CASE SIGNIFICANCE: In this case, the Court ruled that police may justifiably enter a home or building without a warrant if they have an "objectively reasonable" basis (lower than probable cause) to believe that somebody inside is "seriously injured or threatened with such injury." The Court added that "the need to protect or preserve life or avoid serious injury is justification for what would be otherwise illegal absent an exigency or emergency." This reiterates the "danger to third person" or "emergency aid" exception to the warrant requirement. The other notable instances when the police may enter a building or home without a warrant are: (1) when there is danger of physical harm to the officer or destruction of evidence and (2) in cases of "hot pursuit." All three exceptions may be classified under "exigent circumstances."

DAVIS V. WASHINGTON
547 U.S. 813 (2006)

CAPSULE: "Statements are nontestimonial [and therefore admissible in court] when made in the course of police interrogation under circumstances objectively indicating that the primary purpose of interrogation is to enable police assistance to meet an ongoing emergency."

FACTS: After a call and hang-up to 911, the operator reversed the call and Michelle McCottry answered. Based on questioning McCottry, the operator determined she was involved in a domestic disturbance with her former boyfriend, Davis. The operator learned that Davis had just left in a car with another person after hitting McCottry. Officers arrived and observed the injuries to McCottry but had no way to determine the cause of the injuries. Davis was later charged with violating a domestic no-contact order. Over Davis' objection, the 911 tape was admitted into evidence and he was convicted. Davis appealed his conviction, saying that his constitutional right to cross-examination was violated by the admission of the tape-recording into evidence because there was no opportunity to cross-examine.

ISSUE: Are statements made to law enforcement personnel during a 911 call or at a crime scene "testimonial" and thus subject to the requirements of the Sixth Amendment's right to cross-examination and confrontation? NO.

SUPREME COURT DECISION: "Statements are nontestimonial [and therefore admissible in court] when made in the course of police interrogation under circumstances objectively indicating that the primary purpose of interrogation is to enable police assistance to meet an ongoing emergency."

REASON: "The Confrontation Clause of the Sixth Amendment provides: 'In all criminal prosecutions, the accused shall enjoy the right ... to be confronted with the witnesses against him.' In *Crawford v. Washington*, 541 U.S. 36, 53–54 (2004), we held that this provision bars 'admission of testimonial statements of a witness who did not appear at trial unless he was unavailable to testify, and the defendant had had a prior opportunity for cross-examination.' A critical portion of this holding, and the portion central to resolution of the two cases now before us, is the phrase 'testimonial statements.' Only statements of this sort cause the declarant to be a 'witness' within the meaning of the Confrontation Clause. See *id.*, at 51. It is the testimonial character of the statement that separates it from other hearsay that, while subject to traditional limitations upon hearsay evidence, is not subject to the Confrontation Clause." "A 911 call ... and at least the initial interrogation conducted in connection with a 911 call, is ordinarily not designed primarily to 'establis[h] or prov[e]' some past fact, but to describe current circumstances requiring police assistance." "We conclude from all this that the circumstances of McCottry's interrogation objectively indicate its primary purpose was to enable police assistance to meet an ongoing emergency. She simply was not acting as a *witness*; she was not *testifying*." (Emphasis in original.)

CASE SIGNIFICANCE: This is an important case in police work because it holds that tape-recordings of calls to the police may be admissible in court during trial as evidence as long as they are nontestimonial. Every day the police, through the 911 service, receive all kinds of calls that are recorded, including those that may be incriminating to the accused. Davis claimed that admitting the recording violated his right to cross-examination because the taped evidence could not be cross-examined. The Court rejected that claim, ruling that for purposes of admissibility as evidence in court, a distinction should be made between nontestimonial and testimonial evidence. Nontestimonial statements recorded through 911 are admissible, whereas testimonial statements are not.

HERRING V. UNITED STATES
555 U.S. 135 (2009)

CAPSULE: The "good faith" exception for police applies to errors made by non-judicial personnel. A search incident to an arrest based on the erroneous information is also valid.

FACTS: When an officer learned that Herring, who was known to the officer, was at the sheriff's office to retrieve items from an impounded truck, the officer asked the clerk to check the warrants database for that county and a neighboring county. When the clerk discovered that there was an arrest warrant for Herring in the neighboring county, the officer asked to have a copy of the warrant faxed to the office. Meanwhile, the officer pulled Herring over as he left the impound lot and arrested him. A search incident to the arrest yielded drugs and a gun. When the clerk in the neighboring county attempted to retrieve the warrant to fax it, it was determined the warrant had been recalled five months earlier but the database had not been updated. The clerk notified the officers, but the arrest had already taken place and the evidence discovered. At trial, Herring moved to suppress the evidence on the grounds that his initial arrest was illegal. The court denied the motion, citing the good faith exception of *United States v. Leon*, 468 U.S. 897 (1984) for the officer's actions, and Herring was convicted.

ISSUE: Can evidence be admitted into court if it is obtained incident to an arrest based on a warrant that is later determined to have been withdrawn? YES.

SUPREME COURT DECISION: "In light of our repeated holdings that the deterrent effect of suppression must be substantial and outweigh any harm to the justice system, we conclude that when police mistakes are the result of negligence such as that described here, rather than systemic error or reckless disregard of constitutional requirements, any marginal deterrence does not 'pay its way.'" (Internal citations omitted.) "We do not suggest that all recordkeeping errors by the police are immune from the exclusionary rule. In this case, however, the conduct at issue was not so objectively culpable as to require exclusion."

REASON: Because there were conflicts in the lower courts about whether to suppress evidence found in cases similar to this, the Supreme Court accepted this case. In making its decision, the Court relied on elements drawn from previous cases. First, "The fact that a Fourth Amendment violation occurred —*i.e.*, that a search or arrest was unreasonable—does not necessarily mean that the exclusionary rule applies, *Illinois v. Gates*, 462 U.S. 213, 223 (1983). Indeed, exclusion 'has always been our last resort, not our first impulse,' *Hudson v. Michigan*, 547 U.S. 586, 591 (2006)." Second, "When a probable-cause determination was based on reasonable but mistaken assumptions, the person subjected to a search or seizure has not necessarily been the victim of a constitutional violation." "Our cases establish that such suppression is not an automatic consequence of a Fourth Amendment violation. Instead, the question turns on the culpability of the police and the potential of exclusion to deter wrongful police conduct. Here the error was the result of isolated negligence attenuated from the arrest. We hold that in these circumstances the jury should not be barred from considering all the evidence." Third, "To trigger the exclusionary rule, police conduct must be sufficiently deliberate that exclusion can meaningfully deter it, and sufficiently culpable that such deterrence is worth the price paid by the justice system. As laid out in our cases, the exclusionary rule serves to deter deliberate, reckless, or grossly negligent conduct, or in some circumstances recurring or systemic negligence. The error in this case does not rise to that level." In this case, the Court ruled the officers did nothing wrong. In fact, it was the actions of the officers in this case that led to the discovery of the outdated warrant. "These principles are reflected in the holding of *Leon*: 'When police act under a warrant that is invalid for lack of probable cause, the exclusionary rule does not apply if the police acted "in objectively reasonable reliance" on the subsequently invalidated search warrant. 468 U.S., at 922.'" "Similarly, in [*Illinois v.*] *Krull* we elaborated that 'evidence should be suppressed "only if it can be said that the law enforcement officer had knowledge, or may properly be charged with knowledge, that the search was unconstitutional under the Fourth Amendment."' 480 U.S., at 348–349 (quoting *United States v. Peltier*, 422 U.S. 531, 542 [1975])."

CASE SIGNIFICANCE: There is nothing in the Fourth Amendment requiring suppression of evidence obtained in violation of it. The exclusionary rule was created to exclude evidence that would be unfairly prejudicial to citizens and as an effort to deter law enforcement from Fourth Amendment violations. Over the course of many cases, the courts have ruled that police officers have a "good faith" exception to Fourth Amendment violations when they rely on judicial actions that later turn out to be illegal. For example, a judge who does not make certain changes that ultimately render a warrant illegal does not invalidate a search or seizure based on that warrant. These cases left open the issue of whether the good faith exception would still apply if "police personnel were responsible for the error." Both the parties in this case agreed that Herring's arrest was a violation of the Fourth Amendment. The issue was, regardless of the illegality of the arrest, whether the evidence found incident to the arrest should be suppressed. The Court in this case determined that the police actions may have been negligent but they were not malicious and they were not a part of the tactical decisions that led to the arrest. The officers making the arrest and search thought everything had been done properly. As such, they acted in good faith; therefore, the court ruled that their actions should be covered under the good faith exception.

Stop and Frisk

3

INTRODUCTION

"Stop and frisk" is a term in policing that is best understood if construed as two separate acts rather than one continuous act. A stop is justified if the police have "reasonable suspicion" (less than probable cause) that "criminal activity is afoot," that is, an individual has committed, is committing, or is about to commit a crime. The police then ask questions to determine whether the stop is justified based on reasonable suspicion. If the stop is not substantiated, the suspect should be released.

A frisk after a stop is valid for one purpose only: officer protection. Any frisk conducted for any other purpose becomes a "fishing expedition" and is invalid. A valid stop does not always lead to a valid frisk, unless the officer fears for his or her safety. A frisk should not and cannot be used to look for evidence of a crime, unless that crime is the possession of a weapon that constitutes a danger to the officer.

The leading case on stop and frisk is *Terry v. Ohio*, 392 U.S. 1 (1968). In that case, the Supreme Court approved the practice of the police stopping people without probable cause and then asking them questions to determine whether they have committed or are about to commit a crime. The Court held that the police can do this if they have "reasonable suspicion," and that a frisk may follow if there is fear for officer safety. There is no fixed time limit set for the length of an investigatory stop. Instead, it is decided on a case-by-case basis, using reasonableness as the standard. Stops cannot be for any time longer than is necessary for the police to ascertain whether a crime has taken place, is taking place, or is about to take place. A criminal profile alone does not constitute reasonable suspicion for a valid stop; instead, it is merely one factor to be considered in determining whether reasonable suspicion exists.

What starts as a frisk, however, may quickly turn into an arrest if probable cause develops. The suspect can then be subjected to a body search. In this case, the situation will have changed from a stop and frisk to an arrest based on probable cause.

More recent Court decisions hold that an anonymous tip that a person is carrying a gun is not, without more, sufficient to justify a stop and frisk. Another case holds that presence in a high-crime area, combined with an unprovoked flight upon observing police officers, gives officers sufficient grounds to investigate further to determine whether criminal activity has taken place, is taking place, or is about to take place. This is important because the police often face this situation in their work—individuals fleeing upon seeing the police. Flight alone is not likely to justify a stop, but flight plus other circumstances, such as being in a high-crime area, establishes reasonable suspicion that will justify a stop. The most recent Supreme Court decision on stop and frisk holds that the determination of whether or not reasonable suspicion exists must be based on a totality of the circumstances rather than on individual factors that, taken individually, might not justify a legal stop.

The leading cases on stop and frisk are: *Terry v. Ohio, United States v. Sharpe*, and *United States v. Arvizu*. Another case, *Hiibel v. Sixth Judicial District Court of Nevada*, holds that the Fourth Amendment allows officers, pursuant to a stop and frisk, to require a person to provide his or her name, and the person may be arrested for refusing to comply.

TERRY V. OHIO
392 U.S. 1 (1968)

CAPSULE: A stop and frisk based on reasonable suspicion is valid.

FACTS: A plainclothes officer with 39 years of experience, 35 years of which were as a detective and 30 years of which were in the same patrol area, observed two men standing on a street corner. It appeared that the two men were "casing" a store because each walked up and down the street, peering into the store window, and then both returned to the corner to confer. At one point the two men were joined by a third man, who talked to them and then left swiftly. After the officer observed the two rejoining the same third man a couple of blocks away, he approached them, identified himself, and asked for identification. Receiving a mumbled response, the officer patted down the outside clothing of the men. The officer retrieved weapons from Terry and one other man. Terry and the other man were charged with and convicted of carrying concealed weapons.

ISSUE: Is "stop and frisk" valid under the Fourth Amendment? YES.

SUPREME COURT DECISION: The police have the authority to detain a person for questioning even without probable cause to believe the person has committed or is committing a crime. Such an investigatory stop does not constitute an arrest and is permissible when prompted by both the observation of unusual conduct leading to a reasonable suspicion that criminal activity may be afoot and the ability to point to specific and articulable facts to justify the suspicion. Subsequently, an officer may frisk a person if the officer reasonably suspects that he or she is in danger.

REASON: "[T]he police should be allowed to 'stop' a person and detain him briefly for questioning upon suspicion that he may be connected with criminal activity. Upon suspicion that the person may be armed, the police should have the power to 'frisk' him for weapons. If the 'stop' and the 'frisk' give rise to probable cause to believe that the suspect has committed a crime, then the police should be empowered to make a formal 'arrest,' and a full incident 'search' of the person. This scheme is justified in part by the notion that a 'stop' and a 'frisk' amount to a mere 'minor inconvenience and petty indignity,' which can properly be imposed upon the citizen in the interest of effective law enforcement on the basis of a police officer's suspicion." (Footnotes omitted.)

CASE SIGNIFICANCE: The *Terry* case made clear that the stop and frisk practice is valid. Prior to *Terry*, police departments regularly used stop and frisk either by law or by judicial authorization, but its validity was doubtful because the practice was based on reasonable suspicion rather than probable cause, which is necessary in arrest and search cases. The Court held that stop and frisk is constitutionally permissible despite the lack of probable cause for either an arrest or a full search, and despite the fact that a brief detention not amounting to full arrest is a "seizure," requiring some degree of protection under the Fourth Amendment.

ADAMS V. WILLIAMS
407 U.S. 143 (1972)

CAPSULE: A stop and frisk may be based on information provided by another individual.

FACTS: While patrolling a high-crime area of the city in the early hours of the morning, an officer was approached by an informant who had provided him with reliable information in the past. The informant told the officer that Adams, in a nearby automobile, was carrying narcotics and had a gun in his waistband. The officer proceeded to the car, tapped on the window, and asked Adams to open the door. When Adams rolled down the window instead, the officer reached inside the car and removed a revolver from the precise place the informant had said it would be (although it was not visible to the officer). Adams was arrested for unlawful possession of a weapon. A search incident to the arrest revealed more weapons and a quantity of heroin. Adams' motion to suppress the evidence was denied and he was convicted on a weapons and a narcotics charge.

ISSUE: May an officer make a "stop and frisk" under the doctrine set down in *Terry v. Ohio*, based on information provided by an informant? YES.

SUPREME COURT DECISION: Reasonable grounds for a stop and frisk do not rest solely on an officer's personal observations; rather, they may be based on information provided by another individual.

REASON: "The Fourth Amendment does not require a policeman who lacks the precise level of information necessary for probable cause to arrest to simply shrug his shoulders and allow a crime to occur or a criminal to escape. On the contrary, *Terry* recognizes that it may be the essence of good police work to adopt an intermediate response."

CASE SIGNIFICANCE: This case settles the issue of whether information leading to a "stop and frisk" situation can come from an informant and not from direct police observation. It is clear that the police can make an arrest based on information from an informant as long as such information constitutes probable cause. It follows that, if the police can make an arrest based on information from a third person (an informant), the police should also be able to effect a "stop and frisk" (a less intrusive act by the police) based on third-party information—as long as such information constitutes reasonable suspicion.

UNITED STATES V. HENSLEY
469 U.S. 221 (1985)

CAPSULE: Reasonable suspicion based on a "wanted poster" is sufficient for a valid stop.

FACTS: Hensley was wanted for questioning about an armed robbery. The police issued a wanted flyer to other police departments in the area. Knowing of the flyer, and after inquiring without success as to the existence of an arrest warrant, officers stopped the automobile Hensley was driving. Firearms were found in the car and Hensley was arrested. Hensley was convicted of being a convicted felon in possession of a handgun.

ISSUE: May the police stop and briefly detain an individual who is the subject of a wanted flyer? YES.

SUPREME COURT DECISION: When the police have a reasonable suspicion, grounded in specific and articulable facts (in this case the wanted flyer), that an individual was involved in or is wanted in connection with a completed felony, a *Terry* stop may be made to investigate that suspicion.

REASON: "[W]here police have been unable to locate a person suspected of involvement in a past crime, the ability to briefly stop that person, ask questions, or check identification in the absence of probable cause promotes the strong government interest in solving crimes and bringing offenders to justice. Restraining police action until after probable cause is obtained would not only hinder the investigation, but might also enable the suspect to flee in the interim and remain at large. ... The law enforcement interests at stake in these circumstances outweigh the individual's interest to be free of a stop and detention that is no more extensive than permissible in the investigation of imminent or ongoing crimes."

CASE SIGNIFICANCE: *Terry v. Ohio* has been applied primarily in instances when the police have reasonable suspicion that criminal activity may be afoot and when the suspect may be armed and dangerous. *Hensley* authorizes a *Terry*-type stop in cases in which the stop is based on the issuance of a wanted flyer by a police department in another city and not on the possible commission of a criminal offense. Moreover, the Court recognized the need among law enforcement agencies for communication and cooperation, saying: "In an era when criminal suspects are increasingly mobile and increasingly likely to flee across jurisdictional boundaries, this rule is a matter of common sense: it minimizes the volume of information concerning suspects that must be transmitted to other jurisdictions and enables police in one jurisdiction to act promptly in reliance on information from another jurisdiction."

UNITED STATES V. SHARPE
470 U.S. 675 (1985)

CAPSULE: There is no rigid time limit for the length of an investigatory stop; instead, specific circumstances should be taken into account.

FACTS: An agent of the U.S. Drug Enforcement Administration (DEA) was patrolling in an area under surveillance for suspected drug trafficking when he observed Sharpe's automobile driving in tandem with an apparently overloaded truck. After following the two vehicles for 20 miles, the agent radioed for a marked car to assist him in making an investigatory stop. The agent and officer followed the vehicles for several more miles at speeds in excess of the speed limit. The DEA agent stopped the car driven by Sharpe, but the officer was forced to chase the truck, which he stopped a half-mile further on.

The DEA agent radioed for additional uniformed officers to detain Sharpe while the situation was investigated. These officers arrived 10 minutes later. The DEA agent arrived at the location of the truck approximately 15 minutes after it had been stopped. The agent's requests to search the truck were denied, but after he smelled marijuana, he took the keys from the ignition, opened the back of the truck, and found marijuana. The driver was then placed under arrest and the officers returned to arrest Sharpe approximately 40 minutes after his car had been stopped. Both men were charged with and convicted of possession of a controlled substance.

ISSUE: May an individual reasonably suspected of engaging in criminal activity be detained for 20 minutes when the detention is necessary for law enforcement officers to conduct a limited investigation of the suspected criminal activity? YES.

SUPREME COURT DECISION: There is no rigid time limit for the length of an investigatory stop; instead, the following should be taken into account:

1. the purpose of the stop
2. the reasonableness of the time used for the investigation that the officers want to conduct
3. the reasonableness of the means of investigation used by the officers.

Detaining the driver for 20 minutes is considered reasonable in view of the circumstances surrounding this case.

REASON: "While it is clear that 'the brevity of the invasions of the individual's Fourth Amendment interests is an important factor in determining whether the seizure is so minimally intrusive as to be justifiable in reasonable suspicion,' we have emphasized the need to consider the law enforcement purposes to be served by the stop as well as the time reasonably needed to effectuate those purposes." (Citations omitted.)

"Clearly this case does not involve any delay unnecessary to the legitimate investigation of the law enforcement officers. Respondents presented no evidence that the officers were dilatory in their investigation. The delay in this case was attributable almost entirely to the evasive actions of [the driver]. ..."

CASE SIGNIFICANCE: This case answers the question, "How much time is allowed in cases of investigative stops?" The answer is that there is no fixed time allowed; instead, it depends upon the purpose to be served by the stop and the time reasonably needed to carry it out. In this case, the circumstances were such that the detention for 20 minutes was considered reasonable. The Court added that judges should refrain from second-guessing police officers' decisions, particularly when the police are faced with a swiftly developing situation, as was the case here. This means that the benefit of the doubt must be given to the police on questions of how much time is sufficient for an investigative stop. Police officers must be ready to justify the amount of time used for an investigative stop, based on the purpose of the stop and the investigative method used, because an arbitrary delay would be considered unduly intrusive and unreasonable by the courts.

ALABAMA V. WHITE
496 U.S. 325 (1990)

CAPSULE: Reasonable suspicion is a less demanding standard than probable cause, and can be based on an anonymous tip corroborated by independent police work.

FACTS: Acting on an anonymous phone call, police responded to a tip that White would be leaving her apartment at a particular time in a brown Plymouth station wagon with the right taillight lens broken, in the process of going to Dobey's motel, and that she would be in possession of approximately one ounce of cocaine inside a brown attaché case. The police saw White leave her apartment without an attaché case, but she got in a car matching the description given in the telephone call. When the car reached the area where the motel was located, a patrol unit stopped the car and told White that she was suspected of carrying cocaine. After obtaining her permission to search the car, the police found the brown attaché case. Upon request, White provided the combination to the lock; the officers found marijuana and subsequently arrested her. At the station, the officers also found cocaine in her purse. White was charged with and convicted of possession of marijuana and cocaine. She sought to reverse her conviction, saying that the police did not have the necessary reasonable suspicion required by *Terry v. Ohio,* 392 U.S. 1 (1968), for such stops.

ISSUE: Did the anonymous tip, corroborated by independent police work, constitute reasonable suspicion to justify a stop? YES.

SUPREME COURT DECISION: Reasonable suspicion is a less demanding standard than probable cause. It can be established with information different in quantity or content from that required to establish probable cause; it may also be established with the help of an anonymous tip. The stop made by the police in this case was based on reasonable suspicion, therefore the evidence obtained was admissible in court.

REASON: When "an informant is shown to be right about some things, he is probably right about other facts that he has alleged, including the claim that the object of the tip is engaged in criminal activity." It is, thus, not unreasonable in this case to conclude "that the independent corroboration by the police of significant aspects of the informer's predictions imparted some degree of reliability to the other allegations made by the caller. ... What was important was the caller's ability to predict [White's] future behavior, because it demonstrated inside information. ... When significant aspects of the caller's predictions were verified, there was reason to believe not only that the caller was honest but also that he was well informed, at least well enough to justify the stop." Under the totality of circumstances, the anonymous tip, as corroborated, showed sufficient grounds of reliability to justify the investigatory stop of White's car.

CASE SIGNIFICANCE: This case is significant because it categorically states that "reasonable suspicion" is not as demanding a standard as probable cause and that it can be established with information that may be different in quality and quantity from that required for probable cause. The information may also be less reliable. It is important to note, however, that the anonymous tip by telephone given to the police in this case would not, in and of itself, have established reasonable suspicion (as shown in the decision in *Florida v. J.L.*, below). The Court said that "although it is a close question, the totality of the circumstances demonstrates that significant aspects of the informant's story were sufficiently corroborated by the police to furnish reasonable suspicion." What established reasonable suspicion in this case, therefore, was a combination of the anonymous telephone tip and corroboration by the police.

MINNESOTA V. DICKERSON
508 U.S. 366 (1993)

CAPSULE: A frisk that goes beyond that allowed in *Terry* is invalid.

FACTS: During routine patrol, two police officers spotted Dickerson leaving an apartment building that one of the officers knew was a "crack house." Dickerson began walking toward the police, but, upon making eye contact with them, walked in the opposite direction and into an alley. Because of his evasive actions, the police decided to stop Dickerson and investigate further. They pulled into the alley and ordered Dickerson to stop and submit to a pat-down search. The pat-down search revealed no weapons, but the officer continued to search and found a small lump in Dickerson's pocket, which he said he examined with his fingers and determined that it felt like a lump of cocaine in cellophane. The officer reached into Dickerson's pocket and retrieved a small plastic bag of crack cocaine. Dickerson was arrested and charged with possession of a controlled substance.

ISSUE: Was the seizure of the crack cocaine valid under the stop and frisk rule of *Terry v. Ohio*? NO.

SUPREME COURT DECISION: A frisk that goes beyond that allowed under *Terry* is not valid. In this case, the search went beyond the "pat-down search" for weapons allowed by *Terry* because the officer "squeezed, slid, and otherwise manipulated the pocket's content" before knowing it was cocaine.

REASON: The court ruled in *Terry* that a protective search "must be strictly 'limited to that which is necessary for the discovery of weapons which might be used to harm the officer or others nearby.' ... If the protective search goes beyond what is necessary to determine if the suspect is armed, it is no longer valid under *Terry* and its fruits will be suppressed." If an officer, however, "lawfully pats down a suspect's outer clothing and feels an object whose contour or mass makes its identity immediately apparent, there has been no invasion of privacy beyond that already authorized by the officer's search for weapons. ..." In this case, though, the "officer's continued exploration of respondent's pocket after having concluded that it contained no weapon was unrelated to '[t]he sole justification of the search [under *Terry*] … the protection of the police officer and others nearby.'" It therefore amounted to the sort of evidentiary search that is unauthorized by *Terry*.

CASE SIGNIFICANCE: This stop and frisk case further clarifies what is allowed under *Terry v. Ohio*. The Court ruled that the officer's actions in this case went beyond that allowed in *Terry*, arguing the officer did not merely conduct a frisk, but instead "squeezed, slid, and otherwise manipulated the pocket's content." During the initial pat-down, the officer felt a "small lump" in the suspect's jacket pocket, but admitted it was not a weapon. He believed it to be contraband only after he "squeezed, slid, and otherwise manipulated" it. This goes beyond *Terry*, which authorizes a pat-down search only for one purpose: officer safety. That was absent here because the officer admitted that what he felt was not a weapon. The Court's decision might have been different, however, had the officer testified that he knew it was not a weapon when he felt the lump, but that he had probable cause to believe—from his experience as a police officer and the circumstances of this case—that the lump was cocaine. If those were the circumstances, the seizure may have been valid, not under stop and frisk, but under probable cause. A frisk in stop and frisk cases can quickly turn into a valid warrantless search if the officer establishes probable cause (through experience, surrounding circumstances, etc.) that, although the item felt is not a weapon, he or she believes it is in fact contraband, and that belief is reasonable.

ILLINOIS V. WARDLOW
528 U.S. 119 (2000)

CAPSULE: Presence in a high-crime area, combined with unprovoked flight upon observing police officers, gives officers sufficient grounds to investigate further to determine if criminal activity is about to take place.

FACTS: Narcotics officers were caravanning to make arrests in an area known for heavy narcotics trafficking. One officer noticed Wardlow standing next to a building holding an opaque bag. Wardlow looked toward the officers then fled; the officers followed him. When the officers stopped Wardlow, one officer conducted a *Terry*-type pat-down search based on the officer's experience that it was common for there to be weapons in the area of the narcotics trafficking. The officer found a handgun and arrested Wardlow.

ISSUE: Did Wardlow's actions of fleeing in a high-crime area upon seeing police officers create a reasonable suspicion sufficient to justify a *Terry* stop and frisk? YES.

SUPREME COURT DECISION: Wardlow's presence in a high-crime area, combined with unprovoked flight upon observing police officers, gives officers sufficient grounds to investigate further to determine if criminal activity is afoot. The determination of reasonable suspicion must be based on commonsense judgments and inferences of human behavior.

REASON: "While 'reasonable suspicion' is a less demanding standard than probable cause ... the Fourth Amendment requires at least a minimal level of objective justification for making the stop." "An individual's presence in an area of expected criminal activity, standing alone, is not enough to support a reasonable, particularized suspicion that the person is committing a crime," "but a location's characteristics are relevant in determining whether the circumstances are sufficiently suspicious to warrant further investigation." "In this case, moreover, it was not merely respondent's presence in an area of heavy narcotics trafficking that aroused the officers' suspicion, but his unprovoked flight upon noticing the police." "We conclude that [the officer] was justified in suspecting that Wardlow was involved in criminal activity, and, therefore, in investigating further."

CASE SIGNIFICANCE: This case is significant because it addresses the issue of whether the police may stop and frisk a person who flees upon seeing the police. The Court ruled that such flight, under the circumstances of this case, gave the police sufficient reason to stop and frisk. The Court did not answer whether it would have made the same decision if the flight happened in another place not known for heavy narcotics trafficking. Instead the Court concluded that "it was not merely respondent's presence in an area of heavy narcotics trafficking that aroused the officers' suspicion, but his unprovoked flight upon noticing the police," implying that these two factors combined to establish reasonable suspicion. The Court ruled that a "reasonable suspicion determination must be based on commonsense judgments and inferences about human behavior." The implication in this case is that the place where the flight took place was taken into consideration by the Court in giving the police authority to stop. A safe interpretation would be that the Court would look into the "totality of the circumstances" to determine if flight upon seeing the police constitutes reasonable suspicion for a stop and frisk. The police should be prepared to identify "flight plus" factors to be able to establish reasonable suspicion in flight-from-police cases.

FLORIDA V. J.L.
529 U.S. 266 (2000)

CAPSULE: "An anonymous tip that a person is carrying a gun is not, without more, sufficient to justify a police officer's stop and frisk of that person."

FACTS: Police responded to an anonymous tip that a young black male was standing at a particular bus stop wearing a plaid shirt and carrying a gun. When officers observed a person matching that description standing at the bus stop with two other persons, they frisked J.L. and found a pistol. The two other persons were also frisked, but nothing was found. The officers did not see a gun, and they had no reason to suspect any of the three of any illegal conduct.

ISSUE: Is an anonymous tip that a person is carrying a gun, without more, sufficient to justify a stop and frisk of the person? NO.

SUPREME COURT DECISION: "An anonymous tip that a person is carrying a gun is not, without more, sufficient to justify a police officer's stop and frisk of that person." The anonymous tip alone in this case did not amount to reasonable suspicion.

REASON: "Here, the officers' suspicion that J.L. was carrying a weapon arose, not from their own observations, but solely from a call made from an unknown location by an unknown caller. The tip lacked sufficient indicia of reliability to provide reasonable suspicion to make a *Terry* stop: it provided no predictive information and therefore left the police without a means to test the informant's knowledge or credibility." Without some indication of criminal wrongdoing, the police did not possess sufficient reasonable suspicion to warrant the search.

CASE SIGNIFICANCE: This case clarifies what the Court ruled in *Alabama v. White* (above). In *White*, the Court held that reasonable suspicion can be established with the help of an anonymous tip, but more is needed. In *J.L.*, the Court reaffirmed this principle, arguing that an anonymous tip in itself does not amount to reasonable suspicion. What is needed is more indication that would establish that the tip itself was reliable. In *White*, the Court also held that "when significant aspects of the caller's predictions were verified, there was reason to believe not only that the caller was honest but also that he was well informed, at least well enough to justify the stop." Even then, *White* was considered a "close case." In contrast, the anonymous tip in *J.L.* was made from an unknown location by an unknown caller that "a young black male standing at a particular bus stop and wearing a plaid shirt was carrying a gun." There was nothing else beyond that. The Court held that this alone did not amount to reasonable suspicion and was not as reliable as the information received by the officers in *White*. The tip alone in *White* would not have justified a stop; but, based on the tip, police went to the place and observed the suspect's movements, which confirmed what the tip provided. Taken together, the tip plus observation by the police established reasonable suspicion. In sum, the test for reasonable suspicion should be "tip plus more" that would indicate the information given in the tip was reliable. It should be of interest that in this case, the state of Florida and the federal government argued that the Court should create a "firearm exception" to *Terry v. Ohio*, the original stop and frisk case. They suggested that a tip alleging that the suspect had an illegal gun (as in *J. L.*) should justify a stop and frisk even if the information did not amount to reasonable suspicion. The Court rejected this proposed exception, thus holding the same level of standard for stop and frisk in weapons and non-weapons cases.

UNITED STATES V. ARVIZU
534 U.S. 266 (2001)

CAPSULE: "In making reasonable-suspicion determinations, reviewing courts must look at the totality of the circumstances of each case to see whether the detaining officer has a particularized and objective basis for suspecting legal wrongdoing."

FACTS: The U.S. Border Patrol operated a checkpoint in an isolated area of Arizona. A limited number of roads circumvented the checkpoint, and were routinely used by smugglers to avoid the checkpoint. Because of this, sensors were placed along those roads to detect vehicular traffic. When one of the sensors indicated traffic, an officer responded. While following the vehicle for several miles, the officer observed several indicators of suspicious behavior, including: the time the vehicle was on the road coincided with shift change for roving patrols in the area, the roads taken by the vehicle were remote and not well suited for the vehicle type, the vehicle slowed dramatically upon first observing the officer, the driver of the vehicle would not look at the officer when passing, children in the vehicle seemed to have their feet propped up on some cargo, the children waved mechanically at the officer as if being instructed, and the vehicle made turns that would allow it to completely avoid the checkpoint. Based on these observations, the officer stopped the vehicle. After obtaining consent from Arvizu, the officer searched the vehicle and found drugs. The Court of Appeals ruled to suppress the evidence of the search based on an analysis of what it determined to be ten factors related to the stop. Each of the factors was examined individually, and seven were found to not present sufficient ground for reasonable suspicion. Since the majority of these factors were not found in themselves to be sufficient to support reasonable suspicion, the Court of Appeals ruled the search unconstitutional.

ISSUE: What is the proper standard for evaluating the factors used in an officer's decision to make an investigatory stop: consideration of each factor individually, or totality of the circumstances? TOTALITY OF THE CIRCUMSTANCES.

SUPREME COURT DECISION: "In making reasonable-suspicion determinations, reviewing courts must look at the totality of the circumstances of each case to see whether the detaining officer has a particularized and objective basis for suspecting legal wrongdoing."

REASON: "The court's evaluation and rejection of seven of the listed factors in isolation from each other does not take into account the totality of the circumstances, as our cases have understood that phrase. The court appeared to believe that each observation by [the officer] that was by itself readily susceptible to an innocent explanation was entitled to no weight. *Terry* [*v. Ohio*], however, precludes this sort of divide-and-conquer analysis." "When discussing how reviewing courts should make reasonable-suspicion determinations, we have said repeatedly that they must look at the totality of circumstances of each case to see whether the detaining officer has a particularized and objective basis for suspecting legal wrongdoing." "Having considered the totality of the circumstances and given due weight to the factual inferences drawn by the law enforcement officer and District Court Judge, we hold that [the officer] had reasonable suspicion to believe that respondent was engaged in illegal activity."

CASE SIGNIFICANCE: This case settles an issue in stop and frisk cases: how an officer determines the existence of reasonable suspicion. Is it by considering each factor individually, or by focusing on the totality of the circumstances? The Court of Appeals in this case had ruled that seven out of the ten factors cited by the officer, if taken individually, did not establish reasonable suspicion because they were innocent activities and were not in themselves illegal. The Court disagreed, arguing that previous decisions on this issue have always held that totality of the circumstances was the test to follow. This means that, even if the factors identified by the officer individually did not establish reasonable suspicion, taken together they were sufficient to legally stop the vehicle. This case involved stop and search rather than stop and frisk. What was at issue, though, was the legality of the stop, not the legality of the search. The search itself was considered legal because there was valid consent. However, if the stop was illegal because of the absence of reasonable suspicion, the search would also have been illegal because of the illegal stop and, therefore, the evidence would have been excludible. The decision is significant in two ways: (1) it makes it generally easier for officers to establish reasonable suspicion since they can rely on a number of factors to establish reasonable suspicion and (2) the statement by the Court that in determining reasonable suspicion, the process "allows officers to draw on their own experiences and specialized training to make inferences from and deductions about the cumulative information available." This means that what may appear innocent to an untrained person may in fact appear suspicious to a police officer because of his or her training. This reemphasizes an original principle enunciated by the Court in *Terry*, that an officer's training and expertise can be taken into account in determining reasonable suspicion.

HIIBEL V. SIXTH JUDICIAL DISTRICT COURT OF NEVADA ET AL.
542 U.S. 177 (2004)

CAPSULE: The Fourth Amendment allows officers, pursuant to a stop and frisk, to require a person to provide his or her name. The person may be arrested for refusing to comply.

FACTS: The Humbolt County Sheriff's Office received a telephone call from a person who had seen a man assault a woman in a red and silver GMC truck. When an officer arrived at the scene, he found a truck matching the description parked on the side of the road where the caller described. The officer observed skid marks in the gravel behind the vehicle, indicating a sudden stop. The officer also observed a man standing by the truck and a woman sitting inside. The officer approached the man and explained he was investigating the report of an assault. The man appeared intoxicated. The officer asked if he had any identification, but the man refused to produce any. After repeated requests and refusals to identify himself, the man began to taunt the officer by putting his hands behind his back and telling the officer to arrest him. After warning the man he would be arrested if he refused to comply, the officer placed Hiibel under arrest pursuant to a Nevada law allowing officers to detain a person suspected of committing a crime to ascertain his or her identity. The law states that "any person so detained shall identify himself, but may not be compelled to answer any other inquiry of any peace officer."

ISSUE: Can a person be arrested for refusing to identify himself or herself to a police officer? YES, BUT ONLY UNDER CERTAIN CIRCUMSTANCES.

SUPREME COURT DECISION: Requiring a suspect to disclose his or her name in the course of a stop and frisk does not violate the Fourth or the Fifth Amendment.

REASON: Hiibel argued that his Fourth Amendment rights were violated because he could not be compelled to give his name, and his Fifth Amendment rights were violated because his response was testimonial and could incriminate him. The Court rejected both of these arguments. On the Fourth Amendment issue, the Court held that, ordinarily, an "officer is free to ask a person for identification without implicating the Fourth Amendment" as a part of a *Terry* stop. "Here, there is no question that the initial stop was based on reasonable suspicion, satisfying the Fourth Amendment requirements noted in *Brown* [*v. Texas*, 443

U.S. 47, 52 (1979)]." Also, the Nevada statute was more precise than previous laws and only required the person to provide his or her name, not produce a driver's license or other document. "The Nevada statute is consistent with Fourth Amendment prohibitions against unreasonable searches and seizures because it properly balances the intrusion on the individual's interests against the promotion of legitimate government interest." "Hiibel's contention that his conviction violates the Fifth Amendment's prohibition on self-incrimination fails because disclosure of his name and identity presented no reasonable danger of incrimination. The Fifth Amendment prohibits only compelled testimony that is incriminating, and protects only against disclosures that the witness reasonably believes could be used in a criminal prosecution or could lead to other evidence that might be so reasonably used." "In this case, [Hiibel's] refusal to disclose his name was not based on any articulated real and appreciable fear that his name would be used to incriminate him, or that 'it would furnish a link in the chain of evidence needed to prosecute' him." (Internal citations omitted.)

CASE SIGNIFICANCE: This case is significant because it resolves an important issue in law enforcement: whether or not "stop and identify" laws can be constitutional. An earlier California law that required a suspect to furnish an officer "credible and reliable" identification when asked to identify himself or herself was declared unconstitutional because of vagueness or overbreadth. What was at issue in this case was whether the Nevada stop and identify law, which was more specific, was constitutional. The Nevada law [Nev. Rev. Stat. [NRS] Section 199.280 (2003)] provides as follows:

1. Any peace officer may detain any person whom the officer encounters under circumstances which reasonably indicate that the person has committed, is committing, or is about to commit a crime.

   ... .

3. The officer may detain the person pursuant to this section only to ascertain his identity and the suspicious circumstances surrounding his presence abroad. Any person so detained shall identify himself, but may not be compelled to answer any other inquiry of any peace officer.

Hiibel claimed that this law violated his Fourth and Fifth Amendment rights, not simply because it was vague or overly broad. The Court rejected these claims. The alleged violation of the Fifth Amendment privilege against self-incrimination was also rejected by the Court. In this case, Hiibel refused to identify himself "because he thought his name was none of the officer's business," and not because he feared subsequent prosecution; therefore, the Fifth Amendment privilege against self-incrimination could not be successfully invoked.

ARIZONA V. JOHNSON
555 U.S. 323 (2009)

CAPSULE: Officers may order passengers out of a lawfully stopped vehicle and pat them down if there is reasonable suspicion they may be armed and dangerous.

FACTS: Gang Task Force officers were patrolling in a neighborhood associated with Crips. Officers pulled over a vehicle for a registration violation. The vehicle contained three passengers, including Johnson, who was in the back seat. One of the officers noticed Johnson had a hand-held police scanner in his pocket. The officer understood this type of device was used primarily in criminal activity or to avoid the police. Johnson was also wearing clothing consistent with Crip membership. In response to the officer's questions, Johnson admitted being from a town known to the officer as home to a Crip gang and having been to prison. The officer ordered Johnson out of the vehicle to gain information about what gang he might be involved with. Suspecting Johnson might have a weapon, the officer patted him down after he exited the vehicle. During the pat-down, the officer felt the butt of a pistol. At that point, Johnson began to struggle and was handcuffed. Johnson was arrested and convicted of illegal possession of a weapon.

ISSUE: Can officers pat down passengers of a vehicle stopped only for a traffic violation if they have reasonable suspicion the passenger may be armed and dangerous? YES.

SUPREME COURT DECISION: Because the government's "legitimate and weighty" interest in officer safety outweighs the additional intrusion, a driver or passenger, already lawfully stopped, may be required to exit the vehicle. Once outside a stopped vehicle, passengers may be patted down for weapons if the officer has reasonable suspicion that the passengers might be armed and dangerous.

REASON: The Court based its decision in this case on the line of cases related to stops (both personal and vehicular) and frisks (*Terry v. Ohio*). After reviewing the decision in *Terry*, the Court commented that it ruled in *Berkemer v. McCarty* (see Chapter 17) that most traffic stops "resemble, in duration and atmosphere, the kind of brief detention authorized in *Terry*." The Court then relied on three cases to show *Terry's* application to traffic stops. In *Pennsylvania v. Mimms*, 434 U.S. 106 (1977), the Court ruled officers could order the driver out of a vehicle and, citing *Terry*, that, once out of the vehicle, the officer could pat the driver down for weapons if there was reasonable suspicion the driver was armed. The Court extended the decision in *Mimms* to passengers of the vehicle in *Maryland v. Wilson* (see Chapter 10). The Court also stated in dictum of *Knowles v. Iowa* that officers should be able to conduct pat-downs of passengers of lawfully stopped vehicles. Finally, in *Brendlin v. California* (see Chapter 10), the Court ruled that, during a traffic stop, an officer effectively seizes everyone in the vehicle. This ruling meets the first requirement of *Terry* that a person must be lawfully stopped/seized by police. The Court held in *Brendlin* that a vehicle is lawfully stopped "pending inquiry into a vehicular violation," and it is not necessary for the officer to believe anyone in the vehicle is involved in further criminal activity. To meet the second requirement of *Terry*, the officer must have reasonable suspicion that the person is armed and dangerous, which the officer did in this case.

CASE SIGNIFICANCE: This case confirms what the Court had previously intimated—that passengers of lawfully stopped vehicles may be ordered out of the vehicle and patted down if the officer has or develops reasonable suspicion that they may be armed and dangerous. This furthers an officer's ability to take control of a traffic stop and ensures officer safety while the traffic investigation (and any further investigation that might develop) takes place.

UTAH V. STRIEFF
579 U.S. ___, No. 14-1373 (2016)

CAPSULE: The discovery of a valid arrest warrant is a sufficient intervening event to break the causal chain between an unlawful stop and the discovery of evidence incident to an arrest.

FACTS: A detective conducted surveillance of a residence based on an anonymous tip about drug activity. The number of people he observed making brief visits to the house over the course of a week made him suspicious that the occupants were dealing drugs. After observing Strieff leave the residence and walk toward a nearby convenience store, the officer detained him and requested Strieff's identification. The officer learned from dispatch that Strieff had an outstanding arrest warrant for a traffic violation. The officer arrested Strieff, searched him, and found methamphetamine and drug paraphernalia. Strieff moved to suppress the evidence, arguing that it was derived from an unlawful investigatory stop. The trial court denied the motion.

ISSUE: Is the discovery of a valid arrest warrant a sufficient intervening event to break the causal chain between an unlawful stop and the discovery of evidence incident to an arrest? YES.

SUPREME COURT DECISION: "We hold that the evidence the officer seized as part of the search incident to arrest is admissible because the officer's discovery of the arrest warrant attenuated the connection between the unlawful stop and the evidence seized incident to arrest."

REASON: According to the attenuation doctrine, "Evidence is admissible when the connection between unconstitutional police conduct and the evidence is remote or has been interrupted by some intervening circumstance, so that 'the interest protected by the constitutional guarantee that has been violated would not be served by suppression of the evidence obtained'" (internal citations omitted). "The doctrine therefore applies here, where the intervening circumstance is the discovery of a valid, pre-existing, and untainted arrest warrant. Assuming, without deciding, that Officer Fackrell lacked reasonable suspicion to stop Strieff initially, the discovery of that arrest warrant attenuated the connection between the unlawful stop and the evidence seized from Strieff incident to his arrest."

CASE SIGNIFICANCE: This case further clarifies the doctrine of "fruit of the poisonous tree." Officers may not know the attenuation doctrine as one of the exceptions to the Fourth Amendment. This case clarifies that doctrine. The attenuation doctrine provides for admissibility when the connection between unconstitutional police conduct and discovered evidence is sufficiently remote or has been interrupted by some intervening circumstance. "In this case, the warrant was valid, it predated Officer Fackrell's investigation, and it was entirely unconnected with the stop. And once Officer Fackrell discovered the warrant, he had an obligation to arrest Strieff. ... Officer Fackrell's arrest of Strieff thus was a ministerial act that was independently compelled by the pre-existing warrant. And once Officer Fackrell was authorized to arrest Strieff, it was undisputedly lawful to search Strieff as an incident of his arrest to protect Officer Fackrell's safety."

Arrest and Other Seizures of Persons

4

INTRODUCTION

The law of arrest and seizures of persons is of great importance to law enforcement officers. An illegal arrest or seizure of a person violates the constitutional rights of an individual and can lead to lawsuits against the police. Not all detentions constitute an arrest. An arrest is defined as the taking of a person into custody against his or her will for the purpose of criminal prosecution or interrogation (*Dunaway v. New York*, 442 U.S. 200 [1979]). A seizure of a person occurs only when there is governmental termination of freedom of movement through means intentionally applied (*Brower v. County of Inyo*, 489 U.S. 593 [1989]). Both of these legal issues will be addressed in this chapter.

Police arrests may be classified into two general categories: with a warrant and without a warrant. In both categories, probable cause is required. The difference is that, in arrests with a warrant, probable cause has already been determined by a judge or magistrate. In arrests without a warrant, probable cause must be established by the police.

An arrest has four elements: (1) seizure and detention, (2) intention to arrest, (3) arrest authority, and (4) understanding by the person arrested. Seizure and detention can be actual or constructive. Actual seizure takes place when the police take the person into custody with the use of hands or firearms, or by merely touching the individual without the use of force. Constructive seizure takes place without any physical touching, grabbing, holding, or use of force. It occurs when the person peacefully submits to the will and control of the officer. The intent to arrest exists in the mind of the police officer and is therefore difficult for the arrested person to prove; but actions often speak louder than words. For example, if an officer places handcuffs on a suspect or takes the suspect to the police station in a police car, intent to arrest may be present although the officer may not have said: "You are under arrest." Arrest authority is inherent in policing in that every police officer is authorized to make an arrest unless there are specified limitations otherwise. Some jurisdictions limit this authority to the time during which an officer is on duty; other jurisdictions authorize officers to arrest a person even while off-duty if there is probable cause to believe that a crime has been or is being committed.

Whether a person is seized has been addressed by the Supreme Court in a number of cases, starting with *Michigan v. Chesternut*, in which the Court ruled that the test to determine whether a seizure occurs is whether a reasonable person viewing the police conduct would conclude that he or she is free to leave. In *Brower v. County of Inyo*, the Court held that a seizure occurs when there is a "governmental termination of freedom of movement through means intentionally applied." Then, in *California v. Hodari D.*, the Court held that no seizure occurs when an officer seeks to arrest a suspect through a show of authority, but applies no physical force, and the subject does not willingly submit (therefore there was no actual or constructive seizure). Finally, in *Florida v. Bostick* (see Chapter 10), the Court ruled that the test to determine whether a police–citizen encounter on a bus is a seizure is whether a reasonable passenger would feel free to decline the officers' request or otherwise terminate the encounter. In sum, not every encounter with the police is an arrest, or even a seizure. The general test is that it is a seizure only if a reasonable person under the same or similar circumstances would have considered the encounter with the police to result in a termination of freedom to leave.

Two cases have further clarified the authority of the police in arrest or seizure cases. In *Atwater v. City of Lago Vista*, the Court held that the Fourth Amendment does not forbid a warrantless arrest for a minor criminal offense, such as a misdemeanor seatbelt violation, which is punishable only by a fine. This settles an issue that the Court had not addressed before. At present, all 50 states authorize the police to make an arrest even for non-jailable offenses. *Illinois v. McArthur* held that, under emergency circumstances, and where there is need to preserve evidence until the police can obtain a warrant, they may temporarily restrain a person's movement without violating his or her Fourth Amendment rights. This gives the police more power to limit the movement of a suspect who has not been arrested and where the police are sure they have probable cause to obtain a warrant and are in the process of obtaining it.

The leading cases briefed in this section on arrest are *United States v. Watson, Payton v. New York*, and *Atwater v. City of Lago Vista*.

UNITED STATES V. SANTANA
427 U.S. 38 (1975)

CAPSULE: A warrantless arrest that begins in a public place is valid even if the suspect retreats to a private place and is arrested there.

FACTS: An undercover police officer arranged a heroin buy from Patricia McCafferty. After meeting with the officer and driving to the residence of Santana, McCafferty took the officer's $115 of marked bills, went into Santana's house, and returned shortly thereafter. The officer asked McCafferty for the heroin; she gave several envelopes of heroin to him. The officer then placed McCafferty under arrest. When asked where the money was, McCafferty replied that Santana had it. While McCafferty was being taken to the police station, other officers drove to Santana's house where they saw her standing in the doorway with a brown paper bag in her hand. After they identified themselves as police officers, Santana attempted to escape into her house. The officers chased and caught her. During the ensuing scuffle, two bundles of heroin fell to the floor, which the police recovered. Told to empty her pockets, Santana produced $135, of which $70 was the undercover officer's marked money. Santana and others were charged with possession of heroin with intent to distribute.

ISSUE: Is the warrantless arrest of a suspect in a public place valid if the suspect retreats from a public place to a private place? YES.

SUPREME COURT DECISION: A warrantless arrest that begins in a public place is valid even if the suspect retreats to a private place and is arrested there.

REASON: "While it may be true under common law of property that the threshold of one's dwelling is 'private,' as is the yard surrounding the house, it is nonetheless clear that under the cases interpreting the Fourth Amendment, Santana was in a 'public' place, … not in an area where she had any expectation of privacy … She was not merely visible to the public but was exposed to public view, speech, hearing, and touch as if she had been standing completely outside her house." The police, therefore, had probable cause to arrest her and did so in the proper manner. Santana could not, furthermore, thwart her arrest by retreating into her private home. "The District Court was correct in concluding that 'hot pursuit' means some sort of a chase, but it need not be an extended hue and cry 'in and about [the] public streets.' The fact that the pursuit ended almost as soon as it began did not render it any less a 'hot pursuit' sufficient to justify the warrantless entry into Santana's house."

CASE SIGNIFICANCE: In *United States v. Watson*, 423 U.S. 411 (1976), the Court held that the police are not required to obtain a warrant before arresting a person in a public place even if there was time and opportunity to obtain a warrant, as long as there is probable cause. The *Santana* case extends that principle to instances in which the arrest begins in a public place, but ends up in a private place (in this case, the suspect's home) because the suspect goes there. Santana was in a public place when she was standing in the doorway of her house, but ended up in a private place when she retreated. The Court considered what happened as a case of "hot pursuit" and therefore did not require a warrant.

UNITED STATES V. WATSON
423 U.S. 411 (1976)

CAPSULE: An arrest without a warrant in a public place is valid as long as there is probable cause, even if there is time to obtain a warrant.

FACTS: A reliable informant telephoned the postal inspector and informed him that he was in possession of a stolen credit card provided by Watson and that Watson had agreed to furnish the informant with additional cards. The informant agreed to meet with Watson and give a signal if he had additional stolen cards. When the signal was given, officers arrested Watson and took him from the restaurant where he was sitting to the street, where he was given his *Miranda* warnings. When a search revealed no stolen credit cards on Watson, the postal inspector asked if he could look inside Watson's automobile. The inspector told Watson that "if I find anything, it is going to go against you." Watson agreed to the search. Using keys furnished by Watson, the car was searched and an envelope containing stolen credit cards was found. Watson was charged with and convicted of possession of stolen credit cards.

ISSUE: Can officers arrest an individual in a public place with probable cause but without an arrest warrant even if there is time to obtain a warrant? YES.

SUPREME COURT DECISION: An officer may arrest a suspect in a public place without a warrant, even if there is time and opportunity to obtain one, if there is probable cause to believe that a criminal act has been committed.

REASON: "The usual rule is that a police officer may arrest without a warrant one believed by the officer upon reasonable cause to have been guilty of a felony .... Just last term, while recognizing that maximum protection of individual rights could be assured by requiring a magistrate's review of the factual justification prior to any arrest, we stated that 'such a requirement would constitute an intolerable handicap for legitimate law enforcement' and noted that the Court 'has never invalidated an arrest supported by probable cause solely because the officers failed to secure a warrant.'" (Citations omitted.)

"The cases construing the Fourth Amendment thus reflect the ancient common-law rule that a peace officer was permitted to arrest without a warrant for a misdemeanor or felony committed in his presence as well as for a felony not committed in his presence if there was reasonable grounds for making the arrest."

CASE SIGNIFICANCE: This case states that police officers can make an arrest in a public place, without a warrant, based on probable cause, hence dispensing with the warrant requirement even if the police have time to obtain a warrant. The general rule is that a warrant must be obtained before making an arrest, unless the arrest falls under one of the many exceptions to the warrant requirement. This is one of those exceptions—arrest in a public place based on probable cause. The suspect in this case argued that the police should have obtained a warrant because they had time to do so. The Supreme Court ruled that the common law and the laws of most states do not require a warrant to be obtained under these circumstances.

Watson is a federal case involving postal service officers. These officers acted in accordance with a federal law that authorizes officers to "make arrest without warrant for felonies cognizable under the laws of the United States if they have reasonable grounds to believe that the person to be arrested has committed or is committing such a felony." Watson sought to have this law declared unconstitutional, in effect saying that an arrest warrant was constitutionally required whenever there was time to obtain it, even if the arrest is made in a public place. The Court disagreed, saying that this has never been required under common law, the laws of many states, or previous Supreme Court decisions. Note that this case simply says that an arrest warrant is not constitutionally required for arrests made in a public place that are based on probable cause. If a state statute requires that a warrant be obtained, then the statute must be followed. The Court noted, however, that state statutes usually do not require an arrest warrant. The rule stands, therefore, that unless a state statute or case law provides otherwise, the police can make a warrantless arrest in a public place based on probable cause, even if they have time to obtain a warrant.

DUNAWAY V. NEW YORK
442 U.S. 200 (1979)

CAPSULE: Probable cause is needed for the stationhouse detention of a suspect if such detention is accompanied by an interrogation.

FACTS: An informant implicated Dunaway in a murder but could not provide sufficient information to justify the issuance of a warrant. The police, however, ordered Dunaway to be picked up and brought to the police station, where he was taken into custody. Although he was never told that he was under arrest, there was evidence that "he would have been physically restrained if he had attempted to leave." At the station, Dunaway made statements implicating himself in the murder after receiving his *Miranda* warnings. Dunaway was charged with and convicted of murder.

ISSUE: May the police take any suspects into custody, transport them to a police station, and detain them there for interrogation without probable cause to make an arrest? NO.

SUPREME COURT DECISION: The taking of a person into custody against his or her will for the purpose of prosecution or interrogation constitutes an arrest for which probable cause is needed. Probable cause is therefore necessary for the stationhouse detention of a suspect when such detention is accompanied by interrogation (as opposed to just fingerprinting), even if no formal arrest is made.

REASON: "[T]he detention of petitioner was in important respects indistinguishable from a traditional arrest. Petitioner was not questioned briefly where he was found. Instead, he was taken from a neighbor's home to a police car, transported to a police station, and placed in an interrogation room. He was never informed that he was 'free to go'; indeed, he would have been physically restrained if he had refused to accompany the officers or had tried to escape their custody."

"The central importance of the probable cause requirement to the protection of a citizen's privacy afforded by the Fourth Amendment guarantees cannot be compromised in this fashion … . Hostility to seizures based on mere suspicion was a prime motivation for the adoption of the Fourth Amendment, and decisions immediately after its adoption affirmed that 'common rumor or report, suspicion, or even "strong reason to suspect" was not adequate to support a warrant for arrest.'"

CASE SIGNIFICANCE: This case resolves the issue of whether the stationhouse detention of a suspect, accompanied by interrogation, is so restrictive of a person's freedom as to be the equivalent of an arrest, which is illegal without probable cause. In this case, there was no probable cause to arrest Dunaway, but there were reasons for the police to consider him a suspect in connection with a crime being investigated. Dunaway was therefore asked to come to police headquarters. He was never told that he was under arrest, but probably would have been physically restrained had he attempted to leave. He received his *Miranda* warnings, was questioned, and ultimately confessed. The Court held that, because Dunaway was in fact taken into custody by the police and not simply stopped on the street, probable cause was required to take him to the police station. Because probable cause was absent, Dunaway's detention at the stationhouse was illegal and the evidence obtained from him, despite the fact that he was given the *Miranda* warnings, was inadmissible.

PAYTON V. NEW YORK
445 U.S. 573 (1980)

CAPSULE: The police may not validly enter a private home to make a routine, warrantless felony arrest unless justified by exigent circumstances.

FACTS: After two days of intensive investigation, police officers assembled sufficient evidence to establish probable cause to believe that Payton had murdered the manager of a gas station. Officers went to Payton's apartment to arrest him. They had no warrant, although they had time to obtain one. Although light and music emanated from the apartment, there was no response to their knock on the metal door. They summoned emergency assistance and used crowbars to break open the door and enter the apartment. There was no one in the apartment, but in plain view was a .30 caliber shell casing that was seized and later admitted into evidence at Payton's trial. Payton later surrendered to the police and was indicted for murder. In a motion to suppress the evidence, the Court ruled that the search of the house was illegal and suppressed the evidence, but also said that the shell casing was in plain view and admitted it into evidence. Payton was ultimately convicted.

ISSUE: Does the Fourth Amendment guarantee against unreasonable search and seizure require officers to obtain a warrant if making a routine felony arrest when there is time to obtain a warrant? YES.

SUPREME COURT DECISION: In the absence of exigent circumstances or consent, the police may not enter a private home to make a routine, warrantless felony arrest. The evidence was not admissible because there was time to obtain a warrant and there were no exigent circumstances to justify a warrantless, non-consensual search.

REASON: "In terms that apply equally to seizures of property and to seizures of persons, the Fourth Amendment has drawn a firm line at the entrance to the house. Absent exigent circumstances, that threshold may not reasonably be crossed without a warrant."

CASE SIGNIFICANCE: The *Payton* case settled the issue of whether the police can make a warrantless arrest in a routine felony case. The practice was authorized by the state of New York and 23 other states at the time *Payton* was decided. These authorizations are now unconstitutional and officers must obtain a warrant before making a routine felony arrest. If the arrest is not routine (meaning exigent circumstances are present), a warrantless arrest can be made.

MICHIGAN V. SUMMERS
452 U.S. 692 (1981)

CAPSULE: A search warrant carries with it the limited authority to detain the occupants of the premises while the search is conducted.

FACTS: While officers were executing a warrant to search a house for drugs, they encountered Summers descending the front steps of the house. They requested his assistance in gaining entry to the house. He replied that he did not have keys to the front door, but that he would ring someone in over the intercom. Another occupant of the house answered the door but refused to admit the police. The officers gained entry to the house by forcing the door open. Officers detained Summers and eight others in the house while the premises were searched. When narcotics were found in the house, the police determined that Summers was, in fact, the owner of the house and arrested him. During a search of Summers incident to the arrest, officers discovered heroin in his coat pocket.

ISSUE: May the police detain a person on the premises while a search is conducted? YES.

SUPREME COURT DECISION: A warrant to search carries with it the limited authority to detain the occupants of the premises while the search is conducted.

REASON: "The detention of one of the residents while the premises were searched, although admittedly a significant restraint on his liberty, was surely less intrusive than the search itself. Indeed, we may safely assume that most citizens, unless they intend flight to avoid arrest, would elect to remain in order to observe the search of their possessions."

CASE SIGNIFICANCE: This case expands, to a limited extent, the search and seizure power of the police, enabling them to detain persons on the premises while a search is being conducted. A warrant to search for certain items may be used by the police to temporarily deprive a person found on the premises of liberty; such detention being merely a minimal intrusion of the person's Fourth Amendment rights.

WELSH V. WISCONSIN
466 U.S. 740 (1984)

CAPSULE: The warrantless nighttime entry of a suspect's home to effect an arrest for a non-jailable offense violates the Fourth Amendment.

FACTS: A witness saw Welsh's automobile being driven erratically, eventually swerving off the road and stopping in a field. Before the police could arrive, Welsh walked away from the accident. Upon arrival at the scene, the police were told that the driver was either drunk or very sick. The police checked the registration of the car and went to the owner's house without obtaining a warrant. The police gained entry to the house when Welsh's stepdaughter answered the door. Welsh was arrested and convicted for driving while under the influence of intoxicants.

ISSUE: Is a warrantless nighttime entry of a person's home to make an arrest for a non-jailable traffic offense constitutional under the Fourth Amendment? NO.

SUPREME COURT DECISION: The warrantless nighttime entry of a suspect's home to effect an arrest for a non-jailable offense is prohibited by the Fourth Amendment.

REASON: "Before government agents may invade the sanctity of the home, it must demonstrate exigent circumstances that overcome the presumption of unreasonableness that attaches to all warrantless home entries. An important factor to be considered when determining whether any exigency exists is the gravity of the underlying offense for which the arrest is being made. Moreover, although no exigency is created simply because there is probable cause to believe that a serious crime has been committed, application of the exigent circumstances exception in the context of home entry should rarely be sanctioned when there is probable cause that only a minor offense has been committed."

CASE SIGNIFICANCE: Probable cause and exigent circumstances almost always justify a warrantless search or seizure. This means that as long as probable cause and exigent (emergency) circumstances that justify immediate action by the officer are present, a warrantless search or seizure is valid. This case adds a third dimension to this general rule. The Court said that the gravity of the offense must be considered when determining whether a warrantless search or seizure can be undertaken. If the offense is minor and non-jailable, a warrantless entry into a home is not justified, particularly at night. There are, however, unanswered questions in this case. For example, what if the offense is minor but carries a jail term? Or suppose the incident takes place during the day? Or how might current driving while intoxicated (DWI) laws with more severe sentences change this ruling? What is clear from this case is that a warrantless nighttime entry into a person's home to make an arrest for a non-jailable traffic offense is invalid under the Fourth Amendment.

MICHIGAN V. CHESTERNUT
486 U.S. 567 (1988)

CAPSULE: The test to determine whether a seizure of a person occurs is whether a reasonable person, viewing the police conduct and surrounding circumstances, would conclude that the police had restrained the person's liberty so that he or she is not free to leave.

FACTS: Chesternut began to run after observing the approach of a police car. Officers followed him to "see where he was going." As the officers drove alongside Chesternut, they observed him pull a number of packets from his pocket and throw them away. The officers stopped and seized the packets, concluding that they might be contraband. Chesternut was then arrested. A subsequent search revealed more drugs. Chesternut was charged with felony narcotics possession.

ISSUE: Did the officers' investigatory pursuit of Chesternut to "see where he was going" constitute a seizure of him under the Fourth Amendment? NO.

SUPREME COURT DECISION: The appropriate test to determine whether a person has been seized is whether a reasonable person, viewing the police conduct and surrounding circumstances, would conclude that he or she is not free to leave. There is no seizure per se in police investigatory pursuits because the person still has freedom of movement.

REASON: "No bright-line rule applicable to all investigatory pursuits can be fashioned. Rather, the appropriate test is whether a reasonable man, viewing the particular police conduct as a whole and within the setting of all the surrounding circumstances, would have concluded that the police had in some [manner] restrained his liberty so that he was not free to leave ....
Under this test, respondent [Chesternut] was not 'seized' before he discarded the drug packets .... The record does not reflect that the police activated a siren or flashers; commanded respondent to halt or displayed any weapons; or operated the car aggressively to block his course or to control his direction or speed. Thus, respondent could not reasonably have believed that he was not free to disregard the police presence and go about his business. The police, therefore, were not required to have a particularized and objective basis for suspecting him of criminal activity, in order to pursue him."

CASE SIGNIFICANCE: This case provides guidelines to a persistent and difficult question in police work: When is a person considered seized by the police? The question is important because seizure by the police involves the Fourth Amendment and sets in motion constitutional guarantees, particularly the requirements of probable cause and, whenever possible, a warrant. Absent seizure, the police do not have to abide by constitutional guarantees. The Court stated that there is no definitive test to determine seizure; rather, it sets the following guideline: "whether a reasonable man, viewing the particular police conduct as a whole and within the setting of all the surrounding circumstances, would have concluded that the police had in some way restrained his liberty so that he was not free to leave." The standard is not whether the police intended to make a seizure, but whether the suspect would have concluded (as a reasonable person would have) that the police had in some way restrained his or her liberty so that he or she was not free to leave. This is ultimately a question of fact for the judge or jury to decide. Such determination, however, must be made by taking all surrounding circumstances into account, that is, use of siren or flashers, commands to halt, and so forth. If the behavior of the police is passive rather than active, chances are that there is no seizure.

BROWER V. COUNTY OF INYO
489 U.S. 593 (1989)

CAPSULE: The seizure of a person occurs when there is a "governmental termination of freedom of movement through means intentionally applied."

FACTS: In an effort to stop Brower, who had stolen a car and eluded the police in a chase of more than 20 miles, police placed an 18-wheeled truck across both lanes of a highway, behind a curve, with a police car's headlights pointed in a manner that would blind Brower. Brower was killed in the crash as a result of the roadblock. Brower's heirs and estate brought a civil rights action (42 U.S.C. § 1983) for damages against the police, alleging a violation of Brower's constitutional right against unreasonable search and seizure.

ISSUE: Is a roadblock set up by the police to stop a fleeing suspect a form of seizure under the Fourth Amendment? YES.

SUPREME COURT DECISION: A person is seized when there is a "governmental termination of freedom of movement through means intentionally applied." Because Brower was stopped through means intentionally designed to stop him, the stop constituted a seizure.

REASON: "Consistent with the language, history, and judicial construction of the Fourth Amendment, a seizure occurs when governmental termination of a person's movement is effected through means intentionally applied. Because the complaint alleges that Brower was stopped by the instrumentality set in motion or put in place to stop him, it states a claim of Fourth Amendment 'seizure.'"

CASE SIGNIFICANCE: The importance of this case lies in the Court's definition of a "seizure of a person" under the Fourth Amendment. Under the Court's definition of seizure, a roadblock is a form of seizure; and, because the roadblock in this case was set up in such a manner that it was likely to kill Brower, the Court decided that there was possible civil liability for his death. The Court did not say, however, that the police were automatically liable. Instead, it remanded the case to the Court of Appeals to determine whether the District Court erred in concluding that the roadblock was reasonable. If the roadblock was reasonable, then no liability could be imposed on the police. If, however, the roadblock was unreasonable, liability could be imposed.

CALIFORNIA V. HODARI D.
499 U.S. 621 (1991)

CAPSULE: No seizure of a person occurs when an officer seeks to arrest a suspect through a show of authority, but applies no physical force, and the subject does not willingly submit.

FACTS: Two police officers were patrolling a high-crime area in Oakland, California, late one evening. They saw four or five youths huddled around a small red car parked at the curb. When the youths saw the police car approaching, they fled. One officer, who was wearing a jacket with the word "Police" embossed on its front, left the car to give chase. The officer did not follow one of the youths, who turned out to be Hodari, directly; instead, the officer took another route that brought them face to face on a parallel street. Hodari was looking behind as he ran and did not turn to see the officer until they were upon each other, whereupon Hodari tossed away a small rock. The officer tackled Hodari and recovered the rock, which turned out to be crack cocaine. This was used as evidence against Hodari in a subsequent juvenile proceeding.

ISSUE: Had Hodari been "seized" within the meaning of the Fourth Amendment at the time he dropped the crack cocaine? NO.

SUPREME COURT DECISION: No "seizure of a person" occurs under the Fourth Amendment when a law enforcement officer seeks to arrest a suspect through a show of authority, but applies no physical force, and the suspect does not willingly submit. "Seizure" under the Fourth Amendment occurs only when there is either use of physical force or submission by the suspect to the authority of the officer.

REASON: "To say that an arrest is effected by the slightest application of physical force, despite the arrestee's escape, is not to say that for Fourth Amendment purposes there is a continuing arrest during the period of fugitivity. If, for example, Pertoso [the officer] had laid his hands upon Hodari to arrest him, but Hodari had broken away and had then cast away the cocaine, it would hardly be realistic to say that disclosure had been made during the course of an arrest. The present case, however, is even one step further removed. It does not involve the application of any physical force; Hodari was untouched by Officer Pertoso at the time he discarded the cocaine. His defense relies instead upon the proposition that a seizure occurs 'when the officer, by means of physical force or show of authority, has in some way restrained the liberty of a citizen.' Hodari contends that Pertoso's pursuit qualified as a 'show of authority' calling upon Hodari to halt. The narrow question before us is whether, with respect to a show of authority as with respect to application of physical force, a seizure occurs even though the subject does not yield. We hold that it does not."

"The language of the Fourth Amendment, of course, cannot sustain respondent's contention. The word 'seizure' readily bears the meaning of a laying on of hands or application of physical force to restrain movement, even when it is ultimately unsuccessful. It does not remotely apply, however, to the prospect of a policeman yelling 'Stop, in the name of the law!' at a fleeing form that continues to flee. That is no seizure. Nor can the result respondent wishes to achieve be produced—indirectly, as it were—by suggesting that Pertoso's uncomplied-with show of authority was a common-law arrest, and then appealing to the principle that all common-law arrests are seizures. An arrest requires either physical force or, where that is absent, submission to the assertion of authority."

CASE SIGNIFICANCE: There are four elements for a seizure to take place: intention to seize, authority to seize, seizure and detention, and the understanding of the individual that he or she is being seized. This case clarifies one of these elements—seizure and detention. The issue here was whether, at the time Hodari threw away the crack cocaine, he had been seized. Had he been seized before throwing away the crack cocaine, the evidence would have been excluded because at that time there was no probable cause for his seizure. On the other hand, if he had not been seized, the evidence would be admissible because what Hodari did would constitute abandonment.

The Court held that, at the time Hodari dropped the drugs, he had not been "seized" within the meaning of the Fourth Amendment. This is because for "seizure" to be present under the Fourth Amendment, there must be "either the application of physical force, however slight, or, where that is absent, submission to an officer's 'show of authority' to restrain the subject's liberty." There are generally two types of seizures: actual and constructive. Actual seizure is accomplished by taking the person into custody with the use of hands or firearms (denoting use of force without touching the individual) or by merely touching the individual without the use of force. Constructive seizure is accomplished without any physical touching, grabbing, holding, or the use of force. It occurs when the individual peacefully submits to the officer's will and control.

The facts show that Hodari was untouched by the officer before he dropped the cocaine, hence no physical force had been applied. The officer had told Hodari to "halt," but Hodari did not comply and, therefore, he was not seized until he was tackled. There was, therefore, no actual or constructive seizure; hence, one of the elements of a seizure under the Fourth Amendment was missing. Because no illegal seizure had taken place at the time the crack cocaine was tossed away, the evidence recovered by the police was admissible in court.

COUNTY OF RIVERSIDE V. MCLAUGHLIN
500 U.S. 413 (1991)

CAPSULE: The warrantless detention of a suspect for 48 hours is presumptively reasonable. If the time-to-hearing is longer, the burden of proof shifts to the police to prove reasonableness of the delay. If the time-to-hearing is shorter, the burden of proof of unreasonable delay shifts to the suspect.

FACTS: A lawsuit was brought challenging the process of determining probable cause for warrantless arrests by Riverside County, California. The county's policy was to combine probable cause determinations with arraignment proceedings. The policy was close to the California Penal

Code, which says that arraignments must be conducted without unnecessary delay and within two days (48 hours) of arrest, excluding weekends and holidays. The U.S. District Court issued a preliminary injunction requiring the county to provide all persons arrested without a warrant with a probable cause hearing within 36 hours. The Ninth Circuit Court of Appeals affirmed, saying that the county policy of providing a probable cause hearing at arraignment within 48 hours was not in accord with *Gerstein*'s [*v. Pugh*, 420 U.S. 103 (1975)] requirement of promptly providing the probable cause determination after arrest because no more than 36 hours were needed to complete the administrative steps incident to arrest.

There was conflict among the Circuit Courts of Appeals on this issue. The Ninth, Fourth, and Seventh Circuit Courts of Appeals all required a probable cause determination immediately following completion of the administrative procedures incident to arrest. The Second Circuit Court of Appeals allowed flexibility and permitted states to combine probable cause determinations with other pretrial proceedings.

ISSUE: Does the Fourth Amendment require a judicial determination of probable cause immediately (within 36 hours) after completing the administrative steps incident to a warrantless arrest? NO.

SUPREME COURT DECISION: If a probable cause determination is combined with arraignment, it is presumptively reasonable for the arrest-to-hearing period to last up to 48 hours. If more time than that elapses, the government bears the burden of showing that the delay is reasonable. Conversely, if the release is made before 48 hours after arrest, the burden of showing unreasonable delay shifts to the person arrested.

REASON: "Our task in this case is to articulate more clearly the boundaries of what is permissible under the Fourth Amendment. Although we hesitate to announce that the Constitution compels a specific time limit, it is important to provide some degree of certainty so that States and counties may establish procedures with confidence that they fall within constitutional bounds. Taking into account the competing interests articulated in *Gerstein*, we believe that a jurisdiction that provides judicial determinations of probable cause within 48 hours of arrest will, as a general matter, comply with the promptness requirement of *Gerstein*. For this reason, such jurisdictions will be immune from systemic challenges."

"This is not to say that the probable cause determination in a particular case passes constitutional muster simply because it is provided within 48 hours. Such a hearing may nonetheless violate Gerstein if the arrested individual can prove that his or her probable cause determination was delayed unreasonably. Examples of unreasonable delays are delays for the purpose of gathering additional evidence to justify the arrest, a delay motivated by ill will against the arrested individual, or delay for delay's sake. In evaluating whether the delay in a particular case is unreasonable, however, courts must allow a substantial degree of flexibility. Courts cannot ignore the often unavoidable delays in transporting arrested persons from one facility to another, handling late-night bookings where no magistrate is readily available, obtaining the presence of an arresting officer who may be busy processing other suspects or securing the premises of an arrest, and other practical realities."

CASE SIGNIFICANCE: This case defines the allowable time a suspect may be detained by the police without a hearing when a warrantless arrest occurs. In *Gerstein v. Pugh*, the Court held that "the Fourth Amendment requires a prompt judicial determination of probable cause as a prerequisite to an extended pretrial detention following a warrantless arrest." In this case, the Court clarified what the term "prompt" in *Gerstein* means. The Court said that it is presumptively reasonable for the detention to last up to 48 hours. If more than 48 hours elapse, the government bears the burden of showing that the delay was reasonable. On the other hand, release within 48 hours does not necessarily mean that there was no unreasonable delay, but the burden of showing that the delay was unreasonable shifts to the person who has been detained. In the words of the Court, "although we hesitate to announce that the Constitution compels a specific time limit, it is important to provide some degree of certainty so that States and counties may establish procedures with confidence that they fall within constitutional bounds." The Court added that, in evaluating whether the delay in a particular case is unreasonable, courts must allow a substantial degree of flexibility, taking into account practical realities. This includes unavoidable delays in transporting arrested persons, handling late-night bookings, and obtaining the presence of an arresting officer who may be busy doing other jobs. Determinations of unreasonable or reasonable delay are made by lower courts on a case-by-case basis, but using the principle laid out in *McLaughlin* as a standard. This puts more substance and meaning into the word "prompt."

ILLINOIS V. MCARTHUR
531 U.S. 326 (2001)

CAPSULE: Under exigent circumstances, and where police need to preserve evidence until a warrant can be obtained, they may temporarily restrain a person's movements (thus temporarily seizing a person) without violating his or her Fourth Amendment right.

FACTS: A woman asked police officers to accompany her to the trailer where she lived with her husband, McArthur, while she removed her belongings. The woman went inside where McArthur was present, and the officers remained outside. When the woman emerged, she told one of the officers that McArthur had drugs in the trailer. This established probable cause, so the officer knocked on the door and asked permission to search the trailer, which McArthur denied. One officer left to obtain a warrant. When McArthur stepped onto his porch, the other officer prevented him from reentering his trailer unaccompanied. McArthur did reenter the trailer on three occasions while the officer stood in the doorway and observed him. When the other officer returned with a warrant, the officers searched the trailer and found drugs and paraphernalia.

ISSUE: Was the temporary seizure of a suspect while officers obtained a warrant to search his trailer valid? YES.

SUPREME COURT DECISION: Under exigent circumstances, and where there is a need to preserve evidence until the police obtain a warrant, they may temporarily restrain a suspect without violating his or her Fourth Amendment right against unreasonable searches and seizures. The minimal nature of the intrusion and the law enforcement interest at stake justified the brief seizure.

REASON: "When faced with special law enforcement needs, diminished expectations of privacy, minimal intrusions, or the like, the Court has found that certain general, or individual, circumstances may render a warrantless search or seizure reasonable." "Temporarily keeping a person from entering his home, a consequence whenever police stop a person on the street, is considerably less intrusive than police entry into the home itself in order to make a warrantless arrest or conduct a search." "We have found no case in which this Court has held unlawful a temporary seizure that was supported by probable cause and was designed to prevent the loss of evidence while the police diligently obtained a warrant in a reasonable period of time."

CASE SIGNIFICANCE: The Court gave four reasons for this decision:
1. The police had probable cause to believe that the trailer home contained evidence of a crime and unlawful drugs.
2. The police had good reasons to fear that, unless restrained, the suspect would destroy the drugs before they could return with a warrant.
3. The police made reasonable effort to reconcile their law enforcement needs with the demands of the suspect's personal privacy.
4. The police imposed the restraint for a limited time—two hours.

The Court concluded, "[T]he police officers in this case had probable cause to believe that a home contained contraband, which was evidence of a crime. They reasonably believed that the home's resident, if left free of any restraint, would destroy that evidence. And they imposed a restraint that was both limited and tailored reasonably to secure law enforcement needs while protecting privacy interests. In our view, the restraint met the Fourth Amendment's demands."

This case is enlightening; even though the Court allowed the temporary restraint of the suspect while another officer went to obtain a warrant, the decision carefully pointed out the circumstances that justified the restraint. The implication is that temporary restraints by officers must be justified by circumstances similar to this case for the restraint to be valid. How similar is difficult to determine; that will have to be decided on a case-by-case basis.

It is safe to say, however, that the closer the circumstances are to this case, the greater is the likelihood that the police restraint will be deemed valid.

ATWATER V. CITY OF LAGO VISTA
532 U.S. 318 (2001)

CAPSULE: "The Fourth Amendment does not forbid a warrantless arrest for a minor criminal offense, such as a misdemeanor seatbelt violation, punishable only by a fine."

FACTS: A Texas law requires all front seat passengers to wear a seatbelt, a crime punishable by a fine of not more than $50. Texas law also expressly authorizes a police officer to arrest without a warrant if a person is found in violation of the law, although the police may issue a citation in lieu of arrest. Atwater was driving a vehicle with her two young children in the front seat; none was wearing a seatbelt. An officer observed the violation and stopped Atwater, telling her as he approached the vehicle that she was going to jail. Following the release of Atwater's children to a neighbor, the officer handcuffed Atwater, placed her in his police car, and took her to the police station where she was made to remove her shoes, jewelry, eyeglasses, and empty her pockets. Officers later took her mug shot and placed her in a cell for about an hour. She was then taken before a magistrate and released on bond. She later pleaded no contest and paid a $50 fine.

ISSUE: Does the Fourth Amendment forbid a warrantless arrest for a minor criminal offense punishable only by a fine? NO.

SUPREME COURT DECISION: "The Fourth Amendment does not forbid a warrantless arrest for a minor criminal offense, such as a misdemeanor seatbelt violation, punishable only by a fine."

REASON: At common law, commentators disagreed on the ability of police officers to make a warrantless arrest of an individual if the crime committed was not a felony or a misdemeanor involving a breach of the peace. However, during the time of the framing of the Bill of Rights, the states regularly authorized police officers to make warrantless misdemeanor arrests without the requirement of a breach of the peace. When combined with the fact that each of the states currently has laws authorizing arrest for misdemeanors not involving a breach of the peace, Atwater's argument of a constitutional proscription against warrantless arrests for minor violations was not persuasive. Atwater also argued that, even if there was not a constitutional provision against such arrests, the Court should create one, drawing a distinction between crimes for which a sentence of jail time could accrue from those punishable only by a fine. The latter, then, could not result in an arrest without a warrant. "The trouble with this distinction, of course, is that an officer on the street might not be able to tell [if the crime carries a jail sentence] ... [because] penalties for ostensibly identical conduct can vary on account of facts difficult (if not impossible) to know at the scene of the arrest." "For all these reasons, Atwater's various distinctions between permissible and impermissible arrests for minor crimes strike us as very unsatisfactory lines to require police officers to draw on a moment's notice."

CASE SIGNIFICANCE: This case is important because it settles an issue of concern to the police: whether the police can arrest persons who violate laws or ordinances that are not punishable with jail or prison time. At present, all 50 states and the District of Columbia have laws authorizing such warrantless arrests. Texas allows a warrantless arrest even for a minor criminal offense, such as not wearing a seatbelt, which is punishable only by a $50 fine. Atwater paid the fine, but later challenged the constitutionality of the law, arguing that it violated her Fourth Amendment right. She maintained that no such arrests were authorized under common law and that the history and intent of the framers of the Constitution did not allow such arrests. The Court disagreed, saying that it was unclear whether or not such arrests were authorized under common law, and also found that "there is no historical evidence that the framers or proponents of the Fourth Amendment, outspokenly opposed to the infamous general warrants and writs of assistance, were at all concerned about warrantless arrests by local constables and other peace officers." The Court then concluded that: "We simply cannot conclude that the Fourth Amendment, as originally understood, forbade peace officers to arrest without warrant for misdemeanors not amounting to or involving breach of the peace." Given these, the Court held that warrantless arrests for non-jailable offenses are constitutional.

MUEHLER V. MENA
544 U.S. 93 (2004)

CAPSULE: Detaining occupants of the premises in handcuffs for a certain period of time while executing a search warrant does not by itself violate the Fourth Amendment prohibition against unreasonable searches and seizures.

FACTS: Based on information concerning gang-related drive-by shootings, officers obtained a search warrant for a home known to be occupied by gang members. Believing one or more of the suspects in the home might be armed and dangerous, a SWAT team was called to assist in the search. Mena was awakened by officers and placed in handcuffs at gunpoint. Mena and three other individuals were taken to a converted garage where they were held during the search. They remained in handcuffs, but were allowed to move around in the garage. The search revealed several weapons, ammunition, drugs, and gang paraphernalia. Mena was released before officers left the area. She later filed a Section 1983 lawsuit, claiming she was detained for an unreasonably long time and in an unreasonable manner in violation of the Fourth Amendment.

ISSUE: May police handcuff occupants of a home for the duration of a lawfully conducted search? YES.

SUPREME COURT DECISION: Officers may detain in handcuffs occupants of the premises during a search without violating the Fourth Amendment.

REASON: "In *Michigan v. Summers*, 452 U.S. 692 (1981), we held that officers executing a search warrant for contraband have the authority 'to detain the occupants of the premises while a proper search is conducted.' *Id.*, at 705. Such detentions are appropriate, we explained, because the character of the additional intrusion caused by the detention is slight and because the justifications for detention are substantial ... . Against this incremental intrusion, we posited three legitimate law enforcement interests that provide substantial justification for detaining an occupant: 'preventing flight in the event that incriminating evidence is found,' 'minimizing the risk of harm to the officers,' and 'facilitating the orderly completion of the search.' ... The officers' use of force in the form of handcuffs to effectuate Mena's detention in the garage, as well as the detention of the three other occupants, was reasonable because the governmental interests outweigh the marginal intrusion .... In such inherently dangerous situations, the use of handcuffs minimized the risk of harm to both officers and occupants [and] ... the need to detain multiple occupants made the use of handcuffs all the more reasonable." Finally, the Court ruled that "the 2- to 3-hour detention in handcuffs in this case does not outweigh the government's continuing safety interests."

CASE SIGNIFICANCE: Mena filed a Section 1983 case seeking monetary damages from the police, alleging a violation of her constitutional right against unreasonable searches and seizures. She claimed she was illegally detained in handcuffs and for an unreasonably long time. The Court rejected both claims, holding that the detention was consistent with previous cases where the "Court held that officers executing a search warrant for contraband have the authority 'to detain the occupants of the premises while a proper search is conducted.'" Detention in handcuffs by the police was justified in these cases as "minimizing the risk of harm to officers." In this case, there was a valid search in which the police were authorized to "use reasonable force to effectuate the detention." The Court added that "[t]he use of force in the form of handcuffs to detain Mena was reasonable because the governmental interest in minimizing the risk of harm to both officers and occupants, at its maximum when a warrant authorizes a search for weapons and a wanted gang member resides on the premises, outweighs the marginal intrusion." On the allegation that the detention was unreasonably long, the Court replied, "Although the duration of a detention can affect the balance of interest, the 2- to 3-hour detention in handcuffs in this case does not outweigh the government's continuing safety interests." In sum, the Court held that no prior specific rules determine when detention of suspects is unreasonable. The use of handcuffs and the reasonableness of the length of the detention are determined by the circumstances of that case. In this particular case, the circumstances surrounding the search justified the use of handcuffs and the length of the detention.

BAILEY V. UNITED STATES
586 U.S. 186 (2013)

CAPSULE: Detentions incident to the execution of a search warrant must be limited to the immediate vicinity of the premises to be searched.

FACTS: Police obtained a warrant to search an apartment for a handgun. A confidential informant told police he observed the gun when he was at the apartment to purchase drugs. While officers were preparing to execute the search warrant, detectives conducting surveillance saw two men—later identified as Chunon L. Bailey and Bryant Middleton—leave the gated area above the apartment, get in a car, and drive away. The detectives followed the car for approximately a mile before stopping it. They found keys during a pat-down search of Bailey, who initially said he resided in the apartment but later denied it when informed of the search. Both men were handcuffed and driven in a patrol car to the apartment, where the search team had already found a gun and illicit drugs. After the men's arrest, Bailey's keys were seized incident to the arrest. Police discovered that one of Bailey's keys unlocked the apartment's door. At trial, the court ruled Bailey's initial detention was justified under *Michigan v. Summers* (see the case brief earlier in this chapter) as a detention incident to the execution of a search warrant. Bailey was convicted.

ISSUE: Is the seizure of a person reasonable when stopped and detained at some distance away from the premises to be searched when the only justification for the detention was to ensure the safety and efficacy of the search? NO.

SUPREME COURT DECISION: "Detentions incident to the execution of a search warrant are reasonable under the Fourth Amendment because the limited intrusion on personal liberty is outweighed by the special law enforcement interests at stake. Once an individual has left the immediate vicinity of a premises to be searched, however, detentions must be justified by some other rationale." "The rule in *Summers* is limited to the immediate vicinity of the premises to be searched and does not apply here, where Bailey was detained at a point beyond any reasonable understanding of the immediate vicinity of the premises in question."

REASON: "In *Summers*, the Court defined an important category of cases in which detention is allowed without probable cause to arrest for a crime." "The *Summers* rule permits officers executing a search warrant 'to detain the occupant of the premises while a proper search is conducted,' 452 U.S., at 705, even when there is no particular suspicion that an individual is involved in criminal activity or poses a specific danger to the officers, *Muehler v. Mena*, 544 U.S. 93 [2004]. Detention is permitted 'because the character of the additional intrusion caused by detention is slight and because the justifications for detention are substantial.' *Id.*, at 98. In *Summers* and later cases, the detained occupants were found within or immediately outside the residence being searched. Here, however, petitioner left the apartment before the search began and was detained nearly a mile away." "Limiting the rule in *Summers* to the area within which an occupant poses a real threat to the safe and efficient execution of a search warrant ensures that the scope of the detention incident to a search is confined to its underlying justification. Because petitioner was detained at a point beyond any reasonable understanding of immediate vicinity, there is no need to further define that term here. Since detention is justified by the interests in executing a safe and efficient search, the decision to detain must be acted upon at the scene of the search and not at a later time in a more remote place."

CASE SIGNIFICANCE: "In *Summers*, the Court recognized three important law enforcement interests that, taken together, justify detaining an occupant who is on the premises during the search warrant's execution." The first interest was "the interest in minimizing the risk of harm to the officers," "which may include detaining current occupants so the officers can search without fear that the occupants will become disruptive, dangerous, or otherwise frustrate the search." This includes occupants who return to the premises during the search. "The second law enforcement interest is the facilitation of the completion of the search. Unrestrained occupants can hide or destroy evidence, seek to distract the officers, or simply get in the way. But a general interest in avoiding obstruction of a search cannot justify detention beyond the vicinity of the premises." "If officers believe that it would be dangerous to detain a departing individual in front of a residence, they are not required to stop him; and if officers have reasonable suspicion of criminal activity, they can instead rely on *Terry* [*v. Ohio*]." "The third interest is the interest in preventing flight, which also serves to preserve the integrity of the search." "The need to prevent flight, however, if unbounded, might be used to argue for detention of any regular occupant regardless of his or her location at the time of the search, e.g., detaining a suspect 10 miles away, ready to board a plane." None of the three law enforcement interests identified in *Summers* applied in this case, so the Court ruled the stop inadmissible.

Seizures of Things

INTRODUCTION

The Fourth Amendment provides that "The right of the people to be secure in their persons, houses, papers, and effects, against unreasonable searches and seizures, shall not be violated, and no Warrants shall issue, but upon probable cause, supported by Oath or affirmation, and particularly describing the place to be searched, and the person or things to be seized." This provision governs the constitutionality of searches and seizures conducted by the police.

A seizure is defined as the exercise of dominion or control by the government over a person or thing because of a violation of law. The seizures discussed in this chapter are seizures of things or items, as opposed to seizures of persons. "The seizure of property occurs when there is some meaningful interference with an individual's possessory interest in that property" (*United States v. Jacobsen*, 466 U.S. 109 [1984]). The items subject to police seizures fall into four general categories: (1) contraband, such as drugs, counterfeit money, and gambling paraphernalia; (2) fruits of a crime, such as stolen goods; (3) instrumentalities of a crime, such as burglary tools and weapons; and (4) "mere evidence" of a crime, such as clothing containing bloodstains, masks, wigs, and so forth, that are related to criminal activity.

Seizures of these items may either be with a warrant or without a warrant. In both instances, probable cause must be present or the seizure is unconstitutional.

The cases briefed in this section begin with *Schmerber v. California*, 384 U.S. 757 (1966), in which the Court held that drawing blood from a suspect without his or her consent is not a violation of any constitutional right, as long as it is conducted under certain circumstances and using accepted medical methods. There are limits, however, to what the police can seize, even with court permission. For example, in *Winston v. Lee*, 470 U.S. 753 (1985), the Court held that surgery requiring general anesthesia to remove a bullet lodged near a suspect's heart cannot be allowed, even with court permission, unless the government demonstrates a compelling need for it. There are additional cases in this chapter that deal even with the drawing of blood as in the *Schmerber* case. These include *Missouri v. McNeely*, and the recent case, Birchfield v. North Dakota. *Missouri v. McNeely* (2013) expanded *Schmerber* and held that the destruction of evidence authorized in *Schmerber* did not automatically mean officers did not have to have a warrant to obtain such evidence. *Birchfield v. North Dakota* distinguished *Schmerber* in holding that, because of the intrusiveness and because of criminal penalties for refusal, blood tests for DWI require a warrant.

The leading cases briefed in this chapter on seizures in general are *Schmerber v. California* and *Winston v. Lee.*

SCHMERBER V. CALIFORNIA
384 U.S. 757 (1966)

CAPSULE: Drawing blood from a suspect without his or her consent is not a violation of any constitutional right, as long as it is conducted by medical personnel using accepted medical methods.

FACTS: Schmerber was arrested for driving under the influence of alcohol, which resulted in an automobile accident. After reading Schmerber his *Miranda* warnings, and while Schmerber was in a hospital being treated for injuries suffered in the accident, an officer directed a physician to draw a blood sample for purposes of chemical analysis. This was conducted over the objection of Schmerber and against the advice of his counsel. Evidence of the chemical analysis, which indicated intoxication, was admitted in court over Schmerber's objection and he was convicted.

ISSUE: Does the drawing of blood from a defendant over his or her objection violate the Fifth Amendment protection from self-incrimination or the Fourth Amendment protection from unreasonable searches and seizures? NO.

SUPREME COURT DECISION: The drawing of blood from a suspect, without his or her consent, to obtain evidence is not a violation of any constitutional right as long as the removal is accomplished by medical personnel using accepted medical methods.

REASON: "*Breithaupt* [*v. Abram*, 352 U.S. 432 (1957)] was also a case in which police officers caused blood to be drawn from the driver of an automobile involved in an accident, and in which there was ample justification for the officer's conclusion that the driver was under the influence of alcohol. There, as here, the extraction was made by a physician in a simple, medically accepted manner in a hospital environment. There, however, the driver was unconscious at the time the blood was withdrawn and hence had no opportunity to object to the procedure. We affirmed the conviction there resulting from the use of the test in evidence, holding that under such circumstances the withdrawal did not offend 'that "sense of justice" of which we spoke in *Rochin v. California*, 342 U.S. 165.' 352 U.S. at 435. *Breithaupt* thus requires the rejection of petitioner's due process argument and nothing in the circumstances of this case or in supervening events persuades us that this aspect of *Breithaupt* should be overruled."

CASE SIGNIFICANCE: *Schmerber* addressed and settled four constitutional issues that suspects usually raised during pretrial proceedings: right against self-incrimination, right to counsel, right to due process, and right against unreasonable search and seizure. On the first issue (self-incrimination), the Court ruled that the seizure of "real or physical" evidence does not violate Fifth Amendment guarantees because the amendment applies only to testimonial evidence. The second issue (right to counsel) was dismissed by the Court, arguing that there was no right to counsel at this stage. On the issue of the right to due process, the Court concluded that the extraction of blood in this case was valid because it was made by a doctor in a hospital and followed a medically accepted procedure. On the final issue (unreasonable search and seizure), where Schmerber alleged that the police could have obtained a warrant prior to blood removal, the Court ruled that the presence of exigent circumstances (the alcohol would be processed through the body and be lost in a short time) justified the warrantless seizure. This last issue would be distinguished, however, by the Court in *Missouri v. McNeely*, below.

CUPP V. MURPHY
412 U.S. 291 (1973)

CAPSULE: The police may make a warrantless seizure of evidence that is likely to disappear before a warrant can be obtained.

FACTS: Upon learning of his estranged wife's death, Murphy voluntarily went to the police station for questioning. After arriving at the station, where he was met by his lawyer, the police noticed a dark spot on Murphy's finger that they suspected might be dried blood from the murder. Murphy refused an officer's requests to take a sample of scrapings from his fingernails, placed his hands behind his back and in his pockets, and appeared to rub them to remove the spot. Under protest and without a warrant, the police took the fingernail samples. The samples were determined to have traces of the victim's skin, blood cells, and fabric from the victim's nightgown. Murphy was tried and convicted of second-degree murder.

ISSUE: Does seizing evidence that is likely to disappear without consent or formal arrest violate the Fourth Amendment protection from unreasonable searches and seizures? NO.

SUPREME COURT DECISION: The police may seize, without a warrant, evidence that is likely to disappear before a warrant can be obtained. Given the facts of this case—the existence of probable cause, limited intrusion caused by the stationhouse detention, and the destructibility of the evidence—the warrantless seizure by the police did not violate the right against unreasonable search and seizure.

REASON: "Where there is no formal arrest, as in the case before us, a person might [be] … less likely to take conspicuous, immediate steps to destroy incriminating evidence on his person." A full search of Murphy without formal arrest would have been unconstitutional under *Chimel v. California*, 395 U.S. 752 (1969), but the limited intrusion on Murphy was justified here because of probable cause.

CASE SIGNIFICANCE: This case illustrates the "evanescent evidence" exception to the warrant requirement. The general rule is that searches and seizures must be by virtue of a warrant. This rule, however, is subject to many exceptions. One of those exceptions is the "evanescent evidence" rule, which means that the absence of a warrant does not invalidate the seizure if the evidence sought is likely to disappear unless immediately obtained. In this case, the blood on the suspect's fingernails could easily have been rubbed off by the suspect, and the evidence would have disappeared had the police not acted immediately. The likelihood of disappearance of the evidence constituted an emergency that justified the warrantless seizure.

WINSTON V. LEE
470 U.S. 753 (1985)

CAPSULE: Surgery requiring a general anesthetic to remove a bullet from a suspect for use as evidence constitutes an intrusion into the suspect's privacy and security that violates the Fourth Amendment. It cannot be allowed unless the government demonstrates a compelling need for it.

FACTS: In a shoot-out resulting from a robbery, a store owner was wounded in the legs and the assailant appeared to be wounded in the left side of the body. Some time later, officers responding to another call saw the suspect (Lee) eight blocks from the store. He told the officers that he had been wounded when he himself was robbed. The suspect was taken to the same hospital as the store owner. While at the hospital, Lee was identified by the store owner as the man who had shot him. The state asked a court for an order directing Lee to undergo surgery to have the bullet removed.

The doctors first said that there was some danger involved in the operation, but later testified that the bullet was lodged near the surface of the skin and could be easily removed with no danger. While Lee was being prepared for surgery, it was discovered that the bullet was deeper than originally thought and would require surgery under general anesthesia with some risk involved. Lee then moved for a rehearing in the state court which was denied. The case eventually went to the United States Supreme Court.

ISSUE: May a state compel an individual to undergo surgery in a search for evidence of a crime? NO.

SUPREME COURT DECISION: Compelled surgical intrusions into an individual's body may be of such a magnitude that the intrusion is unreasonable even if it may produce evidence of a crime.

REASON: "A compelled surgical intrusion into an individual's body for evidence … implicates expectations of privacy and security of such magnitude that the intrusion may be 'unreasonable' even if likely to produce evidence of a crime. … The unreasonableness of surgical intrusions beneath the skin depends on a case-by-case approach, in which the individual's interests in privacy and security are weighed against society's interests in conducting the procedure. In a given case, the question whether the community's need for evidence outweighs the substantial privacy interest at stake is a delicate one admitting of few categorical answers."

CASE SIGNIFICANCE: This case is significant because it indicates that there are limits to what the government can do in an effort to solve a crime. In this case, the government sought a court order to recover a bullet lodged in the chest of a suspect. The evidence would have been conclusive against the suspect, but the Court held that not even a court of law could order that such surgery be performed because it would have been too intrusive into the suspect's body. In an earlier case (*Schmerber v. California*, 384 U.S. 757 [1966]), the Court held that a state may, over the suspect's protest, have a physician extract blood without violating the suspect's rights. However, according to the *Schmerber* decision, the holding that the Constitution does not forbid minor intrusions into an individual's body under stringently limited conditions in no way indicates that it permits more substantial intrusions or intrusions under other conditions. The Court in *Lee* concluded that the procedure sought was an example of the "more substantial intrusion" cautioned against in *Schmerber*, and therefore held that to permit the procedure would violate the suspect's right to be secure in his person, as guaranteed by the Fourth Amendment, unless a compelling need for it was established by the government. That compelling need was not present in this case.

CITY OF WEST COVINA V. PERKINS
525 U.S. 234 (1999)

CAPSULE: The due process clause does not require the police to provide the owner of property seized with notice of remedies specified by state law for the property's return and the information necessary to use those procedures.

FACTS: Pursuant to a valid search warrant, police officers searched Perkins' home and seized a number of items. The suspect in the crime (March) was a boarder in the Perkins' house. Items seized by the police incriminated March, but some belonged to Perkins. Upon completing the seizure, officers left notice of the search and other information such as the judge who issued the warrant, the officers to contact for information, and an itemized list of property seized. The officers did not leave the warrant number because the case was ongoing and the information was sealed; however, that information was maintained by the court clerk in a file indexed by the address of the home searched. After attempts to secure the return of the property, Perkins filed suit.

ISSUE: When seizing property for a criminal investigation, does the dueprocess clause require that the person from whom property is taken be provided with a detailed notice of the procedures for the return of the seized property and the information needed to use those procedures? NO.

SUPREME COURT DECISION: The due process clause does not require the police to provide the owner of property seized with notice of remedies specified by state law for the property's return and the information necessary to use those procedures.

REASON: "A primary purpose of the notice required by the Due Process Clause is to ensure that the opportunity for a hearing is meaningful. ... It follows that when law enforcement agents seize property pursuant to [a] warrant, due process requires them to take reasonable steps to give notice that the property has been taken so the owner can pursue available remedies for its return. ... No similar rationale justifies requiring individualized notice of state-law remedies which, like those at issue here, are established by published, generally available state statutes and case law. Once the property owner is informed that his property has been seized, he can turn to these public sources to learn about the remedial procedures available to him. The City need not take other steps to inform him of his options."

CASE SIGNIFICANCE: In this case, the Court held that "individualized notice that officers have taken property is necessary in a case such as this one because the owner has no other reasonable means of ascertaining who is responsible for his loss," but that the other requirements specified by state law (such as detailed notice of the state procedures for the return of the seized property and the information necessary to use those procedures, including the search warrant number or a method of obtaining it) are not required by the due process clause.

GROH V. RAMIREZ ET AL.
540 U.S. 551 (2004)

CAPSULE: A search warrant that does not comply with the requirement that the warrant particularly describe the person or things to be seized is unconstitutional. The fact that the application for the warrant (but not the warrant itself) adequately described the things to be seized does not make the warrant valid.

FACTS: Agent Groh prepared an application for a search warrant based on information that weapons and explosives were located on Ramirez's farm. The application was supported by a detailed affidavit listing the items to be seized and describing the basis for his belief that the items were concealed on the property. Groh presented these documents, along with a warrant form he had completed, to a magistrate. The magistrate signed the warrant form. Although the application and affidavit described the contraband expected to be discovered, the warrant form only indicated that the place to be searched was Ramirez's home. The warrant did not incorporate any reference to the itemized list contained in the application or affidavit. The day after the magistrate signed the warrant, officers searched Ramirez's home but found no illegal weapons or explosives. Groh left a copy of the warrant at the home but did not leave a copy of the application. The following day, in response to a request from Ramirez's attorney, Groh faxed a copy of the application. No charges were filed against Ramirez, but he later filed suit claiming his Fourth Amendment rights were violated by the non-specific warrant.

ISSUE: Does a search warrant that does not particularly describe the persons or things to be seized, but has those in the application that was filed with the judge, violate the Fourth Amendment? YES.

SUPREME COURT DECISION: A search warrant that does not contain a particular description of the things to be seized is unconstitutional even if the application for the warrant contains such descriptions.

REASON: "The Fourth Amendment states unambiguously that 'no Warrants shall issue, but upon probable cause, supported by Oath or affirmation, and particularly describing the place to be searched, and the persons or things to be seized.' The warrant in this case complied with the first three of these requirements: It was based on probable cause and supported by a sworn affidavit, and it described with particularity the place of the search. On the fourth requirement, however, the warrant failed altogether." The Court relied on previous cases, including *Massachusetts v. Sheppard*, 468 U.S. 981 (1984), where they stressed that a warrant that does not particularly describe the items to be seized is unconstitutional. The Court then addressed the argument by Groh that the search was based on a particular description because it was in the supporting documents. To this, the Court responded, "The fact that the application adequately described the 'things to be seized' does not save the warrant from its facial invalidity. The Fourth Amendment by its terms requires particularity in the warrant, not the supporting documents." The reason given by the Court for this requirement is, "unless the particular items described in the affidavit are also set forth in the warrant itself (or at least incorporated by reference, and the affidavit present at the search), there can be no written assurance that the Magistrate actually found probable cause to search for, and to seize, every item mentioned in the affidavit." The Court did concede that the particular description could be addressed in supporting documents, however, with the statement that "We do not say that the Fourth Amendment forbids a warrant from cross-referencing other documents. Indeed, most Courts of Appeals have held that a court may construe a warrant with references to a supporting application or affidavit if the warrant uses appropriate words of incorporation, and if the supporting document accompanies the warrant."

CASE SIGNIFICANCE: In this case, the application submitted by the officer to the judge clearly specified the items to be seized; however, the warrant itself did not specify those, and neither did the warrant incorporate by reference the application's itemized list. The Court concluded that the warrant was "plainly invalid." The purpose for the particularity requirement is to have "written assurance" that the judge "actually found probable cause for a search as broad as the affiant requested." The Court also said that "the particularity requirement's purpose is not limited to preventing general searches; it also assures the individual whose property is searched and seized of the executing officer's legal authority, his need to search, and the limits of his power to do so."

This case presents a common dilemma for police officers. Many search warrant forms are computer generated, so they are often cumbersome to fill out and do not provide sufficient space for some descriptions. To overcome these problems with search warrant forms, officers often include references to other documents (affidavits or applications for the warrant), or they provide a brief description and rely on the supporting documents to meet the particularity requirement of the Fourth Amendment. Although the Supreme Court appears to support the procedure of including references to other documents in the search warrant, as long as the documents then accompany the warrant, the Court firmly rejected instances in which the warrant itself does not particularly describe "the place to be searched, and the persons or things to be seized." Officers must be careful, therefore, to make sure the items to be seized are adequately described in the search warrant, or are at least referenced in the warrant and the supporting documents attached to the warrant.

MISSOURI V. MCNEELY
569 U.S. 141 (2013)

CAPSULE: "In those drunk-driving investigations where police officers can reasonably obtain a warrant before a blood sample can be drawn without significantly undermining the efficacy of the search, the Fourth Amendment mandates that they do so."

FACTS: McNeely was stopped for speeding and crossing the center line. He did poorly on field sobriety tests. After refusing a breathalyzer test, he was arrested and taken to a hospital for a blood test. McNeely refused to consent to the blood test, but the officer directed the lab technician to draw the blood. The officer never attempted to obtain a search warrant. McNeely's blood alcohol level was above the legal limit, and he was charged with driving while intoxicated (DWI). McNeely sought to have the blood test excluded at trial. The trial court agreed, indicating there was no exigency to support the blood test without a warrant.

ISSUE: Whether "the natural metabolization of alcohol in the bloodstream presents a *per se* exigency that justifies an exception to the Fourth Amendment's warrant requirement for nonconsensual blood testing in all drunk-driving cases." NO.

SUPREME COURT DECISION: "Exigency in this context must be determined case by case based on the totality of the circumstances." "In those drunk-driving investigations where police officers can reasonably obtain a warrant before a blood sample can be drawn without significantly undermining the efficacy of the search, the Fourth Amendment mandates that they do so."

REASON: The case begins with *Schmerber*, which held that officers could make a warrantless blood test in DWI cases because of the potential for the destruction of evidence (the alcohol dissipating from the blood-stream). The prosecution in this case argued that DWI stops should represent a per se exigency sufficient to allow a warrantless blood draw because the blood alcohol level continually decreases with time, thus representing the possibility of the loss of evidence. The Court did not agree. The Court argued that their decision in *Schmerber* applied a totality of the circumstances approach that was strictly based "on the facts of the present record" (384 U.S. at 772). The Court also made a distinction with *Schmerber* that the laws have changed since that case was decided, and officers are now allowed to apply for a warrant based on sworn testimony communicated by telephone. This can substantially speed up the process and was an option not available in *Schmerber*, furthering the rationale for a case-by-case analysis of the necessity for a warrant.

CASE SIGNIFICANCE: The Court in this case did not rule that there could never be an exigency in a DWI case that would support a warrantless blood draw. The prosecution sought a per se rule allowing a warrantless search. The Court refused to support this position. The Court did leave the door open, however, saying that there are instances where obtaining a warrant is impractical, and dissipation of the blood alcohol level could be one of the factors considered in the totality of circumstances that could support a warrantless blood draw. The Court also pointed out that the warrant process need not significantly delay the blood test because officers could take steps to secure a warrant while the suspect is being transported to a medical facility. The application for law enforcement officers is that the warrant requirement is still strongly in effect for DWI cases. If there is an articulable reason for conducting a blood test without a warrant, officers may do so; but the expectation is that a warrant should be sought in DWI cases.

MARYLAND V. KING
569 U.S. 435 (2013)

CAPSULE: Under certain conditions, officers may take and analyze a cheek swab of a lawfully arrested person as a part of booking procedures.

FACTS: In 2003, a man broke into a woman's home and raped her. Police were not able to identify him but did obtain a DNA sample of the assailant from the victim. In 2009, King was arrested and charged with assault. As a part of a routine booking procedure for serious offenses, his DNA sample was taken by applying a cotton swab to the inside of his cheeks. The DNA matched the DNA taken from the rape victim. King moved to have the DNA excluded at trial because it violated the Fourth Amendment. The petition was overruled by the trial court and King was convicted of the rape.

ISSUE: Does the Fourth Amendment prohibit the collection and analysis of a DNA sample from persons arrested, but not yet convicted, on felony charges? NO.

SUPREME COURT DECISION: "When officers make an arrest supported by probable cause to hold for a serious offense and they bring the suspect to the station to be detained in custody, taking and analyzing a cheek swab of the arrestee's DNA is, like fingerprinting and photographing, a legitimate police booking procedure that is reasonable under the Fourth Amendment."

REASON: The Court ruled that taking the DNA sample was a search within the Fourth Amendment. The Court then relied on previous cases, particularly those involving the collection of fingerprints, in deciding this case. Drawing on *Illinois v. McArthur*, 531 U.S. 326, 330 (2001), the Court reasoned "[w]hen faced with special law enforcement needs, diminished expectations of privacy, minimal intrusions, or the like, the Court has found that certain general, or individual, circumstances may render a warrantless search or seizure reasonable." Specifically, the Court reasoned "Police routinely have used scientific advancements as standard procedures for identifying arrestees. Fingerprinting, perhaps the most direct historical analogue to DNA technology, has, from its advent, been viewed as a natural part of 'the administrative steps incident to arrest.' *County of Riverside v. McLaughlin*, 500 U.S. 44, 58 [413 (1991)]." The Court pointed out that there was a diminished need for a warrant in this instance because the person was already in valid police custody. The Court then turned to the level of intrusion of the collection. The Court noted, "An invasive surgery may raise privacy concerns weighty enough for the search to require a warrant, notwithstanding the arrestee's diminished privacy expectations, but a buccal swab, which involves a brief and minimal intrusion with 'virtually no risk, trauma, or pain' *Schmerber v. California*, 384 U.S. 757, 771, does not increase the indignity already attendant to normal incidents of arrest." Finally, the Court took note of the routine nature of the collection, arguing "[T]he government has an interest in properly identifying 'who has been arrested and who is being tried.'" Based on the combined effect of these circumstances, the Court ruled the collection was constitutional.

CASE SIGNIFICANCE: This case held that officers can collect DNA samples from those arrested and as a part of a routine booking procedure. It is somewhat unclear, however, on the circumstances that may lead to the collection. The Maryland statute in this case was somewhat restrictive— only allowing DNA collection if the person was arrested for violent crimes or burglary, requiring that the test not be conducted until the person was arraigned, and mandating destruction of the DNA sample if the person was not convicted. Law enforcement should be aware that taking of DNA samples is most likely to be supported when it follows the provisions set out by Maryland in this case. Collecting DNA samples for other reasons (say, for less than serious crimes) should be undertaken with caution and may be subject to exclusion in court.

BIRCHFIELD V. NORTH DAKOTA
586 U.S. 186 (2013)

CAPSULE: "The Fourth Amendment permits warrantless breath tests incident to arrests for drunk driving but not warrantless blood tests absent a specific exigency."

FACTS: This case combines three cases in different states. Only the primary (Birchfield) case facts will be discussed. Birchfield drove his car off the highway, and officers observed while he tried to get his car out of the ditch. Upon approaching Birchfield, officers smelled alcohol and noted that he slurred his speech and struggled to stay on his feet. Birchfield agree to several sobriety tests and did poorly on each. The officer informed Birchfield of his obligation under state law to submit to a blood alcohol test (BAC) test. Birchfield consented to a roadside test that revealed his BAC at more than three times the legal limit. The officer then arrested Birchfield. Birchfield refused to have his blood drawn for a confirmatory BAC test.

ISSUE: May motorists lawfully arrested for drunk driving be convicted of a crime or otherwise penalized for refusing to take a warrantless test measuring the alcohol in their bloodstream? NO for blood test, YES for breath test.

SUPREME COURT DECISION: "Taking a blood sample or administering a breath test is a search governed by the Fourth Amendment." "These searches may nevertheless be exempt from the warrant requirement if they fall within, as relevant here, the exception for searches conducted incident to a lawful arrest." "The Fourth Amendment permits warrantless breath tests incident to arrests for drunk driving but not warrantless blood tests." "Motorists may not be criminally punished for refusing to submit to a blood test based on legally implied consent to submit to them. It is one thing to approve implied-consent laws that impose civil penalties and evidentiary consequences on motorists who refuse to comply, but quite another for a State to insist upon an intrusive blood test and then to impose criminal penalties on refusal to submit."

REASON: The Court began by noting that a warrant requirement for every BAC test would be a burden on courts. The Court drew a bright line between breath tests and blood tests. For breath tests, the Court reasoned that there is little physical intrusion, no piercing of the skin, and minimum inconvenience. The Court distinguished blood tests on these criteria, however, ruling that they require a warrant absent a specific exigency. "Because the impact of breath tests on privacy is slight, and the need for BAC testing is great, the Fourth Amendment permits warrantless breath tests incident to arrests for drunk driving. Blood tests, however, are significantly more intrusive, and their reasonableness must be judged in light of the availability of the less invasive alternative of a breath test.

CASE SIGNIFICANCE: Most states have been strengthening DWI laws; and also strengthening laws for refusal to submit to tests. This case combined laws requiring BAC tests. After lengthy discussion of the background of the cases, the Court ruled that BAC breath tests were not intrusive enough to invoke a warrant requirement for them; however, blood tests are more intrusive. Therefore, the general rule is that blood tests will require a warrant, and motorists may not be criminally punished for refusing to submit to them. It is acceptable to apply *criminal* punishment for refusal of a BAC breath test; or it is acceptable to apply *civil* punishment for refusal of a BAC blood test. This case is also interesting in that it provides some detail and references of the history of DWI enforcement that might be a good read for any police officer.

Searches—In General

6

INTRODUCTION

A search is different from a seizure, although both are governed by the same rules. A search is defined as the exploration or examination of an individual's house, premises, or person, to discover things or items that may be used by the government for evidence in a criminal prosecution. In contrast, a seizure is defined as the exercise of dominion or control by the government over a person or thing because of a violation of law. Searching is looking; seizing is taking. If the search yields items that may lawfully be seized, then a seizure takes place. A search usually precedes a seizure.

A search is not limited to homes, buildings, apartments, or other enclosed places. It can take place anywhere, even in a public place (as in a parking lot or a person's computer or Internet account). The rule is that searches (and seizures) must be authorized by a warrant issued by a judge or magistrate—with exceptions, of course. There are four basic requirements for a search warrant to be valid: probable cause, supporting oath or affirmation, particular description of the place to be searched and the things to be seized, and the signature of a magistrate. In reality, however, most seizures, as well as arrests, are made without a warrant. In searches without a warrant, the police bear the burden of establishing probable cause.

The scope of a search is governed by the rule of reasonableness, given the object sought. The following rule succinctly delineates what an officer can and cannot do: "Do not look for an elephant in a matchbox."

The "knock-and-announce" issue has generated several decisions from the Supreme Court. In *Wilson v. Arkansas*, the Court held that the reasonableness requirement of the Fourth Amendment requires officers to knock and announce before entering a place, subject to exceptions determined by state courts. In a subsequent case, the Court held that the Fourth Amendment does not allow a blanket exception to the knock-and-announce requirement in felony drug investigations. The rule on no-knock entries holds even if the entry results in the destruction of property (*United States v. Ramire*). In

Hudson v. Michigan, the Court held that, even if the no-knock rule is violated, it does not automatically require suppression of any evidence seized.

The leading cases briefed in this chapter on searches in general are: *Steagald v. United States, Maryland v. Garrison*, and *Wilson v. Arkansas. United States v. Banks* gives more certainty to the time factor in searches by holding that, after knocking and announcing their presence and intention to search, 15 to 20 seconds is sufficient time for officers to wait before forcing entry into a home to execute a search warrant for drugs.

COOLIDGE V. NEW HAMPSHIRE
403 U.S. 443 (1971)

CAPSULE: A warrant is valid only if issued by a neutral and detached magistrate.

FACTS: A 14-year-old girl left her home in response to a man's request for a babysitter. Thirteen days later, her body was found by the side of a major highway. Police questioned Coolidge in his home concerning the ownership of guns, and asked if he would take a polygraph concerning his whereabouts on the night of the girl's disappearance. He produced three guns voluntarily and agreed to the polygraph. The following Sunday, Coolidge was called to the police station to take the polygraph and for further questioning. While he was being questioned, two officers went to his house and questioned his wife. During the course of the questioning, she voluntarily produced four of Coolidge's guns and the clothes he was believed to have been wearing on the night of the girl's disappearance. After a meeting involving the officers working on the case and the Attorney General, the Attorney General signed an arrest warrant for Coolidge and search warrants for his house and car. Pursuant to those warrants, Coolidge was arrested and his car impounded. The car was searched two days later and twice after that. Evidence presented over Coolidge's objection included gunpowder residue and microscopic particles taken from the car and from the clothes provided by Coolidge's wife, and a .22 caliber rifle also provided by her. Coolidge was charged with and convicted of murder.

ISSUES:

1. Was the warrant authorizing the search of Coolidge's house and car valid? NO.
2. If the warrant was not valid, could the seizure of the evidence in Coolidge's house and car be justified as an exception to the warrant requirement? NO.
3. Were the guns and clothes given to the officers by Coolidge's wife prior to the issuance of the warrant admissible as evidence? YES.

SUPREME COURT DECISIONS:

1. The warrant issued by the state's chief investigator and prosecutor (the State Attorney General) was not issued by a neutral and detached magistrate; hence, the warrant was invalid.

2. The evidence seized from Coolidge's house (vacuum sweepings of the clothes taken from the house) and from the car (particles of gunpowder) could not be admissible as exceptions to the warrant requirement because of the invalid warrant.

3. The guns and clothes given by Coolidge's wife to the police were given voluntarily; hence, they were admissible.

REASONS:

1. "When the right of privacy must reasonably yield to the right of search is, as a rule, to be decided by a judicial officer, not by a policeman or government enforcement agency." A warrant must, therefore, be issued by a neutral and detached magistrate.

2. "Since the police knew of the presence of the automobile and planned all along to seize it, there was no 'exigent circumstance' to justify their failure to obtain a warrant." Such warrantless seizures could not be justified under any of the exceptions to the warrant requirement.

3. "[T]he policemen were surely acting normally and properly when they asked her [Coolidge's wife], as they had asked those questioned earlier in the investigation, including Coolidge himself, about any guns there might be in the house. The question concerning the clothes Coolidge had been wearing the night of the disappearance was logical and in no way coercive. Indeed, one might doubt the competence of the officers involved had they not asked exactly the questions they did ask. And surely when Mrs. Coolidge of her own accord produced the guns and clothes for inspection, rather than simply describing them, it was not incumbent on the police to stop her or avert their eyes."

CASE SIGNIFICANCE: The *Coolidge* case is best known for the principle that a warrant is valid only if issued by a neutral and detached magistrate. If issued by any person who has an interest in the outcome of the case (such as the State Attorney General who was also the state's chief investigator and prosecutor in the case), the warrant is invalid. In this case, because the warrant was invalid, the state sought to justify the admission of the evidence under the various exceptions to the warrant requirement. The Court ruled that the evidence here did not come under such exceptions as "search incident to an arrest," "automobile exception," or the "instrumentality of the crime." The evidence (guns and clothes) given by Coolidge's wife, however, were admissible because they were given, not as the result of improper conduct on the part of the police, but because she wanted to help clear her husband of the crime.

ZURCHER V. STANFORD DAILY
436 U.S. 547 (1978)

CAPSULE: Searches of places belonging to third parties are permissible as long as probable cause exists to believe that evidence of someone's guilt or other items subject to seizure will be found.

FACTS: Responding to a call to quell a disturbance, police were attacked by a group of demonstrators, resulting in several injuries to the officers. There were no police photographers in the vicinity of the attack. Two days later, a special edition of a student newspaper carried articles and photographs of the clash. The District Attorney's Office obtained a warrant to search the newspaper offices. The warrant affidavit contained no allegation that members of the newspaper staff were suspects in the disturbance. The search was conducted pursuant to the warrant and no locked rooms or drawers were opened. The search revealed only the photographs already published and no materials were removed from the paper's offices. Members of the staff filed suit, seeking to have the Court declare the issuance of the warrant illegal and unconstitutional.

ISSUE: Is it constitutional under the Fourth Amendment for a court to issue a warrant for a search of the premises of a third party when the police have probable cause to believe that fruits, instrumentalities, or evidence of a crime are on the premises but do not have probable cause to believe that the possessor of the premises is involved in the crime? YES.

SUPREME COURT DECISION: Searches of property belonging to persons not suspected of crime are permissible as long as probable cause exists to believe that evidence of someone's guilt or other items subject to seizure will be found.

REASON: "A state is not prevented by the Fourth and Fourteenth Amendments from issuing a warrant to search for evidence simply because the owner or possessor of the place to be searched is not reasonably suspected of criminal involvement. The critical element in a reasonable search is not that the property owner is suspected of crime but that there is reasonable cause to believe that the 'things' to be searched for and seized are located on the [premises] to which entry is sought."

CASE SIGNIFICANCE: This case is significant in that it expands the authority of the courts and the police to obtain warrants to search places of third parties, meaning people who are not involved in the commission of a particular crime. Without this decision, it would have been difficult for the police to obtain evidence other than directly from the scene of the crime or from people nearby. This authority, however, cannot be used to conduct a "fishing expedition" for evidence on the premises of a third person. The Court stressed that the search warrant can be issued only if there is probable cause to believe that evidence of someone's guilt or other items subject to seizure will be found.

MINCEY V. ARIZONA
437 U.S. 385 (1978)

CAPSULE: A warrant must be obtained for crime scene investigations, regardless of the seriousness of the offense. The only exception to this rule is if obtaining a warrant would mean the evidence would be lost, destroyed, or removed during the time required to obtain a search warrant.

FACTS: During a narcotics raid on Mincey's apartment, an undercover officer was shot and killed and Mincey and others were wounded. Pursuant to police department policy that officers should not investigate incidents in which they are involved, officers at the scene took no action other than to look for other wounded people and to render medical assistance. About ten minutes after the shooting, homicide investigators arrived at the scene and took charge of the investigation. These officers conducted an extensive search of the apartment that lasted four days, included opening drawers and ripping up carpets, and resulted in the seizure of 200 to 300 objects. The items seized were admitted into evidence during trial. Mincey was convicted of murder, assault, and narcotics offenses.

ISSUE: Does the scene of a homicide represent exigent circumstances that would create an additional exception to the warrant requirement of the Fourth Amendment? NO.

SUPREME COURT DECISION: "The 'murder scene exception' created by the Arizona Supreme Court to the warrant requirement is inconsistent with the Fourth and Fourteenth Amendments, and the warrantless search of petitioner's apartment was not constitutionally permissible simply because a homicide had occurred there."

REASON: "[W]hen the police come upon the scene of a homicide they may make a prompt warrantless search of the area to see if there are other victims or if a killer is still on the premises ... [a]nd the police may seize any evidence that is in plain view during the course of their legitimate emergency activities. ... But a warrantless search must be 'strictly circumscribed by the exigencies which justify its initiation.' *Terry v. Ohio*, 392 U.S., at 25–26. And it simply cannot be contended that this search was justified by any emergency threatening life or limb." "We decline to hold that the seriousness of the offense under investigation itself creates exigent circumstances of the kind that under the Fourth Amendment justify a warrantless search."

CASE SIGNIFICANCE: This case is best understood as an issue under the "exigent circumstances" exception to the warrant requirement. The general rule is that a search warrant must be obtained prior to a search. Among the many exceptions, however, is the presence of exigent circumstances. In this case, the Arizona Supreme Court in previous decisions had carved out a "murder scene" exception, ruling that investigations of murder scenes did not need a warrant because of the seriousness of the offense. The police conducted a warrantless search based on this exception. The importance of this case lies in the Court's statement that "the seriousness of the offense under investigation did not itself create exigent circumstances of the kind that under the Fourth Amendment justify a warrantless search, where there is no indication that evidence would be lost, destroyed, or removed during the time required to obtain a search warrant and there is no suggestion that a warrant could not easily and conveniently have been obtained." In sum, the Court held that a warrant must be obtained for crime scene investigations, regardless of the seriousness of the offense. The only exception to this rule is if obtaining a warrant would mean the evidence would be lost, destroyed, or removed during the time required to obtain a search warrant.

STEAGALD V. UNITED STATES
451 U.S. 204 (1981)

CAPSULE: An arrest warrant does not authorize entry into another person's residence where the suspect may be found.

FACTS: Acting on an arrest warrant issued for a person named Lyons, police entered the home of Steagald to search for Lyons. The entry was made without a warrant. While searching the home of Steagald, the agents found cocaine and other incriminating evidence, but did not find Lyons. Steagald was arrested and convicted on federal drug charges.

ISSUE: May an officer search for the subject of an arrest warrant in the home of a third party, absent exigent circumstances, without a search warrant? NO.

SUPREME COURT DECISION: An arrest warrant is valid for entry into a suspect's place of residence. It does not authorize entry into another person's residence. If the suspect is in another person's home, a search warrant is needed to gain entry into that home, unless there is consent or emergency circumstances that would justify a warrantless search.

REASON: "Two distinct interests were implicated by the search in this case —Lyons' interest in being free from an unreasonable seizure and petitioner's [Steagald's] interest in being free from an unreasonable search of his home. Because the arrest warrant for Lyons addressed only the former interest, the search of petitioner's home was no more reasonable from petitioner's perspective than it would have been if conducted in the absence of any warrant." The search therefore violated the Fourth Amendment.

CASE SIGNIFICANCE: Having an arrest warrant does not authorize the police to enter a third person's home without a search warrant. This is because such an entry violates the Fourth Amendment rights of the third person who may not be involved in the crime. This rule, however, is subject to two exceptions: "exigent circumstances" and consent of the third person.

Exigent circumstances means that the police do not have to obtain a search warrant if circumstances are such that to obtain one would jeopardize the arrest. For example, if the police can establish that obtaining a warrant would allow the suspect to leave the premises and avoid arrest, a warrantless arrest would be justified. Another example would be cases of hot pursuit. If a suspect being pursued by the police enters a third person's home, the police may enter the home without a warrant to capture the suspect. Consent of the third person makes the warrantless search valid as long as the consent is intelligent and voluntary.

MARYLAND V. GARRISON
480 U.S. 79 (1987)

CAPSULE: A warrant that is overbroad in describing the place to be searched, but is based on a reasonable, although mistaken, belief of the officer, is valid.

FACTS: Police officers obtained a warrant to search "the premises known as 2036 Park Avenue third floor apartment," for drugs and drug paraphernalia that supposedly belonged to a person named McWebb. The police reasonably believed there was only one apartment at the location; in fact, there were two apartments on the third floor, one belonging to McWebb and one belonging to Garrison. Before the officers became aware that they were in Garrison's apartment instead of McWebb's, they discovered contraband that provided the basis for Garrison's drug conviction.

ISSUE: Is a search of the wrong address valid if conducted pursuant to a search warrant issued on a reasonable but mistaken belief on the part of the officers that the address was correct? YES.

SUPREME COURT DECISION: The validity of a warrant must be judged in light of the information available to officers when the warrant is sought; thus, a warrant that is overbroad in describing the place to be searched based on a reasonable but mistaken belief of the officer is not in violation of the Fourth Amendment. In this case, the search warrant was valid even though the warrant proved to be too broad to authorize the search of both apartments.

REASON: "On the basis of the information that the officers disclosed, or had a duty to discover and to disclose, to the issuing magistrate, the warrant, insofar as it authorized a search that turned out to be ambiguous in scope, was valid when it [was] issued. The validity of the warrant must be judged in light of the information available to the officers at the time they obtained the warrant. The discovery of facts demonstrating that a valid warrant was unnecessarily broad does not retroactively invalidate the warrant."

CASE SIGNIFICANCE: One of the elements of a valid search is that the warrant must contain a "particular description of the place to be searched."

This means that the warrant must remove any uncertainty about which premises are to be searched. *Garrison* appears to soften the demands of that requirement. Here was a case of mistaken place description, leading to a mistake in the execution of the warrant. Despite this mistake, the Court ruled that the "validity of the warrant must be judged in light of the information available to the officers at the time they obtained the warrant." The fact that later discovery found the warrant to be unnecessarily overbroad did not invalidate the warrant; neither did it affect the admissibility of evidence obtained. It is important to note that the Court found the warrant to be valid on its face, although its broad scope led to an error in the place of execution. There was reasonable effort on the part of the officers to ascertain and identify the place that was the target of the search; nonetheless, a mistake took place. This case should not be interpreted as validating all search warrants when there is a mistake made in the description of the place to be searched. The test as to the validity of search warrants that are "ambiguous in scope" appears to be "whether the officers' failure to realize the overbreadth of the warrant was objectively understandable and reasonable."

CALIFORNIA V. GREENWOOD
486 U.S. 35 (1988)

CAPSULE: A warrantless search and seizure of trash left for collection in an area accessible to the public is valid.

FACTS: Upon receiving information that Greenwood was engaged in drug trafficking, police set up surveillance of his home. Officers observed several vehicles make brief stops at the house during late night and early morning hours, one of which was followed to another residence suspected of drug trafficking. Officers then asked the trash collector to pick up the trash bags Greenwood had left to be collected and turn them over to the police. Once in police possession, officers searched the trash bags and found items indicating drug use. Based on this information, the police obtained a search warrant for Greenwood's home. There, police discovered quantities of cocaine and hashish. Greenwood and a co-conspirator were arrested and charged with felony narcotics charges. After receiving reports of continued drug trafficking, police once again seized Greenwood's garbage and again found evidence of drug use. This resulted in a second search of Greenwood's home, which revealed additional evidence of drug trafficking. Greenwood was arrested again.

ISSUE: Are warrantless searches of garbage left outside the curtilage of the home for regular collection valid under the Fourth Amendment? YES.

SUPREME COURT DECISION: The Fourth Amendment does not prohibit a warrantless search and seizure of trash left for collection in an area accessible to the public.

REASON: "The warrantless search and seizure of the garbage bags left at the Greenwood house would violate the Fourth Amendment only if respondents [Greenwood] manifested a subjective expectation of privacy in their garbage that society accepts as objectively reasonable. ... It may well be that respondents did not expect that the contents of their garbage bags would become known to the police or other members of the public. An expectation of privacy does not give rise to Fourth Amendment protection, however, unless society is prepared to accept that expectation as objectively reasonable. ... Here we conclude that respondents exposed their garbage to the public sufficiently to defeat their claim to Fourth Amendment protection. It is common knowledge that plastic garbage bags left on or at the side of a public street are readily accessible to animals, children, scavengers, snoops, and other members of the public."

CASE SIGNIFICANCE: This case settles an issue that divided federal appellate courts: whether garbage left outside the curtilage of a home for collection is deemed abandoned, and therefore can be seized by the police without a warrant. The Court made it clear that garbage left in that condition no longer enjoys the protection of the Constitution and, therefore, may be seized without a warrant. The test used was whether the original owner of the trash nonetheless enjoyed a "reasonable expectation of privacy" despite its being left outside the curtilage. The Court answered no, ruling that "having deposited their garbage 'in an area particularly suited for public inspection and in a manner of speaking, public consumption, for the express purpose of having strangers take it,' respondents could have no reasonable expectation of privacy in the inculpatory items that they discarded." (Citations omitted.) This case, therefore, allows officers to delve into a person's garbage left at the curb to gather evidence of criminality without a warrant. It is logical to assume that newspaper reporters and other individuals may also do so without violating the original owner's property rights.

WILSON V. ARKANSAS
514 U.S. 927 (1995)

CAPSULE: The Fourth Amendment requires officers to knock and announce before entering a dwelling unless there are exigent circumstances.

FACTS: Wilson conducted several narcotics transactions with an informant over a period of several months. Based on these transactions, police officers obtained an arrest warrant for Wilson and a search warrant for her home. At Wilson's residence, officers identified themselves and stated that they had a warrant as they entered the home through an unlocked door. Once inside the home, officers seized various drugs, a gun, and ammunition. They also found Wilson in the bathroom, flushing marijuana down the toilet. At trial,

Wilson moved for suppression of the evidence, asserting that the search was invalid because the officers did not follow the common-law procedure of "knock and announce" before they entered her home.

ISSUE: Does the Fourth Amendment reasonableness requirement require officers to "knock and announce" before entering a home? YES, ABSENT EXIGENT CIRCUMSTANCES.

SUPREME COURT DECISION: The reasonableness requirement of the Fourth Amendment requires officers to knock and announce before entering a dwelling unless there are exigent circumstances.

REASON: "An examination of the common law of search and seizure ... leaves no doubt that the reasonableness of a search of a dwelling may depend in part on whether law enforcement officers announce their presence and authority prior to entering." This common-law rule of knock and announce dates to at least 1603 and the decision in *Semayne's Case*, 77 Eng. Rep 194, which held: "But before he breaks it, he ought to signify the cause of his coming, and to make request to open doors." "Our own cases have acknowledged that the common-law principle of announcement is embedded in Anglo-American law, but we have never squarely held that this principle is an element of the reasonableness inquiry under the Fourth Amendment. We now so hold." (Citations omitted.)

CASE SIGNIFICANCE: This case holds that, absent exigent circumstances, officers are required to "knock and announce" to meet the reasonableness requirements of the Fourth Amendment. The announcement requirement is based on common-law practice that was woven quickly into the fabric of early American law. The Court stressed, however, that the "Fourth Amendment's flexible requirement of reasonableness should not be read to mandate a rigid rule of announcement that ignores countervailing law enforcement interest." The Court considers "countervailing law enforcement interest" as justifying entries without announcement. Such interest, said the Court, includes threats of physical harm to police, pursuit of recently escaped arrestees, and when there is reason to believe that evidence would be likely to be destroyed if advance notice was given. The Court refrained, however, from presenting a "comprehensive catalog of the relevant countervailing factors."

RICHARDS V. WISCONSIN
520 U.S. 385 (1997)

CAPSULE: The Fourth Amendment does not permit a blanket exception to the knock-and-announce requirement when executing a felony drug warrant. Exceptions must be decided by the court on a case-by-case basis.

FACTS: Police officers obtained a warrant to search Richards' hotel room for drugs and paraphernalia based on information that Richards was one of several individuals dealing drugs out of hotel rooms. The officer's request for a no-knock entry was explicitly denied by the magistrate. One officer knocked on Richard's door and identified himself as a maintenance worker. When Richards opened the door, he saw one of the uniformed officers and slammed the door. At that point, officers identified themselves and began to break down the door. Upon entering the room, officers caught Richards trying to escape through a window. A search of the room revealed cash and cocaine hidden in plastic bags above the bathroom ceiling tiles. The no-knock entry was later justified by the officer based on the rule, in place before *Wilson*, that "police officers are never required to knock and announce when executing a search warrant in a felony drug investigation because of the special circumstances of today's drug culture."

ISSUE: Does the Fourth Amendment allow "a blanket exception to the knock-and-announce requirement for felony drug investigations?" NO.

SUPREME COURT DECISION: The Fourth Amendment does not allow a blanket exception to the knock-and-announce requirement in felony drug investigations. The fact that felony drug investigations may frequently involve threats of physical violence or destruction of evidence (either or both of which may justify not having to knock and announce) does not automatically exempt it from the review of a court to determine the reasonableness of the police decision not to knock and announce in a particular case.

REASON: "[T]he fact that felony drug investigations may frequently present circumstances warranting a no-knock entry cannot remove from the neutral scrutiny of a reviewing court the reasonableness of the police decision not to knock and announce in a particular case. Instead, in each case, it is the duty of a court confronted with the question to determine whether the facts and circumstances of the particular entry justified dispensing with the knock-and-announce requirement. ... In order to justify a 'no-knock' entry, the police must have a reasonable suspicion that knocking and announcing their presence, under the particular circumstances, would be dangerous or futile, or that it would inhibit the effective investigation of the crime by, for example, allowing the destruction of evidence."

CASE SIGNIFICANCE: This case clarifies an issue that was not clearly addressed in *Wilson v. Arkansas. Wilson* held that the knock-and-announce rule is required by the Fourth Amendment, but that there were numerous exceptions to it; such exceptions are to be determined by lower courts. The police in this case sought a blanket exception from this requirement in felony drug investigations, saying that these cases frequently involved threats of physical violence or possible destruction of evidence. The Court rejected this on two grounds. First, it said that there will be situations in which "the asserted governmental safety may not outweigh the individual privacy interests" involved in a particular case. Second, "the blanket exception would threaten to swallow the rule." In other words, if a blanket exception were allowed in felony drug investigations, it might lead to other exceptions (such as in bank robbery cases) that might then completely negate the rule.

UNITED STATES V. RAMIREZ
523 U.S. 65 (1998)

CAPSULE: The Fourth Amendment does not impose a higher standard when officers destroy property during a no-knock entry than the requirement that the police have a reasonable suspicion that knocking and announcing would be dangerous or futile, or would inhibit the effective investigation of the crime.

FACTS: Based on probable cause that an escaped and violent felon was staying at Ramirez's residence, federal agents obtained a no-knock warrant. Early in the morning, officers announced over a loudspeaker that they had a warrant, and simultaneously broke a window in the garage and pointed a weapon through the opening to prevent anyone from obtaining weapons that an informant had suggested were there. After awakening, and believing that he was being burglarized, Ramirez obtained a pistol and shot it through the ceiling of the garage. After police returned fire and announced their presence, Ramirez threw his pistol down and surrendered. The escaped prisoner the agents sought was not found, but Ramirez was taken into custody and charged with being a felon in possession of firearms.

ISSUE: Is there a higher standard when a no-knock entry includes the destruction of property? NO.

SUPREME COURT DECISION: The Fourth Amendment does not impose a higher standard when officers destroy property during a no-knock entry than the requirement that the police have a reasonable suspicion that knocking and announcing would be dangerous or futile, or would inhibit the effective investigation of the crime.

REASON: "Under *Richards* [*v. Wisconsin*], a no-knock entry is justified if police have a 'reasonable suspicion' that knocking and announcing would be dangerous, futile, or destructive to the purposes of the investigation. Whether such a 'reasonable suspicion' exists depends in no way on whether police must destroy property in order to enter."

CASE SIGNIFICANCE: This case extended the decisions in *Wilson v. Arkansas* and *Richards v. Wisconsin* concerning knock-and-announce entries. The standard set by the Supreme Court in knock-and-announce cases is that a no-knock entry is reasonable if officers have reasonable suspicion that obeying the rule would be dangerous or futile or would hamper effective investigation. The trial court in this case had ruled that the search was invalid because there were "insufficient exigent circumstances" to justify the officer's destruction of property. The Court rejected that interpretation and held that reasonable suspicion that obeying the rule would be dangerous or futile or would hamper effective investigation is sufficient to justify entry without knocking and announcing.

MINNESOTA V. CARTER
525 U.S. 83 (1998)

CAPSULE: A person who is in a home for a short period, although with the consent of the owner, has no expectation of privacy under the Fourth Amendment.

FACTS: A law enforcement officer went to an apartment based on information from an informant that he had seen through a ground floor window people putting a white powder into bags. The officer observed the same activity for several minutes through a gap in a closed blind in the apartment. When Carter and an accomplice, Johns, left the apartment, police stopped the car. After observing a handgun in the automobile, officers arrested Carter and Johns. A subsequent search of the automobile revealed drugs and drug paraphernalia. Based on the arrest of Carter and Johns, and pursuant to a search warrant based on the officer's observations, police returned to the apartment and arrested the lessee, Thompson. A search of the apartment pursuant to the warrant revealed additional drugs and drug paraphernalia. Police later learned that Carter and Johns had come to the apartment from another city for the sole purpose of packaging the drugs, that they had never been to the apartment previously, they were only in the apartment for approximately two and one-half hours, and that in return for using the apartment, they gave Thompson one-eighth of an ounce of cocaine.

ISSUE: Is there an expectation of privacy sufficient to invoke the Fourth Amendment for persons who are in a home for a short period of time at the request of the owner? NO.

SUPREME COURT DECISION: "[A]n overnight guest in a home may claim the protection of the Fourth Amendment, but one who is merely present with the consent of the owner may not."

REASON: "Respondents here were obviously not overnight guests, but were essentially present for a business transaction and were only in the home a matter of hours. There is no suggestion that they had a previous relationship with Thompson, or that there was any other purpose to their visit. Nor was there anything similar to the overnight guest relationship in [*Minnesota v.*] *Olson* [495 U.S. 91 (1989)] to suggest a degree of acceptance into the household. While the apartment was a dwelling place for Thompson, it was for these respondents simply a place to do business."

CASE SIGNIFICANCE: This case makes clear previous gaps in Supreme Court decisions concerning the expectation of privacy that persons enjoy in certain places. The expectation of privacy concerns the ability of law enforcement officials to make searches within the guidelines of the Fourth Amendment. The Court had previously stated in *Olson* that overnight guests in a person's house have an expectation of privacy under the Fourth Amendment. In another case, the Court also held that a person had an expectation of privacy in a personal office at work. The Court ruled here, however, that a person in a house for a short period of time does not have that same privilege as an overnight guest.

UNITED STATES V. KNIGHTS
534 U.S. 112 (2001)

CAPSULE: A warrantless search by an officer of a probationer's residence supported by reasonable suspicion and authorized by a condition of probation is valid under the Fourth Amendment.

FACTS: A court imposed as a condition of probation that probationer Knights submit to searches by probation or law enforcement officers of his person, vehicle, and house without a search warrant. An officer investigating vandalism and arson suspected Knights and an accomplice, Simoneau, were involved in the crime. When the officer observed Simoneau's vehicle at Knights' residence, he set up surveillance. Later, Simoneau left Knights' residence with three cylindrical tubes the officer believed to be pipe bombs and threw them in the river. When Simoneau left Knights' residence, the officer followed him. When Simoneau stopped, the officer looked in Simoneau's truck and saw explosive materials and two padlocks matching the description of those taken during the vandalism. Based on this and knowledge of the probation order permitting searches, the officer conducted a search of Knights' apartment. The search revealed more arson and bomb-making materials and a padlock with the vandalized company's name stamped on it.

ISSUE: Is a warrantless search by an officer of a probationer's residence pursuant to a probation condition and supported by reasonable suspicion (but not probable cause) constitutional? YES.

SUPREME COURT DECISION: A warrantless search by an officer of a probationer's residence supported by reasonable suspicion and authorized by a condition of probation is valid under the Fourth Amendment.

REASON: "The degree of individualized suspicion required of a search is a determination of when there is a sufficiently high probability that criminal conduct is occurring to make the intrusion on the individual's privacy interest reasonable." "Although the Fourth Amendment ordinarily requires the degree of probability embodied in the term 'probable cause,' a lesser degree satisfies the Constitution when the balance of governmental and private interests makes such a standard reasonable." Based on these principles, the Court held that "the search of Knights was reasonable under our general Fourth Amendment approach of 'examining the totality of the circumstances' with the probation search condition being a salient circumstance." (Citations omitted.)

CASE SIGNIFICANCE: This case is significant for probationers and parolees. It resolved the issue of whether law enforcement officers can search the residence of a probationer with less than probable cause. The Court held that it could, as long as: (1) there is reasonable suspicion and (2) the search is authorized by the condition of probation. One of the most frequently imposed conditions of probation is that the probationer submit to a search by a probation officer. The Court had earlier decided in *Griffin v. Wisconsin* (483 U.S. 868 [1987]) that a warrantless search by a probation officer of a probationer's home based on reasonable grounds (less than probable cause) was valid because of "special needs," meaning the need to supervise a probationer to accomplish the purpose of probation. The *Griffin* case, however, did not involve a law enforcement officer. In *Knights*, the search was conducted by a sheriff's detective who was authorized by the judge to conduct a search of the probationer. The probationer claimed his Fourth Amendment rights were violated because the search by the officer was investigatory rather than probationary in nature and therefore needed probable cause, like all police searches. The Court disagreed, holding the search was reasonable based on the totality of circumstances. There was a condition of probation imposed by the judge, the probationer was informed of such a condition, and the condition of probation was justified. Given the purposes of probation, and since the probationer was more likely to engage in criminal activity than an ordinary member of the community, the search by the police here was reasonable.

Prior to this case, it was unclear whether or not a judge may authorize police officers to enforce conditions of probation other than those involving arrests for criminal acts. The Court in this case implied that law enforcement can also be authorized by the judge to search probationers' dwellings based on less than probable cause. Note, however, that here, the officer was authorized by the judge to conduct a search of the probationer's residence. Without such an authorization, the search on less than probable cause would likely have been unconstitutional. Also, this case involved a probationer, but it can likely be extended to parolees as long as there is reasonable suspicion and authorization to search by the parole board that sets the conditions of parole.

UNITED STATES V. BANKS
540 U.S. 31 (2003)

CAPSULE: After knocking and announcing their presence and intention to search, 15 to 20 seconds is sufficient time for officers to wait before forcing entry into a home to execute a search warrant for drugs.

FACTS: With information that Banks was selling cocaine from his apartment, officers obtained and executed a search warrant. Upon reaching his apartment, officers announced "police search warrant" and knocked on the door loud enough to be heard by officers at the back door. After waiting 15 to 20 seconds, officers broke down the door with a battering ram. Banks was in the shower and testified he did not hear the officers until they broke the door. The search of the apartment produced weapons, crack cocaine, and other evidence of drug dealing. Banks moved to suppress the evidence, arguing that the officers waited an unreasonably short time before forcing entry, violating the Fourth Amendment.

ISSUE: Does a 15- to 20-second wait before a forcible entry by police violate the Fourth Amendment? NO.

SUPREME COURT DECISION: After knocking and announcing their presence and intention to search, 15 to 20 seconds is sufficient time for officers to wait before forcing entry into a home to execute a search for drugs.

REASON: In this case, the Court rejected a lower court rule of using a list of requirements for forcing entry following a knock and announce, and instead reemphasized that such cases are to be decided on totality of the circumstances. The Court then turned its intention to the circumstances that might require forced entry. They noted that most people keep their doors locked, necessitating use of force when no one answers the knock. The critical issue, then, is what constitutes an exigency. The Court noted that it is exigency that creates a situation authorizing a no-knock warrant; but that same exigency will exist when officers announce their presence and intention to search. The knock and announce essentially "starts the clock" on the potential destruction of evidence. The exigency in this case was that the suspect would attempt to destroy the evidence, typically by flushing it down a drain or toilet. Not answering a knock by police would further indicate this possibility because the bathroom or kitchen will not be near the door but in the interior of the home. The Court recognized that 15 to 20 seconds would be sufficient for a person to begin to destroy evidence such as drugs, but noted that something like a search for a stolen piano would require more time for a person to respond to a knock because of the difficulty in disposing of the evidence.

CASE SIGNIFICANCE: This case is significant because it addresses an important issue of policing: what is a reasonable time in drug cases, after knocking, when officers may gain a valid forcible entry to a dwelling? The officers here had a valid warrant and knocked and announced their presence. After a 15- to 20-second wait, with no response, they used a battering ram and forcibly entered the dwelling. Banks claimed that a 15- to 20-second wait before entry was unreasonable, and therefore violated the Fourth Amendment. He said he was in the shower and did not hear the officers, and that, in any case, it might have taken him more time than that to reach the door. The Court disagreed, arguing that "the facts known to the police are what count in judging a reasonable waiting time, and there is no indication that they knew Banks was in the shower and thus unaware of an impending search." The assertion that it would have taken Banks more time to reach the door was also rejected, the Court arguing that "it is not unreasonable to think that someone could get in a position to destroy the drugs within 15 to 20 seconds." The 15- to 20-second wait considered sufficient in this case may not necessarily suffice in cases other than those involving drugs. An important factor in this case was that the defendant could easily have disposed of the drugs within that short time. Had they waited longer, the suspect could easily have flushed the drugs down the toilet. The Court adhered to a totality of circumstances analysis, in effect holding that whether the time to wait before any forcible entry was too short depends on an analysis of all surrounding circumstances. In this case, those circumstances favored the police.

UNITED STATES V. GRUBBS
547 U.S. 90 (2006)

CAPSULE: There is no constitutional requirement that the person subject to a search be shown the triggering events by police officers for an anticipatory warrant to be valid. Moreover, the fact that the contraband is not yet at the place described in the warrant when it was issued is immaterial as long as there is probable cause to believe it will be there when the warrant is executed.

FACTS: Grubbs purchased a videotape containing child pornography from a Web site operated by undercover Postal Inspectors. Agents arranged for a controlled delivery of the tape. A judge issued an "anticipatory" search warrant for Grubbs' house based on an affidavit from agents describing the procedures for the controlled delivery and that the warrant would not be executed until the tape had been positively delivered and taken into the residence. Two days later, the package was delivered and signed for by Grubbs' wife. Postal Inspectors executed the search warrant. Grubbs consented to interrogation and admitted ordering the tape. Grubbs was given a copy of the search warrant and attachments but not the supporting affidavit that explained when the warrant would be executed. Grubbs was indicted for receiving a visual depiction of a minor engaged in sexually explicit conduct. He appealed, saying that, although he was shown a copy of the search warrant and the attachments, the officers failed to show him the supporting affidavit stating the triggering event, and therefore the anticipatory warrant was invalid.

ISSUE:

1. Must anticipatory warrants indicate the condition upon which the warrant will be triggered to meet the constitutional requirement of particularity? NO.
2. Must the contraband be at the location indicated on the search warrant at the time the search warrant is issued? NO.

SUPREME COURT DECISION: There is no constitutional requirement that the person subject to a search be shown the triggering events by police officers for an anticipatory warrant to be valid. Moreover, the fact that the contraband is not yet at the place described in the warrant when it was issued is immaterial as long as there is probable cause to believe it will be there when the warrant is executed.

REASON: An anticipatory warrant is "a warrant based upon an affidavit showing probable cause that at some future time (but not presently) certain evidence of crime will be located at a specified place." Most anticipatory warrants subject their execution to some condition other than the passage of time (a so-called "triggering condition"). Grubbs argued that, because the evidence was not at the location indicated on the search warrant at the time the search warrant was issued, it violated the Fourth Amendment requirement of only issuing warrants upon probable cause. "Because the probable-cause requirement looks to whether evidence will be found *when the search is conducted,* [emphasis in original] all warrants are, in a sense, 'anticipatory.'" "Thus, when an anticipatory warrant is issued, 'the fact that the contraband is not presently located at the place described in the warrant is immaterial, so long as there is probable cause to believe that it will be there when the warrant is executed.'" (Internal citations omitted.) "For a conditioned anticipatory warrant to comply with the Fourth Amendment's requirement of probable cause, two prerequisites of probability must be satisfied. It must be true not only that *if* the triggering condition occurs 'there is a fair probability that contraband or evidence of a crime will be found in a particular place,' but also that there is probable cause to believe the triggering condition *will occur.*" (Emphasis in original; internal citations omitted.) "In this case, the occurrence of the triggering condition—successful delivery of the videotape to Grubbs' residence—would plainly establish probable cause for the search."

CASE SIGNIFICANCE: An anticipatory warrant is a warrant issued based upon an affidavit showing probable cause that, at some future time, evidence of crime will be found at a certain place. Grubbs in this case challenged the constitutionality of the anticipatory warrant, saying it was invalid because, although he was given a copy of the search warrant and attachments, the police did not show him the affidavit that described the triggering event for the execution of the warrant (the delivery of the tape to his residence and his receiving it). The Court rejected his challenge, ruling this is not a requirement for an anticipatory warrant to be valid. Grubbs also maintained that the anticipatory warrant was invalid because the items to be seized were not in the place described in the warrant when it was issued. The Court disagreed, holding there is no necessity for the item to be there; it suffices that "there is probable cause to believe that it will be there when the warrant is executed." This case is significant because the Court had previously not decided a case questioning the constitutionality of anticipatory warrants, although lower courts had addressed the issue. This case affirms that anticipatory warrants (used by many police departments) are constitutional.

HUDSON V. MICHIGAN
547 U.S. 586 (2006)

CAPSULE: Violation of the knock-and-announce rule does not require exclusion of the seized evidence.

FACTS: Police obtained a warrant authorizing the search for drugs and firearms at Hudson's home. Police executed the warrant by announcing their presence, but waited only 3 to 5 seconds (the usual time is between 15 and 20 seconds) before opening the door and entering Hudson's home. Drugs and a gun were found during the search. Hudson moved to suppress the evidence, alleging that the premature entry by the police violated his Fourth Amendment rights.

ISSUE: Is evidence obtained by the police in violation of the knock-and-announce rule prevented from being introduced at trial? NO.

SUPREME COURT DECISION: Violation of the knock-and-announce rule does not require suppression of the evidence seized.

REASON: In previous cases, the Court held that the knock-and-announce rule was a constitutional requirement. "When the knock-and-announce rule does apply, it is not easy to determine precisely what officers must do. How many seconds' wait are too few? Our 'reasonable wait time,' see *United States v. Banks*, 540 U.S. 31, 41 (2003), standard is necessarily vague." "*Wilson* specifically declined to decide whether the exclusionary rule is appropriate for violation of the knock-and-announce requirement." "Suppression of evidence, however, has always been our last resort, not our first impulse." "[T]he exclusionary rule has never been applied except where deterrence benefits outweigh its substantial social costs." (Internal citations and quotes omitted.) "What the knock-and-announce rule has never protected, however, is one's interest in preventing the government from seeking or taking evidence described in a warrant. Since the interests that *were* violated in this case have nothing to do with the seizure of evidence, the exclusionary rule is inapplicable." "Violation of the warrant requirement sometimes produces incriminating evidence that could not otherwise be obtained. But ignoring knock-and-announce can realistically be expected to achieve absolutely nothing except the prevention of destruction of evidence and the avoidance of life-threatening resistance by occupants of the premises—dangers which, if there is even "reasonable suspicion" of their existence, *suspend the knock-and-announce requirement anyway.* Massive deterrence is hardly required."

CASE SIGNIFICANCE: This case addresses an important issue on the knock-and-announce rule that was not addressed in previous cases. Because the rule is a constitutional requirement, Hudson argued that the evidence obtained in violation of the rule must be excluded under the exclusionary rule. This rule holds that illegally seized evidence can be used as evidence in court. The Court in this case held that the exclusionary rule was not applicable because the purpose of the knock-and-announce rule was to "prevent violence, property damage, and impositions on privacy." The purpose was not to prevent the police from conducting a search for which they had a valid warrant. The Court added that other means could be used by defendants to discourage police violations of the knock-and-announce rule. These are such remedies as civil lawsuits and seeking the discipline of erring police officers. Violation of the knock-and-announce rule can now be added to the growing number of exceptions to the exclusionary rule, meaning that in these cases, the evidence can be used during trial.

SAMSON V. CALIFORNIA
547 U.S. 843 (2006)

CAPSULE: "The Fourth Amendment does not prohibit police officers from conducting a suspicionless search of a parolee."

FACTS: An officer who knew Samson was on parole stopped him and asked about outstanding parole warrants. Samson replied that he had no outstanding warrants, which was confirmed by the officer. Based solely on Samson being on parole, the officer searched Samson, and found methamphetamine in a cigarette box in Samson's shirt pocket. Samson was convicted of drug possession.

ISSUE: Is a suspicionless search of a parolee by a law enforcement officer valid under the Fourth Amendment? YES.

SUPREME COURT DECISION: "The Fourth Amendment does not prohibit police officers from conducting a suspicionless search of a parolee."

REASON: "Whether a search is reasonable 'is determined by assessing, on the one hand, the degree to which it intrudes upon an individual's privacy and, on the other, the degree to which it is needed for the promotion of legitimate governmental interests.'" (Internal citations omitted.) The Court applied that logic in the case of probationers in *United States v. Knights,* 534 U.S. 112 (2001), upholding the search of Knights' apartment based on suspicion and the condition of probation, based on a substantial governmental interest. After pointing out that parolees "have fewer expectations of privacy than probationers, because parole is more akin to imprisonment than probation," the Court concluded that "imposing a reasonable suspicion requirement, as urged by petitioner, would give parolees greater opportunity to anticipate searches and conceal criminality." The Court thus found the balance tipped in favor of suspicionless searches by officers for those on parole.

CASE SIGNIFICANCE: This case affirms the principle generally used by the courts in Fourth Amendment cases involving convicted offenders. Courts adhere to the principle that probationers and parolees have "diminished constitutional rights." The decision in *Samson* was based on two grounds. First, the Court held that parolees do not have a reasonable expectation of privacy (the usual test under the Fourth Amendment) that society could recognize as legitimate. It argued that parolees are released before completion of their time in prison but remain under the custody of the Department of Corrections. In effect, they are prisoners who are entitled to only limited Fourth Amendment rights. A second reason used by the Court was that, as a condition of his parole, Samson signed an agreement that he could be "subject to search or seizure by a parole officer or other peace officer …, with or without a search warrant and with or without cause." This is a standard condition many states use for persons on parole. In effect, the parolee waives his or her constitutional rights under the Fourth Amendment. This provision, together with his diminished constitutional right as a convict, allowed the police to make a valid search even without suspicion.

KENTUCKY V. KING
563 U.S. 452 (2011)

CAPSULE: Police do not "create" an impermissible exigency when they knock on the door of a residence and announce their presence if they have reasonable belief an exigency exists.

FACTS: Police set up a controlled buy of drugs outside an apartment complex. An undercover officer watched the buy take place from an unmarked car in a nearby parking lot. After the buy occurred, the officer radioed uniformed officers to apprehend the suspect. He told the officers the suspect was moving quickly toward the breezeway of an apartment building. Just as the responding officers entered the breezeway, they heard a door shut and detected a strong odor of burnt marijuana. At the end of the breezeway, the officers saw two apartments, but did not know which apartment the suspect had entered. The officers did not hear the undercover officer radio that the suspect was running into the apartment on the right because they had already left their vehicles. Because they smelled marijuana coming from the apartment on the left, they approached the door of that apartment, banged on the door, and announced their presence. The officers then heard movement in the apartment that was consistent with what they believed to be the destruction of evidence. The officers then announced their intention to enter the apartment and kicked in the door. In the apartment they found King and two other people who were smoking marijuana. In subsequent searches, they discovered drugs, cash, and drug paraphernalia. Police eventually entered the apartment on the right and arrested the original suspect. At trial, King filed a motion to suppress the evidence from the warrantless search, but the court held exigent circumstances justified the warrantless entry because no one answered the door and officers heard movement in the apartment that they reasonably believed involved the destruction of evidence.

ISSUE: Do police "create" an impermissible exigency when they knock on the door of a residence and announce their presence? NO.

SUPREME COURT DECISION: The exigent circumstances rule applies only when the police do not create the exigency by engaging or threatening to engage in conduct that violates the Fourth Amendment. The Court in this case held, "We assume for purposes of argument that an exigency existed [because of the noises consistent with destruction of evidence]. Because the officers in this case did not violate or threaten to violate the Fourth Amendment prior to the exigency, we hold that the exigency justified the warrantless search of the apartment."

REASON: The Court recognized that searches and seizures inside a home without a warrant are presumptively unreasonable absent some exceptions. Drawing from *Mincey v. Arizona*, 437 U.S. 385, 394 (1978), the Court opined that one exception was when "the exigencies of the situation make the needs of law enforcement so compelling that [a] warrantless search is objectively reasonable under the Fourth Amendment." (Internal citations omitted.) One of the exigencies recognized by the Court was the need to prevent the imminent destruction of evidence. What the Court had to wrestle with in this case is that the police, to some extent, always create an exigency. The issue is how much creation of exigency by the police is too much. The Court reasoned that, when police knock on a door without a warrant, "they do no more than any private citizen might do." The occupant is then free to open the door or not, or may attempt to destroy evidence. The Court ruled in this case that an exigency did exist; the police actions did not impermissibly create the exigency.

CASE SIGNIFICANCE: This case ruled that officers do not violate the Fourth Amendment by knocking on the door of a residence and announcing their presence. Further, if officers hear noises consistent with destruction of evidence following the knock, they can make a warrantless entry into the residence to investigate without violating the Fourth Amendment.

The Court then provided further guidance to police in this matter. In dicta, the Court stated that it would consider it an unreasonable creation of an exigency for police to threaten to enter when they had no legal basis to do so. The Court denied an argument by King, however, that the officers created an impermissible exigency when they engaged in "conduct that would cause a reasonable person to believe that entry is imminent and inevitable." The Court said the officers' tone, how loud they knocked, or how urgent they sounded were not measurable factors in these cases.

Searches after Arrest

7

INTRODUCTION

Searches after arrest require a separate chapter because of their importance in everyday policing. Although the constitutional rule is that arrests are to be made with a warrant, most arrests are made without a warrant. After a valid arrest, the police may conduct a full search of the arrested person and of the vicinity around him or her. The cases briefed in this chapter define the extent of that search.

The two major cases on searches after an arrest are *United States v. Robinson* and *Chimel v. California*. In *Robinson*, the Court held that a body search is valid when a full-custody arrest occurs. In *Chimel*, the Court authorized the search of the area within a person's immediate control after an arrest. The Court has authorized officers to search the area of immediate control for two reasons: (1) to ensure the safety of the officer and (2) to prevent the destruction of evidence. The problem with *Chimel*, however, is that it does not clearly indicate what is meant by the "area of immediate control." It is clear that this includes the area covered by an arrested person's "wing-span"; however, how much further beyond the wingspan has not been addressed by the Court, other than saying that it is that area from which the arrested person may obtain weapons or destroy evidence.

Most of the cases briefed in this chapter extend the authority of the police to search after an arrest. In *United States v. Edwards*, the Court held that a warrantless search at the place of detention is valid even if a substantial period of time has elapsed between the arrest and the search. In *Maryland v. Buie*, the Court held that a limited protective sweep during an arrest in a home is allowed if justified. In *Illinois v. Lafayette*, the Court ruled that searching the personal effects of a person under lawful arrest is valid if it is part of the administrative procedure incident to the booking and jailing of the suspect.

Other principles set by the Court indicate that there are limits to searches after arrest. For example, the warrantless search of a house after an arrest when the arrest does not take place in a house is justified only in a few cases

(*Vale v. Louisiana*). Although not addressed by the Supreme Court, lower courts have held that body cavity searches after an arrest are unconstitutional unless justified by considerations other than the arrest itself.

The leading cases briefed in this section on searches after arrest are *Chimel v. California* and *United States v. Robinson*.

WARDEN V. HAYDEN
387 U.S. 294 (1967)

CAPSULE: A warrantless search and seizure inside a person's home is valid if probable cause and exigent circumstances are present. "Mere evidence" may be searched, seized, and admitted in court.

FACTS: Police went to Hayden's house pursuant to a call from an individual who had followed a robbery suspect until the suspect entered a house. Hayden's wife consented to a search of the house. Hayden was arrested when it was determined that he was the only man in the house. An officer, attracted to an adjoining bathroom by the sound of running water, found a shotgun and pistol in a flush tank. Another officer, looking for "a man or the money," found clothes fitting the description of those worn by the robber in a washing machine. All items of evidence were admitted at the trial. Hayden was convicted of armed robbery.

ISSUES:
1. Was the search without a warrant valid? YES.
2. Are items considered "mere evidence" (the pistol, shotgun, and clothes), as distinguished from contraband and instrumentalities of crimes, seizable by the police for use as evidence? YES.

SUPREME COURT DECISIONS:
1. The warrantless seizure in this case was valid because probable cause and exigent circumstances were present.
2. There is no difference between "mere evidence" and contraband or instrumentalities of a crime under the provisions of the Fourth Amendment. "Mere evidence" may be searched for, seized, and admitted in court as evidence.

REASON: The search was valid because "[s]peed here was essential, and only a thorough search of the house for persons and weapons could have insured that Hayden was the only man present and that the police had control of all weapons which could be used against them or to effect an escape. ... Nothing in the language of the Fourth Amendment supports the distinction between 'mere evidence' and instrumentalities, fruits of crime, or contraband."

CASE SIGNIFICANCE: This case established that a warrant is not needed if there is probable cause and "exigent" circumstances. This justifies making warrantless searches and seizures. The Court also settled the issue of whether "mere evidence" (as opposed to contraband or illegal items) can be seized by the police. Earlier cases decided by lower courts were divided on the issue. Under this ruling, any evidence, not just contraband, that can help prove the case against a defendant can be seized by the police.

CHIMEL V. CALIFORNIA
395 U.S. 752 (1969)

CAPSULE: After an arrest, police may search the area within a person's immediate control.

FACTS: Chimel was suspected of having robbed a coin shop. Armed with an arrest warrant (but without a search warrant), police officers went to Chimel's house and were admitted by his wife. Chimel was not at home, but was immediately arrested when he arrived. The police asked Chimel if they could "look around." Chimel denied the request, but the officers searched the entire house anyway and discovered some stolen coins. At the trial, the coins were introduced as evidence over Chimel's objection. Chimel was convicted of robbery.

ISSUE: In the course of making a lawful arrest, may officers search the immediate area where the person was arrested without a search warrant? YES.

SUPREME COURT DECISION: After making an arrest, the police may search the area within the person's immediate control. The purpose of such a search is to discover and remove weapons and to prevent the destruction of evidence.

REASON: "When an arrest is made, it is reasonable for the arresting officer to search the person arrested in order to remove any weapons that the latter might seek to use in order to resist arrest or effect his escape. Otherwise, the officer's safety might well be endangered, and the arrest itself frustrated. In addition, it is entirely reasonable for the arresting officer to search for and seize any evidence on the arrestee's person in order to prevent its concealment or destruction. And the area into which an arrestee might reach in order to grab a weapon or evidentiary items must, of course, be governed by a like rule. ... There is ample justification, therefore, for a search of the arrestee's person and the area within his immediate control."

CASE SIGNIFICANCE: *Chimel* categorically states that the police may search the area in the arrestee's "immediate control" when making a valid arrest, whether the arrest takes place with or without a warrant. That area of "immediate control" is defined by the Court as "the area from within which he might gain possession of a weapon or destructible evidence." There is no set rule, however, of what makes up the area of the arrestee's "immediate control." The safest, and most limited, interpretation is a person's wingspan, where it might be possible to grab a weapon or destroy evidence. Another common definition is "lunging distance" but, again, the courts have not specifically defined what constitutes lunging distance. Some lower courts have given a more liberal interpretation to include such areas as the whole room in which the person is arrested.

VALE V. LOUISIANA
399 U.S. 30 (1970)

CAPSULE: The warrantless search of a house after an arrest with a warrant, when the arrest does not take place in a house, is justified only in "a few specifically established and well-delineated exceptions."

FACTS: After obtaining an arrest warrant, the police set up surveillance outside Vale's home. While watching the house, they observed what they suspected to be an exchange of drugs between Vale and a known addict. After the exchange of narcotics, the police blocked the path of the addict, arrested Vale on the front steps of his home, and searched the house without a search warrant. Narcotics were found in a bedroom. Vale was convicted of possession of heroin.

ISSUE: May the police make a warrantless search of a house incident to an arrest without exigent circumstances and when the person was not arrested in the house? NO.

SUPREME COURT DECISION: The warrantless search of a house incident to an arrest when the arrest does not take place in the house is justified only in "a few specifically established and well-delineated exceptions." The facts in this case did not come under one of those exceptions.

REASON: "If a search of a house is to be upheld as incident to an arrest, that arrest must take place inside the house ... not somewhere outside—whether two blocks away, *James v. Louisiana*, 382 U.S. 36 (1965), 20 feet away, *Shipley v. California*, 395 U.S. 818 (1969), or on the sidewalk near the front steps."

CASE SIGNIFICANCE: The Court in this case narrowed the interpretation of the phrase "area of immediate control," where a search incident to an arrest is valid. In this case, the arrest took place at the front steps of the house. The subsequent search of the house did not come under the area of allowable search and, therefore, the evidence obtained was not admissible in court.

UNITED STATES V. ROBINSON
414 U.S. 218 (1973)

CAPSULE: A body search is valid when a full-custody arrest occurs.

FACTS: Based on a previous investigation, a police officer stopped Robinson on the suspicion that he was operating a motor vehicle after his license had been revoked. After making a full-custody arrest with probable cause, the officer made a search of Robinson's person. He felt an unrecognizable object in Robinson's left breast pocket, but admitted in court that he knew it was not a weapon. The officer removed the object, which turned out to be a "crumpled-up cigarette package" that contained fourteen gelatin capsules of heroin. The capsules were admitted as evidence in Robinson's trial and he was convicted of possession of heroin.

ISSUE: Is it constitutional for a police officer to search (as opposed to merely frisking) a person's body after a lawful custodial arrest even though the officer does not fear for his or her personal safety or believe that evidence will be destroyed? YES.

SUPREME COURT DECISION: A body search is valid in any situation in which a full-custody arrest occurs. There is no requirement that officers fear for their safety or believe that they will find evidence of a crime before the body search can be made.

REASON: "A custodial arrest of a suspect based on probable cause is a reasonable intrusion under the Fourth Amendment; that intrusion being lawful, a search incident to the arrest requires no additional justification. It is the fact of the lawful arrest which establishes the authority to search, and we hold that in the case of a lawful custodial arrest a full search of the person is not only an exception to the warrant requirement of the Fourth Amendment, but is also a 'reasonable' search under that Amendment."

CASE SIGNIFICANCE: *Robinson* allows the search of a person's body after a lawful arrest. Prior to *Robinson*, courts allowed a full-body search (as opposed to a frisk) only if the officer feared for his or her personal safety. In this case, the officer had probable cause to make the arrest (therefore the arrest was valid), but admitted that he could not tell what the object was and did not feel that there were reasons to fear for his safety. Under the then-prevailing standard, the search would have been invalid. *Robinson*, therefore, expands the scope of search incident to a valid arrest and does away with the "fear for personal safety" limitation. It differs from *Chimel* in that the *Chimel* case deals with the "area within the arrestee's immediate control," whereas *Robinson* specifically refers to body searches. The suspect's body is obviously within the area of immediate control, but the authority to search it was not necessarily included in *Chimel* because a person's body enjoys greater protection from governmental intrusion than the area around the person.

UNITED STATES V. EDWARDS
415 U.S. 800 (1974)

CAPSULE: After a lawful arrest and detention, any search conducted at the place of detention that would have been lawful at the time of the arrest may be conducted without a warrant, even though a substantial period of time may have elapsed between the arrest and the search.

FACTS: Edwards was arrested shortly after 11:00 P.M., charged with attempting to break into a post office, and taken to jail. Subsequent investigation at the scene of the crime revealed that the attempted entry was made through a wooden window that had been forced open with a pry bar, leaving paint chips on the window sill. The next morning substitute clothes were purchased for Edwards and his clothes were seized and held as evidence. Examination of the clothes revealed paint chips matching those taken from the window. His motion to suppress the evidence seized from his clothes was denied and Edwards was convicted.

ISSUE: Is a warrantless seizure of clothes taken from a suspect several hours after being placed in custody valid under the Fourth Amendment? YES.

SUPREME COURT DECISION: After being lawfully arrested and placed in custody, any search conducted at the place of detention that would have been lawful at the time of the arrest may be conducted without a warrant, even though a substantial period of time may have elapsed between the arrest and the search.

REASON: "This [search and seizure] was and is a normal incident of a custodial arrest and a reasonable delay in effectuating it does not change the fact that Edwards was no more imposed upon than he could have been at the time and place of the arrest or immediately upon arrival at the place of detention."

CASE SIGNIFICANCE: A search incident to an arrest does not have to take place immediately after the arrest as long as such arrest is justified, as in this case. The key is whether the arrest was valid. If the arrest was valid and the suspect is in custody, the search may take place at a later time and the evidence will be admissible in court. There is reason to believe that the Court in this case would have considered the search valid even if substitute clothing was available at the time Edwards was placed in custody.

ILLINOIS V. LAFAYETTE
462 U.S. 640 (1983)

CAPSULE: Searching the personal effects of a person under lawful arrest is valid if it is part of the administrative procedure incident to the booking and jailing of the suspect.

FACTS: After Lafayette was arrested for disturbing the peace, he was taken to the booking room at the police station where an officer removed the contents of a shoulder bag he was carrying. The officer found amphetamine pills. At a pretrial hearing, the prosecutor argued that the search was valid under a previous court ruling and that it was standard procedure to inventory everything in the possession of an arrested person.

ISSUE: Was the warrantless search of defendant's shoulder bag valid pursuant to an administrative inventory search? YES.

SUPREME COURT DECISION: It is not a violation of the Fourth Amendment for the police to search the personal effects of a person under lawful arrest if the search is part of the routine administrative procedure incident to the booking and jailing of the suspect.

REASON: The governmental interests of searching at the station house may be even greater than those supporting a search immediately following arrest because some necessary searches cannot be conducted in public, but all searches may be conducted in private at the station. Furthermore, at the police station, it is proper for police to remove and inventory property found on the person or in the possession of an arrested person. A standardized procedure for making a list or inventory as soon as reasonable after reaching the station not only deters false claims but also inhibits theft or careless handling of articles taken from the arrested person and protects everyone from dangerous weapons. Additionally, "[the] inspection of an arrestee's personal property may assist the police in ascertaining or verifying his identity."

CASE SIGNIFICANCE: In this case, the Court ruled that the warrantless search of the suspect's bag was justified because it was part of a valid inventory search. Lafayette had argued that the search was invalid either as a search incident to a lawful arrest or as part of the inventory search. The Court disagreed, arguing that the police actions in this case were reasonable under the Fourth Amendment, hence giving broad authority to the police when making inventory searches. The Court approved of inventory searches for the following reasons: (1) protection of a suspect's property, (2) deterrence of false claims of theft against the police, (3) security, and (4) identification of the suspect. All these, argued the Court, benefit both the police and the public.

MARYLAND V. BUIE
494 U.S. 325 (1990)

CAPSULE: A limited protective sweep during arrest in a home is allowed if justified.

FACTS: After surveillance, police officers obtained and executed arrest warrants for Buie and an accomplice in connection with an armed robbery. Upon reaching Buie's house, the officers "fanned out through the first and second floors." One of the officers observed the basement so that no one would surprise the officers. This officer shouted into the basement and ordered anyone there to come out. A voice asked who was there. The officer ordered the person to come out three more times before Buie emerged from the basement. After placing Buie under arrest, another officer entered the basement to see whether there was anyone else there. Once in the basement, the officer noticed in plain view a red running suit similar to the one worn by one of the suspects in the robbery. The running suit was admitted as evidence at Buie's trial over his objection, and he was convicted of robbery.

ISSUE: May officers conduct a warrantless protective sweep of the area in which a suspect is arrested to determine whether another person might be there who would be a danger to the officers? YES.

SUPREME COURT DECISION: "The Fourth Amendment permits a properly limited protective sweep in conjunction with an in-home arrest when the searching officer possesses a reasonable belief based on specific and articulable facts that the area to be swept harbors an individual posing a danger to those on the arrest scene."

REASON: "We ... hold that as an incident to the arrest the officers could, as a precautionary matter and without probable cause or reasonable suspicion, look in closets and other spaces immediately adjoining the place of arrest from which an attack could be immediately launched. Beyond that, however, we hold that there must be articulable facts which, taken together with the rational inferences from those facts, would warrant a reasonably prudent officer in believing that the area to be swept harbors an individual posing a danger to those on the scene. This is no more and no less than was required in *Terry* [*v. Ohio*, 392 U.S. 1 (1968)] and [*Michigan v.*] *Long* [463 U.S. 1032 (1983)] and, as in those cases, we think this balance is the proper one."

"We should emphasize that such a protective sweep, aimed at protecting the arresting officers, if justified by the circumstances, is nevertheless not a full search of the premises, but may extend only to cursory inspection of those spaces where a person may be found. The sweep lasts no longer than is necessary to dispel the reasonable suspicion of danger and in any event no longer than it takes to complete the arrest and depart the premises."

CASE SIGNIFICANCE: This case extends and clarifies the decision in *Warden v. Hayden*, above. It is significant because it authorizes the practice in some police departments of conducting a "protective sweep" during an arrest. It is important for police officers to note, however, that *Buie* does not give the police unlimited authority, when making an arrest, to search the whole house. The protective sweep allowed by *Buie* is limited in scope. The following limitations (taken from the language of the court's decision) must be observed:

1. There must be articulable facts which … would warrant a reasonably prudent officer in believing that the area to be swept harbors an individual posing a danger.
2. Such a protective sweep is not a full search of the premises, but may extend only to a cursory inspection of the spaces where a person may be found.
3. The sweep lasts no longer than is necessary to dispel the reasonable suspicion of danger, and in any event no longer than it takes to complete the arrest and depart the premises.

The police must be careful to observe the above limitations, otherwise the search becomes invalid.

While *Buie* does expand the decision in *Warden*, it does not indicate a broadening of the Court's ruling in *Chimel v. California*, in which the Court ruled that once a lawful arrest has been made, the police may search any area within the suspect's "immediate control." The Court itself distinguished *Chimel* from *Buie* as follows:

1. *Chimel* was concerned with a full search of an entire house for evidence of the crime for which the arrest was made, not the more limited intrusion contemplated by a protective sweep.
2. The justification for the search incident to arrest in *Chimel* was the threat posed by the arrestee, not the safety threat posed by unseen third parties in the house.

VIRGINIA V. MOORE
553 U.S. 164 (2008)

CAPSULE: Officers may make a warrantless arrest of a person, even for a misdemeanor crime, if allowed by the Fourth Amendment but prohibited by state law.

FACTS: Police officers stopped a car driven by Moore based on radio traffic indicating he was driving on a suspended license. The officers confirmed Moore had a suspended license and arrested him. Under state law, the officers should have issued Moore a summons instead of arresting him because state law authorized arrest only when suspects fail to stop the violation or when they are likely to ignore the summons. Subsequent to the arrest, they searched Moore and found cash and 16 grams of crack cocaine. Moore was convicted of possessing cocaine with the intent to distribute.

ISSUE: Do police officers violate the Fourth Amendment by making an arrest based on probable cause but prohibited by state law? NO.

SUPREME COURT DECISION: "We conclude that warrantless arrests for crimes committed in the presence of an arresting officer are reasonable under the Constitution, and that while States are free to regulate such arrests however they desire, state restrictions do not alter the Fourth Amendment's protections."

REASON: "When history has not provided a conclusive answer, we have analyzed a search or seizure in light of traditional standards of reasonableness 'by assessing, on the one hand, the degree to which it intrudes upon an individual's privacy and, on the other, the degree to which it is needed for the promotion of legitimate governmental interests.' [*Wyoming v.*] *Houghton*, 526 U.S., at 300; see also *Atwater* [*v. City of Lago Vista*], 532 U.S., at 346." "Applying that methodology, this Court has held that when an officer has probable cause to believe a person committed even a minor crime, the arrest is constitutionally reasonable. *Atwater, supra*, at 354." "Our decisions counsel against changing this calculus when a State chooses to protect privacy beyond the level that the Fourth Amendment requires." "A State is free to prefer one search-and-seizure policy among the range of constitutionally permissible options, but its choice of a more restrictive option does not render the less restrictive ones unreasonable, and hence unconstitutional." "While States are free to require their officers to engage in nuanced determinations of the need for arrest as a matter of their own law, the Fourth Amendment should reflect administrable bright-line rules. Incorporating state arrest rules into the Constitution would make Fourth Amendment protections as complex as the underlying state law, and variable from place to place and time to time. The Court has previously rejected more restrictive laws in favor of the Fourth Amendment."

CASE SIGNIFICANCE: This case essentially merged the cases of *California v. Greenwood* (see Chapter 6) and *Atwater v. City of Lago Vista* (see Chapter 4). In *Greenwood*, the Court ruled that a search of an individual's garbage did not violate the Fourth Amendment even though it violated state law. The justices argued forcefully that the reasonableness of a search within the Fourth Amendment does not hinge on state law. In *Atwater*, the Court ruled that officers could make an arrest for a minor offense punishable only by a fine. The argument there was that officers on the street may not be able to easily determine how an offense will be charged and should not be held to make those snap decisions when making an arrest for an offense that turns out to be only punishable by a fine. In this case, Virginia law prescribed that officers should have issued a summons rather than arrest Moore. Although there is nothing to indicate the officers arrested Moore only to be able to search him, the arrest did lead to a search of Moore that resulted in his conviction on drug charges rather than driving on a suspended license. Moore argued that the officers had no authority to arrest him because it violated state law. The Court reaffirmed that the Fourth Amendment trumps state law in issues of search and seizure (including arrest). While Moore might have been able to have the evidence excluded in a state court because of the state law, a Fourth Amendment challenge was ineffectual because the officers' actions were within the guidelines of the Fourth Amendment and the Fourth Amendment is not subject to the vagaries of state law.

Searches with Consent

INTRODUCTION

The general rule under the Fourth Amendment is that searches must be made with a warrant for the search to be valid. One of the exceptions to this rule is searches with consent. This exception is important because it is used every day by the police in a variety of situations. The requests, "May I search your car?" or "Would you mind if I come in and search your apartment?" or "May I look around?" are routinely heard by the public from the police.

To be valid, consent must be voluntary and intelligent, based on a totality of circumstances. "Voluntary" means the consent was not forced or coerced; "intelligent" means the person giving consent must know what he or she is doing. Mere silence or failure to object to a search does not necessarily indicate valid consent. Written consent is not constitutionally required, but it (or more frequently videotaping the consent) goes a long way toward proving the validity of the consent if later challenged in court.

Aside from the need for the consent to be voluntary and intelligent, there are other important principles in consent searches. First, consent to enter a dwelling does not necessarily mean consent to search. If a container or closet is to be opened after entry, for example, another consent must be sought by the police. Second, warning the occupant that he or she has the right to refuse permission is not necessary for the consent to be valid. Third, the scope of an allowable search depends on the type of consent given. For example, the consent to search a garage does not mean consent to search an adjoining house or barn. Recent rulings by the Court have concerned the ability of one occupant of a dwelling to give consent over the objection of another occupant.

The following types of consent are valid, if voluntary and intelligent: consent given by a wife or husband, by a roommate (as to areas used in common), by the driver of a vehicle (even if he or she is not the owner of the vehicle), and by high school administrators. On the other hand, consent given by a child, a landlord, a lessor, a hotel clerk, a college or university administrator, and a business employee is not valid.

The leading cases briefed in this chapter on searches with consent are *Bumper v. North Carolina, Schneckloth v. Bustamonte,* and *Fernandez v. California.*

STONER V. CALIFORNIA
376 U.S. 483 (1964)

CAPSULE: A hotel clerk cannot give consent to search the room of a hotel guest.

FACTS: Two men were described to the police by eyewitnesses after a robbery of a food market in California. Soon thereafter, a checkbook belonging to Stoner was found in an adjacent parking lot and turned over to the police. Checkbook stubs indicated that checks had been made out to a hotel in a nearby city. Upon checking the records in that city, the police learned that Stoner had a criminal record. The police then obtained a photograph of Stoner. Eyewitnesses identified the man in the photograph as one of the men involved in the robbery. Without an arrest or search warrant, the police went to the hotel where the suspect resided. The hotel clerk notified the police that the suspect was not in his room, but consented to open the room for them. After gaining entrance to the room, the police made an extensive search and discovered articles like those described by the eyewitnesses to the robbery. Stoner was arrested two days later in another state and extradited to California. He was charged with and convicted of armed robbery.

ISSUE: May a hotel clerk give valid consent to a warrantless search of the room of one of the occupants? NO.

SUPREME COURT DECISION: A hotel guest is entitled to protection against unreasonable searches and seizures. This cannot be waived by the consent of a hotel clerk.

REASON: "It is important to bear in mind that it was the petitioner's constitutional right which was at stake here, and not the night clerk's nor the hotel's. It was a right, therefore, which only the petitioner could waive by word or deed."

CASE SIGNIFICANCE: A hotel guest has a reasonable expectation of privacy that cannot be waived by the hotel management simply because the management has the key. A wife can consent to the search of a house, parents can consent to the search of a child's room (with some exceptions), or a roommate to the search of a dormitory room, but a hotel clerk cannot consent to a search of the room of a guest. Note, however, that if the police want to arrest a suspect in a room, the fact that access to the room was made by borrowing a key from the hotel clerk does not invalidate the arrest. The rule on consent, therefore, differs in arrest and in search cases.

BUMPER V. NORTH CAROLINA
391 U.S. 543 (1968)

CAPSULE: Consent obtained by deception through a claim of lawful authority that did not in fact exist is not voluntary. A search conducted by virtue of a warrant cannot later be justified by consent if the warrant turns out to be invalid.

FACTS: During a rape investigation, and prior to his arrest, officers went to Bumper's home where he lived with his grandmother. One of the four officers went to the door and was met by the grandmother. When the officer announced that he had a warrant to search the house (although he did not), the grandmother responded "Go ahead" and opened the door. The officers found a rifle in the kitchen that was seized and entered as evidence. Bumper was subsequently charged with and convicted of rape.

ISSUE: Can a search be justified as lawful on the basis of consent when the alleged consent is given only after the official conducting the search asserts possession of a warrant? NO.

SUPREME COURT DECISION: The alleged consent in this case was not voluntary because it was obtained by deception through a claim of lawful authority that did not exist. A search conducted by virtue of a warrant cannot later be justified by consent if the warrant turns out to be invalid.

REASON: "When a prosecutor seeks to rely upon consent to justify the lawfulness of a search, he has the burden of proving that the consent was, in fact, freely and voluntarily given. This burden cannot be discharged by showing no more than acquiescence to a claim of lawful authority. A search conducted in reliance upon a warrant cannot later be justified on the basis of consent if it turns out that the warrant was invalid. ... When a law officer claims authority to search a home under a warrant, he announces in effect that the occupant has no right to resist the search. The situation is [rife] with coercion—albeit colorably lawful coercion. Where there is coercion there cannot be consent."

CASE SIGNIFICANCE: Consent to search is not valid if permission is given as a result of police misrepresentation or deception. In this case, the police said they had a warrant when, in fact, they did not. Lower courts are divided on the related issue of whether consent is valid if the officer does not have a warrant but threatens to obtain one. That issue has not been resolved by the Supreme Court.

SCHNECKLOTH V. BUSTAMONTE
412 U.S. 218 (1973)

CAPSULE: Voluntariness of consent to search is determined from the totality of circumstances, of which knowledge of the right to refuse consent is a factor but not a requirement.

FACTS: An officer on routine patrol stopped an automobile containing Bustamonte and five others after observing that a headlight and the license plate light were burned out. When the driver could not produce a driver's license, the officer asked if any of the others had any type of identification. Only one, Joe Alcala, was able to produce a driver's license. He explained that the vehicle belonged to his brother. The men were ordered out of the car, and the officer asked Alcala if he could search the car. Alcala replied, "Sure, go ahead." Prior to the search, no one had been threatened with arrest or given the impression they were suspected of any wrongdoing. Alcala assisted in the search by opening the trunk and glove compartment. During the search, the officer found three checks under the left rear seat that had been stolen from a car wash. Bustamonte was convicted of possession of a check with intent to defraud.

ISSUE: Is knowledge by a suspect of the right to refuse consent required for consent to a search to be valid? NO.

SUPREME COURT DECISION: Voluntariness of consent to search is to be determined from the totality of the circumstances, of which consent is one element. Knowledge of the right to refuse consent is not a prerequisite for voluntary consent.

REASON: "Our decision today is a narrow one. We hold only that when the subject of a search is not in custody and the State attempts to justify a search on the basis of his consent, the Fourth and Fourteenth Amendments require that it demonstrate that the consent was in fact voluntarily given and not the result of duress or coercion, expressed or implied. Voluntariness is a question of fact to be determined from all the circumstances, and while the subject's knowledge of a right to refuse is a factor to be taken into account, the prosecution is not required to demonstrate such knowledge as a prerequisite to establishing voluntary consent."

CASE SIGNIFICANCE: In *Miranda v. Arizona*, 384 U.S. 436 (1966), the Court ruled that a suspect must be made aware of the right to remain silent during questioning if responses to questions are later to be admissible in court. *Schneckloth* holds that there is no such requirement in consent search cases. The suspect does not have to be advised that he or she has the right to refuse consent for the search to be valid. All that is required is that the consent be voluntary. The Court also held that "voluntariness is a question of fact to be determined from all the circumstances; and, while the subject's knowledge of a right to refuse is a factor to be taken into account, the prosecution is not required to demonstrate such knowledge as a prerequisite to establishing voluntary consent." The police must prove that consent is voluntary; however, unlike *Miranda*, where the police must say "you have the right to remain silent," the police in consent searches do not have to say "you have the right to refuse consent."

FLORIDA V. ROYER
460 U.S. 491 (1983)

CAPSULE: More serious intrusion of personal liberty than is allowable on suspicion of criminal activity taints the consent and makes the search illegal.

FACTS: Police observed an individual in Miami International Airport who fit a so-called "drug courier profile" of being young, nervous, casually dressed, with heavy American Tourister luggage, and paying for a one-way ticket in cash under an assumed name. Based on this information, the officers approached the suspect. Upon request, but without oral consent, Royer produced an airline ticket with his friend's name and a driver's license with his correct name. When questioned about the discrepancy in names, Royer responded that a friend had bought the ticket under that friend's name. Without returning Royer's airline ticket or license, the officers then informed him that he was suspected of trafficking in narcotics and requested that he follow them to a room 40 feet away. Without consent, Royer's luggage was brought to the room. Although he did not respond to the officer's request to consent to a search of the luggage, Royer produced a key and opened one of the suitcases. Marijuana was found in the suitcase. When Royer said that he did not know the combination to the other suitcase but that he did not object to its being opened, the officers pried open the suitcase and found more marijuana. Royer was then informed he was under arrest. He was convicted of possession of marijuana.

ISSUE: Is evidence obtained through a consent search admissible in court if the initial detention of the suspect was without probable cause, and in violation of the Fourth Amendment? NO.

SUPREME COURT DECISION: At the time the suspect consented to the search of his luggage, "the detention to which he had been subjected was a more serious intrusion of his personal liberty than was allowable on mere suspicion of criminal activity"; thus, the consent was tainted by illegality and could not justify the search.

REASON: "When the detectives identified themselves as narcotics agents, told respondent [Royer] he was suspected of transporting narcotics, and asked him to accompany them to the police room, while retaining his airline ticket and driver's license and without indicating in any way that he was free to depart, respondent was effectively seized for purposes of the Fourth Amendment. At the time respondent produced the key to his suitcase, the detention to which he was then subjected was a more serious intrusion on his personal liberty than is allowable on mere suspicion of criminal activity. What had begun as a consensual inquiry in a public place escalated into an investigatory procedure in a police interrogation room, and respondent, as a practical matter, was under arrest at that time. Moreover, the detectives' conduct was more intrusive than necessary to effectuate an investigative detention otherwise authorized by the *Terry v. Ohio* line of cases."

CASE SIGNIFICANCE: Consent given after an illegal act by the police is not valid because such consent is tainted. For the consent to be valid, the police must be careful that no illegal act precedes it because once the illegal act is committed, consent cannot cure it. The only possible exception is if the taint has somehow been purged by an independent source, inevitable discovery, and so forth. In this case, however, consent did not purge the taint.

ILLINOIS V. RODRIGUEZ
497 U.S. 177 (1990)

CAPSULE: Searches in which the person giving consent has "apparent authority" are valid.

FACTS: After being summoned to a house, the police were met by Gail Fischer, who showed signs of a severe beating. She informed the officers that she had been assaulted by Rodriguez earlier that day in an apartment. Fischer and the police subsequently drove to the apartment of Rodriguez because she stated that Rodriguez would be asleep at that time and that she could let them into the apartment with her key so that they could arrest him. Several times she referred to the apartment as "our" apartment and stated that she had clothes and furniture there. She did not tell the police, however, that she was no longer living there. Upon entrance, without a warrant but with a key and permission provided by Fischer, the police saw in plain view drug paraphernalia and containers filled with cocaine. The officers seized these and other drug paraphernalia found in the apartment where Rodriguez was sleeping. Rodriguez was arrested and charged with possession of a controlled substance with intent to deliver. On appeal, the Circuit Court suppressed the evidence, holding that at the time Fischer consented to the entry of the apartment, she did not have common authority over it because she had moved out several weeks earlier.

ISSUE: Is a warrantless entry and subsequent search, based on the consent of a person whom the police believed to have possessed common authority over the premises, but who in fact did not have such authority, valid? YES.

SUPREME COURT DECISION: The warrantless entry of private premises by the police is valid if based on the consent of a third party whom the police reasonably believed to possess common authority over the premises. The entry is still valid if it is later determined the person did not have such authority.

REASON: The Court conceded that Fischer had no common authority over the apartment; however, the Court ruled that it was sufficient to validate the entry that the officers reasonably believed she did have such authority. Furthermore, the Fourth Amendment only protects against unreasonable searches, not searches performed without the owner's consent. The "reasonableness" clause of the Fourth Amendment "does not demand that the government be factually correct in its assessment." Furthermore, "[t]he Constitution is no more violated when officers enter without a warrant because they reasonably (though erroneously) believe that the person who has consented to their entry is a resident of the premises, than it is violated when they enter without a warrant because they reasonably (though erroneously) believe they are in pursuit of a violent felon who is about to escape."

CASE SIGNIFICANCE: This case reiterates the "apparent authority" rule in searches with consent. The rule says that consent given by a third party whom the police reasonably believe to possess common authority over the premises is valid even if it is later established that the person did not in fact have that authority. In this case, the girlfriend, who gave consent and provided the key, had moved out of the apartment. She led the police to the house and allowed them entry by using her key. She did not tell them that she no longer lived there. The officers reasonably believed that she had authority to give consent; hence, the entry was valid, and the evidence subsequently obtained was admissible. It is important to note, however, that for the "apparent authority" rule to apply, the belief by the police must be reasonable, considering the circumstances.

FLORIDA V. JIMENO
499 U.S. 934 (1991)

CAPSULE: Consent justifies the warrantless search of a container in a car if it is objectively reasonable for the police to believe that the scope of the suspect's consent permitted them to open that container.

FACTS: A Dade County police officer overheard Jimeno arranging what appeared to be a drug transaction over a public telephone. The officer followed Jimeno's car and saw him make an illegal right turn at a red light. The officer stopped Jimeno to issue a traffic citation. After informing Jimeno why he had been stopped, the officer stated that he had reason to believe Jimeno was carrying narcotics in his car and asked permission to search the car. The officer explained that Jimeno did not have to grant permission, but Jimeno stated that he had nothing to hide and gave consent to the search. Pursuant to the search, the officer found a kilogram of cocaine in a brown paper bag located on the floorboard of the passenger compartment. Jimeno was convicted of possession with the intent to distribute cocaine.

ISSUE: Does consent for the police to search a vehicle extend to closed containers found inside the vehicle? YES.

SUPREME COURT DECISION: "A criminal suspect's Fourth Amendment right to be free from unreasonable searches is not violated when, after he gives police permission to search his automobile, they open a closed container found within the car that might reasonably hold the object of the search."

REASON: "The standard for measuring the scope of a suspect's consent under the Fourth Amendment is that of 'objective' reasonableness—what would the typical reasonable person have understood by the exchange between the officer and the suspect? The question before us, then, is whether it is reasonable for an officer to consider a suspect's general consent to a search of his car to include consent to examine a paper bag lying on the floor of the car. We think that it is." "The scope of a search is generally defined by its expressed object. In this case, the terms of the search's authorization were simple. Respondent [Jimeno] granted Officer Trujillo permission to search his car, and did not place any explicit limitation on the scope of the search. Trujillo had informed the respondent that he believed the respondent was carrying narcotics, and that he would be looking for narcotics in the car. We think that it was objectively reasonable for the police to conclude that the general consent to search the respondent's car included consent to search containers within that car which might bear drugs. A reasonable person may be expected to know that narcotics are generally carried in some form of a container. 'Contraband goods rarely are strewn across the trunk or floor of a car.' The authorization to search in this case, therefore, extended beyond the surfaces of the car's interior to the paper bag lying on the car's floor." (Citations omitted.)

CASE SIGNIFICANCE: In an earlier case, *United States v. Ross*, 456 U.S 798 (1982), the Court held that, when the police have probable cause to justify a warrantless search of a car, they may search the entire car and open the trunk and any packages or luggage found therein that could reasonably contain the items for which they have probable cause to search. This case reiterates that holding, although with a different twist because the search was authorized by consent rather than by probable cause.

The issue in this case was whether it was "objectively reasonable for the police to believe that the scope of the suspect's consent permitted them to open the particular container." The issue was not one of probable cause, but the scope of the suspect's consent to search. The

Court concluded that the authorization to search given by the suspect "extended beyond the car's interior surfaces to the bag, since Jimeno did not place any explicit limitation on the scope of the search and was aware that Trujillo [the officer] would be looking for narcotics in the car, and since a reasonable person may be expected to know that narcotics are generally carried in some form of container." The Court added that there is "no basis for adding to the Fourth Amendment's basic test of objective reasonableness a requirement that, if the police wish to search closed containers within a car, they must separately request permission to search each container."

This case defines the extent of what the police can do in cases of searches based on consent. The police do not need specific consent to look into each container. The Court held that, in these cases, the Fourth Amendment is satisfied if, given the circumstances, "it is objectively reasonable for the police to believe that the scope of the suspect's consent permitted them to open the particular container." Conversely, this depends upon what item or items the police are looking for and whether it might be found in that container.

GEORGIA V. RANDOLPH
547 U.S. 103 (2006)

CAPSULE: "[A] warrantless search of a shared dwelling for evidence over the express refusal of consent by a physically present resident cannot be justified as reasonable as to him on the basis of consent given to the police by another resident."

FACTS: After a separation between Randolph and his wife and her return to the household, the wife notified police of a domestic dispute where Randolph took their son away. When officers responded, the wife told them that her husband was a cocaine user. Shortly after the police arrived, Randolph returned. Randolph denied cocaine use, and countered that it was his wife who abused drugs. Later, the wife reaffirmed Randolph's drug use and told police there was "drug evidence" in the house. An officer asked Randolph for permission to search the house, which he unequivocally refused. The officer then asked the wife for consent to search, which she readily gave. She led the officer to a bedroom that she identified as Randolph's, where officers found a section of a drinking straw with a powdery residue suspected to be cocaine. Officers then contacted the District Attorney's office, who instructed him to stop the search and apply for a warrant. When the officers returned to the house, the wife withdrew her consent. The police took the straw to the police station, along with the Randolphs. After obtaining a search warrant, officers returned to the house and seized further evidence of drug use. Randolph was indicted for possession of cocaine.

ISSUE: Is a warrantless search of a shared dwelling valid when one occupant gives consent but another occupant who is present expressly refuses to consent? NO.

SUPREME COURT DECISION: "We therefore hold that a warrantless search of a shared dwelling for evidence over the express refusal of consent by a physically present resident cannot be justified as reasonable as to him on the basis of consent given to the police by another resident."

REASON: In previous cases, the Court recognized the validity of searches based on voluntary consent of an individual who shares common authority over property to be searched. None of the co-occupant consent-to-search cases, however, included the circumstances of a second occupant physically present and refusing permission to search. "[I]t is fair to say that a caller standing at the door of shared premises would have no confidence that one occupant's invitation was a sufficiently good reason to enter when a fellow tenant stood there saying, 'stay out.' Without some very good reason, no sensible person would go inside under those conditions." "The visitor's reticence without some such good reason would show not timidity but a realization that when people living together disagree over the use of their common quarters, a resolution must come through voluntary accommodation, not by appeals to authority." "Since the co-tenant wishing to open the door to a third party has no recognized authority in law or social practice to prevail over a present and objecting co-tenant, his disputed invitation, without more, gives a police officer no better claim to reasonableness in entering than the officer would have in the absence of any consent at all." "So long as there is no evidence that the police have removed the potentially objecting tenant from the entrance for the sake of avoiding a possible objection, there is practical value in the simple clarity of complementary rules, one recognizing the co-tenant's permission when there is no fellow occupant on hand, the other according dispositive weight to the fellow occupant's contrary indication when he expresses it."

CASE SIGNIFICANCE: Consent is an exception to the Fourth Amendment rule requiring probable cause and a warrant in search and seizure cases. This case resolves an issue that was not previously addressed by the Court: whether consent by an occupant of a dwelling over the expressed objection of another occupant authorizes the police to conduct a warrantless search. Previous Supreme Court cases held that one consent sufficed. Those cases, however, did not involve circumstances where the other occupant was present and specifically refused to give consent. In previous cases, the other occupant either was away or did not expressly refuse consent. In this case, the Court held the search invalid because one occupant specifically refused consent. The majority stated, however, that this ruling does not apply to instances when: (1) "the police must enter a dwelling to protect a resident from domestic violence; so long as they have good reason to believe such a threat exists" and (2) in cases where the purpose of the entry is "to give a complaining tenant the opportunity to collect belongings and get out safely, or to determine whether violence (or threat of violence) has just occurred or is about to occur, however much a spouse or other co-tenant objected." The Court also held that this ruling does not apply to cases where the person giving consent is in a position of authority in a "recognized hierarchy," such as parent and child. Finally, the Court ruled that the police could not remove one of the occupants deliberately to prevent the person from refusing consent (see *Fernandez v. California*, below). Despite this ruling, other issues remain unresolved, such as: must the police expressly inform all the occupants that they have a right to refuse consent? How is that consent expressed? Does silence mean consent or refusal? The safer practice is for police officers to make sure occupants of equal status in the house give their expressed consent and obtain that consent in writing.

FERNANDEZ V. CALIFORNIA
571 U.S. 292 (2014)

CAPSULE: The lawful occupant of a house or apartment may consent to a search, even over the potential objection of another lawful occupant, if the other occupant is not present or was removed on objectively reasonable grounds.

FACTS: After observing Abel Lopez cash a check, Walter Fernandez approached Lopez, determined he was Mexican, and indicated he was in a gang. Fernandez then pulled out a knife and cut Lopez on the wrist. Lopez ran from the scene and called 911. At Fernandez's direction, four men emerged from a nearby apartment building and attacked Lopez. After knocking Lopez to the ground, they hit and kicked him and took his cell phone and his wallet. Police officers observed Fernandez run into an apartment building and heard screams coming from one of the apartments. Officers knocked on the apartment door, which was answered by a woman who was battered and bleeding. When the officers asked her to step out of the apartment so they could conduct a protective sweep, Fernandez came to the door and objected. Suspecting that he had assaulted the woman, Roxanne Rojas, officers placed him under arrest. Lopez identified Fernandez as the perpetrator in the robbery, and he was taken to the police station. An hour later, an officer returned to the apartment and, after obtaining the woman's consent, searched the premises. The officer found several items related to the robbery among other contraband. The court overruled Fernandez's motion to suppress the evidence, holding that because he was not present at the time of the consent to the search, the exception to permissible warrantless consent searches of jointly occupied premises that arises when one of the occupants present objects to the search did not apply.

ISSUE: Does the decision in *Georgia v. Randolph* apply when one person with joint authority to consent has been removed by police for objectively reasonable grounds? NO.

SUPREME COURT DECISION: "Putting the exception the Court adopted in *Randolph* to one side, the lawful occupant of a house or apartment should have the right to invite the police to enter the dwelling and conduct a search."

REASON: "Our cases firmly establish that police officers may search jointly occupied premises if one of the occupants consents. See *United States v. Matlock*, 415 U.S. 164 (1974). In *Georgia v. Randolph*, 547 U.S. 103 (2006), we recognized a narrow exception to this rule, holding that the consent of one occupant is insufficient when another occupant is present and objects to the search." "We … refuse to extend *Randolph* to the very different situation in this case, where consent was provided by an abused woman well after her male partner had been removed from the apartment they shared."

CASE SIGNIFICANCE: The Court first established in *Schneckloth v. Bustamonte* (see above) that consent searches were reasonable. The court then established in *United States v. Matlock* that, when multiple occupants are involved, the rule extends to an absent occupant as long as it is given by one of the legal occupants. However, the Court ruled in *Randolph* that, when a physically present inhabitant refuses consent, that refusal "is dispositive as to him, regardless of the consent of a fellow occupant." The Court also held that consent might not be sufficient if "there is evidence that the police have removed the potentially objecting tenant from the entrance for the sake of avoiding a possible objection." The Court in this case made clear, however, that this is not a subjective interpretation of the intent of the officers, but an objective assessment of the reasonableness of the removal. In this case, the Court reasoned, "We therefore hold that an occupant who is absent due to a lawful detention or arrest stands in the same shoes as an occupant who is absent for any other reason." The Court was also not persuaded by Fernandez's argument that the objection he made while at the premises remained effective until he changed his mind and withdrew it. The Court noted several problems with this potential argument, including the duration of the objection (could a person who is sentenced to prison prevent consent from the other occupant for 10 years or more?) and which officers would be bound by the objection (just those officers who were present when the objection was made or a much larger set of officers who may not even know of the objection?).

Vehicle Stops and Searches

9

INTRODUCTION

The Fourth Amendment imposes two requirements for searches and seizures, in general, to be valid: a search warrant or probable cause. The rule is different, however, in vehicular stops and searches because motor vehicles are mobile and can be driven away at any time, making obtaining a warrant impractical. This rule was laid out in *Carroll v. United States*, in which the Supreme Court held that the search of an automobile without a warrant is valid as long as probable cause is present.

Vehicle stops, vehicle searches, and searches of people who happen to be in vehicles must be distinguished because they are governed by different rules. Vehicular stops and searches are addressed in this chapter and are similar in that they do not need a warrant or probable cause. The only requirement for a valid stop is that the police have reasonable suspicion (less than probable cause) of unlawful activity. A vehicle search after a valid stop is governed by a different rule. Such searches do not need a warrant, but probable cause must be present for the search to be valid. Searches involving people in vehicles are addressed in the following chapter.

The search of a vehicle is governed by rules that, over the years, have expanded the power of the police. The Supreme Court has held that police officers may do the following during vehicle searches (assuming the search is valid):

1. Conduct a search of the passenger compartment of a car and of the contents therein if it is incident to a lawful arrest.
2. Search the entire car and open the trunk and any packages or luggage found therein that could reasonably contain the items they are looking for.
3. Search a container in a car if there is probable cause to believe it holds contraband or seizable items, even in the absence of probable cause to search the car.

The leading cases briefed in this chapter on vehicle stops and searches are *Carroll v. United States*, *New York v. Belton*, *United States v. Ross*, *Wyoming v. Houghton,* and *Bond v. United States.*

CARROLL V. UNITED STATES
267 U.S. 132 (1925)

CAPSULE: The warrantless search of an automobile is valid if there exists probable cause to believe it contains contraband.

FACTS: Officers observed the automobile of Carroll while on a regular patrol. The same officers had been in contact with Carroll twice in the four months prior to this sighting. In September, the officers attempted to buy illegal liquor from Carroll, but he was alerted to their true identity and did not produce the contraband. In October, the officers recognized Carroll's automobile returning from Detroit (a city possessing an international boundary and that was known as a city from which illegal liquor was regularly imported). The officers gave chase but failed to apprehend Carroll. Carroll was later stopped by police. He and his companion were ordered out of the car. No liquor was visible in the front seat of the automobile. Officers then opened the rumble seat and looked under the cushions, again finding no liquor. One of the officers then struck the "lazyback" of the seat, tore open the seat cushion, and discovered 68 bottles of gin and whiskey. Carroll was arrested and convicted of transporting intoxicating liquor.

ISSUE: May officers search an automobile without a search warrant but with probable cause that it contains illegal contraband? YES.

SUPREME COURT DECISION: The risk of the vehicle being moved from the jurisdiction, or the evidence being destroyed or carried off, justifies a warrantless search as long as such search is conducted with probable cause that the vehicle that is subject to seizure contains contraband.

REASON: "[T]he guarantee of freedom from unreasonable searches and seizures by the Fourth Amendment has been construed, practically since the beginning of government, as recognizing a necessary difference between a search of a store, dwelling house, or other structure in respect of which a proper official warrant readily may be obtained and a search of a ship, motor boat, wagon, or automobile for contraband goods, where it is not practicable to secure a warrant, because the vehicle can be quickly moved out of the locality or jurisdiction in which the warrant must be sought."

CASE SIGNIFICANCE: The general rule is that searches may be conducted only if a warrant has been issued. There are several exceptions to this rule, however, searches of automobiles being one of them. This case, decided in 1925, created the so-called "automobile exception" to the warrant requirement by ruling that warrantless searches of motor vehicles are valid as long as there is probable cause to believe there are seizable items in the vehicle. The justification for this exception is the mobile nature of the automobile.

CHAMBERS V. MARONEY
399 U.S. 42 (1969)

CAPSULE: If probable cause exists that an automobile contains contraband, a warrantless search is valid even if the automobile is first moved to a police station.

FACTS: Shortly after a gas station attendant and two bystanders gave police a description of two men and the getaway car used in the robbery of the gas station, the police arrested Chambers and three other occupants of a station wagon who fit the description. After the arrest, the car was taken to the police station. The police searched the car and found two revolvers concealed under the dashboard, a glove with the money Chambers had obtained from the gas attendant, and credit cards with the name of another gas station attendant in a different town who had been robbed the previous week. During a warrant-authorized search of Chambers' home the following day, the police found and seized ammunition similar to that found in the guns taken from the station wagon. Chambers was convicted of both robberies.

ISSUE: Is the evidence seized by the police from an automobile, after the automobile has been taken to the police station and searched without a warrant, admissible in court? YES.

SUPREME COURT DECISION: A car may be searched without a warrant as long as probable cause is present. Under the Constitution, there is no difference between seizing and holding a car before presenting the probable cause issue to a magistrate and carrying out an immediate search without a warrant.

REASON: The search made at the police station, some time after the arrest, cannot be justified as a search incident to arrest. "There are, however, alternative grounds arguably justifying the search of the car." Here, the officers had probable cause to arrest the occupants of the car and, therefore, had probable cause to search the car for guns and stolen money. As ruled in *Carroll*, with probable cause, an automobile can be searched without a warrant in circumstances that would not justify a warrantless search of a house or office. "But the circumstances that furnish probable cause to search a particular auto for particular articles are most often unforeseeable. ... Where an effective search is to be made at any time, either the search must be made immediately without a warrant or the car itself must be seized and held without a warrant for whatever period is necessary to obtain a warrant. ... Only in exigent circumstances will the judgment of the police as to probable cause serve as a sufficient authorization for a search. ... For constitutional purposes, we see no difference between ... seizing and holding a car before presenting the probable cause issue to a magistrate and ... carrying out an immediate search without a warrant. Given probable cause to search, either course is reasonable under the Fourth Amendment."

CASE SIGNIFICANCE: This case is significant because it does away with the previous requirement that the police must obtain a warrant to search a vehicle with probable cause if there is time to obtain a warrant. What the former rule said was that, once the police take control of the vehicle and the danger of it being driven away by the suspect is gone because the vehicle is now under police control, a warrant must first be obtained if the vehicle is to be searched further. This case does away with that rule, holding instead that, if the police had probable cause to search the vehicle when it was first stopped, then it can be searched without a warrant even if there is time to obtain a warrant. This case reiterates the rule that warrantless searches of vehicles are valid as long as there is probable cause, even if a warrant could have been obtained.

UNITED STATES V. CHADWICK
433 U.S. 1 (1977)

CAPSULE: The warrantless search of a movable container found in a motor vehicle is invalid in the absence of exigent circumstances.

FACTS: Railroad officials in San Diego observed defendants who fit a "drug courier profile" loading an unusually heavy footlocker, which was leaking talcum powder (often used to mask the smell of marijuana), onto a train. The officials notified federal narcotics agents, who had officers waiting in Boston, the destination of the defendants. The officers in Boston did not obtain a search warrant but brought a dog trained to detect marijuana. The dog signaled the presence of marijuana just before the footlocker was lifted into the trunk of the defendants' automobile. Before the trunk's lid could be closed or the car started, police arrested the three suspects. A search incident to the arrest revealed no weapons, but the keys to the footlocker were taken from one of the suspects. The defendants and the footlocker were taken to the Federal Building. One and one-half hours later, agents opened the footlocker without a search warrant or the defendants' consent. Large amounts of marijuana were found in the footlocker. The defendants were charged with and convicted of possession of marijuana with intent to distribute.

ISSUE: May the police, with probable cause but without a warrant, search a movable container found in a public place? NO.

SUPREME COURT DECISION: The warrantless search of a movable container (in this case, a 200-pound footlocker secured by padlocks) found in a public place is invalid, absent exigent circumstances.

REASON: "The factors which diminish the privacy aspects of an automobile do not apply to respondents' footlocker. ... Unlike an automobile, whose primary function is transportation, luggage is intended as a repository of personal effects ... [and] a person's expectations of privacy in personal luggage are substantially greater than in an automobile. ... Nor does the footlocker's mobility justify dispensing with the added protections of the Warrant Clause ... [Finally] warrantless searches of luggage or other property seized at the time of an arrest cannot be justified as incident to that arrest either if the 'search is remote in time or place from the arrest,' or no exigency exists."

CASE SIGNIFICANCE: In ruling that the warrantless search of the footlocker was unjustified, the Court reaffirmed the general principle that closed packages and containers may not be searched without a warrant. The Court argued that "unlike an automobile, whose primary function is transportation, luggage is intended as a repository of personal effects." A footlocker, by virtue of it being a repository of personal effects, enjoys greater protection and its owner has greater expectations of privacy. The difference between the *Chadwick* case and the case of *United States v. Ross*, 456 U.S. 798 (1982) (in which pieces of evidence obtained without a warrant from a paper bag and a leather pouch were held admissible in court), is that *Chadwick* involved a footlocker, which was luggage and only incidentally loaded in a car when the seizure was made, whereas *Ross* involved a paper bag and a leather pouch, both of which were found in the trunk of the car and therefore could be opened by the police without a warrant. Although not expressly overruled by the Court in *California v. Acevedo* (see below), the decision in this case was severely degraded by that decision.

DELAWARE V. PROUSE
440 U.S. 648 (1979)

CAPSULE: Stopping an automobile at random and without probable cause is unreasonable under the Fourth Amendment.

FACTS: Without observing traffic or equipment violations or suspicious activity, a police officer stopped Prouse's vehicle to check the driver's license and registration. Upon approaching the vehicle, the officer smelled marijuana. He seized a quantity of marijuana in plain view on the floor of the automobile. The officer was not acting pursuant to any departmental regulations governing spot checks. Prouse was convicted of illegal possession of a controlled substance.

ISSUE: May a police officer make a random stop of an automobile simply to check the driving license of the operator and registration of the automobile in the absence of probable cause that its occupants are engaging in illegal activity? NO.

SUPREME COURT DECISION: Stopping an automobile and detaining the driver to check the license and registration is unreasonable under the Fourth Amendment unless there is probable cause to believe that the motorist is unlicensed or that the automobile is in violation of equipment laws, or that its occupants are exhibiting suspicious behavior.

REASON: "The Fourth and Fourteenth Amendments are implicated in this case because stopping an automobile and detaining its occupants constitutes a 'seizure' within the meaning of those Amendments, even though the purpose of the stop is limited and the resulting detention quite brief. The essential purpose of the proscriptions in the Fourth Amendment is to impose a standard of reasonableness upon the exercise of discretion by government officials, including law enforcement agents, in order to 'safeguard the privacy and security of individuals against invasions.'" (Citations omitted.)

CASE SIGNIFICANCE: This case holds that officers cannot arbitrarily stop motor vehicles without probable cause to believe that an illegality or violation has occurred or is occurring. Vehicles may be searched without a warrant, but probable cause must be present. Does this mean that vehicle spot checks are illegal? Not necessarily. The Court in this case argued that this decision does not preclude a state from "developing methods for spot checks that involve less intrusion or that do not involve the unconstrained exercise of discretion." For example, questioning all oncoming traffic at roadblock-type stops is valid and may be used by the police. However, unregulated and random stops are not allowed by the Fourth Amendment. In a similar case (*Heien v. North Carolina*, 574 U.S. ___ [2014]), officers stopped Heien because he had a taillight out. A subsequent search revealed cocaine. At trial, it was determined that the state only required a vehicle "equipped with a stop lamp," invalidating the stop because Heien did have one working stop lamp. The Court ruled that the officers' mistake of law was reasonable and there was reasonable suspicion justifying the stop.

NEW YORK V. BELTON
453 U.S. 454 (1981)

CAPSULE: The police may conduct a warrantless search of the passenger compartment of a car and of the contents therein if it is incident to a lawful arrest.

FACTS: Police stopped an automobile in which Belton was an occupant. A check of driver's licenses and automobile registration revealed that none of the occupants owned the vehicle or were related to the owner. The officer smelled burnt marijuana and saw an envelope marked "Supergold" on the floor of the automobile, which the officer associated with marijuana. After administering *Miranda* warnings, the officer placed the occupants under arrest, picked up the envelope, and found marijuana. He then searched the passenger compartment of the automobile and, on the backseat, found a jacket belonging to Belton. He unzipped one of the pockets of the jacket and discovered cocaine. Belton was convicted of possession of a controlled substance.

ISSUE: Is the warrantless seizure of evidence in the passenger compartment of a car, after a lawful arrest, valid? YES.

SUPREME COURT DECISION: The police may conduct a warrantless search of the passenger compartment of a vehicle incident to a lawful arrest. The search may include containers found within the passenger compartment. The term "container" denotes any object capable of holding another object. It includes closed or open glove compartments, consoles, or other receptacles located anywhere within the passenger compartment, as well as luggage, boxes, bags, clothing, and similar items.

REASON: "[I]n *United States v. Robinson*, 414 U.S. 218 [1973], the Court hewed a straightforward rule ... in the case of a lawful custodial arrest a full search of the person is not only an exception to the warrant requirement of the Fourth Amendment, but is also a 'reasonable' search under that Amendment. ... Accordingly, we hold that when a policeman has made a lawful custodial arrest of the occupant of an automobile, he may, as a contemporaneous incident of that arrest, search the passenger compartment of that automobile. ... It follows from this conclusion that the police may also examine the contents of any containers found within the passenger compartment, for if the passenger compartment is within the reach of the arrestee, so also will containers in it be within his reach."

CASE SIGNIFICANCE: This case defined the extent of allowable searches inside the automobile after a lawful arrest. Prior to this, there was confusion about whether the police may search parts of the automobile outside the driver's "wingspan." The Court expanded the area of allowable search to the whole passenger compartment, including the backseat; it also authorized the opening of containers found in the passenger compartment that might contain the object sought. In this case, Belton's jacket could contain prohibited drugs; its search was therefore valid. This case also authorizes the police to search the interior of the car even if the occupant has been removed from the car or no longer constitutes a danger to the police (but for a distinction, see *Arizona v. Gant*, below). Note, however, that the *Belton* case did not decide whether the trunk could also be searched. This case was decided later in *United States v. Ross*, 456 U.S. 798 (1982).

UNITED STATES V. CORTEZ
449 U.S. 411 (1981)

CAPSULE: In determining reasonable suspicion to make an investigatory stop, the totality of circumstances must be taken into account.

FACTS: Based on footprints found over a period of time, officers concluded that groups of illegal immigrants were walking over a well-defined path from the Mexican border to a highway where they would be picked up by a motor vehicle. A similar set of footprints was found in each group; therefore, officers further concluded that one person was acting as a guide to these groups. Based on the times the tracks were found, officers determined that the crossings occurred on nights during the weekend when the weather was clear. Because the tracks approached the highway and then turned to the east, the officers concluded that the vehicle would approach from and return to the east. Based on these deductions, and the fact that a particular Sunday was the first clear night in three days, officers set up surveillance on the highway. Of the 15–20 vehicles that passed the officers during their surveillance, only two matched the type they were looking for. As one truck passed, the officers obtained a partial license plate number. When the same vehicle passed them again, heading east, they pursued and stopped it. Cortez was driving the truck and a man wearing shoes with soles matching the prints found in the desert was an occupant. The officers told Cortez they were conducting an immigration check. In the back of the truck were six illegal immigrants. Cortez and his companion were convicted of transporting illegal aliens.

ISSUE: May objective facts and circumstantial evidence observed and collected by the police justify an investigative stop of a vehicle? YES.

SUPREME COURT DECISION: In determining reasonable suspicion to make an investigatory stop, the totality of the circumstances must be taken into account. The officers must, however, have a particularized, objective basis for suspecting that the individual stopped is engaged in criminal activity.

REASON: The totality of the circumstances must yield a particularized suspicion containing two elements that must be present before the stop can occur. First, the assessment of the situation must be based on an analysis of all of the circumstances. Second, "the whole picture must yield a particularized suspicion" that the individual being stopped is engaged in criminal activity.

CASE SIGNIFICANCE: The decision to stop must be made with justification. This means that the police cannot arbitrarily stop anyone for investigative purposes. There must be a particularized and objective basis for suspecting that the person stopped has engaged in or will engage in criminal activity. Such suspicion must be based on "the whole picture," as observed by the police. In deciding to make an investigative stop, the experience and training of the law enforcement officer may be taken into account. What may look like innocent activity to an untrained person may look otherwise to a trained officer. Such observation gives an officer a legitimate basis for suspicion that can then justify an investigative stop.

UNITED STATES V. ROSS
456 U.S. 798 (1982)

CAPSULE: When making a valid search of a car, the police may search the entire car and open the trunk and any packages or luggage found therein that could reasonably contain the items for which they have probable cause to search.

FACTS: Police received a telephone tip from a reliable informant that Ross was selling drugs kept in the trunk of his car. The informant provided a detailed description of Ross, his automobile, and the location of the sale. The police drove to the location, spotted the person and car that matched the description given by the informant, and made a warrantless arrest. One of the officers found a bullet on the front seat of the automobile. Without a warrant, officers conducted a more thorough search of the interior of the automobile and discovered a pistol in the glove compartment. Ross was arrested. Officers then took Ross' keys and opened the trunk of his automobile, where they found a closed brown paper bag containing glassine bags of a substance that was later determined to be heroin. The officers then drove the car to police headquarters where another warrantless search of the trunk revealed a zippered leather pouch containing cash. Ross was convicted of possession of heroin with intent to distribute.

ISSUE: During a valid search of an automobile, may the police open the trunk of a car and containers found therein without a warrant or exigent circumstances when they have probable cause to believe the trunk and containers therein could reasonably contain contraband? YES.

SUPREME COURT DECISION: When the police have probable cause to justify the warrantless search of a car, they may search the entire car, and open the trunk and any packages or luggage found therein that could reasonably contain the items for which they have probable cause to search. **REASON:** "If probable cause justifies the search of a lawfully stopped vehicle, it justifies the search of every part of the vehicle and its contents that may conceal the object of the search. ... The scope of a warrantless search of an automobile thus is not defined by the nature of the container in which the contraband is secreted. Rather, it is defined by the object of the search and the places in which there is probable cause to believe that it may be found."

CASE SIGNIFICANCE: The *Ross* case is important because it further defines the scope of police authority in vehicle searches. *United States v. Belton* specifically refused to address the issue of whether the police could open the trunk of a car in connection with a search incident to a valid arrest. *Ross* addressed that issue and authorized such action. *Ross* further stated that any packages or luggage found in the car that could reasonably contain the items for which they have probable cause to search could also be opened without a warrant. *Ross* has, therefore, greatly expanded the scope of allowable warrantless searches, limited only by what is reasonable. Note, however, that this authorization has limits. The police may not open large items taken from the car (such as a footlocker) without a warrant if there is time to obtain one. This is because those items have identities of their own, separate and apart from the car.

MICHIGAN V. LONG
463 U.S. 1032 (1983)

CAPSULE: A limited search of an automobile, after a valid stop, is permissible if the officer has a reasonable belief that the suspect is dangerous and might gain immediate control of a weapon.

FACTS: Officers observed an automobile traveling erratically and at a high rate of speed. When the automobile swerved into a ditch, the officers stopped to investigate. They were met at the rear of the car by Long, who "appeared to be under the influence of something" and did not respond to a request to produce his license. Upon a second request, Long did produce his license. After a second request to see his registration, Long began walking toward the open door of the vehicle. The officers followed him and noticed a large hunting knife on the floorboard of the vehicle. They then stopped Long and frisked him. No other weapons were found. One of the officers shined his flashlight into the car and discovered marijuana. Long was then arrested. The officers then opened the unlocked trunk and discovered approximately 75 pounds of marijuana. Long was convicted of possession of marijuana.

ISSUE: May officers conduct a protective search (similar to a pat-down search authorized in *Terry v. Ohio*) of the passenger compartment of a lawfully stopped vehicle to look for possible weapons? YES.

SUPREME COURT DECISION: The search of an automobile, after a valid stop and limited to the areas in which a weapon may be placed or hidden, is permissible if the officer has a reasonable belief that the suspect is dangerous and might gain immediate control of a weapon.

REASON: "[A]rticles inside the relatively narrow compass of the passenger compartment of an automobile are in fact generally, even if not inevitably, within the area into which an arrestee might reach in order to grab a weapon." (Footnote and quotes omitted.) "If there is reasonable belief that the suspect is dangerous and might gain control of weapons, the officer is justified by self-protection to make search of the interior of the automobile. ... If, while conducting a legitimate *Terry* search of the interior of the automobile, the officer should, as here, discover contraband other than weapons, he clearly cannot be required to ignore the contraband ..."

CASE SIGNIFICANCE: This case gives the police authority to conduct a limited search (similar to a pat-down search of a person) of the passenger compartment of a car if the officers have reasonable belief that they may be in danger. In this case, the officer saw a hunting knife on the floorboard of the driver's side of the car, hence justifying the search of the passenger compartment. Such a search, however, must be limited to the areas in which a weapon may be placed or hidden. If, while conducting such a search, contraband or other illegal items are discovered, they can be seized and may be admitted as evidence into court. The Court added that the fact that the suspect is under the officers' control during the investigative stop does not render unreasonable their belief that the suspect could injure them. This implies that, as long as the officers have probable cause to believe they are in danger, the search may continue even after the suspect has been placed under control, such as when the suspect has been handcuffed.

CALIFORNIA V. CARNEY
471 U.S. 386 (1985)

CAPSULE: Motor homes used on public highways are automobiles for purposes of the Fourth Amendment and therefore a warrantless search is valid.

FACTS: A police agent had uncorroborated information that Carney's motor home was being used to exchange marijuana for sex. He then set up surveillance on the motor home. The agent observed Carney approach a youth who accompanied him to the motor home parked in a nearby lot. Agents followed the youth after he emerged from the motor home and stopped him. The youth said that Carney was exchanging marijuana for sex. At the request of the agents, the youth returned to the motor home and knocked on the door. When Carney stepped out, the agents identified themselves, entered the motor home, and made a search without consent or a warrant. Agents found a quantity of marijuana on a table in the motor home. Agents then arrested Carney and impounded the motor home. A subsequent search of the motor home at the police station revealed additional marijuana.

ISSUE: May police officers make a warrantless search, based on probable cause, of a motor home located in a public place under the automobile exception? YES.

SUPREME COURT DECISION: If a vehicle is being used on public highways or is capable of such use and it is found in a place not regularly used for residential purposes, it may be considered an automobile under the warrantless search doctrine; thus, a warrantless search based on probable cause is justified.

REASON: "When a vehicle is being used on the highways or is capable of such use and is found stationary in a place not regularly used for residential purposes, the two justifications for the vehicle exception come into play. First, the vehicle is readily mobile, and, second, there is a reduced expectation of privacy stemming from the pervasive regulation of vehicles capable of traveling on highways. Here, while respondent's [Carney's] vehicle possessed some attributes of a home, it clearly falls within the vehicle exception. To distinguish between respondent's motor home and an ordinary sedan for purposes of the vehicle exception would require that the exception be applied depending on the size of the vehicle and the quality of its appointments. Moreover, to fail to apply the exception to a vehicle such as a motor home would ignore the fact that a motor home lends itself easily to use as an instrument of illicit drug traffic or other illegal activity."

CASE SIGNIFICANCE: The Court in this case held that motor homes are automobiles for the purposes of the Fourth Amendment and therefore fall under the automobile exception, meaning they can be searched without a warrant. It is important to note, however, that this decision is limited to a motor home that is capable of being used on the road and is located in a place that is not regularly used for residential purposes. The decision specifically states that this case does not resolve whether the automobile exception would apply to a motor home "situated in a way or place that objectively indicates that it is being used as a residence." The police are advised to treat those places as residences that generally need a search warrant.

COLORADO V. BERTINE
479 U.S. 367 (1987)

CAPSULE: Warrantless inventory searches of the person and possessions of arrested individuals are permissible under the Fourth Amendment.

FACTS: Bertine was arrested for driving under the influence of alcohol. After he was taken into custody, and prior to the arrival of a tow truck to impound the van, another officer inventoried the van in accordance with departmental procedures. During the inventory search, the officer opened a backpack in which he found various containers containing controlled substances, drug paraphernalia, and money.

ISSUE: Is evidence seized by opening a closed container without a warrant during an inventory search incident to a lawful arrest admissible? YES.

SUPREME COURT DECISION: Inventory searches without a warrant of the person and possessions of arrested individuals are permissible under the Fourth Amendment:

1. to protect an owner's property while it is under police control
2. to ensure against claims of lost, stolen, or vandalized property
3. to protect the police from danger.

Evidence found in the course of the inventory search, even if found by opening a closed backpack, is admissible.

REASON: "The policies behind the warrant requirement, and the related concept of probable cause, are not implicated in an inventory search, which serves the strong governmental interests in protecting an owner's property while it is in police custody, insuring against claims of lost, stolen or vandalized property, and guarding the police from danger. There was no showing here that the police, who were following standardized caretaking procedures, acted in bad faith or for the sole purpose of investigation. Police, before inventorying a container, are not required to weigh the strength of the individual's privacy interest in the container against the possibility that the container might serve as a repository for dangerous or valuable items."

CASE SIGNIFICANCE: This case allows inventory searches without a warrant even in situations in which containers must be opened. This is significant because prior to this decision it was not clear whether the police, in the course of an inventory search, could open a closed container. The current rule is to allow this type of inventory, as long as the police follow standardized caretaking procedures and they do not act in bad faith or for the sole purpose of investigation. This case synthesized *South Dakota v. Opperman*, 428 U.S. 364 (1976) (inventory search of an impounded vehicle) and *Illinois v. Lafayette*, 462 U.S. 640 (1983) (inventory search of individual possessions while person is in custody).

FLORIDA V. WELLS
495 U.S. 1 (1989)

CAPSULE: Evidence obtained from closed containers during inventory searches is not admissible in court unless authorized by departmental policy.

FACTS: Wells was stopped by the police for speeding and was subsequently arrested for drunk driving. At the station, Wells gave permission for the police to open the trunk after he was told that his car would be impounded. During an inventory search, the police found two marijuana cigarette butts in an ashtray and a locked suitcase in the trunk. The police forced open the suitcase, whereupon a garbage bag full of marijuana was found.

ISSUE: Was the seizure of the marijuana by the police valid? NO.

SUPREME COURT DECISION: A police department's lack of policy regarding the opening of closed containers found during inventory searches requires the suppression of the marijuana found in a locked suitcase that was removed from the trunk of an impounded vehicle and pried open by the police.

REASON: "The individual police officer must not be allowed so much latitude that inventory searches are turned into 'purposeful and general means of discovering evidence of crime.' ... But in forbidding uncanalized discretion to police officers conducting inventory searches, there is no reason to insist they be conducted in a total ... 'all or nothing' fashion" as ruled in *Colorado v. Bertine* (1987). Policies for "opening all containers or for opening no containers are unquestionably permissible ...." It is, however, "equally permissible ... to allow the opening of closed containers whose contents officers determine they [cannot] ascertain from examining the [exterior of the containers.]" To allow "the exercise of judgment based on concerns related to the purposes of an inventory search does not violate the Fourth Amendment."

CASE SIGNIFICANCE: This case stresses the importance of a carefully crafted departmental policy governing the opening of closed containers after vehicle impoundment. The evidence seized in this case was suppressed because there was no departmental policy authorizing the officer's actions. Had the act been authorized by agency policy, the evidence would have been admissible. The main problem in this case was not the opening of the container itself but the absence of a policy authorizing that opening. Courts have held that the absence of a departmental policy, either authorizing the opening of containers or prohibiting such opening, leaves too much discretion to officers such that it has the potential of turning inventory searches into a "general rummaging in order to discover incriminating evidence." It is therefore important that law enforcement departments have a policy governing impoundment inventories. Note that the Court is not concerned with whether that policy allows the opening of the container or not; what the Court is concerned with instead is that there be a policy so that "fishing expeditions" by the police in the process of impoundment inventory are avoided. The Court also argued: "While an 'all or nothing' policy is permissible, one that allows a police officer sufficient latitude to determine whether a particular container should be opened in light of the nature of the search and characteristics of the container itself does not violate the Fourth Amendment." This implies that some latitude to open or not to open a container may be given to the officer by departmental policy; what the court disapproves of is the absence of a policy.

CALIFORNIA V. ACEVEDO
500 U.S. 565 (1991)

CAPSULE: Probable cause to believe that a container in an automobile holds contraband or seizable evidence justifies a warrantless search of that container even in the absence of probable cause to search the vehicle.

FACTS: A Santa Ana, California, police officer received a telephone call from a federal drug enforcement agent in Hawaii who stated that he had intercepted a package containing marijuana that was to have been delivered to the Federal Express Office in Santa Ana and that was addressed to J.R. Daza. The agent arranged to have the package sent to the police officer, who verified the contents as marijuana and took it to the Federal Express Office for a controlled delivery. A man claiming to be Daza picked up the package and took it to an apartment. A short time later, Daza left the apartment and dropped the Federal Express box into a trash bin. At that point, one police officer left the scene of the apartment to obtain a search warrant. A short time later, other officers observed another man leave the apartment carrying a knapsack, which appeared to be half full. The officers stopped the man as he was driving off, searched the knapsack, and found one and one-half pounds of marijuana. Later, Acevedo arrived at the apartment, stayed about 10 minutes, and left carrying a brown paper bag that appeared to be the size of the one that contained the marijuana packages sent from Hawaii. Acevedo placed the bag in the trunk of his car and started to drive away. At that time, the police stopped him, opened the trunk and the bag, and found marijuana.

ISSUE: Does the Fourth Amendment require the police to obtain a warrant to open a closed container in a vehicle if they lack probable cause to search the car but have probable cause to believe that the container itself holds contraband? NO.

SUPREME COURT DECISION: Probable cause to believe that a container in a car holds contraband or seizable evidence justifies a warrantless search of that container even in the absence of probable cause to search the vehicle.

REASON: "Until today, this Court has drawn a curious line between the search of an automobile that coincidentally turns up a container and the search of a container that coincidentally turns up in an automobile. The protections of the Fourth Amendment must not turn on such coincidences. We therefore interpret *Carroll* [*v. United States*] as providing one rule to govern all automobile searches. The police may search an automobile and the containers within it where they have probable cause to believe contraband or evidence is contained."

CASE SIGNIFICANCE: This case, in effect, reverses two earlier Supreme Court rulings. In *United States v. Chadwick*, 433 U.S. 1 (1977) the Court held that the police could seize movable luggage or other closed containers but could not open them without a warrant because a person has a heightened privacy expectation in such containers. In *Arkansas v. Sanders*, 442 U.S. 753 (1979), the Court prohibited the warrantless search of a closed container located in a vehicle when there was probable cause to search only the container but not the vehicle. The Court clarifies the confusion by rejecting these two cases and reiterating instead the Court's ruling in two other cases. The first is *Carroll v. United States*, 267 U.S. 132 (1925), in which the Court held that a warrantless search of an automobile based on probable cause to believe that the vehicle contained evidence of crime, and in the light of the vehicle's likely disappearance, did not contravene the Fourth Amendment's Warrant Clause. The second is *United States v. Ross*, 456 U.S. 798 (1982), in which the Court held that the warrantless search of an automobile includes a search of closed containers found inside the car when there is probable cause to search the vehicle. *Acevedo* goes one step further than *Ross* in that, while *Ross* allows the warrantless search of a container found in a car if there is probable cause to search the car (as long as the opening of the container is reasonable, given the object of the search), *Acevedo* allows the warrantless search of a container as long as there is probable cause to do so—even if there is no probable cause to search the car.

PENNSYLVANIA V. LABRON
518 U.S. 938 (1996)

CAPSULE: There is no need for a warrant in vehicle searches if the vehicle is readily mobile, even if there is time to obtain a warrant.

FACTS: Police observed Labron and others engaging in a series of drug transactions on the street. After arresting the suspects, the police searched the trunk of the car where they had observed the suspects retrieving the drugs. The search revealed bags of cocaine. The search was made without a warrant, although the police had time to obtain one.

ISSUE: Are warrantless searches of vehicles valid even if there is time for the police to obtain a warrant? YES.

SUPREME COURT DECISION: "If a car is readily mobile and probable cause exists to believe it contains contraband, the Fourth Amendment thus permits police to search the vehicle without more." Thus, warrantless searches of vehicles are valid even if there is time to obtain a warrant as long as probable cause is present.

REASON: "Our first cases establishing the automobile exception to the Fourth Amendment's warrant requirement were based on the automobile's 'ready mobility,' an exigency sufficient to excuse failure to obtain a search warrant once probable cause to conduct the search is clear. More recent cases provide a further justification: the individual's reduced expectation of privacy in an automobile, owing to its pervasive regulation ...." (Citations omitted.)

CASE SIGNIFICANCE: This case again extends the authority of the police to make warrantless searches of automobiles. Beginning with *Carroll v. United States*, 267 U.S. 132 (1925), the Court has continually allowed greater freedom to search automobiles without a warrant. This case removed another roadblock to automobile searches: that of the requirement to obtain a warrant to search if there is time to do so. In this holding, the Court seems to have overturned the language in *Coolidge v. New Hampshire*, 403 U.S. 443 (1971), which stated: "Since the police knew of the presence of the automobile and planned all along to seize it, there was no 'exigent circumstance' to justify their failure to obtain a warrant." The difference between this case and *Coolidge* is that, in this case, the car was on the street rather than at the suspect's house. This case makes clear that law enforcement officers may conduct a warrantless search if there is probable cause, even if there is time to obtain a warrant.

KNOWLES V. IOWA
525 U.S. 113 (1998)

CAPSULE: Officers may search a vehicle incident to an arrest, but a search incident to the issuance of a traffic citation, absent consent or probable cause, violates the Fourth Amendment.

FACTS: Knowles was stopped for speeding and issued a citation (although the officer had the authority to arrest him). The officer then conducted a full search of Knowles' car, where he found marijuana and drug paraphernalia. At trial, the officer conceded that he had neither consent nor probable cause for the search and that he relied on state law that permitted "searches incident to citation." The evidence was admitted over Knowles' objection and he was convicted of possession of drug paraphernalia.

ISSUE: May an officer search a vehicle incident to a traffic stop without consent or probable cause? NO.

SUPREME COURT DECISION: While officers may search a vehicle incident to an arrest, a search incident to the issuance of a traffic citation, absent consent or probable cause, violates the Fourth Amendment, even if authorized by state law.

REASON: "We have recognized that the first rationale—officer safety—is "'both legitimate and weighty,'" *Maryland v. Wilson*, 519 U.S. 408, 412 (1997) (quoting *Pennsylvania v. Mimms*, 434 U.S. 106, 110 [1977] [*per curiam*]). The threat to officer safety from issuing a traffic citation, however, is a good deal less than in the case of a custodial arrest. In [*United States v.*] *Robinson*, we stated that a custodial arrest involves 'danger to an officer' because of 'the extended exposure which follows the taking of a suspect into custody and transporting him to the police station.' 414 U.S., at 234–235 .... A routine traffic stop, on the other hand, is a relatively brief encounter and 'is more analogous to a so-called "*Terry* stop" ... than to a formal arrest.' *Berkemer v. McCarty*, 468 U.S. 420, 437 (1984)." "[W]hile the concern for officer safety in this context may justify the 'minimal' additional intrusion of ordering a driver and occupants out of the car, it does not by itself justify the often considerably greater intrusion attending a full field-type search."

CASE SIGNIFICANCE: This case reaffirms the rule that, to be valid, vehicle searches must have either probable cause or consent. There was none in this case, but the officer justified the search because of an Iowa law stating that a search incident to citation "is justified because a suspect may try to hide evidence of his identity or of other crimes." The Court found this unpersuasive and reaffirmed the ruling that, to conduct a search during a traffic stop, officers must have demonstrable probable cause or the consent of the driver.

WYOMING V. HOUGHTON
526 U.S. 295 (1999)

CAPSULE: Police officers with probable cause to search a car may inspect occupants' belongings found in the car that are capable of concealing the object of the search.

FACTS: During a routine traffic stop, an officer stopped an automobile in which Houghton was riding. While questioning the driver, the officer noticed a hypodermic needle in his shirt pocket. When the driver admitted using the needle to use drugs, the occupants in the vehicle were ordered out of the car.

Pursuant to the driver's admission, officers searched the passenger compartment of the vehicle. On the backseat, officers found a purse that Houghton claimed as hers. Methamphetamine and drug paraphernalia were found in the purse and Houghton was arrested for felony possession of drugs.

ISSUE: Do law enforcement officers "violate the Fourth Amendment when they search a passenger's personal belongings inside an automobile that they have probable cause to believe contains contraband?" NO.

SUPREME COURT DECISION: Police officers with probable cause to search a car may inspect passengers' belongings found in the car that are capable of concealing the object of the search.

REASON: "The critical element in a reasonable search is not that the owner of the property is suspected of crime but that there is reasonable cause to believe that the specific 'things' to be searched for and seized are located on the property to which entry is sought" (citing *Zurcher v. Stanford Daily*, 436 U.S. 547 [1978]). "[N]either [*United States v.*] *Ross* itself nor the historical evidence it relied upon admits of a distinction among packages or containers based on ownership." "Passengers, no less than drivers, possess a reduced expectation of privacy with regard to the property that they transport in cars, which 'travel public thoroughfares.'"

CASE SIGNIFICANCE: This is an important decision because it settles an issue that is often raised in vehicle searches, but which the Court had not addressed previously: whether the police may inspect the belongings of passengers in a car. In this case, the arrest of the driver and the search of the driver's property was valid because probable cause was present after the driver admitted that a hypodermic needle in his shirt pocket was used in taking drugs. The officer, however, went beyond that and also searched a purse that the officer knew belonged to a passenger. The passenger was not suspected of any criminal activity, although contraband was later found during the search. The Court held that the search of the passenger's purse was valid under these circumstances based on two reasons: (1) the passenger's reduced expectation of privacy and (2) "the governmental interest in effective law enforcement would be appreciably impaired without the ability to search the passenger's belongings, since an automobile's ready mobility creates the risk that evidence or contraband will be permanently lost while a warrant is obtained."

BOND V. UNITED STATES
529 U.S. 334 (2000)

CAPSULE: A traveler's luggage is an "effect" and is under the protection of the Fourth Amendment. Officers may not physically manipulate (squeeze) the luggage to inspect it without a warrant or probable cause.

FACTS: Bond was riding on a Greyhound bus when an agent boarded the bus to check the immigration status of passengers. After satisfying himself that the passengers were lawfully in the United States, the agent began to walk to the front of the bus. Along the way, he squeezed the soft luggage passengers had placed in overhead storage space. The agent squeezed a canvas bag above Bond's seat and felt that it contained "a brick-like object." Bond admitted owning the bag and agreed to allow the agent to open it, whereupon the agent found a brick of methamphetamine.

ISSUE: Does the physical manipulation of a bus passenger's carry-on luggage by a law enforcement officer violate the Fourth Amendment prohibition against unreasonable searches? YES.

SUPREME COURT DECISION: A traveler's luggage is an "effect" and is under the protection of the Fourth Amendment. Officers may not physically manipulate (squeeze) the luggage to inspect it without a warrant or probable cause.

REASON: A Fourth Amendment analysis involves two issues. The first issue concerns whether an individual has exhibited an expectation of privacy for an effect protected by the Fourth Amendment. A traveler's luggage is clearly an effect within the Fourth Amendment. Here, Bond sought to preserve privacy by using an opaque bag and placing it directly above his seat. The second issue is whether the individual's expectation of privacy is "one that society is prepared to recognize as reasonable." Although there is an expectation that the luggage will be handled by other passengers or bus employees, there is no expectation that the luggage will be physically manipulated in an exploratory manner. Visual inspection of items in public view has been ruled not to be protected by the Fourth Amendment, but a physically invasive inspection is more intrusive than a visual inspection; therefore, the law enforcement officer's physical manipulation of the luggage violated the Fourth Amendment.

CASE SIGNIFICANCE: The government argued that by "exposing the bag to the public, Bond lost a reasonable expectation of privacy that his bag would not be physically manipulated." Bond admitted that "by placing his bag in the overhead compartment, he could expect that it would be exposed to certain kinds of touching and handling." He maintained, however, that the officer's physical manipulation of the luggage "far exceeded the casual contact" that Bond could have expected from other passengers. The Court agreed with Bond, holding: "When a bus passenger places a bag in an overhead bin, he expects that other passengers or bus employees may move it for one reason or another. Thus, a bus passenger clearly expects that his bag may be handled. He does not expect that other passengers or bus employees will, as a matter of course, feel the bag in an exploratory manner. But this is exactly what the agent did here.

We therefore hold that the agent's physical manipulation of petitioner's bag violated the Fourth Amendment."

The Court in this case reiterated two questions that must be asked when analyzing Fourth Amendment cases: (1) whether the individual, by his or her conduct, exhibited an expectation of privacy and (2) whether the individual's expectation of privacy is "one that society is prepared to recognize as reasonable." The Court concluded that the answer to both questions in this case was yes; therefore the conduct of the agent was unconstitutional. This case defines the limit of what police officers can do to pieces of luggage and belongings of passengers. It holds that passengers have a reasonable expectation of privacy as to their belongings while traveling in public transportation and in public places. Officers, therefore, need probable cause to search.

MARYLAND V. PRINGLE
540 U.S. 366 (2003)

CAPSULE: An officer may arrest an occupant of a vehicle based on probable cause that a crime has been committed (or is being committed) in the vehicle and it is not clear who committed it, as long as there is a reasonable inference from the circumstances that the person arrested could have committed the crime.

FACTS: A police officer stopped a car for speeding in which Pringle was an occupant. When the driver of the vehicle opened the glove compartment to retrieve the registration, the officer observed a large amount of rolled up money. After issuing a warning to the driver, the officer sought and received consent to search the vehicle. The search yielded $763 and five plastic bags of cocaine. When none of the occupants of the vehicle admitted to ownership of the drugs and money, the officer arrested all of them and transported them to the police station. Later that morning, Pringle waived his *Miranda* rights and gave an oral and written confession in which he acknowledged that the cocaine belonged to him, that he intended to sell it, and that the other occupants did not know about the drugs. The trial court denied Pringle's motion to suppress his confession as the fruit of an illegal arrest, and he was convicted of possession with the intent to deliver.

ISSUE: Is the arrest of an occupant of a vehicle valid if there is probable cause to believe, from the standpoint of an objectively reasonable police officer, that the occupant was involved in the crime? YES.

SUPREME COURT DECISION: The arrest of an occupant of a vehicle is valid if the officer had probable cause to believe, based on the circumstances of the case, that the occupant could have committed the crime, even if it was not immediately clear who committed the crime.

REASON: "Maryland law authorizes police officers to execute warrantless arrests, *inter alia*, for felonies committed in an officer's presence or where an officer has probable cause to believe that a felony has been committed or is being committed in the officer's presence. ... It is uncontested in the present case that the officer, upon recovering five glassine baggies containing the suspected cocaine, had probable cause to believe a felony had been committed. The sole question is whether the officer had probable cause to believe that Pringle committed the crime. ... [W]e think it an entirely reasonable inference from these facts that any or all three of the occupants had knowledge of, and exercised dominion and control over, the cocaine. Thus a reasonable officer could conclude that there was probable cause to believe Pringle committed the crime of possession of cocaine, either solely or jointly."

CASE SIGNIFICANCE: This case addresses an issue police officers face when making vehicle arrests: whether the officer may arrest all the occupants of a vehicle if there is probable cause to believe one or more of them are involved in the crime. The Court held yes, but based on the specific circumstances of the case. Here, the officer validly searched and seized money and drugs from the vehicle. The three occupants denied ownership of the cocaine and money; so all three were arrested. Pringle was an occupant in the front seat at the time the money and cocaine were discovered. When prosecuted for and convicted of possession with intent to distribute cocaine and possession of cocaine, he appealed, saying his arrest was illegal because there was no probable cause to arrest him (Pringle's later confession, he argued, was the fruit of an illegal arrest). The Court concluded that Pringle's arrest was valid because probable cause was present at the time of arrest. The standard the Court used was: "To determine whether an officer had probable cause to make an arrest, a court must examine the events leading up to the arrest," and then make a decision. The presence of probable cause is determined by asking whether, viewed from the standpoint of an objectively reasonable police officer, the facts amounted to probable cause. Given the circumstances of this case, the Court held, "it is an entirely reasonable inference from the facts here that any or all of the car occupants had knowledge of, and exercised dominion and control over, the cocaine ... either solely or jointly." This case does not give police officers blanket authority to arrest occupants in a car. Instead, each case is different and must be judged based on whether "viewed from the standpoint of an objectively reasonable police officer," the circumstances amounted to probable cause. Given the facts of this case, the Court concluded that probable cause was a reasonable inference. What constitutes a "reasonable inference" that could establish probable cause is ultimately for the courts to decide on a case-by-case basis.

THORNTON V. UNITED STATES
541 U.S. 615 (2004)

CAPSULE: Officers may search the passenger compartment of a vehicle after a lawful arrest even if the suspect was not in the vehicle when arrested.

FACTS: An officer became suspicious of Thornton when he slowed down to avoid driving next to the officer (who was in uniform but in an unmarked car). The officer pulled over so he could get behind Thornton and check his license plate. The check revealed that the tags were not registered to the car Thornton was driving. Before the officer could pull him over, Thornton pulled into a parking lot, parked, and got out of his vehicle. The officer saw Thornton leave the vehicle. The officer then stopped Thornton and asked about the tags on his vehicle. When Thornton began to act nervous and suspicious, the officer, concerned for his safety, asked Thornton if he had any illegal narcotics or weapons on him or in his vehicle. Thornton replied no and consented to a pat-down search. The officer felt a bulge in Thornton's left front pocket and again asked about illegal narcotics. This time, Thornton stated he had drugs, and reached into his pocket and retrieved two bags, one containing marijuana and one containing crack cocaine. The officer handcuffed Thornton, told him he was under arrest, and placed him in the backseat of the patrol car. The officer then searched Thornton's vehicle and discovered a handgun under the driver's seat.

ISSUE: Does a search of the passenger compartment of a vehicle incident to an arrest violate the Fourth Amendment if the suspect was not in the vehicle when arrested? NO.

SUPREME COURT DECISION: Officers may search the passenger compartment of a motor vehicle after a lawful arrest even if the suspect was not in the vehicle when arrested.

REASON: Thornton sought to differentiate the circumstances of this case from *New York v. Belton* based on Belton being inside the vehicle when first encountered by police and Thornton having exited his vehicle. The Court, however, found congruence between the two cases. The Court restated their holding in *Belton* that "when a policeman has made a lawful custodial arrest of the occupant of an automobile, he may, as a contemporaneous incident of that arrest, search the passenger compartment of that automobile." The Court reasoned that "in all relevant aspects, the arrest of a suspect who is next to a vehicle presents identical concerns regarding officer safety and the destruction of evidence as the arrest of one who is inside the vehicle." In fact, the Court noted, "in some circumstances, it may be safer and more effective for the officers to conceal their presence from a suspect until he has left his vehicle." The Court concluded with the statement that: "So long as an arrestee is the sort of 'recent occupant' of a vehicle such as petitioner was here, officers may search that vehicle incident to the arrest."

CASE SIGNIFICANCE: The Court in *Chimel v. California* held that an officer could search the "area of immediate control" of an arrested person for weapons or evidence. This extent of the term "area of immediate control" has been debated in many cases for years. In *New York v. Belton*, the Court held that the area of immediate control included the passenger compartment of a vehicle when officers encountered the suspect in the vehicle. In *Thornton*, the Court extended that ruling to those who are connected with the vehicle (here the officer observed Thornton leaving the vehicle) but who were not in the vehicle when first approached by the officer. The Court in this case did not really set specific boundaries for the "area of immediate control" from the vehicle, stating instead that "while an arrestee's status as a 'recent occupant' may turn on his temporal or spatial relationship to the car at the time of the arrest and search, it certainly does not turn on whether he was inside or outside the car at the moment that the officer first initiated contact with him." Similarly, the Court conceded that "To be sure, not all contraband in the passenger compartment is likely to be readily accessible to a 'recent occupant.'" These statements left unresolved the issue of whether a situation could arise where the occupant of a vehicle could be far enough removed from the vehicle, either temporally or spatially, such that the police can no longer search the car compartment incident to a lawful arrest. This question was addressed by the Court in *Arizona v. Gant* below.

ARIZONA V. GANT
556 U.S. 332 (2009)

CAPSULE: "Police may search a vehicle incident to a recent occupant's arrest only if the arrestee is within reaching distance of the passenger compartment at the time of the search or it is reasonable to believe the vehicle contains evidence of the offense of arrest."

FACTS: Acting on a tip that a residence was being used to sell drugs, officers knocked on the door of the residence and asked to speak to the owner. Gant answered the door and, after identifying himself, stated that the owner was not there but would return later. The officer then left but returned to the house later that evening. In the interim, officers conducted a records check, which revealed there was an outstanding warrant for Gant for driving on a suspended license. When officers returned to the house, they arrested two people outside the house and placed them in police vehicles. One officer recognized Gant as he drove into the driveway. Gant exited the vehicle, closed the door, and approached the officer. They met about 10 feet from Gant's automobile, where the officer immediately arrested him, placed him in handcuffs, and placed him in the backseat of a police vehicle. Two officers then searched Gant's vehicle, finding a gun and also a bag of cocaine in the pocket of a jacket on the backseat. Gant was convicted of possession of drugs for sale and possession of drug paraphernalia.

ISSUE: May officers search a vehicle incident to an arrest if there is no possibility the arrestee can gain access to the passenger compartment and the search is not related to the arrest? NO.

SUPREME COURT DECISION: "We hold that *Belton* does not authorize a vehicle search incident to a recent occupant's arrest after the arrestee has been secured and cannot access the interior of the vehicle. Consistent with the holding in *Thornton v. United States*, 541 U.S. 615 (2004), and following the suggestion in Justice Scalia's opinion concurring in the judgment in that case, *id.*, at 632, we also conclude that circumstances unique to the automobile context justify a search incident to arrest when it is reasonable to believe that evidence of the offense of arrest might be found in the vehicle."

REASON: The rationale for this case is drawn from a varying line of cases. The Court began its reasoning with a quote from *Katz v. United States*, 389 U.S. 347, 357 (1967) that "Warrantless searches 'are *per se* unreasonable,'" and "subject only to a few specifically established and well-delineated exceptions." The Court reasoned that one exception to this rule was stated in *Chimel v. California*, 395 U.S. 752, 763 (1969) where police could search incident to a lawful arrest "the area from within which [an arrestee] might gain possession of a weapon or destructible evidence." This exemption was extended to automobiles in *New York v. Belton*, 453 U.S. 454 (1981) in terms of searches of the passenger compartment of the vehicle, arguing this is an area into which an arrestee might reach. The exemption was further extended in *Thornton v. United States*, 541 U.S. 615 (2004) to recent occupants of a vehicle. The Court in this case refused to extend that ruling to recent occupants of a vehicle if there was no possibility of gaining access to the passenger compartment at the time of the search. The Court also ruled that any search would need to be relevant to the crime of the arrest.

CASE SIGNIFICANCE: This case clarified what the Court meant in previous cases concerning the search of a vehicle following an arrest. Based on *Chimel*, the Court ruled in *Belton* that officers could search the passenger compartment of a vehicle, primarily for weapons, incident to an arrest. The Court extended this logic in *Thornton* to include a person who had recently exited the vehicle. In *Gant*, the Court distinguished *Thornton*.

Here, they argued Gant was far enough away from his vehicle when he made contact with the officer that it was unlikely he could have reached the passenger compartment of his automobile. Even though in both cases the arrestee was handcuffed in the back of a patrol car when the officer conducted the search, in *Thornton*, the search was directly related to the arrest while, in *Gant*, it was not. After this decision, it is still constitutional for officers to search a vehicle incident to an arrest when the arrestee was in the vehicle at the time of arrest. It is probably also constitutional to conduct such a search if the arrestee is in very close proximity to the vehicle, especially if the search is related to the arrest. If the arrestee is physically removed from the vehicle, the only way to conduct the search seems to be if it is directly related to the arrest.

NAVARETTE V. CALIFORNIA
572 U.S. 393 (2014)

CAPSULE: An anonymous 911 call is sufficient to establish reasonable suspicion for an investigative stop if it contains enough information to enable officers to corroborate its veracity and reliability.

FACTS: Officers stopped the pickup truck occupied by Navarette and another man because it matched the description of a vehicle that a 911 caller had recently reported as having run her off the road. As the officers approached the truck, they smelled marijuana. They searched the truck's bed and found 30 pounds of marijuana. They then arrested Navarette. Navarette moved to suppress the evidence, arguing that the officers did not have reasonable suspicion of criminal activity. The court denied the motion, arguing that the officers corroborated the tip with their own observation and the tip indicated sufficiently dangerous conduct to merit an investigative stop without waiting for additional reckless activities.

ISSUE: May officers rely on an anonymous 911 call to establish reasonable suspicion for an investigative stop if there is sufficient information about the activities for officers to corroborate the information? YES.

SUPREME COURT DECISION: "Under the totality of the circumstances, we find the indicia of reliability in this case sufficient to provide the officer with reasonable suspicion that the driver of the reported vehicle had run another vehicle off the road. That made it reasonable under the circumstances for the officer to execute a traffic stop."

REASON: "The Fourth Amendment permits brief investigative stops—such as the traffic stop in this case—when a law enforcement officer has 'a particularized and objective basis for suspecting the particular person stopped of criminal activity.' The 'reasonable suspicion' necessary to justify such a stop 'is dependent upon both the content of information possessed by police and its degree of reliability.' The standard takes into account 'the totality of the circumstances—the whole picture.'" (Citations omitted.) "By reporting that she had been run off the road by a specific vehicle—a silver Ford F-150 pickup, license plate 8D94925—the caller necessarily claimed eyewitness knowledge of the alleged dangerous driving. That basis of knowledge lends significant support to the tip's reliability"; providing officers with the information they needed to corroborate the information and make the stop.

CASE SIGNIFICANCE: This case added some additional clarity to the line of police investigative stops based on anonymous tips. In *Alabama v. White* (see Chapter 3), the Court ruled that a stop can be based on an anonymous tip corroborated by police. The Court cautioned, however, that "an anonymous tip alone seldom demonstrates the informant's basis of knowledge or veracity." In *Florida v. J.L.* (see Chapter 3), the Court determined that no reasonable suspicion arose from a "bare-bones tip" that a young black male in a plaid shirt standing at a bus stop was carrying a gun. However, in this case, the caller gave enough information about the incident and the vehicle (including a license place number) to establish "eyewitness knowledge of the alleged dangerous driving." That basis of knowledge (corroborated by the officers' observation of a truck matching the description in the same general area), supported the officers' reliance on the tip's reliability to establish reasonable suspicion.

BYRD V. UNITED STATES
584 U.S. ___ (2018)

CAPSULE: The fact that a driver in lawful possession or control of a rental car is not listed on the rental agreement does not defeat his otherwise reasonable expectation of privacy.

FACTS: Reed rented a car while Byrd waited outside the rental facility. Reed listed no additional drivers on the rental agreement, but gave the keys to Byrd after leaving the facility. He stored his personal belongings in the trunk of the car. After stopping Byrd for a traffic violation, officers learned the car was rented, that Byrd was not listed as an authorized driver, and that Byrd had prior drug and weapons convictions. Byrd also stated he had a marijuana cigarette in the car. The troopers proceeded to search the car, discovering body armor and 49 bricks of heroin in the trunk. Byrd's objection of an unreasonable search and seizure was overturned at trial based on the rationale that he lacked a reasonable expectation of privacy in a rented car for which he was not an authorized driver.

ISSUE: Does a driver have a reasonable expectation of privacy in a rental car when he or she is not listed as an authorized driver on the rental agreement? YES.

SUPREME COURT DECISION: "As a general rule, someone in otherwise lawful possession and control of a rental car has a reasonable expectation of privacy in it even if the rental agreement does not list him or her as an authorized driver."

REASON: "One of the main rights attaching to property is the right to exclude others," and "one who owns or lawfully possesses or controls property will in all likelihood have a legitimate expectation of privacy by virtue of the right to exclude." *Rakas v. Illinois*, 439 U.S. 128. "The Government's contention that drivers who are not listed on rental agreements always lack an expectation of privacy in the car rests on too restrictive a view of the Fourth Amendment's protections. But Byrd's proposal that a rental car's sole occupant always has an expectation of privacy based on mere possession and control would, without qualification, include thieves or others who have no reasonable expectation of privacy." The Court in this case also relied on *Jones v. United States*, 362 U.S. 257, 259 (1960). In this case, Jones was declared to have a reasonable expectation of privacy in a friend's apartment because he "had complete dominion and control over the apartment and could exclude others from it." The Court concluded that the expectation of privacy comes from a right to exclude others, and would apply to a house or an automobile.

CASE SIGNIFICANCE: While this case is limited in scope, it has an important consequence for officers. The rental agreement has little to do with a person's expectation of privacy for the rented automobile. Sole possessors of the vehicle generally have an expectation of privacy. However, as the Court noted, probable cause or consent to search would overcome the expectation of privacy. As long as officers treat rented automobiles as owned and follow any normal search requirements, they should be able to make a search.

Searches of People in Vehicles

INTRODUCTION

Also falling under the automobile exception are the searches of people who are stopped in an automobile. As with vehicle searches, searches of occupants in vehicles are excluded from the warrant requirement because motor vehicles are mobile and can be driven away at any time, making obtaining a warrant impractical. Such searches do not need a warrant, but probable cause must be present or the search is invalid.

Court decisions have established that, after a vehicle is stopped, the officer may legally do the following:

1. order the driver to exit the vehicle
2. order the occupants to exit the vehicle
3. ask the driver to produce a driver's license and other documents required by state law
4. ask questions of the driver and occupants.

The Court has also held that the reasonableness of a traffic stop does not depend on the initial motives of the police officer.

It is important to note that vehicle stops and searches also include passengers traveling on public transportation. The foundation of this, and other searches of persons in vehicles, is found in *Florida v. Bostick*. This case held that, like the driver of a vehicle, the passenger is seized within the meaning of the Fourth Amendment during a traffic stop. This is applied in public transportation issues where the Court also held that the Fourth Amendment permits police officers to approach bus passengers, ask questions, and request their consent to search, provided that a reasonable person would understand that he or she is free to refuse.

The leading cases briefed in this chapter on searches of people in vehicles are *Florida v. Bostick*, *Whren v. United States*, *Ohio v. Robinette*, and *Brendlin v. California*.

FLORIDA V. BOSTICK
501 U.S. 429 (1991)

CAPSULE: The test to determine whether a police–citizen encounter on a bus is a seizure is whether, taking into account all the circumstances, a reasonable passenger would feel free to decline the officers' requests or otherwise terminate the encounter.

FACTS: Without any suspicion and with the intention of catching drug smugglers, two uniformed law enforcement officers boarded a bus in Fort Lauderdale, Florida, that was en route from Miami to Atlanta. The officers approached Bostick and asked for identification and his bus ticket. The officers then asked Bostick for consent to search his bag and told Bostick he could refuse consent. Bostick consented to the search of his luggage and cocaine was found. He later sought to suppress the evidence in court, alleging that it was improperly seized.

ISSUE: Did the police conduct in this case constitute a seizure of Bostick under the Fourth Amendment, such that he felt compelled to consent to the officers' request? NO.

SUPREME COURT DECISION: "The Florida Supreme Court erred in adopting a per se rule that every encounter on a bus is a seizure. The appropriate test is whether, taking into account all of the circumstances surrounding the encounter, a reasonable passenger would feel free to decline the officers' requests or otherwise terminate the encounter."

REASON: "Our cases make it clear that a seizure does not occur simply because a police officer approaches an individual and asks a few questions. So long as a reasonable person would feel free 'to disregard the police and go about his business,' the encounter is consensual and no reasonable suspicion is required. The encounter will not trigger Fourth Amendment scrutiny unless it loses its consensual nature."

"Since *Terry* [*v. Ohio*, 392 U.S. 1 (1968)], we have held repeatedly that mere police questioning does not constitute a seizure. In *Florida v. Royer*, 460 U.S. 491 (1983) (plurality opinion), for example, we explained that 'law enforcement officers do not violate the Fourth Amendment by merely approaching an individual on the street or in another public place, by asking him if he is willing to answer some questions, by putting questions to him if the person is willing to listen, or by offering in evidence in a criminal prosecution his voluntary answers to such questions.'"

"There is no doubt that if this same encounter had taken place before Bostick boarded the bus or in the lobby of the bus terminal, it would not rise to the level of a seizure. The Court has dealt with similar encounters in airports and has found them to be 'the sort of consensual encounters that implicate no Fourth Amendment interests.' We have stated that even when officers have no basis for suspecting a particular individual, they may generally ask questions of that individual and request consent to search his or her luggage—as long as the police do not convey a message that compliance with their requests is required."

CASE SIGNIFICANCE: This case is significant because it clarifies what test is to be used when determining whether an encounter on public transportation constitutes a seizure. The Florida Supreme Court had adopted an inflexible rule stating that the Broward County Sheriff's practice of "working the buses" was per se unconstitutional. The U.S. Supreme Court ruled that the "result of this decision is that police in Florida, as elsewhere, may approach persons at random in most public places, ask them questions and seek consent to a search, but they may not engage in the same behavior on a bus."

The Court rejected this rule, arguing that "the appropriate test is whether, taking into account all of the circumstances surrounding the encounter, a reasonable passenger would feel free to decline the officers' requests or otherwise terminate the encounter." This ruling replaces the Florida Supreme Court's single fact basis with a totality of circumstances standard.

WHREN V. UNITED STATES
517 U.S. 806 (1996)

CAPSULE: The temporary detention of a motorist upon probable cause to believe that he has violated the traffic laws does not violate the Fourth Amendment's prohibition against unreasonable seizures, even if a reasonable officer would not have stopped the motorist absent some additional law enforcement objective.

FACTS: Plainclothes vice officers were patrolling a high drug activity area in an unmarked car when they noticed a vehicle with temporary license plates and youthful occupants waiting at a stop sign. The truck remained stopped at the intersection for what appeared to be an unusually long time while the driver stared into the lap of the passenger. When the officers made a U-turn and headed toward the vehicle, it made a sudden right turn without signaling and sped off at an "unreasonable" speed. The officers overtook the vehicle when it stopped at a red light. When one of the officers approached the vehicle, he observed two large plastic bags of what appeared to be crack cocaine in Whren's hands. At trial, Whren sought to suppress the evidence, arguing that plainclothes officers would not normally stop traffic violators and that there was no probable cause to make a stop on drug charges; therefore, the stop on the traffic violation was merely a pretext to determine whether Whren had drugs. This motion to suppress was denied and Whren and his accomplice were convicted of drug charges.

ISSUE: Is the temporary detention of a motorist who the police have probable cause to believe has committed a civil traffic violation constitutional under the Fourth Amendment if the officer in fact had some other law enforcement objective? YES.

SUPREME COURT DECISION: "The temporary detention of a motorist upon probable cause to believe that he has violated the traffic laws does not violate the Fourth Amendment's prohibition against unreasonable seizures, even if a reasonable officer would not have stopped the motorist absent some additional law enforcement objective."

REASON: "We think these cases [discussed in the preceding paragraphs] fore-close any argument that the constitutional reasonableness of traffic stops depends on the actual motivations of the individual officers involved. We of course agree with petitioners that the Constitution prohibits selective enforcement of the law based on considerations such as race. But the constitutional basis for objecting to intentionally discriminatory application of laws is the equal protection clause, not the Fourth Amendment. Subjective intentions play no role in ordinary, probable-cause Fourth Amendment analysis."

CASE SIGNIFICANCE: This case is important because it gives law enforcement officers an additional tool to make valid searches and seizures. In this case, the defendant alleged that what the police did was illegal because they did not have probable cause to search him for drugs. Although it was true that they had probable cause to believe that he committed a civil traffic violation (turning suddenly without signaling, and speeding off at an unreasonable speed), that alone would not ordinarily have caused the police to make a stop. He claimed that the stop was merely a pretext to enable the officers to search for drugs, which they in fact found. The Court disagreed, holding that the officers' probable cause to believe the motorist had committed a traffic violation made the stop valid even if the actual purpose was to look for drugs. The Court in effect argued that whether ordinarily the police officers "would have" made the stop is not the test for validity; instead, the test is whether the officers "could have" made the stop. The message for the police from this case is this: the real purpose of the stop does not render the stop and subsequent search invalid if there was in fact a valid reason for the stop.

OHIO V. ROBINETTE
519 U.S. 33 (1996)

CAPSULE: The Fourth Amendment does not require police officers to inform motorists who are lawfully stopped for traffic violations that the legal detention has concluded before any subsequent interrogation or search will be found to be consensual.

FACTS: After a deputy stopped Robinette for speeding, he asked Robinette to step out of the car, where he was issued a verbal warning. After the deputy returned Robinette's license, he asked "One question before you get gone: are you carrying any illegal contraband in your car?" When Robinette replied "no," the deputy asked if he could search the car. Robinette consented and the deputy searched the car, where he found a small amount of marijuana and a pill that turned out to be methylenedioxy-methamphetamine. The evidence was admitted over Robinette's objection and he was convicted of possession of a controlled substance. Robinette later claimed that he should have been informed that he was "free to go" for the consent to search the car to be valid.

ISSUE: Does the Fourth Amendment require "that a lawfully seized defendant must be advised that he is 'free to go' before his consent to search will be recognized as voluntary?" NO.

SUPREME COURT DECISION: The Fourth Amendment does not require "police officers to inform motorists lawfully stopped for traffic violations that the legal detention has concluded before any subsequent interrogation or search will be found to be consensual."

REASON: The Court ruled in *Pennsylvania v. Mimms*, 434 U.S. 106 (1977) "that once a motor vehicle has been lawfully detained for a traffic violation, the police officers may order the driver to get out of the vehicle without violating the Fourth Amendment's proscription of unreasonable searches and seizures." The Court then found that "there is no question that, in light of the admitted probable cause to stop Robinette for speeding, [the deputy] was objectively justified in asking Robinette to get out of the car ...." Using the standard of the totality of the circumstances, the Court ruled that: (1) "voluntariness is a question of fact to be determined from all the circumstances"; (2) while "knowledge of the right to refuse consent is one factor to be taken into account, the government need not establish such knowledge as the *sine qua non* of an effective consent"; and (3) it would "be unrealistic to require police officers to always inform detainees that they are free to go before a consent to search may be deemed voluntary."

CASE SIGNIFICANCE: There is no requirement under the Fourth Amendment for the officer to first inform the detained motorist that "you are free to go" before consent to search the car will be held to be voluntary and therefore valid. The Court added that "the voluntariness of a consent to search is a question of fact to be determined from all the circumstances," and not on a per se rule that requires an officer to inform the motorist that he or she is "free to go." This case confirms and extends the Court's ruling that the totality of circumstances applies in search and seizure cases. Here, the Court ruled that officers may obtain consent to search a vehicle from stopped motorists without the requirement to first inform them that they are free to go.

MARYLAND V. WILSON
519 U.S. 408 (1997)

CAPSULE: "[A]n officer making a traffic stop may order passengers to get out of the car pending completion of the stop."

FACTS: A state trooper attempted to stop a car, in which Wilson was a passenger, for speeding and an irregular license plate. After activating his blue lights, the trooper followed the car for more than a mile before it stopped. During this time, two of the three passengers in the car kept looking back at the trooper, ducking below the line of sight and then reappearing. As the trooper approached the car after it stopped, the driver got out and met him halfway. The trooper reported that the driver was trembling and appeared very nervous, but did produce a valid driver's license. When the driver returned to the car to retrieve the rental papers, the trooper noticed that Wilson was sweating and appeared very nervous. When the trooper ordered Wilson out of the car, a quantity of crack cocaine fell to the ground. Wilson was arrested and charged with possession of cocaine with intent to distribute.

ISSUE: After stopping a car, may an officer order the passengers to exit the vehicle? YES.

SUPREME COURT DECISION: After a valid traffic stop, the officer may also order the passengers, not just the driver, to exit the car.

REASON: In *Pennsylvania v. Mimms*, 434 U.S. 106 (1977), the Supreme Court ruled that "[t]he touchstone of our analysis under the Fourth Amendment is always 'the reasonableness in all the circumstances of the particular governmental intrusions on a citizen's personal security' ... and ... that reasonableness depends on 'a balance between the public's interest and the individual's right to personal security.'" Here, the Court ruled that "[o]n the public interest side of the balance, the same weighty interest in officer safety is present regardless of whether the occupant of the stopped car is a driver or passenger. Regrettably, traffic stops may be dangerous encounters. ... On the personal liberty side of the balance, the case for the passengers is in one sense stronger than that for the driver. There is probable cause to believe that the driver has committed a minor vehicular offense, but there is no such reason to stop or detain the passengers. But as a practical matter, the passengers are already stopped by virtue of the stop of the vehicle. The only change in their circumstances which will result from ordering them out of the car is that they will be outside of, rather than inside of, the stopped car." "While there is [therefore] not the same basis for ordering the passengers out of the car as there is for ordering the driver out, the additional intrusion on the passenger is minimal. We therefore hold that an officer making a traffic stop may order passengers to get out of the car pending completion of the stop."

CASE SIGNIFICANCE: In *Mimms*, the Supreme Court ruled that a law enforcement officer may order the driver to exit the car. It was not clear from *Mimms*, however, whether that rule also extended to passengers. The Court in *Wilson* clarified this issue and ruled that it did; thus, both the driver and passenger can now be ordered by the police to exit the car after a stop. The reason for this rule is simple: officer safety. The Court argued that the government's "legitimate and weighty" interest in protecting officers prevails against the minimal infringement on the liberties of both the car driver and the passengers. Although a passenger has a stronger claim of liberty than the driver (who is suspected to have committed a traffic offense), the passenger nonetheless "has the same motivation as a driver to use a weapon concealed in the car to prevent the officer from finding evidence of more serious crime." Given this danger, the Court held that the car driver and the passengers can be made to exit the car. The Court stopped short, however, of ruling that officers could forcibly detain the passenger for the entire duration of the stop absent exigent circumstances.

UNITED STATES V. DRAYTON
536 U.S. 194 (2002)

CAPSULE: The Fourth Amendment permits police officers to approach bus passengers, to ask questions, and to request their consent to search, provided that a reasonable person would understand that he or she is free to refuse. There is no requirement in the Fourth Amendment for officers to advise the persons of their right to refuse to cooperate.

FACTS: Drayton and Clifton Brown were traveling on a Greyhound bus from Ft. Lauderdale, Florida, to Detroit, Michigan, when it made a scheduled stop in Tallahassee, Florida. While the bus driver left to complete paperwork, three police officers boarded the bus as a part of a drug interdiction program. One of the officers knelt in the driver's seat and watched the passengers. The other two officers went to the back of the bus. One officer stayed at the back to watch passengers while the other began to move forward, speaking with individual passengers as he went. He asked passengers about their travel and attempted to match passengers with luggage. To avoid blocking the aisle, the officer stood behind the passenger's seat while speaking. Passengers who declined to speak to the officer or who left the bus were allowed to do so. As the officer approached Drayton and Brown, he leaned forward from the rear and spoke in a tone just loud enough for them to hear. When asked if they had any bags, they both pointed to a single bag overhead. The officer examined the bag and found nothing. Both Drayton and Brown were wearing heavy coats and baggy pants despite the warm weather. Based on the officer's experience that this was typical for persons trafficking narcotics, he asked Brown if he could check his person. Brown agreed, leaned forward in his seat, and opened his jacket. The officer patted down Brown and felt objects on his legs consistent with drug packages he had detected on other occasions. The officer then asked Drayton if he could check him, to which Drayton agreed. A pat-down of Drayton's thighs produced evidence of similar objects.

ISSUE: Does the Fourth Amendment require police officers to advise bus passengers of their right not to cooperate when asked questions and to refuse consent to a search? NO.

SUPREME COURT DECISION: The Fourth Amendment permits police officers to approach bus passengers, ask questions, and request their consent to search, provided a reasonable person under the same circumstances would understand that he or she is free to refuse to cooperate. The Fourth Amendment does not require officers to advise persons of their right to refuse to cooperate when asked questions and to refuse consent to a search.

REASON: Law enforcement officers do not violate the Fourth Amendment prohibition of unreasonable seizures merely by approaching individuals on the street or in other public places and putting questions to them if they are willing to listen. Even when law enforcement officers have no basis for suspecting a particular individual, they may pose questions, ask for identification, and request consent to search luggage—provided they do not induce cooperation by coercive means. If a reasonable person would feel free to terminate the encounter, then he or she has not been seized. (Citations omitted.) "Applying the [*Florida v.*] *Bostick* framework to the facts of this particular case, we conclude that the police did not seize respondents when they boarded the bus and began questioning passengers. The officers gave the passengers no reason to believe that they were required to answer the officers' questions."

CASE SIGNIFICANCE: The Court in this case held that the police are not required to inform bus passengers of their right to refuse to cooperate when asked questions or when seeking consent to search, as long as a reasonable individual under the same circumstances would have believed that he or she did not have to cooperate. The Court stressed that "law enforcement officers do not violate the Fourth Amendment's prohibition of unreasonable seizures merely by approaching individuals on the street or in other public places and putting questions to them if they are willing to listen." This is true even if the officers do not have any basis for suspecting that an individual is involved in a criminal act. Officers are free to "pose questions, ask for identification, and request consent to search luggage provided they do not induce cooperation by coercive means." There is no seizure under the Fourth Amendment if a reasonable person would feel free to terminate the encounter.

As in most cases involving the Fourth Amendment, the decision in this case was based on a totality of the circumstances. The Court held: "'While knowledge of the right to refuse consent is one factor to be taken into account, the government need not establish such knowledge as the *sine qua non* of an effective consent.' Nor do this Court's decisions suggest that even though there are no *per se* rules, a presumption of invalidity attaches if a citizen consented without explicit notification that he or she was free to refuse to cooperate. Instead, the Court has repeated that the totality of the circumstances must control, without giving extra weight to the absence of this type of warning."

This decision informs law enforcement officers that no specific information about an individual's right to refuse to cooperate need be given, but that the confrontation itself should not be coercive and the officer must be prepared to establish, if the legality of the act is later challenged, that the totality of the circumstances was such that a reasonable person would have felt free to refuse to cooperate. It should be noted that the reality is that most suspects answer questions by the police and give permission to search even if they have something to hide. What makes suspects do that despite awareness that the police will find something incriminating is difficult to tell. Encounters with the police may be deemed by some to be so inherently coercive that they do not feel free to refuse. Or they may think that refusal to search in itself creates added suspicion and that the police can then go ahead and search anyway. Whatever the reason, suspects giving consent to the police to search even if they have something to hide, which will likely be discovered, is an interesting topic.

BRENDLIN V. CALIFORNIA
551 U.S. 1 (2007)

CAPSULE: Like the driver, the passenger of a vehicle is seized within the meaning of the Fourth Amendment during a traffic stop.

FACTS: Officers stopped a vehicle to verify a temporary license tag, even though the officers admitted there was nothing unusual about the permit. The officer recognized the occupant of the vehicle, Brendlin, as potentially on parole and asked him to identify himself. After verifying that Brendlin was a parole violator and had a warrant for his arrest, the officer arrested him. A search incident to the arrest revealed a syringe cap. A pat-down search of the driver revealed syringes and marijuana. Drug production equipment was found in a search of the vehicle. After Brendlin's motion to suppress the evidence as fruits of a stop without probable cause was denied, he pleaded guilty to drug charges.

ISSUE: Is the passenger of a vehicle "seized" within the meaning of the Fourth Amendment during a traffic stop? YES.

SUPREME COURT DECISION: "[Like the driver Simeroth] Brendlin was seized from the moment Simeroth's car came to a halt on the side of the road, and it was error to deny his suppression motion on the ground that seizure occurred only at the formal arrest."

REASON: "A person is seized by the police and thus entitled to challenge the government's action under the Fourth Amendment when the officer, 'by means of physical force or show of authority,' terminates or restrains his freedom of movement *'through means intentionally applied.'* Thus, an 'unintended person … [may be] the object of the detention,' so long as the detention is 'willful' and not merely the consequence of 'an unknowing act.'" (Internal citations omitted; emphasis in original.) "The law is settled that in Fourth Amendment terms a traffic stop entails a seizure of the driver 'even though the purpose of the stop is limited and the resulting detention quite brief.' *Delaware v. Prouse*, 440 U.S. 648, 653 (1979). And although we have not, until today, squarely answered the question whether a passenger is also seized, we have said over and over *in dicta* that during a traffic stop an officer seizes everyone in the vehicle, not just the driver." "We resolve this question by asking whether a reasonable person in Brendlin's position when the car stopped would have believed himself free to 'terminate the encounter' between the police and himself. We think that in these circumstances any reasonable passenger would have understood the police officers to be exercising control to the point that no one in the car was free to depart without police permission." (Internal citations omitted.)

CASE SIGNIFICANCE: This case settles an issue that the Court had not previously decided authoritatively: whether, like the driver, a car occupant is also "seized" under the Fourth Amendment when the driver of the vehicle is stopped. A unanimous Court ruled "yes" by asking whether a reasonable person in the position of the occupant would have "believed" himself or herself to be intentionally detained and subject to the authority of the police. Applying this standard, the Court held that, under the circumstances of this case, Brendlin would have reasonably believed he was intentionally detained and subject to police authority. In view of the reasonableness of this belief, Brendlin was seized under the Fourth Amendment and therefore could assert his Fourth Amendment right against unreasonable search and seizure. The Court added that, to accept the state's arguments that detention of passengers started only after Brendlin was arrested, would "invite police officers to stop cars with passengers regardless of probable cause or reasonable suspicion of anything illegal." It is important to note, however, that the Court stressed that the ruling in this case does not extend to instances of incidental motor vehicle restrictions, such as when motorists are forced to slow down or stop because other vehicles are being detained. It is also important to note that the Court in this case resolved a narrow legal issue: whether a vehicle passenger is seized when the vehicle is stopped. It said "yes" and therefore Brendlin could challenge the constitutionality of the seizure of the evidence used against him.

Roadblocks

11

INTRODUCTION

The final component of vehicle stops and searches is when police set up roadblocks in efforts to prevent illegal activity such as drinking and driving (as opposed to setting up a roadblock in an attempt to seize a particular person). The practice of establishing roadblocks to detect people drinking and driving became popular among police in the late 1980s. The constitutionality was challenged and the Court held these kinds of police actions are constitutional under limited circumstances (*Michigan Department of State Police v. Sitz*). In another case, however, the Court ruled that highway checkpoints whose primary purpose is to detect evidence of ordinary criminal wrongdoing violated the Fourth Amendment (*Indianapolis v. Edmond*). Finally, in *Illinois v. Lidster*, the Court ruled that police checkpoints set up for the purpose of obtaining information from motorists about a hit-and-run accident are valid under the Fourth Amendment. These cases show that roadblocks must meet a standard of individualized suspicion absent some compelling societal interest. This means roadblocks designed to enhance safety on the roads are acceptable, whereas roadblocks designed to detect "ordinary criminal wrongdoing" are not.

The leading cases briefed in this chapter on roadblocks are *Michigan Department of State Police v. Sitz* and *Indianapolis v. Edmond*.

MICHIGAN DEPARTMENT OF STATE POLICE V. SITZ
496 U.S. 444 (1990)

CAPSULE: Sobriety checkpoints are constitutional.

FACTS: The Michigan State Police established a highway checkpoint program pursuant to guidelines that governed checkpoint operations, site selection, and publicity. Under these guidelines, checkpoints would be set up at selected sites along state roads and all vehicles passing through the checkpoints would be stopped and the drivers checked for signs of intoxication. If intoxication was noted, the vehicle would be pulled to the side of the road for further tests; all other drivers would be permitted to resume their journey. During the only operation of the checkpoint, which lasted approximately one hour and 15 minutes, 126 vehicles were checked, with an average delay of 25 seconds per vehicle. Two individuals were arrested for driving under the influence of alcohol.

ISSUE: Is the use of a sobriety checkpoint that stops all vehicles a violation of the Fourth and Fourteenth Amendments? NO.

SUPREME COURT DECISION: Sobriety checkpoints, in which the police stop every vehicle, do not violate the Fourth and Fourteenth Amendment protections against unreasonable searches and seizures and are therefore constitutional.

REASON: The Court ruled that sobriety checkpoints are a form of seizure, but such a seizure is reasonable because the intrusion on motorists stopped briefly at sobriety checkpoints is slight. In *United States v. Martinez-Fuerte*, 428 U.S. 543 (1976), the Court used a balancing test to uphold checkpoints for detecting illegal aliens. The Court held that the state has a substantial interest in preventing illegal aliens from entering the United States. This substantial interest, when balanced against the degree of intrusion placed on motorists passing through the checkpoint, supported the constitutionality of the procedure under the Fourth Amendment. In this case, the Court decided that "[t]he intrusion resulting from the brief stop at the sobriety checkpoint is for constitutional purposes indistinguishable from the checkpoint stops we upheld in *Martinez-Fuerte*," thus the two cases were decided similarly by the Court.

CASE SIGNIFICANCE: For a long time, lower courts had conflicting opinions about the constitutionality of sobriety checkpoints. Courts in 21 states had upheld sobriety checkpoints, while courts in 12 states had declared them unconstitutional. The Supreme Court declared that the police may establish highway checkpoints in an effort to catch drunk drivers.

Although the Court admitted that sobriety checkpoints constitute a form of seizure and therefore come under the Fourth Amendment, the intrusion on the driver is minimal and therefore considered reasonable, particularly in light of the state interest involved. Balancing the state interest involved and the individual constitutional rights invoked, the Court came down on the side of the state, thus giving the police an added weapon in the fight against drunk driving.

In an earlier decision, the Court ruled that police officers were not authorized to stop a single vehicle for the sole purpose of checking the driver's license and vehicle registration (*Delaware v. Prouse*, 440 U.S.

648 [1979]). In *Prouse*, the Court disapproved of random stops in an effort to apprehend unlicensed drivers and unsafe vehicles because there was no empirical evidence to indicate that such stops would be an effective means of promoting road safety. In *Sitz*, however, the Court argued that the detention of each of the 126 vehicles resulted in the arrest of two drunk drivers, or approximately 1.5 percent of the drivers. This is a higher percentage than the number of aliens (0.12 percent) found in the *Martinez-Fuerte* case. The Court in *Sitz* decided in favor of the state for three reasons: (1) the balance of the state's interest in preventing drunk driving, (2) the extent to which sobriety checkpoints can reasonably be said to advance that state interest, and (3) the minimal degree of intrusion on individual motorists who are stopped briefly. Police departments should note that the sobriety checkpoint procedures declared constitutional by the Court in *Sitz* were a product of careful study and thinking. The *Sitz* case does not allow police to make random stops; what it does authorize are well-conceived and carefully structured sobriety checkpoints, such as that of Michigan. Although sobriety checkpoints are constitutional, they may be prohibited by departmental policy or state law.

INDIANAPOLIS V. EDMOND
531 U.S. 32 (2000)

CAPSULE: Highway checkpoints whose primary purpose is to detect evidence of ordinary criminal wrongdoing violate the Fourth Amendment.

FACTS: Indianapolis police began a program of vehicle checkpoints in an effort to detect illegal drugs. The roadblocks operated during daylight hours and were clearly marked by signs. The locations of the roadblocks were planned well in advance, and a predetermined number of vehicles were to be stopped. At the stop, an officer required the driver to produce a driver's license and registration. The officer would check for signs of impairment in the driver and conduct a plain view observation of the vehicle from the outside while a narcotics detection dog was walked around the outside of the vehicle. Only if the officer developed particularized suspicion of illegality was the driver detained and further investigation conducted; and officers had no discretion to stop any vehicle out of sequence. The total time of the stop was to be less than five minutes. Edmond and others were stopped at the checkpoints.

ISSUE: Do roadblocks that have the primary purpose of crime control violate the Fourth Amendment? YES.

SUPREME COURT DECISION: Highway checkpoints whose primary purpose is to detect evidence of ordinary criminal wrongdoing violate the Fourth Amendment.

REASON: "We have never approved a checkpoint program whose primary purpose was to detect evidence of ordinary criminal wrongdoing. Rather our checkpoint cases have recognized only limited exceptions to the general rule that a seizure must be accompanied by some measure of individualized suspicion. We suggested in [*Delaware v.*] *Prouse* that we would not credit the 'general interest in crime control' as justification for a regime of suspicionless stops, 440 U.S. at 659, n. 18. Consistent with this suggestion, each of the checkpoint programs that we have approved was designed primarily to serve purposes closely related to the problems of policing the border or the necessity of ensuring roadway safety. Because the primary purpose of the Indianapolis narcotics checkpoint program is to uncover evidence of ordinary criminal wrongdoing, the program contravenes the Fourth Amendment."

CASE SIGNIFICANCE: The general rule in Fourth Amendment cases is that searches and seizures are unreasonable unless there is individualized suspicion of criminal wrongdoing. In roadblocks, there is no individualized suspicion of wrongdoing. There are exceptions to this need for individualized suspicion, however, which are: (1) when the purpose of the roadblock is securing the border, (2) when the purpose is apprehending drunken drivers, and (3) when the purpose is verifying drivers' licenses and registrations. Setting up checkpoints to control the flow of drugs was sought by the City of Indianapolis as another exception. The Court rejected this contention, concluding that the purpose of the checkpoint was general law enforcement, which could not be allowed because it was too general. The Court argued that "if this case were to rest at such a high level of generality, there would be little check on the authorities' ability to construct roadblocks for almost any conceivable law enforcement purpose." The drug problem is severe, but the Court did not think it justified setting up roadblocks. The Court concluded, "We have never approved a checkpoint program whose primary purpose was to detect evidence of ordinary criminal wrongdoing. Rather, our checkpoint cases have recognized only limited exceptions to the general rule that a seizure must be accompanied by some measure of individualized suspicion. We suggested in *Prouse* that we would not credit the 'general interest in crime control' as justification for a regime of suspicionless stops." The lesson for law enforcement from this case is this: properly designed roadblocks for traffic and illegal immigration purposes are valid, but roadblocks for general crime control are unconstitutional. If the purpose is crime control, there must be individualized suspicion before the officer can stop motor vehicles.

ILLINOIS V. LIDSTER
540 U.S. 419 (2004)

CAPSULE: Police checkpoints set up for the purpose of obtaining information from motorists about a hit-and-run accident are valid under the Fourth Amendment.

FACTS: Police set up a highway checkpoint to obtain information from motorists about a hit-and-run accident. The checkpoint was established at about the same time of night and at the same location as the hit-and-run. Officers stopped each vehicle for 10 to 15 seconds, asked the occupants if they saw anything related to the accident, and handed them a flyer asking for their assistance. As Lidster approached the checkpoint, his van swerved, almost hitting an officer. When the officer smelled alcohol on Lidster's breath, he directed him to a side street where another officer administered a sobriety test and then arrested Lidster.

ISSUE: Does a checkpoint designed to obtain information from motorists about a hit-and-run accident violate the Fourth Amendment? NO.

SUPREME COURT DECISION: Police checkpoints set up to obtain information from motorists about a hit-and-run accident are valid under the Fourth Amendment. When officers have probable cause that a stopped person is engaged in illegal activity, they may take appropriate action.

REASON: This case is another in the line of cases related to police checkpoints (included in this chapter). In this case, the purpose was not to determine whether a vehicle's occupants were engaged in crime, but to request the assistance of motorists related to a crime in which they were likely not involved. The Court rejected a rule of automatic unconstitutionality for such stops, arguing that they will normally lack individualized suspicion, but that does not automatically make them unconstitutional. The Court relied on previous cases to support its argument that sometimes special law enforcement concerns justify highway stops without individualized suspicion.

CASE SIGNIFICANCE: This case is significant because it adds more information concerning the validity of roadblocks set up by the police. Not all police roadblocks are constitutional under the Fourth Amendment. In this case, the Court held that, whether a roadblock is constitutional (given the absence of individualized suspicion that the person stopped has committed a crime) is to be determined by: (1) "the gravity of the public concerns served by the seizure," (2) "the degree to which the seizure advances the public interest," and (3) "the severity of the interference with individual liberty." The roadblock set up here was valid because the purpose was not for general "crime control," but had a much more specific purpose—to seek information about a hit-and-run incident that took place about a week earlier. Moreover, "each stop required only a brief wait in line and contact with police for only a few seconds." In sum, police checkpoints set up for a specific purpose are valid, but checkpoints whose purpose is to obtain information for general crime control are unconstitutional.

Electronic Surveillance

12

INTRODUCTION

The law on electronic surveillance has changed drastically over the years. In *Olmstead v. United States*, the Supreme Court held that wiretapping does not violate the Fourth Amendment if there is no trespass into a constitutionally protected area. This enabled the police to conduct legal wiretaps as long as they did not illegally intrude into a person's dwelling.

This rule was changed in *Katz v. United States*, when the Court expressly overruled *Olmstead* and held that any form of electronic surveillance (including wiretapping) that violates a reasonable expectation of privacy constitutes a search under the Fourth Amendment. This means that electronic surveillance is unconstitutional anywhere if it violates a person's reasonable expectation of privacy. Trespass into a building was no longer a requirement for an unlawful electronic search; thus electronic surveillance could be illegal, even if conducted in a public place, if a person had a reasonable expectation of privacy. This change was inevitable because technology had become so sophisticated that surveillance could be conducted without entering a person's dwelling.

The other cases in this chapter hold that evidence obtained as a result of permission given to the police to listen in on a conversation by a "friend" is admissible as evidence in court. The Court has also held that the use of electronic devices to record or listen to a conversation constitutes a search under the Fourth Amendment; therefore, safeguards are needed for the search to be valid. The warrantless use of a homing device in a public place does not constitute a search, but becomes a search if it involves a private residence or the police intrude on a constitutionally protected space (even a vehicle in certain circumstances).

At present, the rules on electronic surveillance are governed by federal and state laws. The main federal law governing electronic surveillance is Title III of the Omnibus Crime Control and Safe Streets Act of 1968. This law is long and complex, but it basically states that law enforcement officers (federal, state, and local) cannot tap or intercept wire communications or use electronic devices to intercept private conversations, except: (1) if there is a court order authorizing the wiretap or (2) if consent is given by one of the parties to the conversation. In addition, a court order authorizing the wiretap can be issued only if state law authorizes it, subject to the provisions of Title III of the Omnibus Crime Control and Safe Streets Act. On the other hand, consent given by one of the parties to the conversation may be prohibited by state law. In sum, the police must comply with state and federal laws if they wish to obtain a warrant.

Electronic surveillance of terrorism and terrorists is a growing concern and topic for law and for policing. Neither *Katz* or the other early Supreme Court cases addressed whether their requirements applied to foreign intelligence or foreign terrorism within the U.S. The Omnibus Crime Control and Safe Streets Act was passed largely in response to the *Katz* decision. Title III of the Act contains a provision in 18 U.S.C. § 2511(3) that gives the President power to act against "any other clear and present danger" to the U.S. In *United States v. United States District Court for the Eastern District of Michigan*, 407 U.S. 297 (1972), the Court dismissed this provision for domestic groups if they attempt to "attack and subvert the existing structure of the Government"; and instead reiterated the necessity of a warrant. The Court did not, however, address foreign intelligence or foreign terrorism, even within the U.S. (although it did recognize the potential difficulty in distinguishing between domestic and foreign powers—just not in the present case). More recently, the Foreign Intelligence Surveillance Act (FISA) of 1978, and the related court dedicated to it, have revised the discussion of electronic surveillance on U.S. soil. This topic is not addressed in this book because most FISA work is a federal law enforcement issue, not local law enforcement; and, there are no openly available Supreme Court cases that directly apply to day-to-day law enforcement actions in this area. When such a case exists, it will certainly be briefed here (as we did with *Riley*).

The leading cases on electronic surveillance briefed in this chapter on electronic surveillance are *Katz v. United States* and *United States v. Jones*.

OLMSTEAD V. UNITED STATES
277 U.S. 438 (1928)

CAPSULE: Wiretapping does not violate the Fourth Amendment unless there is a trespass into a "constitutionally protected area." (This case was overruled by *Katz v. United States*, 389 U.S. 347 [1967].)

FACTS: Olmstead and co-conspirators of a conglomerate involved in importing and distributing illegal liquor were convicted of conspiracy to violate the National Prohibition Act. Information leading to the arrests was gathered primarily by intercepting messages from the telephones of the conspirators. The information was obtained by placing wiretaps on the telephone lines outside the conspirators' offices and homes. The wiretaps were installed without trespass on any property of the conspirators.

ISSUE: Do telephone wiretaps violate the Fourth Amendment protection from illegal searches and seizures? NO.

SUPREME COURT DECISION: Wiretapping does not violate the Fourth Amendment unless there is a trespass into a "constitutionally protected area." (Note: this doctrine was expressly overruled by the Supreme Court in *Katz v. United States*, 389 U.S. 347 [1967].)

REASON: "The [Fourth] Amendment does not forbid what was done here. There was no searching. There was no seizure. The evidence was secured by the use of the sense of hearing and that only. There was no entry of the houses or offices of the defendants."

CASE SIGNIFICANCE: The *Olmstead* case is significant because it represents the old rule on wiretaps. This was the first major case decided by the Court on electronic surveillance, and reflects the old concept that evidence obtained through a bugging device placed against a wall to overhear a conversation in an adjoining office was admissible because there was no actual trespass. The rule lasted from 1928 to 1967. In 1967, the Court decided *Katz v. United States*, 389 U.S. 347, which held that any form of electronic surveillance (including wiretapping) that violates a reasonable expectation of privacy constitutes a search. Under the new rule, the search may be unreasonable even though no physical trespass occurred.

ON LEE V. UNITED STATES
343 U.S. 747 (1952)

CAPSULE: Evidence obtained as a result of permission given by a "friend" who allowed the police to listen in on a conversation is admissible in court.

FACTS: A federal undercover agent who was an old acquaintance and former employee of On Lee entered his laundry wearing a radio transmitter and engaged On Lee in a conversation. Self-incriminating statements made by On Lee at that time and later in another conversation were listened to on a radio receiver by another federal agent located outside the laundry. The conversations were submitted as evidence at On Lee's trial over his objection. He was convicted of selling opium.

ISSUE: Is electronic eavesdropping through a consenting party a violation of the Fourth Amendment's protection from unreasonable searches and seizures? NO.

SUPREME COURT DECISION: There is no violation of a suspect's Fourth Amendment right if a "friend" allows the police to listen in on a conversation; hence, the evidence obtained is admissible in court.

REASON: The conduct of the officers in this case did not constitute the kind of search and seizure that is prohibited by the Fourth Amendment. There was no trespass when the undercover agent entered the suspect's place of business, and his subsequent conduct did not render his entry a trespass. The suspect here claimed that the undercover officer's entrance constituted a trespass because consent was obtained by fraud, and that the other agent was a trespasser because, by means of the radio receiver outside the laundry, the agent overheard what went on inside. The Court, however, rejected these allegations.

CASE SIGNIFICANCE: This case allows the police to obtain evidence against a suspect by bugging or listening to a conversation as long as the police have the permission of one of the parties to the conversation and such practice is not prohibited by state law. The Supreme Court in this case ruled that the Fourth Amendment does not protect persons against supposed friends who turn out to be police informers. Thus, a person assumes the risk that whatever is said to another person may be reported by that person to the police; there being no police "search" in such cases. It follows that, if the "friend" allows the police to listen in on a telephone conversation with a suspect, there is no violation of the suspect's constitutional right. The evidence can be used in court.

KATZ V. UNITED STATES
389 U.S. 347 (1967)

CAPSULE: Any form of electronic surveillance, including wiretapping, that violates a reasonable expectation of privacy, constitutes a search under the Fourth Amendment. No physical trespass is required.

FACTS: Katz was convicted of transmitting wagering information across state lines. The evidence against Katz consisted of a conversation overheard by FBI agents who had attached an electronic listening device to the outside of a public telephone booth from which the calls were made.

ISSUE: Is a public telephone booth a constitutionally protected area such that evidence collected by an electronic listening or recording device is obtained in violation of the right to privacy of the user of the booth? YES.

SUPREME COURT DECISION: Any form of electronic surveillance, including wiretapping, that violates a reasonable expectation of privacy, constitutes a search. No physical trespass is required.

REASON: "The government stresses the fact that the telephone booth from which the petitioner made his call was constructed partly of glass, so that he was as visible after he entered it as he would have been if he had remained outside. But what he sought to exclude when he entered the booth was not the intruding eye, it was the uninvited ear. He did not shed his right to do so simply because he made his calls from a place where he might be seen. No less than an individual in a business office, in a friend's apartment, or in a taxicab, a person in a telephone booth may rely upon the protection of the Fourth Amendment. One who occupies it, shuts the door behind him, and pays the toll that permits him to place a call is surely entitled to assume that the words he utters into the mouthpiece will not be broadcast to the world. To read the Constitution more narrowly is to ignore the vital role that the public telephone has come to play in private communication."

CASE SIGNIFICANCE: The *Katz* decision expressly overruled the decision 39 years earlier in *Olmstead v. United States*, 277 U.S. 438 (1928), which held that wiretapping did not violate the Fourth Amendment unless there was some trespass into a "constitutionally protected area." In *Katz*, the Court held that the coverage of the Fourth Amendment does not depend on the presence or absence of a physical intrusion into a given enclosure. The current test is that a search exists, and therefore comes under the Fourth Amendment protection, whenever there is a "reasonable expectation of privacy." The concept that the Constitution "protects people rather than places" is significant because it makes the protection of the Fourth Amendment "portable," meaning that it is carried by persons wherever they go as long as their behavior and circumstances are such that they are entitled to a reasonable expectation of privacy. This was made clear by the Court when it stated that "No less than an individual in a business office, in a friend's apartment, or in a taxicab, a person in a telephone booth may rely upon the protection of the Fourth Amendment. One who occupies it, shuts the door behind him, and pays the toll that permits him to place a call is surely entitled to assume that the words he utters into the mouthpiece will not be broadcast to the world." *Katz*, therefore, made a significant change in the concept of the right to privacy and expanded the coverage of that right, particularly as applied to Fourth Amendment cases. It is the current standard by which the legality of search and seizure cases is tested.

UNITED STATES V. KARO
468 U.S. 705 (1984)

CAPSULE: The warrantless monitoring of a beeper (homing device) in a private residence violates the Fourth Amendment.

FACTS: Upon learning that Karo and co-conspirators had ordered ether from a government informant, to be used in extracting cocaine from clothing imported into the United States, government agents obtained a court order authorizing the installation of a beeper (a homing device) in one of the cans. With the informant's consent, Drug Enforcement Administration (DEA) agents substituted one of their cans containing a beeper for one of the cans to be delivered to respondent. Over several months, the beeper enabled the agents to monitor the can's movement to a variety of locations, including several private residences and two commercial storage facilities. Agents obtained a search warrant for one of the homes, relying in part on information derived through the use of the beeper. Based on the evidence obtained during the search, Karo and co-conspirators were arrested and charged with various drug offenses.

ISSUE: Did the monitoring of a beeper without a warrant violate the defendant's Fourth Amendment rights? YES.

SUPREME COURT DECISION: The warrantless monitoring of a beeper in a private residence violates the Fourth Amendment rights of individuals to privacy in their own homes and therefore cannot be conducted without a warrant. (The Court, however, reversed the decision on other grounds.)

REASON: "The monitoring of a beeper in a private residence, a location not opened to visual surveillance, violates the Fourth Amendment rights of those who have a justifiable interest in the privacy of the residence. Here, if a DEA agent had entered the house in question without a warrant to verify that the ether was in the house, he would have engaged in an unreasonable search within the meaning of the Fourth Amendment. The result is the same where, without a warrant, the government surreptitiously uses a beeper to obtain information that it could not have obtained from outside the curtilage of the house. There is no reason in this case to deviate from the general rule that a search of a house should be conducted pursuant to a warrant."

CASE SIGNIFICANCE: A year earlier, in *United States v. Knotts*, 459 U.S. 276 (1983), the Court held that the use of beepers in a car on a public road by the police does not constitute a search because there is no reasonable expectation of privacy. The Court ruled this search reasonable because the monitoring device was placed in a chloroform can with the permission of the owner and before the can came into Knotts' possession. Moreover, the Court added that the Fourth Amendment does not prohibit the police from supplementing their sensory faculties with technological aids to help police identify a car's location. The *Karo* and *Knotts* cases were decided differently because their facts were different. In *Knotts*, the agents learned nothing from the beeper that they could not have visually observed, hence there was no Fourth Amendment violation. Moreover, the monitoring in *Knotts* occurred in a public place, whereas the beeper in *Karo* intruded on the privacy of a home. The two cases are, therefore, complementary, not inconsistent, in legal principles. Later, the Court ruled in *United States v. Jones* that, even though the monitoring of a vehicle on public highways was constitutional, installing the device on constitutionally protected grounds made the search unconstitutional.

The Court held *in dicta* that a warrant for the monitoring of a beeper should contain:

1. the object into which the beeper would be installed
2. the circumstances leading to the request for the beeper
3. the length of time for which beeper surveillance is requested.

KYLLO V. UNITED STATES
533 U.S. 27 (2001)

CAPSULE: Using a technological device to explore details of a home that would previously have been unknowable without physical intrusion is a search and is presumptively unreasonable without a warrant.

FACTS: Officers who suspected Kyllo of growing marijuana in his home used a thermal-imaging device to examine the heat radiating from his house. The thermal-imaging device was used from across the street and took only a few minutes. The scan showed that the roof over the garage and a side wall of Kyllo's house were relatively hot compared to the rest of his house and substantially hotter than neighboring homes. Based on this information, utility bills, and tips from informants, officers obtained a search warrant for Kyllo's home. The search revealed more than 100 marijuana plants.

ISSUE: "[W]hether the use of a thermal-imaging device aimed at a private home from a public street to detect relative amounts of heat within the home constitutes a 'search' within the meaning of the Fourth Amendment." YES.

SUPREME COURT DECISION: Where the government uses a device that is not in general public use to explore details of the home that would have been unknowable without physical intrusion, the surveillance is a search and is presumptively unreasonable without a warrant.

REASON: "At the very core of the Fourth Amendment stands the right of a man to retreat into his own home and there be free from unreasonable governmental intrusions. With few exceptions, the question whether a warrantless search of a home is reasonable and hence constitutional must be answered no." (Citations omitted.) "We think that obtaining by sense-enhancing technology any information regarding the interior of the home that could not otherwise have been obtained without physical intrusion into a constitutionally protected area constitutes a search, at least where (as here) the technology in question is not in general public use. "On the basis of this criterion, the information obtained by the thermal imager in this case was the product of a search."

CASE SIGNIFICANCE: This case addresses the use of thermal-imaging devices in law enforcement, an issue of concern in many jurisdictions because of technological advances. The government argued that thermal imaging does not constitute a search because: (1) it detects "only heat radiating from the external surface of the house" and therefore there is no entry, and (2) it did not "detect private activities occurring in private areas" because everything that was detected was on the outside. The Court disagreed, concluding that the Fourth Amendment draws "a firm line at the entrance of the house." It conceded that, while no significant compromise of the homeowner's privacy occurred in this case, "we must take the long view, from the original meaning of the Fourth Amendment forward." Acknowledging that "it would be foolish to contend that the degree of privacy secured to citizens by the Fourth Amendment has been entirely unaffected by the advance of technology," it nonetheless concluded that "the Fourth Amendment is to be construed in the light of what was deemed an unreasonable search and seizure when it was adopted, and in a manner that will conserve public interest as well as the interest and rights of individual citizens." In sum, there is a limit to electronic surveillance even if it does not directly intrude into individual privacy. The limit here was drawn "when the government uses a device that was not in general public use, to explore details of a private home that would previously have been unknowable without physical intrusion."

UNITED STATES V. JONES
565 U.S. 400 (2012)

CAPSULE: Whether or not the use of a GPS device for tracking a vehicle is admissible in court has more to do with the method of attachment than with the data retrieved from the device.

FACTS: Jones was suspected of trafficking in drugs. Based on surveillance, evidence from a camera observing the nightclub owned by Jones, and a wiretap of Jones' cell phone, law enforcement officers obtained a search warrant allowing them to install a Global Positioning System (GPS) tracking device on a vehicle registered to Jones' wife. The warrant authorized installation in the District of Columbia and within 10 days, but agents installed the device on the eleventh day and in Maryland. The vehicle's movements were tracked for 28 days. Based on the tracking, Jones and others were arrested for drug trafficking.

ISSUE: "[W]hether the attachment of a Global-Positioning-System (GPS) tracking device to an individual's vehicle, and subsequent use of that device to monitor the vehicle's movements on public streets, constitutes a search or seizure within the meaning of the Fourth Amendment." YES.

SUPREME COURT DECISION: "The Government's attachment of the GPS device to the vehicle, and its use of that device to monitor the vehicle's movements, constitutes a search under the Fourth Amendment." In this case, the government illegally intruded on Jones' "effect," making the search unconstitutional.

REASON: The Court concluded that it is important to be clear about what occurred in this case: there were two potential ways the Court could interpret this case (and therefore decide on the precedents set by that interpretation)—as a wiretap or more as a physical search. The Court rejected the Government's argument that the proper interpretation for the case was the "reasonable expectation of privacy" rule drawn from *Katz v. United States*, 389 U.S. 347, 351 (1967), stating that the intrusion in this case was more fundamental than that in *Katz*. Instead, the Court reasoned the government physically occupied private property for the purpose of obtaining information, arguing "We have no doubt that such a physical intrusion would have been considered a 'search' within the meaning of the Fourth Amendment when it was adopted." The Court made a distinction between this case and *United States v. Karo*, 468 U.S. 705 (1984), in that Karo was not in possession of the container when police attached a beeper; therefore, there was no unconstitutional intrusion (see also *On Lee v. United States*, 343 U.S. 747 (1952) where there was no search or seizure when an informant, who was wearing a concealed microphone, was invited into the defendant's business). The Court also rejected the government's argument in *New York v. Class*, 475 U.S. 106, 114 (1986), that "[t]he exterior of a car … is thrust into the public eye, and thus to examine it does not constitute a 'search.'" The Court ruled that, by attaching the device to the Jeep, officers encroached on a protected area, arguing "In *Class* itself we suggested that this would make a difference, for we con-cluded that an officer's momentary reaching into the interior of a vehicle did constitute a search. 475 U.S., at 114–115."

CASE SIGNIFICANCE: The Court largely left alone the issue of the use of GPS devices in general, focusing instead on the method of attachment and if there were any intrusions that would have made their use unconstitu-tional. Whether use of a GPS device constitutes a search within the Fourth Amendment is, therefore, still unclear according to the Supreme Court. It can be assumed based on a previous case (*United States v. Knotts*, 459 U.S. 276 [1983]) that the use would be approved as long as the device was not attached or monitored in a constitutionally protected area. This rationale is not completely clear, however, since the Court in *Knotts* argued that part of what made that search constitutional was that the tracking device was placed in a can with the owner's permission before it came into Knotts' possession. This may make placing a tracking device on a vehicle difficult to meet constitutional muster. What is clear, however, is that the Court decided that whether the search is admissible in court depends on law enforcement agents maintaining constitutional practices. The Court again examined electronic monitoring of the movement of persons in *Grady v. North Carolina*, 575 U.S. ___ 2015 (per curiam). Although the Court remanded the case to determine if the use of satellites to track the whereabouts of sex offenders constitutes a reasonable search, the Court affirmed that such satellite tracking is a search under the Fourth Amendment. This will likely continue to be a source of jurisprudence in the coming years.

Plain View and Open Fields Searches

13

INTRODUCTION

The plain view doctrine states that items within the sight of an officer who is legally in a place from which the view is made may be seized without a warrant as long as such items are immediately recognizable as subject to seizure. Items in plain view are not protected by the Fourth Amendment guarantee against unreasonable searches and seizures; thus, no warrant or probable cause is necessary for a valid seizure. There are, however, three requirements for the plain view doctrine to apply:

1. The item must be within the officer's sight.
2. The officer must legally be in the place from which the item is seen.
3. It must be immediately apparent to the officer that the item is subject to seizure.

The requirement that the item be within the officer's sight means that the item must be noted through the sense of sight and not through the use of the other senses. If the officer is not legally in the place from which the item is seen, the seizure of the item is illegal and therefore it cannot be used as evidence. It must also be immediately clear to the officer that the item seen is subject to seizure. If the officer does not immediately know the item is seizable (such as if the item is identified as seizable only after touching or looking at it more closely), the plain view doctrine does not apply because other methods were used to determine "seizability."

"Inadvertence," meaning the accidental finding by the officer of the item rather than prior knowledge that the item is in a particular place, was a fourth requirement for plain view. In *Horton v. California*, however, the Court ruled: "The Fourth Amendment does not prohibit the warrantless seizure of evidence in plain view even though the discovery of the evidence was not inadvertent," thus doing away with the inadvertence requirement. In reality, most items seized under plain view are discovered by the officers inadvertently and not because they know beforehand that seizable items can be found in a location.

The open fields doctrine states that items in open fields are not protected by the Fourth Amendment and may be properly seized by an officer without a warrant or probable cause. Plain view and open fields are similar in that, in both situations, there is no need for a search warrant or probable cause for the police to be able to seize the items. They are different, however, in two ways:

1. Under the plain view doctrine, the seizable property is usually in a house or another enclosed place (such as a car), whereas under the open fields doctrine, the item is found in a non-enclosed area, such as in a parking lot, a public street, or a park that is accessible to the public.

2. Under the plain view doctrine, the item seized is limited to what is in the officer's sight. By contrast, items known or observed through the use of the officer's other senses (smell, hearing, touching, and tasting) also fall under the open fields doctrine.

In *United States v. Dunn*, 480 U.S. 294 (1987), the Supreme Court held that the warrantless search of a barn that is not part of the curtilage of a house is valid (curtilage is the grounds and buildings immediately surrounding a dwelling). In that case, the Court listed four factors that determine whether an area is considered part of the curtilage and therefore not considered an open field. These four factors are so vague, however, that they are of little practical help to law enforcement officers and judges in determining where the curtilage ends and where open fields begin.

The leading cases briefed in this chapter on the doctrines of plain view and open fields are *Oliver v. United States*, *United States v. Dunn*, and *Horton v. California*.

TEXAS V. BROWN
460 U.S. 730 (1983)

CAPSULE: "Certain knowledge" that evidence seen is incriminating is not necessary under the plain view doctrine. Probable cause suffices.

FACTS: An officer stopped Brown's vehicle at night at a routine driver's license checkpoint. The officer asked Brown for his driver's license and shined his flashlight into the automobile. When Brown withdrew his hand from his pocket, the officer observed an opaque, green party balloon, which was knotted one-half inch from the tip, fall from Brown's hand onto the seat. Based on his experience, the officer knew that such balloons were frequently used to transport drugs. Responding to the officer's second request to produce a driver's license, Brown reached across and opened the glove compartment. The officer shifted his position to get a better view of the glove compartment and observed several small plastic vials, a quantity of a white powdery substance, and an open package of party balloons. After rummaging through the glove compartment, Brown informed the officer that he did not have a driver's license. The officer picked up the balloon, which had a white powdery substance in the tied-off portion, and showed it to another officer who also recognized the balloon as one possibly containing narcotics. The officers placed Brown under arrest. A search of Brown's vehicle incident to the arrest revealed several plastic bags containing marijuana and a bottle of milk sugar (often mixed with heroin before selling). Brown was charged with and convicted of possession of heroin.

ISSUE: Must an officer have certain knowledge that an object in plain view is contraband or evidence of criminal activity before it may be seized under the plain view doctrine? NO.

SUPREME COURT DECISION: Items must be "immediately recognizable" as subject to seizure if they are to fall under the plain view doctrine, but "certain knowledge" that incriminating evidence is involved is not necessary. Probable cause is sufficient to justify a seizure. The use of a flashlight by an officer during the evening to look into the inside of a car does not constitute a search under the Fourth Amendment. The items discovered still fall under plain view.

REASON: "In the *Coolidge* [*v. New Hampshire*, 403 U.S. 443 (1971)] plurality's view, the 'plain view' doctrine permits the warrantless seizure by police of private possessions where three requirements are satisfied. First, the police officer must lawfully make an 'initial intrusion' or otherwise properly be in a position from which he or she can view a particular area. Second, the officer must discover incriminating evidence 'inadvertently,' which is to say, he or she may not 'know in advance the location of [certain] evidence and intend to seize it,' relying on the plain view doctrine only as a pretext. Finally, it must be 'immediately apparent' to the police that the items they observe may be evidence of a crime, contraband, or otherwise subject to seizure." (Citations omitted.) The "immediately apparent" language in *Coolidge*, however, does not require an officer to "know" that items are contraband or evidence of criminal activity; probable cause is sufficient.

CASE SIGNIFICANCE: There are four basic elements of the plain view doctrine. They are:

1. awareness of the item must be gained solely through the sense of sight
2. the officer must be legally present in the place from which the items are viewed
3. discovery of the items must be inadvertent
4. the items must be immediately recognizable as subject to seizure.

This case clarifies the fourth requirement, that "immediate recognizability" does not mean "certain knowledge." All that is needed is probable cause. In this case, the officer shined his flashlight into the car's interior and saw an opaque green party balloon, knotted about one-half inch from the tip. The officer also saw white powder in the open glove compartment. In court, the officer testified that he had learned from experience that tied-off balloons are often used to transport narcotics. The Supreme Court concluded that the officer had probable cause to believe that the balloon contained narcotics and that a warrantless seizure was, therefore, justified under the plain view doctrine.

OLIVER V. UNITED STATES
466 U.S. 170 (1984)

CAPSULE: "No Trespassing" signs do not effectively bar the public from viewing open fields; therefore, the expectation of privacy by the owner of an open field does not exist. The police may enter and investigate unoccupied or undeveloped areas outside the curtilage without either a warrant or probable cause.

FACTS: Acting on reports that marijuana was being grown on the petitioner's farm, but without a search warrant, probable cause, or exigent circumstances, police officers went to the farm to investigate. They drove past Oliver's house to a locked gate with a "No Trespassing" sign, and with a footpath around one side. Officers followed the footpath around the gate and found a field of marijuana more than one mile from the petitioner's house. Oliver was charged with and convicted of manufacturing a controlled substance.

ISSUE: Does the open fields doctrine apply when the property owner attempts to establish a reasonable expectation of privacy by posting a "No Trespassing" sign, using a locked gate, and planting marijuana more than one mile from the house? YES.

SUPREME COURT DECISION: Because open fields are accessible to the public and the police in ways that a home, office, or commercial structure would not be, and because fences or "No Trespassing" signs do not effectively bar the public from viewing open fields, the expectation of privacy by an owner of an open field does not exist. Consequently, the police may enter and search unoccupied or underdeveloped areas outside the curtilage without either a warrant or probable cause.

REASON: "The test of a reasonable expectation of privacy is not whether the individual attempts to conceal criminal activity, but whether the government's intrusion infringes upon the personal and societal values protected by the Fourth Amendment. Because open fields are accessible to the public and because fences or 'No Trespassing' signs, etc. are not effective bars to public view of open fields, the expectation of privacy does not exist and police are justified in investigating these areas without a warrant."

CASE SIGNIFICANCE: This case makes clear that the "reasonable expectation of privacy" doctrine under the Fourth Amendment, as established in *Katz v. United States*, 389 U.S. 347 (1967), does not apply when the property involved is an open field. The Court stressed that steps taken to protect privacy, such as planting the marijuana on secluded land and erecting a locked gate (but with a footpath along one side) and posting "No Trespassing" signs around the property, do not establish any reasonable expectation of privacy. This case allows law enforcement officers to make warrantless entries and observations without probable cause in open fields, thus affording them greater access to remote places where prohibited plants or drugs might be concealed.

CALIFORNIA V. CIRAOLO
476 U.S. 207 (1986)

CAPSULE: The naked-eye observation by the police of a suspect's backyard, which is part of the curtilage, does not violate the Fourth Amendment.

FACTS: After receiving an anonymous telephone tip that Ciraolo was growing marijuana in his backyard, police went to his residence to investigate. Realizing that the area in question could not be viewed from ground level, officers used a private plane and flew over the home at an altitude prescribed by law. Officers trained in the detection of marijuana readily identified marijuana plants growing in Ciraolo's yard. Based on that information and an aerial photograph of the area, officers obtained a search warrant for the premises. A search was made pursuant to the warrant and numerous marijuana plants were seized. Ciraolo was charged with and convicted of cultivation of marijuana.

ISSUE: May officers make an aerial observation of an area within the curtilage of a home without a search warrant? YES.

SUPREME COURT DECISION: The constitutional protection against unreasonable searches and seizures is not violated by the naked-eye aerial observation of a suspect's backyard, which is a part of the curtilage, by the police.

REASON: "That the area is within the curtilage does not itself bar all police observation. The Fourth Amendment protection of the home has never been extended to require law enforcement officers to shield their eyes when passing by a home on public thoroughfares. Nor does the mere fact that an individual has taken measures to restrict some views of his activities preclude an officer's observations from a public vantage point where he has a right to be and which renders the activities clearly visible."

CASE SIGNIFICANCE: The term "curtilage" refers to the grounds and buildings immediately surrounding a dwelling. Ordinarily, the curtilage is not considered an open field and hence is protected against unreasonable searches and seizures. This means that searching a curtilage area requires a warrant. In this case, however, the Court held that there was no need for a warrant because the naked-eye aerial observation of a suspect's backyard was not a search within the meaning of the Fourth Amendment. The Court held that the fact that an area falls within the curtilage does not in itself prohibit all police observation. This case, therefore, expands police power to observe the curtilage without a warrant through aerial observation.

UNITED STATES V. DUNN
480 U.S. 294 (1987)

CAPSULE: The warrantless observation of a barn that is not part of the curtilage is valid. Four factors determine whether an area is considered part of the curtilage.

FACTS: After learning that a co-defendant purchased large quantities of chemicals and equipment used in the manufacture of controlled substances, drug agents obtained a warrant to place an electronic tracking beeper in some of the equipment. The beeper ultimately led agents to Dunn's farm. The farm was encircled by a perimeter fence with several interior fences of the type used to hold livestock. Without a warrant, officers entered the premises over the perimeter fence, interior fences, and a wooden fence that encircled a barn, approximately 50 yards from respondent's home. The officers were led to the barn by the odor of chemicals and the sound of a running motor. Without entering the barn, officers stood at a locked gate and shined a flashlight into the barn where they observed what appeared to be a drug laboratory. Officers returned twice the next day to confirm the presence of the laboratory, each time without entering the barn. Based on information obtained from these observations, officers obtained a search warrant and seized the drug lab from the barn and a quantity of controlled substances from the house.

ISSUE: Is a barn located approximately 50 yards from a house and surrounded by a fence different from that of the house, part of the curtilage that cannot be observed without a warrant? NO.

SUPREME COURT DECISION: The interior of the barn that was observed but not entered by police was not a part of the curtilage and, therefore, the warrantless observation by the police was valid. Whether an area is considered a part of the curtilage of a home rests on four factors:

1. the proximity of the area to the home
2. whether the area is in an enclosure surrounding the home
3. the nature and uses of the area
4. the steps taken to conceal the area from public view.

Applying these factors, the barn in this case could not be considered a part of the curtilage.

REASON: "Under *Oliver* [*v. United States*, 466 U.S. 170 (1984)] and *Hester* [*v. United States*, 265 U.S. 57 (1924)], there is no constitutional difference between police observations conducted while in a public place and while standing in an open field."

CASE SIGNIFICANCE: This case is important because, for the first time, the Court laid out the standards for determining whether a particular building falls within the curtilage of the main house. Applying the four factors enumerated above, the Court concluded that the barn observed but not entered by the police did not fall within the curtilage of the main building and therefore did not need a warrant to be observed. These four factors take into account such elements of consideration as proximity, enclosure, uses, and steps taken to protect the area. The problem with these factors is that they are necessarily subjective and therefore lend themselves to imprecise application. Nonetheless, they are an improvement over the complete lack of guidelines under which the lower courts decided prior cases.

ARIZONA V. HICKS
480 U.S. 321 (1987)

CAPSULE: Probable cause to believe that items seen are contraband or evidence of criminal activity is required for the items to be seized under the plain view doctrine.

FACTS: A bullet, fired through the floor of Hicks' apartment and injuring a man below, prompted the police to enter Hicks' apartment to search for the shooter, weapons, and other victims. The police discovered three weapons and a stocking cap mask. An officer noticed several pieces of stereo equipment that seemed to be out of place in the ill-appointed apartment. Based on this suspicion, he read and recorded the serial numbers of the equipment, moving some of the pieces in the process. A call to police headquarters verified that one of the pieces of equipment was stolen. A subsequent check of the serial numbers of the other pieces of equipment revealed they were also stolen. A search warrant was then obtained and the other equipment was seized. Hicks was charged with and convicted of robbery.

ISSUE: May an officer make a plain view search with less than probable cause to believe the items being searched are contraband or evidence of criminal activity? NO.

SUPREME COURT DECISION: Probable cause to believe that items being searched are, in fact, contraband or evidence of criminal activity is required for the items to be searched under the plain view doctrine.

REASON: "[M]oving the equipment ... did constitute a 'search' separate and apart from the search for the shooter, victims, and weapons that was the lawful objective of [the officer's] entry into the apartment. Merely inspecting those parts of the turntable that came into view during the latter search would not have constituted an independent search, because it would have produced no additional invasion of respondent's privacy interest. But taking action, unrelated to the objectives of the authorized intrusion, which exposed to view concealed portions of the apartment or its contents, did produce a new invasion of respondent's privacy unjustified by the exigent circumstance that validated the entry."

CASE SIGNIFICANCE: The plain view doctrine states that items within the sight of an officer who is legally in the place from which the view is made, and who had no prior knowledge that the items were present, may properly be seized without a warrant as long as the items are immediately recognizable as subject to seizure. This case holds that, even after the officer has seen an object in plain view, he or she may not search or seize it unless there is probable cause to believe that the object is contraband, or that it is useful as evidence in court. Therefore, if, at the moment the object is picked up, the officer did not have probable cause but only "reasonable suspicion" (as was the case here), the seizure is illegal. The plain view doctrine as the basis for a warrantless seizure may be invoked by the police only if there is probable cause to believe the item is contraband or useful evidence; it may not be invoked based on "reasonable suspicion" or any other level of certainty that is less than probable cause.

HORTON V. CALIFORNIA
496 U.S. 128 (1990)

CAPSULE: "Inadvertent discovery" of evidence is no longer a necessary element of the plain view doctrine.

FACTS: A police officer determined that there was probable cause to search Horton's home for the evidence of a robbery and weapons used in the robbery. The affidavit filed by the officer referred to police reports that described both the weapons and the stolen property, but the warrant that was issued authorized a search only for the stolen property. When the officer went to Horton's home to execute the warrant, he did not find the stolen property, but found weapons in plain view and seized them. At the trial, the officer testified that while he was searching Horton's home for the stolen property, he was also interested in finding other evidence related to the robbery. Horton argued on appeal that the weapons should have been suppressed during the trial because their discovery was not "inadvertent."

ISSUE: Is inadvertence a necessary element of the plain view doctrine? NO.

SUPREME COURT DECISION: "The Fourth Amendment does not prohibit the warrantless seizure of evidence in plain view even though the discovery of the evidence was not inadvertent. Although inadvertence is a characteristic of most legitimate plain view seizures, it is not a necessary condition."

REASON: Justice Stewart [in *Coolidge v. New Hampshire*, 403 U.S. 443 (1971)] concluded that the inadvertence requirement was necessary to avoid a violation of the express constitutional requirement that a valid warrant must particularly describe the things to be seized. He explained: "The rationale of the exception to the warrant requirement, as just stated, is that a plain view seizure will not turn an initially valid (and therefore limited) search into a 'general' one, while the inconvenience of procuring a warrant to cover an inadvertent discovery is great. But where the discovery is anticipated, where the police know in advance the location of the evidence and intend to seize it, the situation is altogether different. The requirement of a warrant to seize imposes no inconvenience whatever, or at least none which is constitutionally cognizable in a legal system that regards warrantless searches as '*per se* unreasonable' in the absence of 'exigent circumstances.'"

In *Horton*, the Court stated: We find two flaws in this reasoning. First, evenhanded law enforcement is best achieved by the application of objective standards of conduct, rather than standards that depend upon the subjective state of mind of the officer. The fact that an officer is interested in an item of evidence and fully expects to find it in the course of a search should not invalidate its seizure if the search is confined in area and duration by the terms of a warrant or a valid exception to the warrant requirement. If the officer has knowledge approaching certainty that the item will be found, we see no reason why he or she would deliberately omit a particular description of the items to be seized from the application of a search warrant. Specification of the additional item could only permit the officer to expand the scope of the search. On the other hand, if he or she has a valid warrant to search for one item and merely a suspicion concerning the second, whether or not it amounts to probable cause, we fail to see why that suspicion should immunize the second item from seizure if it is found during a lawful search for the first. Second, the suggestion that the inadvertence requirement is necessary to prevent the police from conducting general searches, or from converting specific warrants into general warrants, is not persuasive because that interest is already served by the requirements that no warrant issue unless it 'particularly describes the place to be searched and the persons or things to be seized,' and that a warrantless search be circumscribed by the exigencies that justify its initiation."

CASE SIGNIFICANCE: This case does away with the requirement that, for the plain view doctrine to apply, the discovery of the evidence must be purely accidental. The police officer in this case knew the evidence was there because it was described in the officer's affidavit; but, for some reason, the warrant issued by the magistrate authorized a search only for the stolen property. Nonetheless, the officer saw the weapons in plain view during the search and seized them. Expressly rejecting the inadvertence requirement, the Court held that the seizure was valid because:

1. The items seized from petitioner's home were discovered during a lawful search authorized by a valid warrant.
2. When they were discovered, it was immediately apparent to the officer that they constituted incriminating evidence.
3. The officer had probable cause, not only to obtain a warrant to search for the stolen property, but also to believe that the weapons and handguns had been used in the crime he was investigating.
4. The search was authorized by the warrant.

Note that most seizures by the police under plain view are likely to be inadvertent, meaning the police had no prior knowledge the item was there. What *Horton* held was that, even if the police know an item is to be found in a place, the item can be seized under plain view as long as the four elements outlined above are present.

Searches by Dogs

14

INTRODUCTION

Developing from their use in the U.S. military and in drug detection, police use of dogs to aid in their work is increasingly common. Actually, the use of dogs in policing is almost older than policing itself. The Egyptians used dogs in guarding and policing the pyramids before there was any formalized police force. Currently, dogs are employed for a variety of uses in policing, including bomb detection, border/customs searches, drug detection, and as "second officers" on patrol. The aspect of the use of dogs in police work that is most likely to come to the attention of the courts is their use in searches. The first true test of the use of a dog as a search mechanism was heard in *United States v. Place*. In this case, the Court ruled that the sniff of a dog is not a search within the Fourth Amendment. This case, together with the effectiveness of drug detection dogs, has led to their widespread use in policing. The use of dogs, however, does have attendant issues as police officers use dogs in a variety of ways. An increasing number of cases related to the use of dogs in policing are reaching the Supreme Court. This chapter covers those cases, and provides context for officers in how they can use dogs legally to further their work.

The leading cases briefed in this chapter are *United States v. Place* and *Florida v. Jardines*.

UNITED STATES V. PLACE
462 U.S. 696 (1983)

> **CAPSULE:** The sniff of a dog does not constitute a search within the meaning of the Fourth Amendment.
>
> **FACTS:** When Place's behavior aroused the suspicion of police at Miami International Airport, officers approached him and asked for identification. Place consented to a search of the two suitcases he had checked, but, because his flight was about to depart, the officers decided not to search the luggage. When the officers noted discrepancies in the tags on Place's

luggage, they called Drug Enforcement Administration (DEA) authorities in New York. When Place arrived at LaGuardia Airport, he was approached by two DEA agents. When Place refused to consent to a search of his luggage, one of the agents told him that they were going to take the luggage to a federal judge to obtain a search warrant. The agents then took the luggage to Kennedy Airport where it was subjected to a "sniff test" by a trained narcotics detection dog. The dog reacted positively to one of the suitcases. The agents later obtained a search warrant and discovered cocaine.

ISSUE: Does the Fourth Amendment prohibit police from "temporarily detaining personal luggage for exposure to a trained narcotics detection dog on the basis of reasonable suspicion that the luggage contains narcotics"? NO.

SUPREME COURT DECISION: The investigative procedure of subjecting luggage to a "sniff test" by a well-trained drug detection dog does not constitute a "search" within the meaning of the Fourth Amendment.

REASON: "In this case, the Government asks us to recognize the reasonableness under the Fourth Amendment of warrantless seizures of personal luggage from the custody of the owner on the basis of less than probable cause, for the purpose of pursuing a limited course of investigation, short of opening the luggage, that would quickly confirm or dispel the authorities' suspicion. Specifically, we are asked to apply the principles of *Terry v. Ohio* [see Chapter 3], to permit such seizures on the basis of reasonable, articulable suspicion, premised on objective facts, that the luggage contains contraband or evidence of a crime. In our view, such application is appropriate." A sniff by a trained drug detection dog does not require the luggage to be opened. "It does not expose non-contraband items that otherwise would remain hidden from public view, as does, for example, an officer's rummaging through the contents of the luggage. Thus, the manner in which information is obtained through this investigative technique is much less intrusive than a typical search. Moreover, the sniff discloses only the presence or absence of narcotics, a contraband item. Thus, despite the fact that the sniff tells the authorities something about the contents of the luggage, the information obtained is limited." "We are aware of no other investigative procedure that is so limited both in the manner in which the information is obtained and in the content of the information revealed by the procedure. Therefore, we conclude that the particular course of investigation that the agents intended to pursue here—exposure of respondent's luggage, which was located in a public place, to a trained canine—did not constitute a 'search' within the meaning of the Fourth Amendment."

CASE SIGNIFICANCE: In this case, the Court ruled that a sniff by a trained dog was not a search within the meaning of the Fourth Amendment. This case opened the legal door for police use of trained dogs in an investigative role.

ILLINOIS V. CABALLES
543 U.S. 405 (2005)

CAPSULE: An examination by drug detection dog conducted during a lawful traffic stop that reveals no information other than the location of an illegal substance that no individual has any right to possess does not violate the Fourth Amendment.

FACTS: An officer stopped Caballes for speeding and radioed the dispatcher. Hearing the radio transmission, another officer drove to the scene with his drug detection dog. While the first officer wrote Caballes a warning ticket, the K-9 officer walked his dog around Caballes' car. The dog alerted on the trunk. Based on that alert, the officers searched the trunk and found marijuana. Caballes sought suppression of the evidence, arguing that, because there was no suspicion of him being involved in drug activity, use of the dog violated the Fourth Amendment.

ISSUE: Does the Fourth Amendment require reasonable, articulable suspicion to justify using a drug detection dog to sniff a vehicle during a legitimate traffic stop? NO.

SUPREME COURT DECISION: "A dog sniff conducted during a ... lawful traffic stop that reveals no information other than the location of [an illegal] substance that no individual has any right to possess does not violate the Fourth Amendment."

REASON: "In our view, conducting a dog sniff would not change the character of a traffic stop that is lawful at its inception and otherwise executed in a reasonable manner, unless the dog sniff itself infringed respondent's constitutionally protected interest in privacy. Our cases hold that it did not. ... We have held that any interest in possessing contraband cannot be deemed 'legitimate,' and thus, governmental conduct that only reveals the possession of contraband 'compromises no legitimate privacy interest.' ... Accordingly, the use of a well-trained narcotics detection dog—one that 'does not expose non-contraband items that otherwise would remain hidden from public view,' *Place*, 462 U.S. at 707—during a lawful traffic stop, generally does not implicate legitimate privacy interest. In this case, the dog sniff was performed on the exterior of respondent's car while he was lawfully seized for a traffic violation. Any intrusion on respondent's privacy expectations does not rise to the level of a constitutionally cognizable infringement."

CASE SIGNIFICANCE: This case ruled that the use by the police of dogs to sniff cars during a lawful stop is valid. The defendant here was validly stopped for speeding, but not for drug possession. While the first officer wrote a warning ticket, another officer, who had driven to the scene, walked the dog around Caballes' car. The dog indicated the presence of drugs in the car trunk, so the officers opened the trunk, found marijuana, and then arrested Caballes. On appeal, Caballes argued that the use of the dog to sniff for drugs in the absence of any "specific and articulable facts to suggest drug activity" extended the routine traffic stop and converted it into a drug investigation. The Court disagreed and held the seizure valid, concluding, "in our view, conducting a dog sniff would not change the character of a traffic stop that is lawful at its inception and otherwise executed in a reasonable manner." The Court added that no privacy interest was violated because "the dog sniff was performed on the exterior of respondent's car while he was lawfully seized for a traffic violation. Any intrusion on respondent's privacy expectation does not rise to the level of a constitutionally cognizable infringement." In sum, if the stop of a motor vehicle is valid, the use of dogs to sniff the car for drugs is also valid, even if the reason for the stop was not drug-related.

FLORIDA V. HARRIS
568 U.S. 237, No. 11-817 (2013)

CAPSULE: The proper standard to determine the appropriateness of a search by a dog is totality of the circumstances, not a rigid checklist of records.

FACTS: An officer pulled over Harris for a routine traffic stop. Observing Harris' nervousness and an open beer can, the officer sought consent to search Harris' truck. When Harris refused, the officer executed a sniff test with his trained drug detection dog. The dog alerted at the driver's-side door handle, leading the officer to conclude he had probable cause for a search. The search did not produce anything the dog was trained to detect, but did reveal pseudoephedrine and other ingredients for manufacturing methamphetamine. Harris was arrested and charged with illegal possession of those ingredients. While Harris was out on bail, the officer pulled over Harris again, and again, the dog alerted on the door handle. This time, nothing was found. At a suppression hearing, the officer testified about his and the dog's extensive training in drug detection. Harris' attorney did not contest the quality of that training, focusing instead on the dog's expired certification and performance in the field, particularly in the two stops of Harris' truck. The trial court denied the motion to suppress, but the Florida Supreme Court reversed.

ISSUE: Must states present exhaustive records of a dog's performance to establish a dog's reliability for detection? NO.

SUPREME COURT DECISION: Because training and testing records supported the dog's reliability in detecting drugs and Harris' testimony failed to undermine that evidence, the officer had probable cause to search Harris' truck.

REASON: "The test for probable cause is not reducible to 'precise definition or quantification.'" "In evaluating whether the State has met this practical and common-sensical standard, we have consistently looked to the totality of the circumstances." "A gap as to any one matter, we explained, should not sink the State's case; rather, that 'deficiency … may be compensated for, in determining the overall reliability of a tip, by a strong showing as to … other indicia of reliability.' So too here, a finding of a drug-detection dog's reliability cannot depend on the State's satisfaction of multiple, independent evidentiary requirements." "The question—similar to every inquiry into probable cause—is whether all the facts surrounding a dog's alert, viewed through the lens of common sense, would make a reasonably prudent person think that a search would reveal contraband or evidence of a crime. A sniff is up to snuff when it meets that test." "For that reason, evidence of a dog's satisfactory performance in a certification or training program can itself provide sufficient reason to trust his alert." "The record in this case amply supported the trial court's determination that [the dog's] alert gave [the officer] probable cause to search the truck."

CASE SIGNIFICANCE: Use of dogs in drug detection and preliminary searches is becoming increasingly commonplace. As a result, there is more emphasis on the legal issues surrounding such searches. This case, in essence, clarifies how to qualify a dog as an "expert witness" for a search. The Florida court held that "the fact that the dog has been trained and certified is simply not enough to establish probable cause." It then ruled that "[T]he State must present … the dog's training and certification records, an explanation of the meaning of the particular training and certification, field performance records (including any unverified alerts), and evidence concerning the experience and training of the officer handling the dog, as well as any other objective evidence known to the officer about the dog's reliability." The Supreme Court overruled this procedure as unnecessarily restrictive. It held that these factors could be taken into account in a probable cause hearing; but that none of them would make the search valid or invalid. Instead, a totality of the circumstances was the standard by which a search by a dog should be admitted or not admitted as evidence.

FLORIDA V. JARDINES
569 U.S. 1, No. 11-564 (2013)

CAPSULE: Using a police dog to sniff within the boundaries of the curtilage of a house is a search that is in violation of the Fourth Amendment.

FACTS: Police received a tip that marijuana was being grown in the home of Jardines. Police then established surveillance on Jardines' home. One of the officers approached Jardines' home accompanied by a K-9 handler and his dog. The dog was on a six-foot leash. As the dog approached Jardines' front porch, he indicated the presence of a drug in the air. After sniffing the base of the front door, the dog sat, which is the trained behavior upon discovering the odor's strongest point. The officer pulled the dog away from the door and returned to his vehicle. On the basis of the indication by the dog, officers applied for and received a warrant to search the residence. The search revealed marijuana plants, and Jardines was charged with trafficking in cannabis. At trial, Jardines moved to suppress the marijuana plants on the grounds that the K-9 investigation was an unreasonable search.

ISSUE: Is using a drug detection dog on a homeowner's porch to investigate the contents of the home a "search" within the meaning of the Fourth Amendment? YES.

SUPREME COURT DECISION: "The government's use of trained police dogs to investigate the home and its immediate surroundings is a 'search' within the meaning of the Fourth Amendment."

REASON: The Court began by reestablishing that the Fourth Amendment is clear concerning searches of houses, stating, "when it comes to the Fourth Amendment, the home is first among equals. At the Amendment's 'very core' stands 'the right of a man to retreat into his own home and there be free from unreasonable governmental intrusion.' This right would be of little practical value if the State's agents could stand in a home's porch or side garden and trawl for evidence with impunity ...." "We therefore regard the area 'immediately surrounding and associated with the home'—what our cases call the curtilage—as 'part of the home itself for Fourth Amendment purposes.'" "The officers were gathering information in an area belonging to Jardines and immediately surrounding his house in the curtilage of the house, which we have held enjoys protection as part of the home itself. And they gathered that information by physically entering and occupying the area to engage in conduct not explicitly or implicitly permitted by the homeowner." "Since the officers' investigation took place in a constitutionally protected area, we turn to the question of whether it was accomplished through an unlicensed physical intrusion." "This implicit license typically permits the visitor to approach the home by the front path, knock promptly, wait briefly to be received, and then (absent invitation to linger longer) leave. Complying with the terms of that traditional invitation does not require fine-grained legal knowledge; it is generally managed without incident by the Nation's Girl Scouts and trick or treaters." "But introducing a trained police dog to explore the area around the home in hopes of discovering incriminating evidence is something else. There is no customary invitation to do that." "To find a visitor knocking on the door is routine (even if sometimes unwelcome); to spot that same visitor exploring the front path with a metal detector, or marching his bloodhound into the garden before saying hello and asking permission, would inspire most of us to, well, call the police. The scope of a license express or implied is limited not only to a particular area but also to a specific purpose." "That the officers learned what they learned only by physically intruding on Jardines' property to gather evidence is enough to establish that a search occurred."

CASE SIGNIFICANCE: This case dealt with two major issues, not necessarily involving the search by the dog. The first is whether the police intruded on the area of the home protected by the Fourth Amendment (the curtilage, as repeatedly discussed in legal cases). The Court ruled that the police did break the line of curtilage. The second issue was whether the activities were "an unlicensed physical intrusion." Since the Court had previously ruled that sniffs by dogs were not a search within the meaning of the Fourth Amendment, it was somewhat unclear whether that would be the case here. The Court ruled, however, that the dog had (1) entered the curtilage of the home, and (2) conducted activities that were beyond what would be ordinary for a person who might be visiting the house. As a result, the dog sniff at the front door was considered a search in violation of the Fourth Amendment.

RODRIGUEZ V. UNITED STATES
575 U.S. ___, No. 13-9972 (2015)

CAPSULE: "Absent reasonable suspicion, police extension of a traffic stop in order to conduct a dog sniff violates the Constitution's shield against unreasonable seizures."

FACTS: A K-9 officer stopped Rodriguez for driving on the highway shoulder. After issuing a warning and concluding the traffic stop, the officer asked for consent to walk his dog around the vehicle. When Rodriguez refused, the officer detained him until another officer arrived. The officer's dog alerted to the presence of drugs. A search revealed methamphetamine. Approximately 8 minutes elapsed from the warning to the time the dog alerted.

ISSUE: May police routinely extend an otherwise-completed traffic stop, absent reasonable suspicion, to conduct a dog sniff? NO.

SUPREME COURT DECISION: "Absent reasonable suspicion, police extension of a traffic stop in order to conduct a dog sniff violates the Constitution's shield against unreasonable seizures."

REASON: A traffic stop's "tolerable duration is determined by the seizure's 'mission,' which is to address the traffic violation that warranted the stop ...." "Authority for the seizure ends when tasks tied to the traffic infraction are—or reasonably should have been—completed. The Fourth Amendment may tolerate certain unrelated investigations that do not lengthen the roadside detention, but a traffic stop 'become[s] unlawful if it is prolonged beyond the time reasonably required to complete th[e] mission' of issuing a warning ticket" (internal citations omitted). "A dog sniff is not fairly characterized as part of the officer's traffic mission"; therefore, it cannot prolong the duration of the stop. "The critical question is not whether the dog sniff occurs before or after the officer issues a ticket, but whether conducting the sniff adds time to the stop."

CASE SIGNIFICANCE: In *Illinois v. Caballes*, the Court held that a dog sniff conducted during a lawful traffic stop does not violate the Fourth Amendment. As a result, many law enforcement agencies are issuing dogs for regular patrol, and using them to search for drugs. This case presents the question whether the Fourth Amendment allows a dog sniff conducted after completion of a traffic stop. The Court ruled that it does not. An officer should have specific suspicion or probable cause to extend any traffic stop that includes a dog sniff. It appears to remain legal for officers to conduct a dog sniff that does not prolong the stop (such as having one officer conduct the sniff while another officer conducts the traffic stop—see *Illinois v. Caballes*).

Computer/Cell Phone Searches

15

INTRODUCTION

It is indisputable that cell phones and computers have become a central part of modern life. People routinely now use their cell phones as a central repository for almost every facet of their life—either on the phone itself or in the connections it makes to online entities, such as Instagram. Computers are also central and critical to people's lives, although perhaps less so than even a few years ago with the rise of cell phone technology. All of the documents, letters, pictures, and other depictions of life may be placed on a person's computer as a central storage facility. As such, cell phones and computers are also central to the lives of those who break the law. Not only may they keep their personal lives on their cell phones and computers, they may also keep records of their criminal activities on them—either explicitly in documents, photos, e-mails, etc., or implicitly through those they call or the places they visit, that are contained in the location data or computer history. It follows, then, that law enforcement agents will increasingly come into contact with phones and computers as they investigate crimes. Every person who is arrested is likely to have a cell phone on his or her person. The extent to which police officers can and should attempt to retrieve information from cell phones is now central in law enforcement discussion.

There are only a few, but growing number, of cases reaching the Supreme Court related to cell phones and computers that are directly applicable to police, rather than challenges of laws, etc. (such as challenging the federal child pornography laws). The Court in *Riley* took the somewhat unusual approach of providing a tremendous amount of discussion on the judges' thoughts regarding digital evidence. It addressed the role of cell phones in modern life, including the relationship between "physical evidence" of the phone, "digital evidence" of what is on the phone, and even "connected evidence," such as information from the cloud that may be accessed by the phone. This case, in its entirety, is another of the "must reads" in police law.

The Court commented in *Riley* that, particular to cell phones but also applicable to computers, "[o]ne of the most notable distinguishing features of modern cell phones is their immense storage capacity." It then reasoned that "the storage capacity of cell phones has several interrelated consequences for privacy. First, a cell phone collects in one place many distinct types of information—an address, a note, a prescription, a bank statement, a video—that reveal much more in combination than any isolated record. Second, a cell phone's capacity allows even just one type of information to convey far more than previously possible. The sum of an individual's private life can be reconstructed through a thousand photographs labeled with dates, locations, and descriptions; the same cannot be said of a photograph or two of loved ones tucked into a wallet. Third, the data on a phone can date back to the purchase of the phone, or even earlier. A person might carry in his pocket a slip of paper reminding him to call Mr. Jones; he would not carry a record of all his communications with Mr. Jones for the past several months, as would routinely be kept on a phone."

The Court also took note of the nature of cell phones and computers beyond what is contained on them. The Court addressed the interconnected nature of cell phones by noting that "the scope of the privacy interests at stake is further complicated by the fact that the data viewed on many modern cell phones may in fact be stored on a remote server. Thus, a search may extend well beyond papers and effects in the physical proximity of an arrestee, a concern that the United States recognizes but cannot definitively foreclose."

The Court also recognized the difficulty of separating digital data from more traditional evidence. In rejecting the analogue test (comparison of digital evidence to pre-digital counterparts) the Court argued, "In addition, an analogue test would launch courts on a difficult line-drawing expedition to determine which digital files are comparable to physical records. Is an e-mail equivalent to a letter? Is a voicemail equivalent to a phone message slip? It is not clear how officers could make these kinds of decisions before conducting a search, or how courts would apply the proposed rule after the fact."

In recognizing the critical nature of proper law enforcement investigations and balancing it with privacy rights in a technological world that could not have been imagined by the writers of the Constitution, the Court attempted to provide its rationale for the decision. In the dissent, Justice Alito outlined the complexities of this debate in his statement: "The Court strikes this balance in favor of privacy interests with respect to all cell phones and all information found in them, and this approach leads to anomalies. For example, the Court's broad holding favors information in digital form over information in hard-copy form. Suppose that two suspects are arrested. Suspect number one has in his pocket a monthly bill for his land-line phone, and the bill lists an incriminating call to a long-distance number. He also has in his wallet a few snapshots, and one of these is incriminating. Suspect number two has in his pocket a cell phone, the call log of which shows a call to the same incriminating number. In addition, a number of photos are stored in the memory of the cell phone, and one of these is incriminating. Under established law, the police may seize and examine the phone bill and the snapshots in the wallet without obtaining a warrant, but under the Court's holding today, the information stored in the cell phone is out."

It is unlikely this will be the final case concerning cell phones and computers (and their crossover, as the line between cell phones and computers continues to blur). But *Riley* was a substantial case in determining the near-term future of law enforcement investigations; and the Court provided a strong statement of its reasoning and debates that will aid in future police actions.

The leading cases briefed in this chapter on computer/cell phone searches are *Riley v. California*, *Carpenter v. United States*, and *Packingham v. United States*.

RILEY V. CALIFORNIA
573 U.S. 373 (2014)

> **CAPSULE:** "The police generally may not, without a warrant, search digital information on a cell phone seized from an individual who has been arrested."
>
> **FACTS:** The *Riley* decision is based on two cases (*Riley* itself and *United States v. Wurie*, No. 13–212) with similar facts—both including a search of a cell phone taken from a person incident to an arrest. Since they are similar, only the facts from the *Riley* case are discussed below. Riley was stopped for a traffic violation. His car was impounded because of traffic violations. An inventory search was conducted that revealed weapons, which led to Riley's arrest on weapons charges. An officer searching Riley incident to the arrest seized a cell phone from Riley's pants pocket. The officer accessed information on the phone and noticed the repeated use of a term associated with a street gang. At the police station two hours later, a detective specializing in gangs further examined the phone's contents. Based in part on photographs and videos that the detective found, Riley was charged in connection with a shooting that occurred a few weeks earlier.
>
> **ISSUE:** May officers search the contents of a cell phone taken incident to an arrest without a warrant? NO.
>
> **SUPREME COURT DECISION:** "Modern cell phones are not just another technological convenience. With all they contain and all they may reveal, they hold for many Americans 'the privacies of life,' *Boyd* [*v. United States*, 116 U.S. 616 (1886)], *supra*, at 630. The fact that technology now

allows an individual to carry such information in his hand does not make the information any less worthy of the protection for which the Founders fought. Our answer to the question of what police must do before searching a cell phone seized incident to an arrest is accordingly simple—get a warrant."

REASON: The Court in this case based its finding on precedents governing search incident to an arrest (*Chimel v. California, United States v. Robinson,* and *Arizona v. Gant*). They then stated overall reasoning concerning cell phone searches based on the jurisprudence in these cases.

On the reasoning from *Chimel*, where a search incident to arrest was warranted to protect the officer or limit destruction of evidence, the Court held, "The digital data stored on cell phones does not present either *Chimel* risk." "Digital data stored on a cell phone cannot itself be used as a weapon to harm an arresting officer or to effectuate the arrestee's escape. Law enforcement officers remain free to examine the physical aspects of a phone to ensure that it will not be used as a weapon—say, to determine whether there is a razor blade hidden between the phone and its case. Once an officer has secured a phone and eliminated any potential physical threats, however, data on the phone can endanger no one." "To the extent that a search of cell phone data might warn officers of an impending danger, e.g., that the arrestee's confederates are headed to the scene, such a concern is better addressed through consideration of case-specific exceptions to the warrant requirement, such as exigent circumstances."

Turning to the application of *Robinson*, the Court reasoned "while *Robinson's* categorical rule strikes the appropriate balance in the context of physical objects, neither of its rationales has much force with respect to digital content on cell phones. On the government interest side, *Robinson* concluded that the two risks identified in *Chimel*—harm to officers and destruction of evidence—are present in all custodial arrests. There are no comparable risks when the search is of digital data. In addition, *Robinson* regarded any privacy interests retained by an individual after arrest as significantly diminished by the fact of the arrest itself. Cell phones, however, place vast quantities of personal information literally in the hands of individuals. A search of the information on a cell phone bears little resemblance to the type of brief physical search considered in *Robinson*."

On the potential for destruction of evidence from *Chimel* and, to a lesser extent, *Gant*, the Court reasoned, "As an initial matter, those broad concerns [vulnerability to remote wiping and data encryption] are distinct from *Chimel's* focus on a defendant who responds to arrest by trying to conceal or destroy evidence within his reach. The [government] also gives little indication that either problem is prevalent or that the opportunity to perform a search incident to arrest would be an effective solution. And, at least as to remote wiping, law enforcement currently has some technologies of its own for combatting the loss of evidence."

Applying all of the principles above, the Court then turned to the use of cell phones in modern society. The Court began this reasoning by noting "Cell phones differ in both a quantitative and a qualitative sense from other objects that might be kept on an arrestee's person." Cell phones, the Court argued, have "privacy concerns far beyond those implicated by the search of a cigarette pack, a wallet, or a purse." The ruling in previous cases that inspecting the contents of an arrestee's pockets involves no substantial additional intrusion on privacy beyond the arrest itself cannot be extended to the search of digital data because of the expansive nature of what may be viewed on a cell phone.

The prosecution offered several potential ways to search cell phones incident to arrest that were rejected by the Court. The first was to use the rationale in *Gant* of "allowing a warrantless search of an arrestee's cell phone whenever it is reasonable to believe that the phone contains evidence of the crime of arrest." The Court rejected this argument because *Gant* was based on "circumstances unique to the vehicle context" that did not apply here. The next proposal was "a rule that would restrict the scope of a cell phone search to those areas of the phone where an officer reasonably believes that information relevant to the crime, the arrestee's identity, or officer safety will be discovered." The Court opined that this would likely turn into an expansive search because officers could not always tell where the information they sought would be found and would rely on the plain view doctrine to admit into evidence anything they found while looking for the approved information. Finally, the prosecution argued for an "analogue rule" that would allow officers to search for anything that could have been obtained from a pre-digital counterpart. The Court rejected this argument, stating "the fact that a search in the pre-digital era could have turned up a photograph or two in a wallet does not justify a search of thousands of photos in a digital gallery. The fact that someone could have tucked a paper bank statement in a pocket does not justify a search of every bank statement from the last five years. ... In Riley's case, for example, it is implausible that he would have strolled around with videotapes, photo albums, and an address book all crammed into his pockets."

The Court concluded by conceding, "We cannot deny that our decision today will have an impact on the ability of law enforcement to combat crime. Cell phones have become important tools in facilitating coordination and communication among members of criminal enterprises, and can provide valuable incriminating information about dangerous criminals. Privacy comes at a cost."

CASE SIGNIFICANCE: Some would argue this case is a serious blow to effective law enforcement. The Court argued that the ruling would have an influence on policing, but tried to allay any fears by outlining what police could do to search phones. The bottom line of the holding is that "Our holding, of course, is not that the information on a cell phone is immune from search; it is instead that a warrant is generally required before such a search, even when a cell phone is seized incident to arrest." The Court then pointed out that warrants may be obtained with increasing efficiency that could lessen the impact of denying searches incident to an arrest. The Court also gave law enforcement a way to search through exigent circumstances, stating, "In light of the availability of the exigent circumstances exception, there is no reason to believe that law enforcement officers will not be able to address some of the more extreme hypotheticals that have been suggested: a suspect texting an accomplice who, it is feared, is preparing to detonate a bomb, or a child abductor who may have information about the child's location on his cell phone." For law enforcement, therefore, this case rules that cell phones cannot be searched simply as incident to an arrest, but officers have the ability to obtain a warrant for any information on the phone (which is becoming more routine in law enforcement and computer forensic investigations), and there are many exceptions to the warrant requirement (particularly exigent circumstances) that would apply to cell phone searches.

PACKINGHAM V. UNITED STATES
582 U.S. ___ No. 15-1194 (2017)

CAPSULE: Laws broadly preventing sex offenders from accessing social media websites are contrary to First Amendment protections.

FACTS: Packingham had sex with a 13-year-old girl and pled guilty to taking indecent liberties with a child. He was required to register as a sex offender and was barred from gaining access to commercial social networking sites. In response to having a traffic ticket dismissed, Packingham posted a statement on his personal profile (under an assumed name) on Facebook. Officers investigating violations of the law preventing access to social media saw the post and, through examining traffic court cases, linked the post to Packingham. Evidence obtained through a search warrant confirmed this was Packingham's Facebook profile. Packingham was indicted and his motion to dismiss on the grounds that the charges violated his First Amendment rights were denied.

ISSUE: Does North Carolina's law preventing access to social media websites violate the First Amendment? YES.

SUPREME COURT DECISION: "It is well established that, as a general rule, the Government 'may not suppress lawful speech as the means to suppress unlawful speech.' *Ashcroft* v. *Free Speech Coalition*, 535 U. S., at 255. That is what North Carolina has done here. Its law must be held invalid."

REASON: "A fundamental principle of the First Amendment is that all persons have access to places where they can speak and listen, and then, after reflection, speak and listen once more." While there may have been a time when it was unclear where the most important places for speech were, "today the answer is clear. It is cyberspace—the 'vast democratic forums of the Internet' in general, *Reno* v. *American Civil Liberties Union*, 521 U. S. 844, 868 (1997), and social media in particular."

"This case is one of the first this Court has taken to address the relationship between the First Amendment and the modern Internet. As a result, the Court must exercise extreme caution before suggesting that the First Amendment provides scant protection for access to vast networks in that medium." The rule must be that "the law must not 'burden substantially more speech than is necessary to further the government's legitimate interests.'" "By prohibiting sex offenders from using those websites, North Carolina with one broad stroke bars access to what for many are the principal sources for knowing current events, checking ads for employment, speaking and listening in the modern public square, and otherwise exploring the vast realms of human thought and knowledge." "In sum, to foreclose access to social media altogether is to prevent the user from engaging in the legitimate exercise of First Amendment rights. It is unsettling to suggest that only a limited set of websites can be used even by persons who have completed their sentences. Even convicted criminals—and in some instances especially convicted criminals—might receive legitimate benefits from these means for access to the world of ideas, in particular if they seek to reform and to pursue lawful and rewarding lives."

CASE SIGNIFICANCE: In this case, the Court took substantial steps to apply the First Amendment to social media. It builds on cases such as *Ashcroft v. Free Speech Coalition* that strikes down laws that are so broad as to infringe on constitutional rights. While it may seem these cases favor criminals over the state, they only do so to the extent that laws must be written narrowly, in line with the legitimate interests of the state, and within the guidelines of the Constitution. Even in this case, the Court left the door open for North Carolina to enact a law that would pass constitutional muster, stating the "First Amendment permits a State to enact specific, narrowly tailored laws that prohibit a sex offender from engaging in conduct that often presages a sexual crime, like contacting a minor or using a website to gather information about a minor." The significance for law enforcement in this case is that it helps set bounds for where officers may investigate such criminal activity and where it is ill advised to do so.

CARPENTER V. UNITED STATES
585 U.S. ___ No. 16-402 (2018)

CAPSULE: "Whether the Government employs its own surveillance technology as in *Jones* or leverages the technology of a wireless carrier, we hold that an individual maintains a legitimate expectation of privacy in the record of his physical movements as captured through CSLI."

FACTS: Agents identified the cell phone numbers of several robbery suspects, then prosecutors were granted a court order to obtain the suspects' cell phone records. These records contained time stamped cell-site location information (CSLI). From this information, agents tracked Carpenter's movements over 127 days (12,898 location points). Over his objection, prosecutors used the robbery locations at trial to show he was near four of the locations at the time the robberies occurred.

ISSUE: Does the Government conduct a search under the Fourth Amendment when it accesses historical cell phone records that provide a comprehensive chronicle of the user's past movements? YES. Must the Government obtain a warrant to acquire those files? YES.

SUPREME COURT DECISION: "Given the unique nature of cellphone location records, the fact that the information is held by a third party does not by itself overcome the user's claim to Fourth Amendment protection. Whether the Government employs its own surveillance technology as in *Jones* or leverages the technology of a wireless carrier, we hold that an individual maintains a legitimate expectation of privacy in the record of his physical movements as captured through CSLI." "Having found that the acquisition of Carpenter's CSLI was a search, we also conclude that the Government must generally obtain a warrant supported by probable cause before acquiring such records."

REASON: The Court has ruled that individuals have a reasonable expectation of privacy in their physical movements. "Allowing government access to cell-site records—which 'hold for many Americans the "privacies of life,"' *Riley v. California*, 573 U.S. 373 (2014)—contravenes that expectation. In fact, historical cell-site records present even greater privacy concerns than the GPS monitoring considered in *Jones*: They give the Government near perfect surveillance and allow it to travel back in time to retrace a person's whereabouts, subject only to the five-year retention policies of most wireless carriers." "The Government did not obtain a warrant supported by probable cause before acquiring Carpenter's cell-site records. It acquired those records pursuant to a court order under the Stored Communications Act, which required the Government to show 'reasonable grounds' for believing that the records were 'relevant and material to an ongoing investigation.' 18 U. S. C. §2703(d). That showing falls well short of the probable cause required for a warrant. Consequently, an order issued under §2703(d) is not a permissible mechanism for accessing historical cell-site records. Not all orders compelling the production of documents will require a showing of probable cause. A warrant is required only in the rare case where the suspect has a legitimate privacy interest in records held by a third party. And even though the Government will generally need a warrant to access CSLI, case-specific exceptions —e.g., exigent circumstances—may support a warrantless search."

CASE SIGNIFICANCE: This case involves two competing rationales. The first is the protection from GPS monitoring established in *U.S. v. Jones.* The other involves "a person's expectation of privacy in information voluntarily turned over to third parties. See *United States v. Miller,* 425 U. S. 435 (no expectation of privacy in financial records held by a bank), and *Smith, 442 U. S.* 735" (no expectation of privacy in records of dialed telephone numbers conveyed to telephone company). In *Jones,* the Court foreshadowed the rationale in this case in its comment that "longer term GPS monitoring in investigations of most offenses impinges on expectations of privacy"—regardless whether those movements were disclosed to the public at large. While this decision is prescriptive, it does not mean law enforcement cannot obtain third party records or that a warrant is always required for cell information. Specifically, the Court stated that "This decision is narrow. It does not express a view on matters not before the Court; does not disturb the application of *Smith* and *Miller* or call into question conventional surveillance techniques and tools, such as security cameras; does not address other business records that might incidentally reveal location information; and does not consider other collection techniques involving foreign affairs or national security." But the best approach for officers needing CSLI is to obtain a warrant.

Use of Force

16

INTRODUCTION

The use of force is often necessary in police work, particularly when making an arrest. Force used in policing is categorized into two types: deadly force and non-deadly force. Deadly force is force that is likely to produce death or serious bodily injury. All other kinds of force are non-deadly force.

Cases involving the use of force are difficult to decide because they are never alike. In use of deadly force cases, the safest rule is: follow department policy strictly. Almost all law enforcement agencies presently have clear policies on the use of deadly force. These policies may be more restrictive than those allowed by the Constitution or state law. The more limiting department policies should be followed by the police.

In non-deadly force cases, the rule is: the police should use only reasonable force, meaning only as much force as is needed to accomplish a legitimate goal, such as subduing a resisting suspect. The difficulty lies in determining what force is reasonable under the circumstances. Regardless of circumstances, the rule is that the police must never use punitive force (force that aims to punish rather than to accomplish a legitimate goal).

The leading cases briefed in this chapter are *Tennessee v. Garner*, *Graham v. Connor*, and *Scott v. Harris*.

TENNESSEE V. GARNER
471 U.S. 1 (1985)

CAPSULE: The police may not use deadly force to prevent the escape of a suspect unless it is necessary and the officer has probable cause to believe the suspect poses a significant threat of death or serious physical injury to the officer or to others.

FACTS: Memphis police officers were dispatched to answer a "prowler inside" call. At the scene, they saw a woman standing on her porch and gesturing toward the adjacent house. She told them she heard glass breaking and that someone was breaking in next door. While one officer radioed the dispatcher, the other went behind the adjacent house. He heard a door slam and saw someone run across the backyard. The fleeing suspect, Garner, stopped at a six-foot-high chain-link fence at the edge of the yard. With the aid of a flashlight, the officer was able to see Garner's face and hands. He saw no sign of a weapon, and, although not certain, was "reasonably sure" that Garner was unarmed. While Garner was crouched at the base of the fence, the officer called out "Police, halt" and took a few steps toward him. Garner then began to climb over the fence. Believing that if Garner made it over the fence he would elude capture, the officer shot him. Garner was taken by ambulance to a hospital, where he died. Ten dollars and a purse taken from the house were found on his body.

ISSUE: Is the use of deadly force to prevent the escape of an individual suspected of a non-violent felony constitutional? NO.

SUPREME COURT DECISION: "Deadly force may not be used unless it is necessary to prevent escape and the officer has probable cause to believe that the suspect poses a significant threat of death or serious physical injury to the officer or others."

REASON: "The use of deadly force to prevent the escape of all felony suspects, whatever the circumstances, is constitutionally unreasonable. It is not better that all felony suspects die than that they escape. Where the suspect poses no immediate threat to the officer and no threat to others, the harm resulting from failing to apprehend him does not justify the use of deadly force to do so. It is no doubt unfortunate when a suspect who is in sight escapes, but the fact that the police arrive a little late or are a little slower of foot does not always justify killing the suspect. A police officer may not seize an unarmed, nondangerous suspect by shooting him dead. The Tennessee statute is unconstitutional insofar as it authorizes the use of deadly force against such fleeing suspects."

CASE SIGNIFICANCE: This case clarifies the extent to which the police may use deadly force to prevent the escape of an unarmed felon. The Court made it clear that deadly force may be used only if the officer has probable cause to believe that the suspect poses a threat of serious physical harm to the officer or others. In addition, when feasible, the suspect must first be warned. The decision rendered unconstitutional existing laws in more than one-half of the states that imposed no restrictions on the use of force by police officers to prevent the escape of an individual suspected of a felony. State laws and departmental rules can set narrower limits on the use of force (as in rules stating that use of deadly force may be used only in instances of self-defense), but broader limits are unconstitutional. The

Court based the decision on the Fourth Amendment, arguing that "there can be no question that apprehension by the use of force is a seizure subject to the reasonableness requirement of the Fourth Amendment."

GRAHAM V. CONNOR
490 U.S. 396 (1989)

CAPSULE: Police officers may be held liable under the Constitution for using excessive force. The test for liability is "objective reasonableness" rather than "substantive due process."

FACTS: Graham, a diabetic, asked a friend, Berry, to drive him to a convenience store to buy orange juice, which he needed to counteract the onset of an insulin reaction. They went to the store, but Graham saw many people ahead of him in line so he hurried out and asked Berry to drive him, instead, to a friend's house. Officer Connor became suspicious after he saw Graham hastily enter and leave the store. He followed Berry's car, made an investigative stop, and ordered Graham and Berry to wait while he determined what happened at the store. Other officers arrived, handcuffed Graham, and ignored Graham's attempt to explain his condition. An encounter ensued in which Graham sustained multiple injuries. Graham was later released when Officer Connor learned that nothing had happened at the store. Graham brought a Section 1983 lawsuit against the police alleging a violation of his Fourth Amendment constitutional protection from excessive force.

ISSUE: May police officers be held liable under Section 1983 for using excessive force? YES. What should be the standard for liability? OBJECTIVE REASONABLENESS.

SUPREME COURT DECISION: Police officers may be held liable under the Constitution for using excessive force. Such liability must be judged under the Fourth Amendment's "objective reasonableness" standard, rather than under a "substantive due process" standard.

REASON: "The 'reasonableness' of a particular use of force must be judged from the perspective of a reasonable officer on the scene, rather than with the 20/20 vision of hindsight. The Fourth Amendment is not violated by an arrest based on probable cause, even though the wrong person is arrested, nor by the mistaken execution of a valid search warrant on the wrong premises. With respect to a claim of excessive force, the same standard of reasonableness at the moment applies: 'Not every push or shove, even if it may later seem unnecessary in the peace of a judge's chamber,' violates the Fourth Amendment. The calculus of reasonableness must embody allowance for the fact that police officers are often forced to make split-second judgments—in circumstances that are tense, uncertain, and rapidly evolving—about the amount of force that is necessary in a particular situation." (Citations omitted.)

CASE SIGNIFICANCE: This case gives police officers some protection in civil liability cases involving the use of force. The old "substantive due process" test used by many lower courts prior to the *Graham* case required the courts to consider whether the officer acted in "good faith" or "maliciously and sadistically for the very purpose of causing harm." This meant that the officer's "subjective motivations" were of central importance in deciding whether the force used was unconstitutional. The *Graham* case requires a new test: that of "objective reasonableness" under the Fourth Amendment. This means that the reasonableness of an officer's use of force must be judged "from the perspective of a reasonable officer on the scene, rather than with the 20/20 vision of hindsight." This makes a big difference in determining whether such use of force was reasonable. This test recognizes that police officers often make split-second judgments in situations that involve their own lives and must, therefore, be judged in the context of "a reasonable officer at the scene."

SCOTT V. HARRIS
550 U.S. 372 (2007)

CAPSULE: "A police officer's attempt to terminate a dangerous high-speed car chase that threatens the lives of innocent bystanders does not violate the Fourth Amendment, even when it places the fleeing motorist at risk of serious injury or death."

FACTS: A Georgia county deputy clocked Harris' vehicle traveling at 73 miles per hour on a road with a 55-mile-per-hour speed limit. When the deputy attempted to pull Harris over, he sped away, initiating a high-speed chase down a two-lane road at speeds exceeding 85 miles per hour. Officer Scott heard the radio communication and joined the pursuit, along with other officers. After turning into the parking lot of a shopping center, the suspect, Harris, evaded officers by making a sharp turn, colliding with Scott's police car. This maneuver made Scott the lead pursuit vehicle. Six minutes and nearly 10 miles later, Scott attempted to terminate the pursuit. Prior to this, Scott received permission for the maneuver from his supervisor. Scott used his push bumper to ram the rear of Harris' vehicle, causing Harris to lose control of the vehicle. It left the roadway and crashed. Harris was badly injured and rendered a quadriplegic.

ISSUES:

1. Can police officers constitutionally stop a motorist from fleeing by taking actions that place the motorist or bystanders at risk of serious injury or death? YES.

2. Do police officers violate "clearly established" federal law by using what amounts to deadly force during a high-speed chase? NO.

SUPREME COURT DECISION:

1. "A police officer's attempt to terminate a dangerous high-speed car chase that threatens the lives of innocent bystanders does not violate the Fourth Amendment, even when it places the fleeing motorist at risk of serious injury or death."

2. Police officers do not violate "clearly established" federal law when they use what amounts to deadly force during a high-speed chase under circumstances similar to this case; therefore, they are not civilly liable under federal law.

REASON: "In determining the reasonableness of the manner in which a seizure is effected, '[w]e must balance the nature and quality of the intrusion on the individual's Fourth Amendment interests against the importance of the governmental interests alleged to justify the intrusion' [*United States v. Place*, 462 U.S. 696, 703 (1983)]. Scott defends his actions by pointing to the paramount governmental interest in ensuring public safety, and respondent [Harris] nowhere suggests this was not the purpose motivating Scott's behavior. Thus, in judging whether Scott's actions were reasonable, we must consider the risk of bodily harm that Scott's actions posed to respondent in light of the threat to the public that Scott was trying to eliminate. Although there is no obvious way to quantify the risks on either side, it is clear from the videotape that respondent posed an actual and imminent threat to the lives of any pedestrians who might have been present, to other civilian motorists, and to the officers involved in the chase." "It was respondent, after all, who intentionally placed himself and the public in danger by unlawfully engaging in the reckless, high-speed flight that ultimately produced the choice between two evils that Scott confronted. Multiple police cars, with blue lights flashing and sirens blaring, had been chasing respondent for nearly 10 miles, but he ignored their warning to stop. By contrast, those who might have been harmed had Scott not taken the action he did were entirely innocent. We have little difficulty in concluding it was reasonable for Scott to take the action that he did."

CASE SIGNIFICANCE: This case is a significant case for police officers because it affords them protection from civil liability under federal law (42 U.S.C. § 1983) if they use deadly force (in this case the chase of the suspect's motor vehicle and the maneuvers used by the police to stop the suspect's vehicle) in connection with a vehicle chase as long as the suspect's behavior constitutes a danger to the public. The suspect in this case became a quadriplegic as a result of the police chase. He sued the police officer, arguing the officer violated his "clearly established" constitutional right (a requirement for plaintiff to succeed in Section 1983 civil liability cases in federal law) under the Fourth Amendment by ramming the fleeing suspect's vehicle in a high-speed chase. The Court rejected this allegation, ruling that the officer's actions were reasonable under the Fourth Amendment because the videotape of the car chase showed that, contrary to Harris' claim, his driving posed "an imminent threat to the lives of any pedestrians who might have been present, to other civilian motorists, and to the officers involved in the chase." The Court argued that it is reasonable for police officers to use deadly force to prevent harm to innocent bystanders, even if such use of deadly force puts the fleeing motorist at serious risk of injury or death. In this case, the Court took the rather unusual step of viewing the video of the motor vehicle chase to make a finding of fact (usually a function of the trial court): that the behavior of the suspect constituted a danger to the safety of others. The Court then weighed the need to prevent the harm the suspect could have inflicted on others as opposed to the harm the officer could have inflicted, and did inflict, on the suspect. It concluded that the use of deadly force was reasonable. It also concluded that there was no violation of a "clearly established" constitutional right because lower court decisions on this issue varied and therefore the right was not clearly established. This is a case of balancing public safety against the constitutional rights of the accused. Under the circumstances of this case, public safety prevailed. Although this was a motor vehicle case, it is reasonable to assume that the same standard of "an imminent threat to the lives of others" will likely be applied by the Court in non-motor vehicle cases.

For some, this case may seem to be in conflict with *Brower v. County of Inyo*, 489 U.S. 593 (1989), in Chapter 4. In that case, the Court ruled that when police take steps to terminate the freedom of a person "through means intentionally applied," it is a seizure within the Fourth Amendment. That is consistent with this case. Where some cause for conflict does arise is in what happens next. In *Brower*, the Court ruled that if the police actions were not reasonable, they could be held civilly liable. The Court also indicated that the seizure in this case could be unreasonable, and the police, therefore, liable; although it stopped short of this ruling and remanded to the lower court for this determination. In *Scott*, the Court seemed to create a lower standard for police—such that they could take steps similar to that of *Brower* without creating liability. The difference, however, seems to be in the "legal fiction" of the cases. In *Brower*, the primary question was whether a seizure had occurred—an issue that had not been decided by the Court. The Court there ruled that a seizure did occur (the same as in *Scott*). In *Brower*, there was no primary issue of liability. So, even though the Court commented on it, there was no real ruling on civil liability other than the Court recognizing that, in all seizure cases, if the actions of the officers are unreasonable, liability could ensue. In *Scott*, the second primary issue was whether officers violated a "clearly established constitutional right" that is required for civil liability to attach. The Court ruled that the actions of the officers were not unreasonable in light of the situation and, since the courts differed on similar previous cases, there was no clearly established constitutional right. So, in this case, there was no civil liability. As with many issues in law enforcement, there is no absolute rule on this issue. The best course of action for officers, therefore, is to work to ensure that their actions are reasonable under the law.

PLUMHOFF V. RICKARD
572 U.S. 765 (2014)

CAPSULE: The Fourth Amendment does not prohibit officers from using deadly force to terminate a dangerous car chase, and the officers were entitled to qualified immunity for their conduct because they violated no clearly established law.

FACTS: Officers pulled Rickard over because the car he was driving had only one operating headlight. One officer asked Rickard if he had been drinking, and Rickard responded that he had not. Because Rickard failed to produce his driver's license upon request and appeared nervous, the officer asked him to step out of the car. Rather than comply with the officer's request, Rickard sped away. After a lengthy and high-speed chase, Rickard's car spun off the street and into Plumhoff's patrol car. Officers approached Rickard's car and pounded on the windows while he attempted to free his car and resume the flight. At that point, Plumhoff fired three shots into Rickard's car. Rickard managed to drive away, almost hitting an officer in the process. As Rickard left, officers fired 12 shots toward Rickard's car. Rickard then lost control of the car and crashed into a building. Rickard and his passenger died from some combination of gunshot wounds and injuries suffered in the crash that ended the chase. Rickard's daughter filed a Section 1983 suit against the officers, mayor, and chief of police of West Memphis, alleging that the officers used excessive force in violation of the Fourth and Fourteenth Amendments. The officers' motion for summary judgment based on qualified immunity was denied.

ISSUE: Were the officer's actions in this case a violation of the Fourth Amendment? NO. Were the officers entitled to qualified immunity for their actions? YES.

SUPREME COURT DECISION: "Under the circumstances present in this case, we hold that the Fourth Amendment did not prohibit petitioners from using the deadly force that they employed to terminate the dangerous car chase that Rickard precipitated. In the alternative, we note that petitioners are entitled to qualified immunity for the conduct at issue because they violated no clearly established law."

REASON: "The record conclusively disproves respondent's claim that the chase in the present case was already over when petitioners began shooting. Under the circumstances at the moment when the shots were fired, all that a reasonable police officer could have concluded was that Rickard was intent on resuming his flight and that, if he was allowed to do so, he would once again pose a deadly threat for others on the road. Rickard's conduct even after the shots were fired—as noted, he managed to drive away despite the efforts of the police to block his path—underscores the point." "In light of the circumstances we have discussed, it is beyond serious dispute that Rickard's flight posed a grave public safety risk, and here, as in *Scott* [*v. Harris*], the police acted reasonably in using deadly force to end that risk." "We now consider respondent's contention that, even if the use of deadly force was permissible, petitioners acted unreasonably in firing a total of 15 shots. We reject that argument. It stands to reason that, if police officers are justified in firing at a suspect in order to end a severe threat to public safety, the officers need not stop shooting until the threat has ended." "Here, during the 10-second span when all the shots were fired, Rickard never abandoned his attempt to flee. Indeed, even after all the shots had been fired, he managed to drive away and to continue driving until he crashed. This would be a different case if petitioners had initiated a second round of shots after an initial round had clearly incapacitated Rickard and had ended any threat of continued flight, or if Rickard had clearly given himself up. But that is not what happened." "We have held that petitioners' conduct did not violate the Fourth Amendment, but even if that were not the case, petitioners would still be entitled to summary judgment based on qualified immunity."

CASE SIGNIFICANCE: This case had two substantive parts that are important to law enforcement: whether officers used excessive force and whether they should have been granted qualified immunity. Normally, in cases like this, qualified immunity is the major part of the decision; but the Court in this case specifically singled out the actions of the officers as "'beneficial' in 'develop-[ing] constitutional precedent' in an area that courts typically consider in cases in which the defendant asserts a qualified immunity defense." Here, the Court ruled the officers' conduct was justified. The Court then stated that, regardless of the constitutionality of their actions, the officers were entitled to qualified immunity because their actions did not violate a clearly established law. Based on *Scott v. Harris* (above) and a later *per curiam* decision that supported *Scott*, the Court reasoned that the officers' actions were in line with this case; therefore, they were not in violation of a clearly established law.

COUNTY OF LOS ANGELES, CALIFORNIA, ET AL. V. MENDEZ, ET AL.

581 U.S. ___ (2017)

CAPSULE: The standard for use of force claims is set out in *Graham* as the totality of the circumstances. "An earlier Fourth Amendment violation cannot transform a later, reasonable use of force into an unreasonable seizure."

FACTS: Based on a felony arrest warrant, deputies were searching for a parolee-at-large who was deemed to be armed and dangerous. When officers learned of his presence near a particular house, they planned for a multi-officer search. During the planning, deputies were made aware that Mendez and his wife were living on the property in the back yard. When deputies arrived at the house, three of them knocked on the front door while two went around the back of the house. In that area were three metal storage sheds and a one room wooden shack. The doorway was covered by a blanket. Without a search warrant, officers searched the metal sheds. Without announcing their presence, they then entered the shack, where Mendez and his wife were napping. When the officers entered, Mendez rose up from the bed holding a BB gun he used to kill rodents. One deputy yelled "Gun!" and both deputies opened fire, shooting 15 times. Both Mendez and his wife sustained injuries; with Mendez's leg being amputated below the knee. Mendez and his wife filed suit claiming excessive force. The Ninth Circuit affirmed the lower court's ruling that the force used was constitutional under *Graham*; but that the officers were liable for damages due to the Circuit's "provocation rule," which holds that "an officer's otherwise reasonable (and lawful) defensive use of force is unreasonable as a matter of law, if (1) the officer intentionally or recklessly provoked a violent response, and (2) that provocation is an independent constitutional violation."

ISSUE: "If law enforcement officers make a 'seizure' of a person using force that is judged to be reasonable based on a consideration of the circumstances relevant to that determination, may the officers nevertheless be held liable for injuries caused by the seizure on the ground that they committed a separate Fourth Amendment violation that contributed to their need to use force?" NO.

SUPREME COURT DECISION: "A different Fourth Amendment violation cannot transform a later, reasonable use of force into an unreasonable seizure." "The framework for analyzing excessive force claims is set out in *Graham*. If there is no excessive force claim under Graham, there is no excessive force claim at all. To the extent that a plaintiff has other Fourth Amendment claims, they should be analyzed separately."

REASON: The Ninth Circuit's provocation rule examines all actions leading up to the use of force. If officers "recklessly or purposely" violated a person's rights in the previous actions, the provocation rule would look to see if those actions could have been a proximate cause of the force. If so, officers could be held liable for the force, even though it was reasonable, because of the previous actions. In this case, since the deputies violated Mendez's rights in the warrantless entry and knock-and-announce, they, in effect provoked the confrontation that led to the use of force. The Court provided a statement of why the provocation rule was an "unwarranted and illogical extension of *Graham*." The Court reasoned that the provocation rule only comes into play after the use of force has been deemed reasonable under *Graham*. The Court rejected this thinking, ruling that "A different Fourth Amendment violation cannot transform a later, reasonable use of force into an unreasonable seizure." In confirming the rule of law, the Court stated, "Our case law sets forth a settled and exclusive framework for analyzing whether the force used in making a seizure complies with the Fourth Amendment." Also reaffirming the decision in *Tennessee v. Garner*, the Court stated "The reasonableness of the use of force is evaluated under an 'objective' inquiry that pays 'careful attention to the facts and circumstances of each particular case.' *Graham*, supra, at 396. And '[t]he "reasonableness" of a particular use of force must be judged from the perspective of a reasonable officer on the scene, rather than with the 20/20 vision of hindsight.' *Ibid.*" The Court refused to address the issue of the true proximate cause of the warrantless entry; but did open the door for Mendez to be successful on remand. On that part of the case, the Court stated, "On remand, the court should revisit the question whether proximate cause permits respondents to recover damages for their shooting injuries based on the deputies' failure to secure a warrant at the outset."

SIGNIFICANCE: The Court reiterated the rule of law established in *Graham v. Connor* and other case law. The proper determination of the use of excessive force is the totality of the circumstances at the time of the use of force. There may be proximate causes that can be considered in this determination; but not solely looking at a separate and previous constitutional violation.

What Constitutes Interrogation for *Miranda* Purposes?

INTRODUCTION

The *Miranda* warnings must be given whenever there is a "custodial interrogation." Custodial means the person is under arrest or is deprived of freedom in a significant way. Interrogation means that the suspect is asked questions by the police that tend to link the person to a crime. There are instances in which the police must give the *Miranda* warnings even if no actual interrogation or questioning takes place (*Brewer v. Williams*). In that case, the Supreme Court ruled that the police must give the *Miranda* warnings even if no questioning takes place if the behavior of the police constitutes the functional equivalent of an interrogation, meaning that the behavior is likely to elicit a confession even in the absence of questioning. In *Brewer*, the officers gave the suspect the "Christian burial" speech in which the officer called the suspect "Reverend" and indicated that the parents of the missing girl ought to have the opportunity to give a Christian burial for their child, who had been kidnapped on Christmas Eve. The suspect then confessed. The Court reasoned that, although there was no actual interrogation, the police officers' behavior amounted to the "functional equivalent" of an interrogation because it was likely to elicit a confession.

The Court has held in two subsequent cases that the following instances did not constitute the functional equivalent of an interrogation:

1. When officers, who had the suspect in the backseat of the car, talked between themselves about how terrible it would be if one of the handicapped students from a school near the crime scene were to find a loaded shotgun (supposedly the weapon used in the shotgun robbery of a taxicab driver) and get hurt. This led the suspect to interrupt the police and tell them the location of the shotgun.
2. When the police recorded a conversation, in the presence of an officer, between a suspect and his wife.

In sum, interrogation takes place when the police ask questions of a suspect that tend to link him or her to a crime. There are instances, however, when the *Miranda* warnings must be given even if the police are not asking questions of a suspect, as illustrated in the *Brewer* case.

The leading cases briefed in this chapter on custodial interrogation for *Miranda* purposes are *Brewer v. Williams* and *Rhode Island v. Innis*.

BREWER V. WILLIAMS
430 U.S. 387 (1977)

CAPSULE: Under the *Miranda* rule, interrogations can be "actual" (as when questions are asked) or the "functional equivalent" thereof.

FACTS: The day before Christmas, a 10-year-old girl disappeared from a YMCA building in Des Moines, Iowa. A short time later, Williams, an escapee from a mental hospital and a religious person, was seen leaving the YMCA with a large bundle wrapped in a blanket. A 14-year-old boy who helped him carry the bundle reported that he had seen "two legs in it and they were skinny and white." Williams' car was found the next day in Davenport, 160 miles east of Des Moines. Items of clothing belonging to the missing child and a blanket like the one used to wrap the bundle were found at a rest stop between the YMCA in Des Moines and where the car was found in Davenport. Assuming that the girl's body could be found between the YMCA and the car, a massive search was conducted. Meanwhile, Williams was arrested by police in Davenport and was arraigned. Williams' counsel was informed by the police that Williams would be returned to Des Moines without being interrogated. During the trip, an officer began a conversation with Williams in which he said that the girl ought to be given a Christian burial before a snowstorm, which might prevent the body from being found. As Williams and the officer neared the town where the body was hidden, Williams agreed to take the officer to the child's body. The body was found about two miles from one of the search teams. At the trial, a motion to suppress the evidence was denied and Williams was convicted of first-degree murder.

ISSUE: Was what the police did in talking to Williams about a "Christian burial" the "functional equivalent" of interrogating a suspect without providing him his right to counsel? YES.

SUPREME COURT DECISION: Interrogation takes place, not only when direct questions are asked, but also when, as in this case, the police officers, knowing the defendant's religious interest, make remarks designed to appeal to that interest and therefore induce a confession. In this case, the police officer's "Christian burial" speech was equivalent to an interrogation; therefore, Williams was entitled to the assistance of counsel at that time.

REASON: "There can be no serious doubt ... that Detective Leaming deliberately and designedly set out to elicit information from Williams just as surely as—and perhaps more effectively than—if he had formally interrogated him. Detective Leaming was fully aware before departing from Des Moines that Williams was being represented in Davenport by [lawyer] Kelly and in Des Moines by [lawyer] McKnight. Yet he purposely sought during Williams' isolation from his lawyers to obtain as much information as possible. Indeed Detective Leaming conceded as much when he testified at Williams' trial."

CASE SIGNIFICANCE: There are two important principles for the police in this case. The first is that once a suspect has been formally charged with an offense and has a lawyer, he or she should not be interrogated unless there is a valid waiver or the lawyer is present. The second is that conversations with or appeals to the suspect that may induce a confession constitute an interrogation that then requires both *Miranda* warnings and the right to counsel.

This case declares that "interrogation" by the police does not simply mean asking direct questions. In this case, the police had been told by the lawyers for the suspect that he was not to be interrogated while being transported from Davenport to Des Moines. The police assured the lawyers that Williams would not be interrogated. There was, in fact, no interrogation, but the police officer gave Williams what became known as the "Christian burial speech" in which he addressed Williams as "Reverend" and pleaded that "the parents of this little girl should be entitled to a Christian burial for the little girl who was snatched away from them on Christmas Eve and murdered." The Court concluded that the speech was the functional equivalent of an interrogation and therefore violated the suspect's right to counsel.

RHODE ISLAND V. INNIS
446 U.S. 291 (1980)

CAPSULE: The conversation in this case was merely a dialogue between police officers and did not constitute the "functional equivalent" of an interrogation; hence no *Miranda* warnings were needed.

FACTS: Police arrested Innis for the abduction and killing of a taxicab driver. The officer advised Innis of his *Miranda* rights and did not converse with him. When a sergeant and captain arrived at the scene, Innis was again advised of his *Miranda* rights. He replied that he understood his rights and wanted to speak to an attorney. Innis was placed in a police car to be transported to the police station. En route, two of the officers engaged in a conversation between themselves concerning Innis' shotgun, which had not been recovered. When one of the officers expressed concern that children from a nearby school for the handicapped might find the weapon and hurt themselves, Innis interrupted the conversation, saying that the officers should return to the scene so that he could show them where the shotgun was hidden. Upon returning to the scene, Innis was again advised of his *Miranda* rights. He again stated that he understood his rights but wanted to remove the gun before one of the children found it. He then led the police to the shotgun.

ISSUE: Did the conversation between the two police officers that prompted Innis to lead them to the shotgun constitute a custodial interrogation in the absence of his lawyer? NO.

SUPREME COURT DECISION: "Interrogation" refers not only to express questioning, but also the "functional equivalent" of questioning that involves any words or actions by the police that they should know are reasonably likely to elicit an incriminating response. In this instance, no such interrogation occurred—the conversation was merely a dialog between two police officers; therefore, the evidence obtained by the police was admissible.

REASON: "Here there was no express questioning of respondent; the conversation between the two officers was, at least in form, nothing more than a dialogue between them to which no response from respondent was invited. Moreover, respondent [Innis] was not subjected to the 'functional equivalent' of questioning since it cannot be said that the officers should have known that their conversation was reasonably likely to elicit an incriminating response from respondent. There is nothing in the record to suggest that the officers were aware that respondent [Innis] was peculiarly susceptible to an appeal to his conscience concerning the safety of handicapped children, or that the police knew that respondent was unusually disoriented or upset at the time of his arrest. Nor does the record indicate that, in the context of a brief conversation, the officers should have known that respondent [Innis] would suddenly be moved to make a self-incriminating response."

CASE SIGNIFICANCE: The *Miranda* case held that the *Miranda* warnings must be given whenever a suspect is subjected to "custodial interrogation." Subsequent cases have held that there is interrogation, not only if questions are asked of a suspect, but also if police behavior amounts to the "functional equivalent" of actual questioning (*Brewer v. Williams*). What the police did in this case, however, was not the "functional equivalent" of interrogation. As the Court reasoned, "the conversation between the two officers was, at least in form, nothing more than a dialogue between them to which no response from respondent was invited." It is important for police officers to know that "interrogation" does not necessarily mean asking questions of the suspect. There are situations in which the behavior of the police constitutes the "functional equivalent" of an interrogation (as in *Brewer*), but that was not the case here.

ARIZONA V. MAURO
481 U.S. 520 (1987)

CAPSULE: A conversation between a suspect and his wife, which was recorded in the presence of an officer, did not constitute the "functional equivalent" of an interrogation.

FACTS: The police received a call that a man had just entered a store claiming that he had killed his son. When officers reached the store, Mauro admitted to committing the act and directed officers to the body. He was then arrested and advised of his *Miranda* rights. He was taken to the police station where he was again given the *Miranda* warnings. Mauro told officers that he did not wish to make any more statements until a lawyer was present. At that time, all questioning ceased. Following questioning in another room, Mauro's wife insisted on speaking with him. Police allowed the meeting on the condition that an officer be present and tape the conversation. The tape was used to impeach Mauro's contention that he was insane at the time of the murder.

ISSUE: Does a conversation between a suspect and a spouse that is recorded by an officer constitute an interrogation under *Miranda v. Arizona*? NO.

SUPREME COURT DECISION: A conversation between a suspect and a spouse, which is recorded in the presence of an officer, does not constitute the functional equivalent of an interrogation under *Miranda* or *Rhode Island v. Innis*. Evidence obtained during the conversation is, therefore, admissible in court.

REASON: "The purpose of *Miranda* … is to prevent the government from using the coercive nature of confinement to extract confessions that would not be given in an unrestrained environment. This purpose is not implicated here, since respondent was not subjected to compelling influences, psychological ploys, or direct questioning. There is no evidence that the police allowed the wife to meet with respondent in order to obtain incriminating statements. Moreover, police testimony, which the trial court found credible, indicated a number of legitimate reasons for an officer's presence at the meeting, including the wife's safety and various security considerations. Furthermore, an examination of the situation from respondent's perspective demonstrated the improbability that he would have felt he was being coerced to incriminate himself simply because he was told his wife would be allowed to speak to him."

CASE SIGNIFICANCE: This case further explains the meaning of the term "interrogation" as used in *Miranda*. In an earlier case (*Brewer v. Williams*), the Court held that "interrogation" does not have to mean the actual asking of questions by the police; rather, it includes instances that amount to the "functional equivalent" of interrogation, meaning "words or actions by the police which they know are reasonably likely to elicit an incriminating response." The term "functional equivalent" is subjective and difficult to determine. Whatever its meaning may be, what the police did in this case (allowing the wife to talk with the husband and recording the conversation) was not the "functional equivalent" of an interrogation; hence, anything the suspect said during that conversation could be used against him in court.

CHAVEZ V. MARTINEZ
538 U.S. 760 (2004)

CAPSULE: "Statements compelled by police interrogation may not be used against a defendant in a criminal case, but it is not until such use that the Self-Incrimination Clause is violated."

FACTS: Officers were questioning an individual about suspected drug activity when they heard a bicycle approaching on a darkened path. They ordered the rider, Martinez, to dismount the bicycle, spread his legs, and place his hands behind his head. He complied, and an officer found a knife in his waistband during a pat-down search. An altercation ensued with the police and Martinez was shot several times. Chavez, a patrol supervisor, arrived several minutes later and accompanied Martinez to the hospital. Chavez interviewed Martinez in the hospital while he was receiving medical treatment. The interview lasted 10 minutes over a 45-minute period, with Chavez leaving the emergency room periodically to allow medical personnel to attend to Martinez. During the interview, Martinez admitted to taking a gun from one of the officer's holsters, and he admitted to heroin use. At one point, Martinez stated "I am not telling you anything until they treat me," but Chavez nonetheless continued the interview. At no point was Martinez given his *Miranda* warnings. Martinez was never charged with a crime and his answers were never used against him in any criminal prosecution. Martinez filed a Section 1983 suit against Chavez, claiming his Fifth and Fourteenth Amendment rights were violated by the interrogation.

ISSUE: Do statements taken in violation of *Miranda* violate the Fifth Amendment protection against self-incrimination even if they are not used in a criminal trial? NO.

SUPREME COURT DECISION: "Statements compelled by police interrogation may not be used against a defendant in a criminal case, but it is not until such use that the Self-Incrimination Clause is violated." Therefore, the police in this case are not liable under Section 1983 because no constitutional right of the suspect was violated.

REASON: In this case, the Court reemphasized that statements made in violation of the Fifth Amendment cannot be used against the person in legal proceedings, "but it is not until their use in a criminal case that a violation of the Self-Incrimination Clause occurs. ... Here, Martinez was never made to be a 'witness' against himself in violation of the Fifth Amendment's Self-Incrimination Clause because his statements were never admitted as testimony against him in a criminal case." The Court stated that, although conduct by police prior to trial may cause the constitutional violation (such as taking an illegal confession), it is not until the trial itself that the privilege applies. The Court argued that there are several instances where witnesses can be compelled to testify without violating the Fifth Amendment, such as testifying before a grand jury or the compelled testimony of a witness who has been granted immunity. "Even for persons who have a legitimate fear that their statements may subject them to criminal prosecution, we have long permitted the compulsion of incriminating testimony so long as those statements (or evidence derived from those statements) cannot be used against the speaker in any criminal case." Turning specifically to the facts here, the Court held, "the fact that Martinez did not know his statements could not be used against him does not change our view. ... [and] Chavez's failure to read *Miranda* warnings to Martinez did not violate Martinez's constitutional rights and cannot be the grounds for a Section 1983 action." The Court further stated "our views on the proper scope of the Fifth Amendment's Self-Incrimination Clause do not mean that police torture or other abuse that results in a confession is constitutionally permissible so long as the statements are not used at trial ...." What the Court ruled here was simply that the officer's conduct did not interfere with Martinez's medical attention to a level where it constituted a violation of Martinez's constitutional right.

CASE SIGNIFICANCE: This case is best understood as a Section 1983 civil liability case for a possible violation of a suspect's constitutional right. A Section 1983 case, filed by a plaintiff primarily seeking monetary compensation from a police officer, succeeds only if there is a proven violation of a constitutional right or of a right guaranteed by federal law. The suspect in this case filed a Section 1983 case alleging his constitutional privilege against self-incrimination was violated when he was not given the *Miranda* warnings and the interrogation continued despite his telling the police that "I am not telling you anything until they treat me." The Court held that "mere compulsive questioning" by the police does not violate the Constitution, neither does police questioning constitute a criminal case. It is true that statements compelled through police interrogation cannot be used against a defendant in a criminal trial, "but it is not until such use that the Self-Incrimination Clause is violated." The Court concluded that "failure [by the police] to read *Miranda* warnings to Martinez did not violate Martinez's constitutional rights and cannot be grounds for a Section 1983 action. And the absence of a 'criminal case' in which Martinez was compelled to be a witness against himself defeats his core Fifth Amendment claim."

DAVIS V. WASHINGTON
547 U.S. 813 (2006)

CAPSULE: "Statements are nontestimonial [and therefore admissible in court] when made in the course of police interrogation under circumstances objectively indicating that the primary purpose of interrogation is to enable police assistance to meet an ongoing emergency."

FACTS: After a call and hang-up to 911, the operator reversed the call and Michelle McCottry answered. Based on questioning McCottry, the operator determined she was involved in a domestic disturbance with her former boyfriend, Davis. The operator learned that Davis had just left in a car with another person after hitting McCottry. Officers arrived and observed the injuries to McCottry but had no way to determine the cause of the injuries. Davis was later charged with violating a domestic no-contact order. Over Davis' objection, the 911 tape was admitted into evidence and he was convicted. Davis appealed his conviction, saying that his constitutional right to cross-examination was violated by the admission of the tape-recording into evidence because there was no opportunity to cross-examine.

ISSUE: Are statements made to law enforcement personnel during a 911 call or at a crime scene "testimonial" and thus subject to the requirements of the Sixth Amendment's right to cross-examination and confrontation? NO.

SUPREME COURT DECISION: "Statements are nontestimonial [and therefore admissible in court] when made in the course of police interrogation under circumstances objectively indicating that the primary purpose of interrogation is to enable police assistance to meet an ongoing emergency."

REASON: "The Confrontation Clause of the Sixth Amendment provides: 'In all criminal prosecutions, the accused shall enjoy the right ... to be confronted with the witnesses against him.' In *Crawford v. Washington*, 541 U.S. 36, 53–54 (2004), we held that this provision bars 'admission of testimonial statements of a witness who did not appear at trial unless he was unavailable to testify, and the defendant had had a prior opportunity for cross-examination.' A critical portion of this holding, and the portion central to resolution of the two cases now before us, is the phrase 'testimonial statements.' Only statements of this sort cause the declarant to be a 'witness' within the meaning of the Confrontation Clause. See *id.*, at 51. It is the testimonial character of the statement that separates it from other hearsay that, while subject to traditional limitations upon hearsay evidence, is not subject to the Confrontation Clause." "A 911 call ... and at least the initial interrogation conducted in connection with a 911 call, is ordinarily not designed primarily to 'establis[h] or prov[e]' some past fact, but to describe current circumstances requiring police assistance." "We conclude from all this that the circumstances of McCottry's interrogation objectively indicate its primary purpose was to enable police assistance to meet an ongoing emergency. She simply was not acting as a *witness*; she was not *testifying*." (Emphasis in original.)

CASE SIGNIFICANCE: This is an important case in police work because it holds that tape-recordings of calls to the police may be admissible in court during trial as evidence as long as they are nontestimonial. Every day the police, through the 911 service, receive all kinds of calls that are recorded, including those that may be incriminating to the accused. Davis claimed that admitting the recording violated his right to cross-examination because the taped evidence could not be cross-examined. The Court rejected that claim, ruling that for purposes of admissibility as evidence in court, a distinction should be made between nontestimonial and testimonial evidence. Nontestimonial statements recorded through 911 are admissible, whereas testimonial statements are not.

Confessions and Admissions: Cases Affirming *Miranda*

18

INTRODUCTION

By any standard, *Miranda* is a landmark case in policing. It has had a lasting and pervasive influence on police investigations, and is the best-known case in law enforcement. The *Miranda* rule holds that evidence obtained by the police during custodial interrogation of a suspect is not admissible in court to prove guilt unless the suspect was given the *"Miranda* warnings" and there was a valid waiver by the suspect. There are, of course, exceptions to this rule.

Miranda is important because it changed the way courts determine the admissibility of an admission or confession obtained from an in-custody suspect. Prior to *Miranda*, the test for admissibility was whether the admission or confession was voluntary or involuntary, on a case-by-case basis. In contrast, under *Miranda*, the test consists of three questions: (1) Were the *Miranda* warnings given by the police? (2) Was there a waiver by the suspect? (3) If there was a waiver, was the waiver voluntary and intelligent? If the answer to all three questions is "yes," the admission or confession is admissible. Conversely, if the answer to any of the questions is "no," the evidence is not admissible.

Miranda warnings must be given whenever there is a custodial interrogation. That phrase is best understood if discussed as two separate requirements. Custodial means the suspect is under arrest or is deprived of his or her freedom in a significant way. Interrogation denotes that the suspect is asked questions by the police that are likely to elicit an incriminating response (typically linking the suspect to a crime).

As the cases briefed in this chapter indicate, subsequent cases have affirmed the *Miranda* rule. Arguably, the most significant of these cases is *Edwards v. Arizona*, in which the Supreme Court held that an accused who, after having been given the *Miranda* warnings, invokes the right to remain silent and to have a lawyer present, cannot be interrogated further for the same crime until a lawyer is made available. In *Berkemer v. McCarty*, the Court held that the

Miranda rule applies to felony and misdemeanor offenses. The only type of interrogation in which the *Miranda* warnings are not required is the roadside questioning of a motorist detained pursuant to a routine traffic stop.

Dickerson v. United States is important because it holds that *Miranda* governs the admissibility in federal and state courts of confessions and admissions and that any law passed by Congress that seeks to overturn the *Miranda* decision is unconstitutional. This is a significant decision because it affirms that the *Miranda* warnings are required by the Constitution and are not simply judge-made rules.

Aside from *Miranda*, the other important cases in this chapter on Confessions and Admissions: Cases Affirming *Miranda* are *Edwards v. Arizona*, *Berkemer v. McCarty*, and *Dickerson v. United States*.

BROWN V. MISSISSIPPI
297 U.S. 278 (1936)

CAPSULE: Confessions obtained as a result of coercion and brutality are not admissible in court.

FACTS: A deputy sheriff and others went to Brown's home and asked him to accompany them to the house of a deceased person. While there, Brown was accused of the murder. When he denied the accusation, he was hanged by the neck from a tree limb, let down, and hanged again. Persisting in his claim of innocence, he was tied to a tree and whipped, but was later released. Several days later, the same deputy returned to Brown's home and arrested him. On the way to the jail, Brown was again beaten by the deputy, who said he would continue beating Brown until Brown confessed. Brown did confess and was held in jail. Two other suspects were taken to the same jail. There they were forced to strip by the same deputy and others and were laid over chairs where they were whipped with a leather strap with a buckle on it. When they finally confessed, the officers left, saying that if they changed their story they would be whipped again. The next day the three were brought before the sheriff and others, at which time they confessed to the crimes. Trial began the next day. The suspects testified that the confessions were false and were obtained by torture. The rope marks on the suspects' necks were clearly visible and none of the participants in the beatings denied they had taken place. The suspects were convicted of murder and sentenced to death.

ISSUE: Are confessions obtained by brutality and torture by law enforcement officers a violation of the due process rights guaranteed by the Fourteenth Amendment? YES.

SUPREME COURT DECISION: Confessions obtained as a result of coercion and brutality by law enforcement officers violate the due process clause of the Fourteenth Amendment and are therefore inadmissible in court.

REASON: "The State is free to regulate the procedure of its courts in accordance with its own conceptions of policy, unless in so doing it 'offends some principle of justice so rooted in the traditions and conscience of our people as to be ranked fundamental.' ... [T]he freedom of the State in establishing its policy is the freedom of constitutional government and is limited by the requirement of due process of law. Because a State may dispense with a jury trial, it does not follow that it may substitute trial by ordeal. The rack and torture chamber may not be substituted for the witness stand. The State may not permit an accused to be hurried to conviction under mob domination—where the whole proceeding is but a mask—without supplying corrective process."

CASE SIGNIFICANCE: This case was decided by the Court in 1936, before the Fifth Amendment right against self-incrimination was made applicable to the states. Instead of using the Fifth Amendment, the Court used the due process clause of the Fourteenth Amendment because the Fourteenth Amendment has always applied to state criminal proceedings. This case renders inadmissible in court any evidence obtained as a result of physical torture. The methods used by the law enforcement officers in *Brown* were extreme, hence it was easy to prohibit their use. Subsequently, the Court ruled that any type of physical coercion was also prohibited. Still later, even psychological coercion was prohibited. All of these culminated in *Miranda v. Arizona* (see below), in which the test for admissibility shifted from voluntariness to one of "were *Miranda* warnings given?" *Brown* represents the first case in which evidence obtained as a result of physical torture in a state court criminal proceeding was held inadmissible by the Supreme Court. If a case similar to *Brown* were decided today, the evidence would be excluded based on the exclusionary rule and not on the Fourteenth Amendment due process clause.

MIRANDA V. ARIZONA
384 U.S. 436 (1966)

CAPSULE: Evidence obtained by the police during custodial interrogation of a suspect is not admissible in court to prove guilt unless the suspect was given the *Miranda* warnings and there is a valid waiver.

FACTS: Miranda was arrested at his home and taken to a police station for questioning in connection with a rape and kidnapping. Miranda was 23 years old, poor, and had completed only one-half of the ninth grade. The officers interrogated him for two hours, in which time they obtained a written confession.

ISSUE: Must the police inform a suspect who is subject to a custodial interrogation of his or her constitutional rights involving self-incrimination and right to counsel prior to questioning? YES.

SUPREME COURT DECISION: Evidence obtained by the police during a custodial interrogation of a suspect cannot be used in court unless the suspect was informed of the following rights prior to the interrogation:

1. the right to remain silent
2. that any statement made can and will be used against him or her in a court of law
3. the right to have an attorney present during questioning
4. if the suspect cannot afford an attorney, one will be appointed for him or her prior to questioning.

REASON: "The Fifth Amendment privilege is so fundamental to our system of constitutional rule and the expedient of giving an adequate warning as to the availability of the privilege so simple, we will not pause to inquire in individual cases whether the defendant was aware of his rights without a warning being given. Assessments of the knowledge the defendant possessed, based on information as to his age, education, intelligence, or prior contact with authorities, can never be more than speculation; a warning is a clear-cut fact. More important, whatever the background of the person interrogated, a warning at the time of the interrogation is indispensable to overcome its pressures and to ensure that the individual knows he is free to exercise the privilege at that point in time. ... The warning of the right to remain silent must be accompanied by the explanation that anything said can and will be used against the individual in court. This warning is needed in order to make him aware not only of the privilege, but also of the consequences of forgoing it. It is only through an awareness of these consequences that there can be any assurance of real understanding and intelligent exercise of the privilege. Moreover, this warning may serve to make the individual more acutely aware that he is faced with a phase of the adversary system—that he is not in the presence of persons acting solely in his interest." "The circumstances surrounding in-custody interrogation can operate very quickly to overbear the will of one merely made aware of his privilege by his interrogators. Therefore, the right to have counsel present at interrogation is indispensable to the protection of the Fifth Amendment privilege under the system we delineate today. Our aim is to assure the individual's right to choose between silence and speech remains unfettered throughout the interrogation process ...." "We have concluded that without proper safeguards the process of in-custody interrogation of persons suspected or accused of crime contains inherently compelling pressures which work to undermine the individual's will to resist and to compel him to speak where he would not otherwise do so freely. In order to combat these pressures and to permit a full opportunity to exercise the privilege against self-incrimination, the accused must be adequately and effectively apprised of his rights and the exercise of those rights must be fully honored."

CASE SIGNIFICANCE: *Miranda v. Arizona* is, arguably, the most widely known case ever to be decided by the U.S. Supreme Court. It also has had the deepest influence on day-to-day police work, and has led to changes that have since become an accepted part of routine police procedure. No other law enforcement case has generated more controversy inside and outside police circles. Supporters of the *Miranda* decision hail it as properly protective of individual rights, whereas critics have accused the Supreme Court of being soft on crime and coddling criminals. The 5–4 split among the justices served to fan the flames of the controversy in its early stages, with opponents of the ruling hoping that a change in Court composition would hasten its demise. That has not happened, and neither is it likely to happen in the immediate future. *Miranda* has survived the test of time and, although cases have eroded the influence of *Miranda*, a complete overruling, even by a conservative Court, appears remote.

Miranda is unique in that seldom does the Court tell the police exactly what ought to be done. In this case, the court literally told police what warnings should be given if the evidence obtained from a custodial interrogation is to be admitted in court. *Miranda* also clarified some of the ambiguous terms used in *Escobedo v. Illinois*, 378 U.S. 478 (1964). "By custodial interrogation," stated the Court, "we mean questioning initiated by law enforcement officers after a person has been taken into custody or otherwise deprived of his freedom of action in any significant way." It then added in a footnote: "This is what we meant in *Escobedo* when we spoke of an investigation which had focused on an accused." Yet the "focus" test was abandoned by the Court in later cases, preferring to use the "custodial interrogation" test to determine whether the *Miranda* warnings needed to be given. The *Escobedo* case brought the right to counsel to the police station prior to trial; the *Miranda* case went beyond the police station and brought the right to counsel out into the street if a custodial interrogation is to take place.

EDWARDS V. ARIZONA
451 U.S. 477 (1981)

CAPSULE: An accused who, after having been given the *Miranda* warnings, invokes the right to remain silent and to have a lawyer present, cannot be interrogated further by the police until a lawyer is made available.

FACTS: Edwards was arrested pursuant to a warrant. At the police station, he was read his *Miranda* warnings and indicated that he understood them and would answer questions. After being informed that an accomplice had made a sworn statement implicating him, Edwards sought to "make a deal," but later changed his mind and said that he wanted to speak to an attorney before making a deal. At that point questioning ceased. The next morning, two other officers went to the jail and asked to see Edwards. Edwards told the detention officer that he did not wish to speak to the officers; but was told that he had no choice in the matter. Edwards was again informed of his *Miranda* rights. He indicated that he would talk but first wanted to hear the taped statement of the accomplice. After listening to the statement, Edwards made a statement implicating himself in the crime.

ISSUE: If a suspect has been given the *Miranda* warnings and invokes the right to remain silent or to have counsel, may that suspect be later interrogated by the police if the *Miranda* warnings are given again? NO.

SUPREME COURT DECISION: An accused who, after having been given the *Miranda* warnings, invokes the right to silence and to have a lawyer, cannot be interrogated further by the police until a lawyer has been made available. An exception to this rule is if the accused initiates further communication, exchanges, or conversations with the police.

REASON: "We think it clear that Edwards was subjected to custodial interrogation on January 20 within the meaning of [*Rhode Island v.*] *Innis* and that this occurred at the insistence of the authorities. His statement, made without having access to counsel, did not amount to a valid waiver and hence was inadmissible." "When an accused asks for counsel, a valid waiver of that right cannot be established by showing only that he responded to further police-initiated custodial interrogation, even if he has been advised of his rights. We further hold that an accused, such as Edwards, having expressed his desire to deal with the police only through counsel, is not subject to further interrogation by the authorities until counsel has been made available to him, unless the accused himself initiates further communication, exchanges, or conversations with the police."

CASE SIGNIFICANCE: The principle is clear: once a suspect invokes his or her rights after having been given the *Miranda* warnings, interrogation must cease. Further, the police cannot later interrogate the suspect again, even with another reading of the *Miranda* warnings, until the suspect has been provided with a lawyer. If the suspect, however, on his or her own, initiates further communication or conversation with the police, the confession will be admissible. In such instances, there is a need for the suspect to be given the *Miranda* warnings again.

BERKEMER V. MCCARTY
468 U.S. 420 (1984)

CAPSULE: The *Miranda* rule applies to misdemeanor offenses. It does not apply to the roadside questioning of a motorist detained pursuant to a routine traffic stop.

FACTS: After following McCarty's car for two miles and observing it weave in and out of a lane, an officer stopped the car and asked McCarty to get out of the vehicle. McCarty had difficulty standing while getting out of the car. The officer decided that McCarty would be charged with a traffic offense, thus terminating his freedom to leave the scene. McCarty was not told he would be taken into custody, but was required to take a field sobriety test, which he failed. While still at the scene of the stop, McCarty was asked whether he had been using any intoxicants, to which he replied that he had consumed two beers and several marijuana cigarettes. McCarty was then formally arrested and taken to jail. A test given to McCarty to determine his blood-alcohol level did not detect any alcohol. The officer resumed the questioning, in which McCarty admitted to consuming alcohol. At no point was McCarty given *Miranda* warnings. McCarty pleaded no contest and was found guilty of operating a motor vehicle while under the influence.

ISSUES:

1. Must *Miranda* warnings be given when interrogating in-custody suspects charged with misdemeanor traffic offenses? YES.
2. Does the roadside questioning of a motorist detained for a traffic violation constitute a custodial interrogation under *Miranda v. Arizona*? NO.

SUPREME COURT DECISIONS:

1. A person subjected to custodial interrogation must be given *Miranda* warnings regardless of the nature or severity of the offense.
2. The roadside questioning of a motorist detained pursuant to a routine traffic stop does not constitute a custodial interrogation, hence no *Miranda* warnings need be given.

REASON: "In the years since the decision in *Miranda*, we have frequently reaffirmed the central principle established by that case: if the police take a suspect into custody and then ask him questions without informing him of the rights enumerated above, his responses cannot be introduced into evidence to establish his guilt." "Petitioner asks us to carve an exception out of the foregoing principle. When the police arrest a person for allegedly committing a misdemeanor traffic offense and then ask him questions without telling him his constitutional rights, petitioner argues his responses should be admissible against him. We cannot agree."

"One of the principal advantages of the doctrine that suspects must be given warnings before being interrogated while in custody is the clarity of that rule. … The exception to *Miranda* proposed by petitioner would substantially undermine this crucial advantage of the doctrine. The police often are unaware when they arrest a person whether he may have committed a misdemeanor or a felony."

"Two features of an ordinary traffic stop mitigate the danger that a person questioned will be induced 'to speak where he would not otherwise do so freely.' *Miranda v. Arizona*, 384 U.S. at 476. First, detention of a motorist pursuant to a traffic stop is presumably temporary and brief. The vast majority of roadside detentions last only a few minutes. ... Second, circumstances associated with the typical traffic stop are not such that the motorist feels completely at the mercy of the police."

CASE SIGNIFICANCE: This case settles two legal issues that had long divided lower courts. The first part of the decision made clear that once a suspect has been placed under arrest for any offense, be it a felony or a misdemeanor, the *Miranda* warnings must be given before interrogation. It is a rule that is easier for the police to follow than the requirement of determining whether the arrest is for a felony or a misdemeanor before giving the warning. The Court argued that the purpose of the *Miranda* warnings, which is to ensure that the police do not coerce or trick captive suspects into confessing, is applicable equally to misdemeanor or felony cases. The second part of the decision is equally important in that it identifies an instance in which the warnings need not be given. There is no custodial interrogation in a traffic stop because it is usually brief and the motorist expects that, although he or she may be given a citation, in the end the motorist will most likely be allowed to continue on his or her way. However, if the motorist who has been temporarily detained is later arrested, the *Miranda* warnings must be given if an interrogation then is to take place.

ARIZONA V. ROBERSON
486 U.S. 675 (1988)

CAPSULE: An accused who has invoked the right to counsel may not be subjected to a police-initiated interrogation even if the interrogation concerns a different crime.

FACTS: After being arrested at the scene of a burglary, Roberson was advised of his *Miranda* rights and indicated that he wanted to speak to a lawyer before answering any questions. Three days later, while Roberson was still in custody, a different officer, unaware of Roberson's request for counsel, gave him the *Miranda* warnings and interrogated him concerning a different burglary. Roberson made incriminating statements concerning the crime.

ISSUE: If an accused has invoked the right to counsel, may the police, after giving the *Miranda* warnings again, interrogate the same suspect about a different crime? NO.

SUPREME COURT DECISION: An accused who has invoked the right to counsel may not be subjected to a police-initiated interrogation even if the interrogation concerns a different crime.

REASON: "The *Edwards* rule applies to bar police-initiated interrogation following a suspect's request for counsel in the context of a separate investigation." "The bright-line prophylactic *Edwards* rule benefits the accused and the State alike. It protects against the inherently compelling pressures of custodial interrogation [on] suspects who feel incapable of undergoing such questioning without the advice of counsel, by creating a presumption that any subsequent waiver of the right to counsel at the authorities' behest was coercive and not purely voluntary. Moreover, it provides clear and unequivocal guidelines that inform police and prosecutors with specificity what they may do in conducting custodial interrogation, and that inform courts under what circumstances statements obtained during interrogation are not admissible."

CASE SIGNIFICANCE: *Edwards v. Arizona*, 451 U.S. 477 (1981), held that if an accused asks for counsel after having been given the *Miranda* warnings, that accused cannot be further interrogated by the police. This case differs from *Edwards* in that the interrogation was for a different offense. Nonetheless, the Court held that the rule is the same: an accused who had invoked the right to counsel may not be subjected to police interrogation again, even if it is for a different offense. Although the Court did not explicitly say so, it may be assumed that the exception in *Edwards*, in which interrogations are allowed if the suspect initiates the communication or conversation, also applies to interrogations for a different offense.

MINNICK V. MISSISSIPPI
498 U.S. 146 (1990)

CAPSULE: Once a suspect requests a lawyer, the interrogation must stop— whether the suspect confers with the lawyer or not.

FACTS: Minnick and a fellow prisoner, Dyess, escaped from a jail in Mississippi and broke into a mobile home in search of weapons. In the course of the burglary, they were interrupted by the arrival of the owner, another man, and an infant. Dyess and Minnick used the stolen weapons to kill the two adults. Dyess and Minnick ultimately split up and Minnick was arrested in California. The day following his arrest, Minnick was told that he would have to talk to FBI agents. After being read his *Miranda* warnings, Minnick refused to sign a waiver form but made statements to the agents. After making incriminating statements, the agents reminded Minnick of his *Miranda* rights, at which time Minnick stated "come back Monday when I have a lawyer" and that he would make a more complete statement then. After the FBI interview, an appointed attorney met with Minnick on two or three occasions, although it is unclear whether all of these conferences were in person. Two days later, a deputy from Mississippi arrived to question Minnick. Minnick was again told that he would have to talk to the deputy and that he could not refuse. The deputy advised Minnick of his rights and he again declined to sign a waiver. Minnick did, however, describe the escape and subsequent murders. At trial, Minnick moved to suppress all statements made while in custody. The court suppressed statements made to the FBI because Minnick had not been afforded counsel, but refused to suppress statements made to the deputy.

ISSUE: Once a person invokes *Miranda* rights, can the police initiate an interrogation once counsel has been appointed but is not present during questioning? NO.

SUPREME COURT DECISION: Once a suspect requests a lawyer, the interrogation must stop—whether the defendant confers with the lawyer or not. The Fifth Amendment is violated when the suspect requests a lawyer, is given an opportunity to confer with a lawyer, and then is forced to talk with the police without the lawyer being present. Prior consultation with the lawyer is not enough. The lawyer must be present at all subsequent questioning; otherwise, the evidence obtained is not admissible.

REASON: The decision in *Edwards v. Arizona* strengthened *Miranda* by mandating that, once a person invokes his or her rights under *Miranda*, the police cannot initiate further interrogations until counsel has been made available to the person. The lower courts in this case interpreted that to mean that, once counsel has been appointed, police could initiate an interrogation and, if the person waived his or her *Miranda* privileges, statements could be taken and used in court. The Supreme Court disagreed, stating "a fair reading of *Edwards* and subsequent cases demonstrates that we have interpreted the rule to bar police-initiated interrogation unless the accused has counsel with him at the time of questioning. ... We decline to remove protection from police-initiated questioning based on isolated consultations with counsel who is absent when the interrogation resumes. ... [T] he need for counsel to protect the Fifth Amendment privilege comprehends not merely a right to consult with counsel prior to questioning, but also to have counsel present during any questioning."

CASE SIGNIFICANCE: This case is an extension of *Edwards v. Arizona*. This case, decided nine years later, holds that once a lawyer is assigned, the police cannot force the suspect to answer questions without the lawyer being present, even though there was prior opportunity for the suspect to talk with the lawyer. It is a strict rule aimed at making the *Miranda* rights more meaningful. The fact that the suspect had the opportunity to confer with the lawyer or that consultation with the lawyer did in fact take place does not give the police authority to ask the suspect questions again. If they want to ask the suspect questions, the lawyer must be present—otherwise, the evidence obtained is not admissible in court. In sum, the rule is: once the suspect invokes the right to have a lawyer, the police must cease interrogation and not initiate it again. The only exceptions are if the suspect initiates such conversation or if the lawyer is present.

ARIZONA V. FULMINANTE
499 U.S. 279 (1991)

CAPSULE: A finding of coercion need not depend on actual violence by a government agent; a credible threat is sufficient to make a confession involuntary.

FACTS: Fulminante was suspected of having murdered his stepdaughter. His statements to the police concerning her disappearance were inconsistent, but no charges were filed against him. Fulminante left Arizona for New Jersey, where he was later convicted on an unrelated federal charge of possession of a firearm. While incarcerated in a federal prison in New York, Fulminante was befriended by a fellow inmate, Sarivola, who was serving a 60-day sentence for extortion. Sarivola later became a paid informant for the FBI. Sarivola told Fulminante that he knew Fulminante was getting tough treatment from the other inmates because of a rumor that he was a child murderer. Sarivola offered Fulminante protection in exchange for the truth. Fulminante admitted to Sarivola that he had driven his stepdaughter "to the desert on his motorcycle, where he choked her, sexually assaulted her, and made her beg for her life, before shooting her twice in the head." After Fulminante's release from prison, he also confessed to Sarivola's wife about the same crime. Fulminante was indicted in Arizona for first-degree murder. He sought to exclude the confession to Sarivola, alleging that it was coerced and thus barred by the due process clauses of the Fifth and Fourteenth Amendments. He also challenged his confession to Sarivola's wife as "fruit" of the first confession. Both confessions were admitted by the trial court. Fulminante was convicted and sentenced to death.

ISSUES: Was Fulminante's confession coerced because he was fearful of violence in prison? YES.

SUPREME COURT DECISION: Fulminante's confession was coerced because it was motivated by a fear of physical violence if he were not to be protected by Sarivola.

REASON: "Although the question is a close one, we agree with the Arizona Supreme Court's conclusion that Fulminante's confession was coerced. The Arizona Supreme Court found a credible threat of physical violence unless Fulminante confessed. Our cases have made clear that a finding of coercion need not depend upon actual violence by a government agent; a credible threat is sufficient."

CASE SIGNIFICANCE: This case raised a number of issues on which the justices were sharply divided; one of which was an issue related to the courts (harmless error), which is not discussed here. On the issue of whether Fulminante's confession was coerced, the Court agreed with the finding of the Arizona courts that "Sarivola's promise was extremely coercive," and that "the confession was obtained as a direct result of extreme coercion and was tendered in the belief that the defendant's life was in jeopardy if he did not confess." Because the confession was coerced, it could not be admissible in court. This case is important to law enforcement because it extended the possibility of a coerced confession to that based on a threat of violence. Furthermore, the violence does not have to come from the police; it can come from any source—such as the threat of harm in prison as in this case. So, police should be careful that there is no perceived threat of coercion or violence if statements are to be admissible in court.

DICKERSON V. UNITED STATES
530 U.S. 428 (2000)

CAPSULE: *Miranda v. Arizona* governs the admissibility in federal and state courts of confessions and admissions given during custodial interrogation by the police. Any law passed by Congress that seeks to overturn the *Miranda* decision is unconstitutional.

FACTS: Dickerson was arrested and made incriminating statements to police. Before his trial, he moved to suppress the statements because he had not received his *Miranda* warnings prior to being interrogated. His statements were voluntary, but they were made without having been given the *Miranda* warnings. The Federal District Court granted the motion to suppress, but the Court of Appeals overturned it, stating that 18 U.S.C. Section 3501, passed by Congress in response to the *Miranda* decision, prevailed and only required a finding by a court that the confession was given voluntarily. 18 U.S.C. Section 3501 was passed by Congress in 1966, right after the *Miranda* decision came out, but the constitutionality of that law never reached the United States Supreme Court because it was not enforced by the federal government—up until this case. That law sought to overturn the Court's decision in *Miranda* by providing that the admissibility of confessions and admissions in federal court is determined by whether or not they were voluntarily made, not by whether or not they complied with the *Miranda* warnings.

ISSUE: Is a law passed by Congress seeking to overturn the United States Supreme Court ruling in *Miranda v. Arizona* constitutional? NO.

SUPREME COURT DECISION: *Miranda v. Arizona* governs the admissibility in federal and state courts of statements given during custodial interrogation by the police. Any law passed by Congress seeking to overturn the *Miranda* decision is unconstitutional because it is a constitutional rule, not a rule of evidence.

REASON: "Congress retains the ultimate authority to modify or set aside any judicially created rules of evidence and procedure that are not required by the Constitution." "But Congress may not legislatively supersede our decisions interpreting and applying the Constitution. This case therefore turns on whether the *Miranda* Court announced a constitutional rule or merely exercised its supervisory authority to regulate evidence in the absence of congressional direction." "[W]e conclude that *Miranda* announced a constitutional rule that Congress may not supersede legislatively."

CASE SIGNIFICANCE: This is a highly significant case because it settled an important issue: whether the *Miranda* decision continues to govern the admissibility of confessions and admissions or whether it could be negated by laws passed by Congress or by state legislatures. The Court held that *Miranda* is a constitutional rule, not just a rule of evidence, and therefore it cannot be undone by legislation. The *Miranda* decision is here to stay, unless overturned by the Court itself. Had the decision been otherwise, federal cases would have been governed by the provisions of the federal law. Some state legislatures would likely have passed similar legislation, causing the admissibility of statements to be governed by different rules. This is significant because, since the *Miranda* decision came out in 1966, scholars have debated whether or not *Miranda* is a constitutional rule that could not be superseded by legislation or whether it was merely a rule of evidence. The Court in *Dickerson* settled that controversy, concluding that *Miranda* is a constitutional rule unless overturned by the Court. It cannot be superseded by legislation passed by Congress or state legislatures. This case reaffirms the authority of *Miranda v. Arizona*.

KAUPP V. TEXAS
538 U.S. 626 (2003)

CAPSULE: A confession must be suppressed if obtained during a detention where officers did not have probable cause for an arrest and where the detention amounted to the functional equivalent of an arrest.

FACTS: Officers investigating the disappearance of a girl focused on her half-brother and Kaupp. Her half-brother ultimately confessed to killing her, and implicated Kaupp in the murder. Because the brother failed a polygraph test three times and Kaupp had passed his polygraph, officers did not believe they had probable cause for an arrest warrant based solely on the brother's confession. An attempt to get a "pocket warrant" to question Kaupp was also refused by the prosecutor. At least three officers then went to Kaupp's home at 3:00 A.M. and, after his father let them in, went to his bedroom, awakened him with a flashlight, and told him "we need to go and talk." Kaupp was then handcuffed and taken, dressed only in a T-shirt and boxer shorts, to a patrol car. After going to the scene where the body had been recovered, officers then took him to the sheriff's office. There, Kaupp was taken to an interview room where the handcuffs were removed and he was read his *Miranda* warnings. After initially denying any involvement in the crime, he ultimately admitted to having some part, although he did not confess to the murder for which he was later tried. In rejecting Kaupp's motion to suppress his confession, the court held that Kaupp consented to go with the officers when he answered "Okay" when the officers told him "we need to go and talk." The court also agreed with the police that handcuffing was for officer safety and was routine, and that Kaupp did not resist the use of handcuffs or act in other uncooperative ways.

ISSUE: May a confession be admitted in evidence when obtained after officers create a situation where a reasonable person would not have felt free to leave and where the police had no probable cause for an arrest? NO.

SUPREME COURT DECISION: A confession must be suppressed if it is obtained during a detention where officers did not have probable cause for an arrest and where the detention amounted to the functional equivalent of an arrest.

REASON: The Court in this case relied on a number of previous holdings to reinforce the legal factors that represent the functional equivalent of an arrest. Addressing Kaupp's reply of "Okay" to the officers, the Court stated "there is no reason to think Kaupp's answer was anything more than 'a mere submission to a claim of lawful authority,'" and in no way implied consent. The Court also stated that "as for lack of resistance, failure to struggle with a cohort of deputy sheriffs is not a waiver of the Fourth Amendment protection." Again relying on previous cases, the Court stated that, "'at some point in the investigative process, police procedures can qualitatively and quantitatively be so intrusive with respect to a suspect's freedom of movement and privacy interests as to trigger the full protection of the Fourth and Fourteenth Amendments.' It cannot seriously be suggested that when the detectives began to question Kaupp, a reasonable person in his situation would have thought he was sitting in the interview room as a matter of choice, free to change his mind and go home to bed." Finally, the Court noted that "although certain seizures may be justified on something less than probable cause, see, e.g., *Terry v. Ohio*, 392 U.S. 1 (1968), we have never 'sustained against Fourth Amendment challenge the involuntary removal of a suspect from his home to a police station and his detention there for investigative purposes ... absent probable cause or judicial authorization.'"

The Court concluded, "since Kaupp was arrested before he was questioned, and because the state does not even claim that the sheriff's department had probable cause to detain him at that point, well-established precedent requires suppression of the confession."

CASE SIGNIFICANCE: The significance of this case lies in its further clarification of what constitutes an arrest when the perceptions of the police and the suspect differ. In this case, a 17-year-old boy was asked by the police to go with them to the police station because "we need to talk." The suspect answered, "Okay," which the police interpreted to mean consent. Ten or fifteen minutes into the interrogation at the police station, the defendant implicated himself. The police maintained that the suspect was not under arrest at the time he confessed; therefore, the evidence was admissible. The Court rejected that, ruling that "a seizure of the person within the meaning of the Fourth and Fourteenth Amendments occurs when, 'taking into account all of the circumstances surrounding the encounter, the police conduct would have communicated to a reasonable person that he was not at liberty to ignore the police presence and go about his business.'"

FELLERS V. UNITED STATES
540 U.S. 519 (2004)

CAPSULE: The proper standard to be used when determining whether statements made by a defendant after an indictment are admissible in court is the Sixth Amendment right to counsel, not the Fifth Amendment privilege against self-incrimination.

FACTS: After a grand jury indicted Fellers, officers went to his home to arrest him. While there, after he invited them in, they told Fellers they had come to discuss his involvement in drug distribution, that they had a warrant for his arrest, and that he had been indicted. They then asked Fellers questions concerning the involvement of others in drug distribution. Fellers made incriminating statements concerning other individuals and his involvement with them. Officers then took Fellers to the police station, where he was advised of his *Miranda* rights and signed a waiver of those rights. Fellers reiterated his previous statements and made other statements concerning his involvement in drugs.

ISSUE: What standard should be used to determine the admissibility of statements given to the police after a suspect has been indicted—the Sixth Amendment right to counsel standard or the Fifth Amendment self-incrimination standard?

SUPREME COURT DECISION: The proper standard to determine whether statements made after an indictment should be admitted is the

Sixth Amendment protection of right to counsel, not the Fifth Amendment protection against self-incrimination.

REASON: The issue in this case was whether the actions of the officers at Fellers' home were something that could be waived pursuant to *Oregon v. Elstad*, 470 U.S. 298 (1985), or whether it was a Sixth Amendment violation. To address this, the Court stated, "The Sixth Amendment right to counsel is triggered 'at or after the time that judicial proceedings have been initiated ... whether by way of formal charge, preliminary hearing, indictment, information, or arraignment.' We have held that an accused is denied 'the basic protections' of the Sixth Amendment 'when there [is] used against him at his trial evidence of his own incriminating words, which federal agents ... deliberately elicited from him after he had been indicted and in the absence of his counsel.'" (Internal citations omitted.)

Concluding that the Sixth Amendment applied in this case, the Court stated, "there is no question that the officers in this case 'deliberately elicited' information from petitioner. Indeed, the officers, upon arriving at petitioner's house, informed him that their purpose in coming was to discuss his involvement. ... Because the ensuing discussion took place after petitioner had been indicted, outside the presence of counsel, and in the absence of any waiver of petitioner's Sixth Amendment rights ...," the statements made violated the Sixth Amendment.

CASE SIGNIFICANCE: The defendant in this case claimed that his Sixth Amendment right to counsel and his Fifth Amendment *Miranda* rights were both violated when the statements he made at his home and later at the police station were used against him. Fellers was under indictment when both questionings took place. If the Fifth Amendment privilege against self-incrimination were to be used as the standard for admissibility, then his statement while in custody would have been admissible because he was given the *Miranda* warnings and had waived his Fifth Amendment privilege before giving the confession. However, he claimed that the in-custody statement was nonetheless inadmissible because it violated his Sixth Amendment right to counsel in that it was the "fruit" of an unlawful interrogation at his home and therefore should be excluded even if he was given the *Miranda* warnings. The Court agreed, arguing that, in previous cases "this Court has consistently applied the deliberate-elicitation standard in subsequent Sixth Amendment cases ... and has expressly distinguished it from the Fifth Amendment custodial-interrogation standard." It then added that "there is no question here that the officers 'deliberately elicited information from Fellers at his home.' Because the police officers interrogated Fellers at home without counsel after he was indicted, the absence of his lawyer made his statement in his home inadmissible. Therefore, the subsequent statement in jail was also inadmissible because it was 'fruit of the poisonous tree.'" The lesson for the police in this case is: once a suspect has been indicted and has a lawyer, the police must refrain from interrogating the suspect even after giving the

Miranda warnings. The *Miranda* warnings may make the statement admissible under the Fifth Amendment protection against self-incrimination, but the same statement may be inadmissible because it violates the Sixth Amendment right to counsel.

MISSOURI V. SEIBERT
542 U.S. 600 (2004)

CAPSULE: Giving the *Miranda* warnings after the police purposefully obtain an unwarned confession violates the *Miranda* rule; therefore, statements made even after the *Miranda* warnings are given are not admissible in court even if they repeat those given before the *Miranda* warnings.

FACTS: Seibert's son had cerebral palsy. When he died in his sleep, Seibert feared charges of neglect because of bedsores on his body. In her presence, two of her teenaged sons and two of their friends planned to burn the family's mobile home to conceal the death of the son. They also planned to leave a mentally ill teenager who was living with the family in the mobile home to avoid the appearance that the son had been left alone. In the fire, the mentally ill teenager died. Five days later, the police awoke Seibert at 3:00 A.M. in the hospital where one of her sons was being treated for burns. She was arrested and taken to the police station. The officer making the arrest was told not to read her the *Miranda* warnings. At the station, Seibert was left in an interrogation room for about 20 minutes and then she was interrogated for about 40 minutes without being read her *Miranda* warnings. After she admitted she knew the teenager was meant to die in the fire, she was given a 20-minute break. The officer then turned on a tape recorder, gave Seibert the *Miranda* warnings, obtained a signed waiver of rights, and then resumed the interrogation. At the beginning of the interrogation, the officer confronted Seibert with her pre-warning statements and essentially walked her back through the statements she made prior to her *Miranda* warnings. At a suppression hearing to exclude the statements, the officer admitted he made a conscious decision to withhold the *Miranda* warnings based on an interrogation technique he was taught by police trainers— which was to question first, give the warnings, then repeat the questioning "until I get the answer she's already provided once."

ISSUE: Are statements made after a suspect is given the *Miranda* warnings that repeat a statement given when officers intentionally did not give *Miranda* warnings admissible in court? NO.

SUPREME COURT DECISION: Giving the *Miranda* warnings after an interrogation and an unwarned confession has intentionally first been obtained by the police does not effectively comply with *Miranda*'s constitutional requirement, even if it repeats the statements made before the warnings were given; therefore, statements obtained are not admissible in court.

REASON: "The object of question-first is to render *Miranda* warnings ineffective by waiting for a particularly opportune time to give them, after the suspect has already confessed. ... The threshold issue when interrogators question first and warn later is thus whether it would be reasonable to find that in these circumstances the warnings could function effectively as *Miranda* requires. Could the warnings effectively advise the suspect that he had a real choice about giving an admissible statement at that juncture? Could they reasonably convey that he could choose to stop talking even if he had talked earlier? For unless the warnings could place a suspect who has just been interrogated in a position to make such an informed choice, there is no practical justification for accepting the formal warnings as compliance with *Miranda*, or for treating the second state of interrogation as distinct from the first, unwarned and inadmissible segment. ... By any objective measure, applied to the circumstances exemplified here, it is likely that if the interrogators employ the technique of withholding warnings until after interrogation succeeds in eliciting a confession, the warnings will be ineffective in preparing the suspect for successive interrogations, close in time and similar in content. ... Upon hearing the warnings only in the aftermath of interrogation and just after making a confession, a suspect would hardly think he had a genuine right to remain silent, let alone persist in so believing once the police began to lead him over the same ground again. ... Thus, when the *Miranda* warnings are inserted in the midst of coordinated and continuing interrogation, they are likely to mislead and 'depriv[e] a defendant of knowledge essential to his ability to understand the nature of his rights and the consequences of abandoning them' *Moran v. Burbine*, 475 U.S. 412 (1986)."

CASE SIGNIFICANCE: The Court in this case struck down an established practice in some police departments. In an earlier case, *Oregon v. Elstad*, 470 U.S. 298 (1985), the Court admitted a confession obtained after the police gave the *Miranda* warnings—even though the suspect had previously made statements before the warnings were given. This practice was subsequently used by police training organizations, such as the Police Law Institute, in what became known as the "question-first" technique of interrogation. In this procedure, police first interrogate a person without the *Miranda* warnings. Once a confession is obtained, the *Miranda* warnings are then given, the officer resumes the interrogation, and obtains a warned confession similar to the unwarned confession that was given. In *Seibert*, the Court held this practice violated *Miranda* and therefore held the evidence inadmissible.

The Court indicated that there were several distinctions between this case and *Elstad* (where the evidence obtained was admissible despite a prior unwarned statement). These included "the completeness and detail of the question and answers in the first round of interrogation, the overlapping content of the two statements, the timing and setting of the first and the second statements, the continuity of police personnel, and the degree to which the interrogator's questions treated the second round as continuous with the first." The overriding consideration in these types of "two-interrogation" cases is whether the two interrogations (the unwarned and the warned) can be seen as separate and distinct interrogations where a reasonable person would believe he or she is free to disregard the first and assert his or her rights on the second. In the *Seibert* case, the Court stated, "At the opposite extreme are the facts here [as opposed to the facts in the *Elstad* case], which by any objective measure reveal a police strategy adapted to undermine the *Miranda* warnings. The unwarned interrogation was conducted at the stationhouse, and the questioning was systematic, exhaustive, and managed with psychological skill. When the police were finished there was little, if anything, of incriminating potential left unsaid. The warned phase of questioning proceeded after a pause of only 15 to 20 minutes, in the same place as the unwarned segment. When the same officer who had conducted the first phase recited the *Miranda* warnings, he said nothing to counter the probable misimpression that the advice that anything Seibert said could be used against her also applied to the details of the inculpatory statement previously elicited. In particular, the police did not advise that her prior statement could not be used."

The end result is that the issue of whether a subsequent warned admission or confession is admissible after the suspect has given an unwarned admission or confession depends on the facts and circumstances of the case. If the facts and circumstances are closer to *Elstad*, the statement may be admissible, but if they are closer to *Seibert*, the statement may not be admissible.

MONTEJO V. LOUISIANA
556 U.S. 778 (2009)

CAPSULE: "When a court appoints counsel for an indigent defendant in the absence of any request on his part, there is no basis for a presumption that any subsequent waiver of the right to counsel will be involuntary."

FACTS: Montejo was arrested for robbery and murder. Montejo waived his *Miranda* rights and was interrogated at the sheriff's office. He ultimately admitted he killed the victim in a botched burglary. Three days later, Montejo was brought before a judge in a preliminary hearing, and the court ordered the Office of Indigent Defender be appointed to represent him. Later that day, officers went to the jail and requested Montejo to accompany them to find the murder weapon. After some discussion, he waived his *Miranda* rights and agreed to accompany the officers. During the ride, he wrote an inculpatory letter of apology to the widow. Only after returning did Montejo meet with his attorney. At trial, the letter was admitted over defense objection that it violated the precedent set forth in *Michigan v. Jackson*, 475 U.S. 625 (1986) that "if police initiate interrogation after a defendant's assertion, at an arraignment or similar proceeding, of his right to counsel, any waiver of the defendant's right to counsel for that police-initiated interrogation is invalid," 475 U.S., at 636. The Louisiana Supreme Court, relying on a federal circuit of appeals decision, reasoned that the Sixth Amendment was not triggered unless the defendant requested a lawyer or otherwise invoked his Sixth Amendment right; otherwise, the proper inquiry was whether he knowingly, intelligently, and voluntarily waived his rights under *Miranda*. Because Montejo did not speak at his arraignment, he did not specifically ask for an attorney, so the court looked to his *Miranda* waiver as prevailing.

ISSUE: Must courts presume that following appointment of counsel in the absence of any request on the part of the defendant, any waiver is invalid? NO.

SUPREME COURT DECISION: "When a court appoints counsel for an indigent defendant in the absence of any request on his part, there is no basis for a presumption that any subsequent waiver of the right to counsel will be involuntary." *Michigan v. Jackson*, 475 U.S. 625 (1986) is overruled.

REASON: The Court took the time in this case to review the rules of the states and found them to vary widely in whether a defendant had to assert his or her right to counsel or not. An additional problem in establishing a nationwide, bright-line rule, is that "police who did not attend the hearing would have no way to know whether they could approach a particular defendant." The Court stated unequivocally that, once adversarial proceedings have begun, defendants have the right to counsel at all "critical stages" of the process—interrogation by police being one of those stages. The Court also noted that the right to counsel may be waived by a voluntary, knowing, and intelligent waiver (*Miranda*). The rule that police may not contact a person once he or she invoked Miranda protections was established in *Edwards v. Arizona*. The Court noted that "*Jackson* represented a 'wholesale importation of the Edwards rule into the Sixth Amendment'" waivers. Here, the Court reasoned that "*Edwards* and *Jackson* are meant to prevent police from badgering defendants into changing their minds about their rights, but a defendant who never asked for counsel has not yet made up his mind in the first instance."

CASE SIGNIFICANCE: This case was born from great confusion over when police may approach a suspect after arraignment, where some states required an affirmative action on the part of the defendant and some did not. Montejo argued that Jackson held that it would not matter whether the defendant requested assistance of counsel for police to be prevented from asking the defendant to talk and administering *Miranda* warnings. The Court ruled that this made *Jackson* too broad and that it did not automatically apply. Further, the Court ruled that, even if a defendant had been appointed counsel, a valid *Miranda* waiver would overcome that invocation. While the relationship between a request for right to counsel and subsequent requests by police is still somewhat unclear, it would appear that a valid waiver of *Miranda* should allow police that opportunity. Once a defendant has invoked the *Miranda* protections, however, *Edwards* should be the prevailing rule, and police should not re-approach the defendant.

MARYLAND V. SHATZER
559 U.S. 96 (2010)

CAPSULE: Once a suspect invokes his or her *Miranda* rights, a break in custody of more than 14 days overcomes the *Edwards* rule and allows officers to re-contact the suspect for interrogation.

FACTS: In 2003, a police detective attempted to question Shatzer, who was in prison on a different conviction, about allegations that he sexually abused his son. Shatzer invoked his *Miranda* rights, so the detective terminated the interview and closed the investigation. Shatzer was released back into the general prison population. Because of new information, the case was reopened in 2006. A different detective again attempted to interview Shatzer, who was still incarcerated. This time, Shatzer waived his *Miranda* rights and made statements incriminating himself. After making the statements, Shatzer asked for an attorney and the detective ended the interview. The trial court refused to suppress the statements over Shatzer's argument that *Edwards v. Arizona*, 451 U.S. 477 (1981) prevented officers from re-interviewing Shatzer without an attorney present. The court held *Edwards* did not apply because Shatzer had experienced a break in *Miranda* custody between the 2003 and 2006 interviews.

ISSUE: Does a break in custody end the presumption of involuntariness established in *Edwards*? YES.

SUPREME COURT DECISION: "Because Shatzer experienced a break in *Miranda* custody lasting more than two weeks between the first and second attempts at interrogation, *Edwards* does not mandate suppression of his March 2006 statements."

REASON: In *Edwards v. Arizona* the Court created a presumption that once a suspect invokes *Miranda* rights, any waiver of those rights can only come from the suspect. If the police attempt a subsequent custodial interrogation, it is presumed to be involuntary. In *Shatzer*, the Court reiterated that *Edwards*' "fundamental purpose is to '[p]reserv[e] the integrity of an accused's choice to communicate with police only through counsel,' *Patterson v. Illinois*, 487 U.S. 285, 291 (1988), by 'prevent[ing] police from badgering a defendant into waiving his previously asserted *Miranda* rights,' [*Michigan v.*] *Harvey*, [494 U.S. 344, 350 (1990)]." In *Edwards*, the Court reasoned that a suspect's subsequent waiver was considered coerced if the suspect had been held uninterrupted in custody since the first refusal because "he remains cut off from his normal life and companions, 'thrust into' and isolated in an 'unfamiliar,' 'police-dominated atmosphere,' *Miranda*, 384 U.S., at 456–457, where his captors 'appear to control [his] fate,' *Illinois v. Perkins*, 496 U.S. 292, 297 (1990)." However, when "a suspect has been released from his pretrial custody and has returned to his normal life for some time before the later attempted interrogation, there is little reason to think that his change of heart regarding interrogation without counsel has been coerced." If a break in custody did not terminate *Edwards*, police would be prevented from ever interviewing a suspect who has invoked *Miranda*, even if they knew nothing of the invocation and the later crime was completely removed from the earlier one. As a result "[w]e conclude that such an extension of *Edwards* is not justified; we have opened its 'protective umbrella,' *Solem* [*v. Helm*] 463 U.S. [277], at 644, n. 4, far enough. The protections offered by *Miranda*, which we have deemed sufficient to ensure that the police respect the suspect's desire to have an attorney present the first time police interrogate him, adequately ensure that result when a suspect who initially requested counsel is reinterrogated after a break in custody that is of sufficient duration to dissipate its coercive effects."

CASE SIGNIFICANCE: The extension of *Edwards* to *Miranda* mandated that, once a suspect invoked his or her *Miranda* rights, police could not initiate another interview, even for another crime, without the suspect's attorney present. The only way a subsequent interview could take place was if the suspect initiated the contact with police. This prevented police from badgering a suspect with repeated requests for interviews while the suspect was still in custody, but also often prevented police from interviewing the suspect in wholly unrelated cases and where the request for an interview was separated by time. The Court ruled in this case that a break in custody of 14 days is sufficient to dissipate *Edwards*, reasoning that it "provides plenty of time for the suspect to get reacclimated to his normal life, to consult with friends and counsel, and to shake off any residual coercive effects of his prior custody." This case was somewhat complicated because Shatzer remained in prison between the interviews, but the Court reasoned that "when previously incarcerated suspects are released back into the general prison population, they return to their accustomed surroundings and daily routine. ... Their continued detention is relatively disconnected from their prior unwillingness to cooperate in an investigation." Therefore, Shatzer's release back into the general prison population constituted a sufficient break in *Miranda* custody.

J.D.B. V. NORTH CAROLINA
564 U.S. 261 (2011)

CAPSULE: A child's age must be considered as a factor in deciding issues of custody and *Miranda* warnings.

FACTS: J.D.B., 13 years old, was stopped and questioned concerning two burglaries when he was observed behind one of the houses in the neighborhood. Later that week, he was removed from his classroom by a uniformed police officer, escorted to a conference room, and questioned by police and school officials for 30–45 minutes. J.D.B.'s guardian was not informed of the questioning. J.D.B. was given neither *Miranda* warnings nor the opportunity to speak to his guardian; nor was he told he was free to leave the room. At one point, J.D.B. asked if he would still be in trouble if he returned the stolen items. J.D.B. eventually confessed to the break-ins. At that point, the officer told J.D.B. that he could refuse to answer questions and he was free to leave. When the officer asked if he understood, J.D. B. nodded. He then provided further detail about the break-ins and wrote a statement at the officer's request.

ISSUE: Is the age of a child subjected to police questioning relevant to the custody analysis of *Miranda v. Arizona*? YES.

SUPREME COURT DECISION: "It is beyond dispute that children will often feel bound to submit to police questioning when an adult in the same circumstances would feel free to leave. Seeing no reason for police officers or courts to blind themselves to that commonsense reality, we hold that a child's age properly informs the *Miranda* custody analysis."

REASON: Citing *Miranda v. Arizona* (see above), the Court began by recognizing that "[b]y its very nature, custodial police interrogation entails 'inherently compelling pressures.'" The Court reasoned that this type of environment can "compel him to speak where he would not otherwise do so freely." The Court relied on research concerning confessions indicating that custodial interrogation can cause people to confess to crimes they never committed, and that the pressure and the potential for false confessions are even worse for juveniles. Again returning to *Miranda*, the Court reiterated that "if a suspect makes a statement during custodial interrogation, the burden is on the Government to show, as a 'prerequisit[e]' to the statement's admissibility ... that the defendant 'voluntarily, knowingly and intelligently' waived his rights." Turning to the question of the context of age in legal issues, the Court noted "'[o]ur history is replete with laws and judicial recognition' that children cannot be viewed simply as miniature adults. We see no justification for taking a different course here. So long as the child's age was known to the officer at the time of the interview, or would have been objectively apparent to any reasonable officer, including age as part of the custody analysis requires officers neither to consider circumstances 'unknowable' to them, nor to 'anticipat[e] the frailties or idiosyncrasies' of the particular suspect whom they question." (Internal citations omitted.) The Court concluded that, in most circumstances, a child's age affects "how a reasonable person in the suspect's position would perceive the ability to leave," stating "[t]hat is, a reasonable child subjected to police questioning will sometimes feel pressured to submit when a reasonable adult would feel free to go." Based on this analysis, the Court concluded that J.D.B.'s age was a relevant factor.

CASE SIGNIFICANCE: Some police agencies had been relying on a secondary decision in *Yarborough v. Alvarado*, 541 U.S. 652 (2004), stating "The state court's failure to consider Alvarado's age and inexperience does not provide a proper basis for finding that the state court's decision was an unreasonable application of clearly established law." Many had taken this ruling to mean that the Court was holding that age should not be considered in *Miranda* and custody analyses. The Court in this case made it clear, however, that age is a factor to be considered. The Court turned to research indicating that juveniles had a high likelihood of making false confessions due to the pressures of custodial interrogation (see Drizin, S. and Leo, R., The Problem of False Confessions in the Post-DNA World, 82 *N.C.L. Rev.*, 891, 906–907 [2004]). The Court was also clear, however, that age is not a deciding factor, stating "This does not mean that a child's age will be a determinative, or even a significant, factor in every case, but it is a reality that courts cannot ignore." In cases where it is obvious that the interrogation will be of a young person, proper steps should be taken to ensure the spirit of *Miranda* is followed.

Confessions and Admissions: Cases Weakening *Miranda*

INTRODUCTION

Since 1966, when *Miranda* was decided, the Supreme Court has continued to refine the *Miranda* rule—either affirming or weakening it by determining instances in which the *Miranda* rule does or does not apply. The *Miranda* case, decided by a 5-to-4 vote, was intensely controversial in the law enforcement community when it was decided. Over the years, however, reservations about the adverse effects of *Miranda* in police work diminished. At present, its acceptance is assured even among those who administer it. The *Miranda* rule has become an integral part of policing.

That does not mean, however, that *Miranda* has stood as originally decided. Over the years, the Supreme Court has decided cases detailing when *Miranda* warnings are not necessary (e.g. when there is concern for public safety, as decided in *New York v. Quarles*) and has otherwise diminished the strict rule of *Miranda* (i.e., the warnings need not be given in the exact form as worded in *Miranda*). This chapter briefs some of the more significant cases that, in various ways, eroded the strict rule of *Miranda*.

The leading cases briefed in this chapter on Confessions and Admissions: Cases Weakening *Miranda* are *New York v. Quarles*, *Oregon v. Elstad*, and *Duckworth v. Eagan*. A more recent significant case, *Salinas v. Texas* (2013), held that a suspect in an interrogation must expressly invoke the privilege against self-incrimination. It is not enough to simply remain silent in response to officers' questions.

SOUTH DAKOTA V. NEVILLE
459 U.S. 553 (1983)

CAPSULE: The admission into evidence of a suspect's refusal to submit to a blood-alcohol test does not violate the suspect's privilege against self-incrimination.

FACTS: South Dakota law directed a person suspected of driving while intoxicated to submit to a blood-alcohol test and authorized revocation of the driver's license of any person who refused to take the test. The statute permitted such refusal to be used against the driver as evidence of guilt during the trial. Neville was arrested for driving while intoxicated. He was asked to submit to a blood-alcohol test and warned that he could lose his license if he refused to take the test. He was not warned, however, that the refusal could be used against him during trial. Neville refused to take the test. During trial, Neville sought to exclude the evidence obtained, claiming that it violated his right to protection against compulsory self-incrimination.

ISSUE: Does a state law that allows the admission into evidence of a suspect's refusal to submit to a blood-alcohol test violate the suspect's Fifth Amendment right against self-incrimination? NO.

SUPREME COURT DECISION: The admission into evidence of a defendant's refusal to submit to a blood-alcohol test does not violate the suspect's Fifth Amendment right against self-incrimination. A refusal to take such a test, after a police officer has lawfully requested it, is not an act coerced by the officer, and thus is not protected by the Fifth Amendment. A law that allows the accused to refuse to take a blood-alcohol test and provides that such refusal may be admitted in evidence against him or her is constitutional.

REASON: "The simple blood-alcohol test is so safe, painless, and commonplace that respondent concedes, as he must, that the state could legitimately compel the suspect, against his will, to accede to the test. Given, then, that the offer of taking a blood-alcohol test is clearly legitimate, the action becomes no less legitimate when the State offers a second option of refusing the test, with the attendant penalties for making that choice. Nor is this a case where the State has subtly coerced respondent into choosing the option it had no right to compel, rather than offering a true choice. To the contrary, the State wants respondent to choose to take the test, for the inference of intoxication arising from a positive blood-alcohol test is far stronger than that arising from a refusal to take the test. ... We recognize, of course, that the choice to submit or refuse to take a blood-alcohol test will not be an easy or pleasant one for a suspect to make. But the criminal process often requires suspects and defendants to make difficult choices. We hold, therefore, that a refusal to take a blood-alcohol test, after a police officer has lawfully requested it, is not an act coerced by the officer, and thus is not protected by the privilege against self-incrimination."

CASE SIGNIFICANCE: This case legitimizes the practice, established by law in many states, of giving suspected DWI offenders a choice to take or refuse blood-alcohol tests, but to use the refusal as evidence of guilt later in court. The defendant in this case argued that introducing such evidence in court, in effect, coerces the suspect to waive constitutional protection against self-incrimination because of the consequence. The Court rejected this contention, arguing that any incrimination resulting from a blood-alcohol test is physical in nature, not testimonial, and hence is not protected by the Fifth Amendment; therefore, a suspect has no constitutional right to refuse to take the test. The Court reasoned that the offer to the suspect to take the test is clearly legitimate and becomes no less legitimate when the state offers the option of refusing the test but prescribes consequences for making that choice. The Court added that the failure by the police to warn Neville that his refusal to take the test could be used as evidence against him during the trial was not so fundamentally unfair as to deprive him of "due process" rights. The evidence obtained was, therefore, admissible during trial.

NEW YORK V. QUARLES
467 U.S. 649 (1984)

CAPSULE: Concern for public safety represents an exception to the *Miranda* rule.

FACTS: Officers were approached by a woman claiming that she had just been raped by an armed man. She described him and said that he had entered a nearby supermarket. The officers drove the woman to the supermarket and one officer went in while the other radioed for assistance. The officer in the supermarket quickly spotted Quarles, who matched the description provided by the woman, and a chase ensued. The officer ordered Quarles to stop and place his hands over his head. The officer frisked Quarles and discovered an empty shoulder holster. After handcuffing Quarles, the officer asked him where the gun was. Quarles nodded in the direction of some empty cartons and responded, "the gun is over there." The gun was retrieved from the cartons and Quarles was placed under arrest and read his *Miranda* warnings. Quarles indicated that he would answer questions without an attorney present and admitted that he owned the gun.

ISSUE: Were the suspect's initial statements and the gun admissible in evidence despite the failure of the officer to give him the *Miranda* warnings prior to asking questions that led to the discovery of the gun? YES.

SUPREME COURT DECISION: Responses to questions asked by a police officer that are reasonably prompted by concern for public safety are admissible in court even though the suspect was in police custody and was not given the *Miranda* warnings.

REASON: "We hold that on these facts there is a 'public safety' exception to the requirement that *Miranda* warnings be given before a suspect's answers may be admitted into evidence, and that the availability of that exception does not depend upon the motivation of the individual officers involved. In a kaleidoscopic situation such as the one confronting these officers, where spontaneity rather than adherence to a police manual is necessarily the order of the day, the application of the exception which we recognize today should not be made to depend on post hoc findings at a suppression hearing concerning the subjective motivation of the arresting officer. Undoubtedly most police officers, if placed in Officer Kraft's position, would act out of a host of different, instinctive, and largely unverifiable motives—their own safety, the safety of others, and perhaps as well the desire to obtain incriminating evidence from the suspect."

CASE SIGNIFICANCE: *New York v. Quarles* carves out a "public safety" exception to the *Miranda* rule. The Supreme Court argued that the case presents a situation in which concern for public safety must be paramount to adherence to the literal language of the rules enunciated in *Miranda*. Here, although Quarles was in police custody and therefore should have been given the *Miranda* warnings, concern for public safety prevailed. In this case, reasoned the Court, the gun was concealed somewhere in the supermarket and therefore posed more than one danger to the public. The Court hinted, however, that the "public safety" exception needs to be interpreted narrowly, and added that police officers can and will distinguish almost instinctively between questions necessary to secure their own safety or the safety of the public and questions designed solely to elicit testimony evidence from a suspect.

OREGON V. ELSTAD
470 U.S. 298 (1985)

CAPSULE: A confession made after proper *Miranda* warnings and waiver of rights is admissible even if the police obtained an earlier voluntary but unwarned admission from the suspect.

FACTS: Officers went to a burglary suspect's home with a warrant for his arrest. Elstad's mother answered the door and led the officers to her son's room. One officer waited with Elstad while the other explained his arrest to the mother. The officer told Elstad that he was implicated in the burglary, to which he responded "Yes, I was there." Elstad was then taken to the police station where he was advised of his *Miranda* rights for the first time. Elstad indicated that he understood his rights and wanted to talk to the officers. He then made a full statement that was typed, reviewed, and read back to Elstad for corrections, then signed by the officer and Elstad.

ISSUE: Do voluntary but unwarned statements made prior to *Miranda* warnings render all subsequent statements inadmissible under the Fifth Amendment's protection from self-incrimination? NO.

SUPREME COURT DECISION: If a confession is made after proper *Miranda* warnings and waiver of rights, the Fifth Amendment does not make it inadmissible solely because the police obtained an earlier voluntary but unwarned admission from the suspect that was not admissible.

REASON: "Far from establishing a rigid rule, we direct courts to avoid one; there is no warrant for presuming coercive effect where the suspect's initial inculpatory statement, though technically in violation of *Miranda*, was voluntary. The relevant inquiry is whether, in fact, the second statement was also made voluntarily. As in any such inquiry, the finder of fact must examine the surrounding circumstances and the entire course of police conduct with respect to the suspect in evaluating the voluntariness of his statements. The fact that a suspect chooses to speak after being informed of his rights is, of course, highly probative. We find that the dictates of *Miranda* and the goals of the Fifth Amendment proscription against use of compelled testimony are fully satisfied in the circumstances of this case by barring the use of the unwarned statement in the case in chief. No further purpose is served by imputing 'taint' to subsequent statements obtained pursuant to a voluntary and knowing waiver."

CASE SIGNIFICANCE: This case weakens the *Miranda* doctrine by holding that "a suspect who has once responded to unwarned yet noncoercive questioning is not thereby disabled from waiving his or her rights and confessing after he or she has been given the requisite *Miranda* warnings." The suspect in this case alleged that the "statement he made in response to questioning at his house (without *Miranda* warnings) 'let the cat out of the bag,' ... and tainted the subsequent confessions as 'fruit of the poisonous tree.'" In most cases, the courts have held that any evidence obtained as a result of an illegal act by the police is inadmissible in court because it is, indeed, fruit of the poisonous tree. Such was not the case here, however, because while the statement "Yes, I was there" from Elstad was inadmissible because it was in response to a police question asked before the *Miranda* warnings were given, such an act by the police was not, in itself, illegal. As long as subsequent facts prove that the second statement, after *Miranda* warnings were given, was valid, the fact that no warnings were given earlier does not render the second statement inadmissible. The police should note, however, that the rule still holds that if the police commit an illegal act, any evidence obtained as a result of that illegal act is inadmissible as "fruit of the poisonous tree." See also *Missouri v. Seibert* in the previous chapter for illegal police activity directly related to this case that does render the statements inadmissable in court.

COLORADO V. CONNELLY
479 U.S. 157 (1986)

CAPSULE: Statements made when the mental state of the defendant interfered with his "rational intellect" and "free will" are not automatically excludable. Their admissibility is governed by state rules of evidence.

FACTS: Connelly approached a police officer and confessed that he had murdered someone and wanted to talk to the officer about it. The officer advised Connelly of his *Miranda* rights. Connelly indicated that he understood his rights and wanted to talk about the murder. After a homicide detective arrived, Connelly was again advised of his *Miranda* rights and again indicated that he understood them and still wanted to speak with the police. Connelly was then taken to the police station, where he made a full statement of the facts, and agreed to take the officers to the scene of the murder. When he became visibly disoriented, he was sent to a state hospital where, in an interview with a psychiatrist, Connelly revealed that he was following the advice of God in confessing to the murder. He was found incompetent to assist in his own defense but competent to stand trial.

ISSUE: Is a suspect's waiver of the *Miranda* rights valid even for statements made when the suspect was not fully rational? YES.

SUPREME COURT DECISION: The admissibility of statements made when the mental state of the defendant interfered with his "rational intellect" and "free will" is governed by state rules of evidence rather than previous court decisions regarding coerced confessions and the *Miranda* waivers. Such evidence therefore is not automatically excluded; its admissibility instead depends upon state rules.

REASON: "We have ... observed that 'jurists and scholars have recognized that the exclusionary rule imposes a substantial cost on the societal interest in law enforcement by its proscription of what concededly is relevant evidence.' ... Moreover, suppressing respondent's statements would serve absolutely no purpose in enforcing constitutional guarantees. The purpose of excluding evidence seized in violation of the Constitution is to substantially deter future violations of the Constitution. ... Only if we were to establish a brand new constitutional right—the right of a criminal defendant to confess to his crime only when totally rational and properly motivated—could respondent's present claim be sustained."

CASE SIGNIFICANCE: The Supreme Court indicated in this case that confessions and admissions are involuntary and invalid under the Constitution only if coercive police activity is involved. If the waiver is caused by anything other than police behavior, admissibility of the confession should depend on the state's rules of evidence. It is clear in this case that the *Miranda* warnings were repeatedly given and that there was a waiver. Such waiver, however, was later challenged as involuntary because it was promoted by the "voice of God." The Court held that this was not sufficient to render the waiver involuntary because the police did not act improperly or illegally. As long as police behavior is legal, a waiver is considered voluntary under the Constitution and its admissibility is governed by state law. This means that if state law allows its admissibility, such evidence can be used.

CONNECTICUT V. BARRETT
479 U.S. 523 (1987)

CAPSULE: A suspect's oral confession is admissible even if the suspect tells the police that he or she will not make a written statement without a lawyer present.

FACTS: Barrett was arrested in connection with a sexual assault. On arrival at the police station, Barrett was advised of his *Miranda* rights and signed a statement acknowledging he understood his rights. Barrett stated that he would not give a written statement in the absence of counsel, but that he would talk to the police about the incident. In two subsequent interrogations, Barrett was again advised of his rights and signed a statement of understanding. On both occasions he gave an oral statement admitting his involvement in the assault but refused to make a written statement. Because of a malfunction in the tape recorder, an officer reduced the confession to writing based on his recollection of the conversation.

ISSUE: Is there a valid waiver of the *Miranda* rights if a defendant requests assistance of counsel and refuses to make written statements, but makes oral statements voluntarily to the police? YES.

SUPREME COURT DECISION: The oral confession made by a suspect is admissible as evidence in court even if the suspect told the police he would talk with them but would not make a written statement without a lawyer present. The waiver of *Miranda* rights by Barrett is valid because he was not "threatened, tricked, or cajoled" into speaking to the police.

REASON: "Respondent's statements to the police made it clear his willingness to talk about the sexual assault, and, there being no evidence that he was 'threatened, tricked, or cajoled' into speaking to the police, the trial court properly found that his decision to do so constituted a voluntary waiver of his right to counsel. Although the *Miranda* rules were designed to protect defendants from being compelled by the government to make statements, they also gave defendants the right to choose between speech and silence."

"Respondent's invocation of his right to counsel was limited by its terms to the making of written statements, and did not prohibit all further discussions with the police. Requests for counsel must be given broad, all-inclusive effect only when the defendant's words, understood as ordinary people would understand them, are ambiguous. Here, respondent clearly and unequivocally expressed his willingness to speak to police after the sexual assault."

CASE SIGNIFICANCE: The issue in this case was the validity of the waiver of *Miranda* rights. The defendant told the police that he would talk with them, but would not make a written statement without a lawyer present. Ordinarily, a waiver is unconditional; here, the waiver was conditional in that the suspect did agree to make oral statements without a lawyer present. He later challenged his incriminating oral statements as inadmissible because he had asked for a lawyer, even though he agreed to make an oral statement. The Supreme Court rejected the challenge, holding that the sole test for the admissibility of an oral confession was voluntariness. There was a voluntary waiver of rights here, although the defendant refused to make a written statement. What this case tells the police is that the waiver of rights does not have to be complete or unconditional to be valid. Refusal to have a statement in writing does not make a confession inadmissible, as long as the police can establish that the *Miranda* warnings were given and the waiver was intelligent and voluntary.

COLORADO V. SPRING
479 U.S. 564 (1987)

CAPSULE: The waiver of *Miranda* rights is valid even if the suspect believes that the interrogation will focus on minor crimes but the police later shift the questioning to cover a different and more serious crime.

FACTS: Spring and a companion shot and killed a man during a hunting trip in Denver. An informant told federal agents that Spring was engaged in interstate trafficking in stolen firearms and that he had participated in the murder. Pursuant to that information, agents set up an undercover operation and arrested Spring in Kansas City. Agents advised Spring of his *Miranda* rights upon arrest. At the agent's office, Spring was again advised of his *Miranda* rights and signed a statement that he understood and waived his rights. Agents then asked Spring about his involvement in the firearms transactions leading to his arrest. He was also asked if he had ever shot a man, to which he responded affirmatively, but denied the shooting in question. Thereafter, Colorado officials questioned Spring. He was again read his *Miranda* warnings and again signed a statement asserting that he understood and waived his rights. This time, Spring confessed to the Colorado murder. A written statement of his confession was prepared, which Spring read, edited, and signed.

ISSUE: Must a suspect be informed of all crimes on which he or she is to be questioned before there can be a valid waiver of the Fifth Amendment privilege against self-incrimination? NO.

SUPREME COURT DECISION: A suspect's waiver of *Miranda* rights is valid even if he or she believes the interrogation will focus on minor crimes but the police shift the questioning to cover a different and more serious crime.

REASON: "Respondent's March 30 decision to waive his Fifth Amendment privilege was voluntary absent evidence that his will was overborne and his capacity for self-determination critically impaired because of coercive police conduct. His waiver was also knowingly and intelligently made, that is, he understood that he had the right to remain silent and that anything he said could be used as evidence against him. The Constitution does not require that a suspect know and understand every possible consequence of a waiver of the Fifth Amendment privilege. Here, there was no allegation that respondent failed to understand that privilege or that he misunderstood the consequences of speaking freely."

CASE SIGNIFICANCE: The confession was held valid in this case because there was no deception or misrepresentation by the police in obtaining the confession. Here, the police first questioned Spring about firearms transactions (a lesser offense) and, after he incriminated himself on these, the police asked him about a more serious offense, the murder, and Spring again incriminated himself. Spring, in challenging the validity of the waiver, argued that he should have been informed first of the offense for which he would be interrogated. The Court held that the police did not have to do so as long as there was no intention on the part of the police to mislead or deceive Spring. Although not expressly stated by the Court, there was also the implication that Spring could have stopped the interrogation when the officers shifted to the more serious crime. Since he did not, the waiver applied to both crimes. The principle is that a valid waiver of the *Miranda* rights allows the police to ask questions of the suspect about any crime as long as the interrogation does not involve misrepresentation or deception. There is no need to repeat the *Miranda* warnings if the suspect is asked about a different crime.

DUCKWORTH V. EAGAN
492 U.S. 195 (1989)

CAPSULE: The *Miranda* warnings need not be given in the exact form as worded in *Miranda v. Arizona*; what is needed is that they convey to the suspect his or her rights.

FACTS: Duckworth, when first questioned by Indiana police in connection with a stabbing, was in custody and made incriminating statements after having signed a waiver form that provided, among other things, that if he could not afford a lawyer, one would be appointed for him "if and when you go to court." Twenty-nine hours later, he was interrogated again and signed a different waiver form. He confessed to the stabbing and led officers to a site where they recovered relevant physical evidence. Over respondent's objection, his two statements were admitted into evidence at trial. Duckworth was charged with and convicted of attempted murder. He challenged his confession as inadmissible, arguing that the first waiver form did not comply with the requirements of *Miranda*; therefore, his confessions were not admissible.

ISSUE: Was the waiver form used by the police in this case (which informed the suspect that an attorney would be appointed for him "if and when you go to court") sufficient to comply with the requirements of *Miranda v. Arizona?* YES.

SUPREME COURT DECISION: The *Miranda* warnings need not be given in the exact form as outlined in the case; they must simply convey to the suspect his or her rights. The initial warning given to Duckworth in this case—namely, the right to remain silent, that anything said could be used against him in court, that he had the right to talk to a lawyer for advice before and during questioning even if he could not afford to hire one, that he had the right to stop answering questions at any time until he talked to a lawyer, and that the police could not provide him with a lawyer but one would be appointed for him "if and when you go to court"—complied with all the requirements of the *Miranda* case. The evidence obtained was, therefore, admissible.

REASON: "We think it must be relatively commonplace for a suspect, after receiving *Miranda* warnings, to ask when he will obtain counsel. The 'if and when you go to court' advice simply anticipates the question. Second, *Miranda* does not require that attorneys be producible on call, but only that the suspect be informed, as here, that he has the right to an attorney before and during questioning, and that an attorney would be appointed for him if he could not afford one. The Court in *Miranda* emphasized that it was not suggesting that 'each police station must have a "stationhouse lawyer" present at all times to advise prisoners.' If the police cannot provide appointed counsel, *Miranda* requires only that the police not question a suspect unless he waives his right to counsel. Here, respondent did just that."

CASE SIGNIFICANCE: This case clarifies two unclear points in the *Miranda* case. The first point is whether the police must use the exact wording in the *Miranda* decision to warn a suspect of his or her rights. The Court ruled no. It is sufficient that the warnings, however worded, "reasonably convey to a suspect his rights." Note, however, that, although the warnings need not be adopted verbatim from the *Miranda* case, the substance of the warnings, as indicated above, must be conveyed to the suspect. The second point addresses whether the police must immediately produce a lawyer if a suspect asks for one. The Court also ruled no. There is no requirement that the police produce a lawyer on call. The police need to inform the suspect that he or she has the right to an attorney and to an appointed attorney if he or she cannot afford one. If the suspect wants a lawyer and the police cannot immediately provide one, the interrogation simply stops; there is no obligation to provide a lawyer immediately. If the interrogation continues, however, any evidence obtained cannot be used in court.

PENNSYLVANIA V. MUNIZ
496 U.S. 582 (1990)

CAPSULE: The police may validly ask routine questions of persons suspected of driving while intoxicated and videotape their responses without giving them the *Miranda* warnings.

FACTS: An officer stopped Muniz's vehicle and directed him to perform three standard field tests. Muniz performed these tests poorly and informed the officer that he failed the tests because he had been drinking. The officer then arrested Muniz and took him into custody. After informing him that his actions and voice would be videotaped, Muniz was processed through procedures for receiving persons suspected of driving while intoxicated. Without being given his *Miranda* warnings, he was asked seven questions regarding his name, address, height, weight, eye color, date of birth, and age. He was also asked an eighth question, which he was unable to answer: the date of his sixth birthday. An officer then directed Muniz to perform each of the sobriety tests he had performed during the initial stop, which he again completed poorly. While performing these tests, Muniz attempted to explain his difficulties in completing the tasks and often requested further instruction on the tests. An officer then asked Muniz to submit to a breathalyzer test and read him the law regarding sanctions for failing or refusing the test. After asking several questions and commenting on his state of inebriation, Muniz refused to submit to the test. At this point, Muniz was read his *Miranda* warnings for the first time. He then waived his rights and admitted in further questioning that he had been driving while intoxicated. The evidence obtained by the police in the form of Muniz's responses and the videotape of Muniz's performance during booking was submitted into court over his objection and he was convicted of driving under the influence of alcohol.

ISSUE: Do the police need to give drunk driving suspects the *Miranda* warnings when asking routine questions and videotaping the proceedings? NO.

SUPREME COURT DECISION: The police may ask persons suspected of driving while intoxicated routine questions and videotape their responses without giving *Miranda* warnings. The questions and videotape do not elicit testimonial responses that are protected by the Fifth Amendment.

REASON: "The privilege against self-incrimination protects an 'accused from being compelled to testify against himself, or otherwise provide the state with evidence of a testimonial or communicative nature,' but not from being compelled by the state to produce 'real or physical evidence.' To be testimonial, the communication must, explicitly or implicitly, relate to a factual assertion or disclose information." "Muniz's answers to direct questions are not rendered inadmissible by *Miranda* merely because the slurred nature of his speech was incriminating. Requiring a suspect to reveal the physical manner in which he articulates words, like requiring him to reveal the physical properties of the sound of his voice, by reading a transcript, does not, without more, compel him to provide a 'testimonial' response for the purposes of the privilege." "However, Muniz's response to the sixth birthday question was incriminating not just because of his delivery, but because the content of his answer supported an inference that his mental state was confused. His response was testimonial because he was required to communicate an expressed or implied assertion of the fact or belief and, thus, was confronted with the 'trilemma' of truth, falsity, or silence, the historical abuse against which the privilege against self-incrimination was aimed."

CASE SIGNIFICANCE: This case aids the police in obtaining evidence for prosecutions in drunk driving cases. Another case, decided by the Court a few days earlier, holds that sobriety checkpoints in which the police stop every vehicle do not violate the Constitution (*Michigan Department of State Police v. Sitz*, 496 U.S. 444 [1990]). Within a week's time, the Court gave the police a virtual one-two punch in DWI cases. This case holds that the police may ask questions of a drunk driving suspect and videotape the whole proceeding without giving the suspect the *Miranda* warnings. This case, however, approved only "routine" questions (namely, eye color, date of birth, and current age). The fact that the answers to the seven questions were slurred and therefore incriminating did not render the evidence inadmissible. Note, however, that Muniz's answer to the question about the date of his sixth birthday was excluded because "the content of his answer supported the inference that his mental state was confused."

Four justices who voted with the majority said that this decision constitutes a new exception to the *Miranda* rule, and that this routine booking exception is justified because the questions asked are not intended to obtain information for investigatory purposes. Four other justices, however, argued that the *Miranda* rule simply did not apply to such questions and therefore did not consider the ruling an exception to the *Miranda* rule. Despite this disagreement, the fact remains that, when asking routine questions, the *Miranda* warnings need not be given and the videotaping of the proceedings is constitutional.

From the perspective of police officers, this case means that they now have greater leeway in handling DWI cases. From a legal perspective, however, the main issue is what kind of self-incriminating evidence is admissible in court. The rule is that the Fifth Amendment prohibition against self-incrimination (which is protected by the *Miranda* rule) prohibits only testimonial or communicative self-incrimination and does not prohibit physical self-incrimination. The asking of routine questions, the answers to which were slurred, and the videotaping of the proceedings were self-incriminatory, but such incrimination was physical; the *Miranda* warnings were, therefore, not needed and the evidence was admissible in court. Note, however, that Muniz's answer to the question about the date of his sixth birthday was excluded because "the content of his answer supported the inference that his mental state was confused." In sum, if the evidence obtained was physical instead of mental in nature, the evidence was admissible in court, even without the *Miranda* warnings being given.

MCNEIL V. WISCONSIN
501 U.S. 171 (1991)

CAPSULE: An accused's request for a lawyer at a bail hearing after being charged with an offense does not constitute an invocation of rights under *Miranda* for other offenses for which the accused has not yet been charged.

FACTS: McNeil was arrested in Omaha, Nebraska, pursuant to a warrant charging him with an armed robbery in a suburb of Milwaukee, Wisconsin. In that case, McNeil asked for and was represented by a public defender at a bail hearing for that offense. While in detention because of that charge, he was asked by the police about a murder and related crimes in a nearby town. McNeil was advised of his *Miranda* rights; and he signed forms waiving them and then made statements incriminating himself in those crimes. Over the next four days, McNeil was interviewed twice more, each time being read his *Miranda* warnings and signing statements that he waived his rights. Ultimately, McNeil confessed to the murder, attempted murder, and armed burglary. McNeil sought to suppress his confession, arguing that his request for a lawyer during the bail hearing for the armed robbery charge constituted an invocation of his *Miranda* rights, thus precluding any further police interrogation.

ISSUE: Does an accused's request for counsel at a bail hearing constitute an invocation of his rights under *Miranda* for other unrelated offenses for which he has not yet been charged? NO.

SUPREME COURT DECISION: An accused's request for a lawyer at a bail hearing after being charged with an offense does not constitute an invocation of rights under *Miranda* for other offenses for which the accused has not yet been charged.

REASON: "In *Michigan v. Jackson*, 475 U.S. 625 (1986) we held that once this right to counsel has attached and has been invoked, any subsequent waiver during a police-initiated custodial interview is ineffective. … In *Edwards v. Arizona*, 451 U.S. 477 (1981), we established a second layer of prophylaxis for the *Miranda* right to counsel: once a suspect asserts the right, not only must the current interrogation cease, but he may not be approached for further interrogation until counsel has been made available to him. … The *Edwards* rule, moreover, is not offense-specific: once a suspect invokes the

Miranda right to counsel for interrogation regarding one offense, he may not be reapproached regarding any offense unless counsel is present. ... The Sixth Amendment right, however, is offense-specific. It cannot be invoked once for all future prosecutions, for it does not attach until a prosecution is commenced. ... To exclude evidence pertaining to charges as to which the Sixth Amendment right to counsel had not attached at the time the evidence was obtained, simply because other charges were pending at that time, would unnecessarily frustrate the public's interest in the investigation of criminal activities." (Citations omitted.)

CASE SIGNIFICANCE: In several decisions that followed *Miranda v. Arizona*, the Supreme Court strengthened *Miranda* by holding that once a person has invoked his or her right to counsel, the person could not be subjected to any further police-initiated questioning for any crime (*Edwards v. Arizona*) and unless counsel is present (*Minnick v. Mississippi*, 498 U.S. 146 [1990]). This case is slightly different in that the accused maintained that, when he invoked his Sixth Amendment right to counsel during a bail hearing for armed robbery, he was in effect also invoking his Fifth Amendment (*Miranda*) rights for the other offenses with which he had not yet been charged; therefore, police interrogation for the other offenses could not take place. The Court disagreed, reasoning that his invocation of *Miranda* during that bail hearing did not apply to the other cases with which he had not yet been charged, particularly because he voluntarily waived his *Miranda* rights when interrogated by the police concerning those cases. The Court ruled that "requesting the assistance of an attorney at a bail hearing does not satisfy the minimum requirement of some statements that can reasonably be construed as an expression of a desire for counsel in dealing with custodial interrogation by the police." In other words, the request for counsel at a bail hearing is different from a request for counsel when being interrogated by the police for a crime.

DAVIS V. UNITED STATES
512 U.S. 452 (1994)

CAPSULE: After a knowing and voluntary waiver of *Miranda* rights, law enforcement officers may continue questioning until and unless the suspect clearly requests an attorney.

FACTS: Davis and Keith Shackleford were playing pool in which Shackleford lost a game and a $30 wager but refused to pay. Shackleford was later beaten to death with a pool cue. An investigation into the murder revealed Davis' presence on the evening of the murder and that he was absent without authorization from his naval duty station the next morning. The investigation also found that only privately owned pool cues could be taken from the club and that Davis had two of them, one of which was subsequently found to have a bloodstain on it. Investigative agents were told by others that Davis had either admitted committing the murder or had recounted details that clearly indicated his involvement. Davis was interviewed by Naval Investigative Service agents. As required by military law, the agents advised Davis that he was a suspect, that he was not required to make a statement, that any statement made could be used against him at a trial, and that he was entitled to speak to an attorney and to have the attorney present during questioning. Davis waived his rights to remain silent and to counsel both orally and in writing. An hour and a half into the interview, Davis stated "Maybe I should talk to a lawyer." When agents inquired if Davis was asking for an attorney, he replied that he was not. After a short break, agents reminded Davis of his rights and the interview continued. After another hour, Davis said "I think I want a lawyer before I say anything else." At that time, questioning ceased. At his court-martial hearing, a motion to suppress the statements obtained prior to requesting an attorney was denied and Davis was convicted of murder.

ISSUE: After a knowing and voluntary waiver of the *Miranda* rights, does a suspect's statement during custodial interrogation that does not qualify as an unambiguous invocation of the right to counsel require officers to cease questioning? NO.

SUPREME COURT DECISION: "Invocation of the *Miranda* right to counsel 'requires, at a minimum, some statement that can reasonably be construed to be an expression of a desire for the assistance of an attorney.' *McNeil v. Wisconsin*, 501 U.S. 171 (1991) at 178. But if a suspect makes a reference to an attorney that is ambiguous or equivocal in that a reasonable officer in light of the circumstances would have understood only that the suspect might be invoking the right to counsel, our precedents do not require the cessation of questioning."

REASON: "The rationale underlying *Edwards* [*v. Arizona*] is that the police must respect a suspect's wishes regarding his right to have an attorney present during custodial interrogation. But when the officers conducting the questioning reasonably do not know whether or not the suspect wants a lawyer, a rule requiring the immediate cessation of questioning 'would transform the *Miranda* safeguards into wholly irrational obstacles to legitimate police investigative activity' *Michigan v. Mosley*, 423 U.S. 96, 102 (1975)."

CASE SIGNIFICANCE: This 5-to-4 decision by the Court represents a modification of the *Edwards* rule. The *Edwards* case stated that, once a suspect asks for a lawyer, questioning by the police must cease. In this case, the suspect argued that the statement, "Maybe I should talk to a lawyer" constituted an invocation of the right to a lawyer under *Miranda*; hence police interrogation should have stopped. The Court disagreed, reasoning that the statement was an ambiguous request for counsel and therefore did not trigger the protections under *Edwards* or *Miranda*. Had the request been unambiguous to a reasonable investigator, the result would have been different. A statement such as, "I think I want a lawyer before I say anything else" (as Davis said later in the interview, and when questioning stopped) would likely have been considered an unambiguous request. That the case was decided on such a close vote indicates that the other justices did not think that the preceding phrase, "Maybe ..." made a significant difference in the tone of the request. This case holds that the request for the right to counsel must be clear and unambiguous (as judged from the perspective of a reasonable interrogator) where there was a previous valid and intelligent waiver, before the *Edwards* rule applies.

UNITED STATES V. PATANE
542 U.S. 630 (2004)

CAPSULE: Failure to give a suspect the *Miranda* warnings does not require suppression of the physical fruits of the suspect's unwarned but voluntary statements.

FACTS: Patane was arrested for harassing his ex-girlfriend. He was released on bond, subject to a restraining order that prohibited him from contacting her. Patane violated the restraining order by contacting his ex-girlfriend by phone. An officer investigating the matter was provided information by a probation officer that Patane illegally possessed a pistol. The officer went to Patane's home and inquired about his attempts to contact his girlfriend. The officer then arrested Patane for violating the restraining order. When another officer attempted to read Patane his *Miranda* warnings, Patane interrupted and said he knew his rights. Neither officer attempted to further warn Patane about his *Miranda* rights. The officer then asked Patane about the pistol. Patane was initially reluctant to discuss the matter, but upon the officer's insistence told him where the pistol was located. He then gave the officer permission to retrieve the pistol and it was seized by the officer. Patane was arrested for being a felon in possession of a firearm.

ISSUE: Does the failure to give a suspect the *Miranda* warnings require suppression of the physical fruits of the unwarned but voluntary statements? NO.

SUPREME COURT DECISION: Failure to give a suspect the *Miranda* warnings does not require suppression of the physical fruits of the suspect's unwarned but voluntary statements.

REASON: The Court based its ruling on three foundations: the relationship between the self-incrimination clause and physical evidence, the requirement to provide *Miranda* warnings for physical evidence, and the relationship to the exclusionary rule.

On the first issue of the self-incrimination clause, the Court stated, "the *Miranda* rule is a prophylactic employed to protect against violation of the Self-Incrimination Clause. The Self-Incrimination Clause, however, is not implicated by the admission into evidence of the physical fruit of a voluntary statement. ... The core protection afforded by the Self-Incrimination Clause is a prohibition on compelling a criminal defendant to testify against himself at trial." The court in *Elstad*, upon which Patane partially based his arguments, agreed that the Fifth Amendment was not concerned with non-testimonial evidence.

Even if this were so, the Court indicated in the second foundation issue that "[o]ur cases make clear the related point that a mere failure to give *Miranda* warning does not, by itself, violate a suspect's constitutional rights or even the *Miranda* rule. ... And although it is true that the Court requires the exclusion of the physical fruit of actually coerced statements, it must be remembered that statements taken without sufficient *Miranda* warnings are presumed to have been coerced only for certain purposes and then only when necessary to protect the privilege against self-incrimination. ... It follows that police do not violate a suspect's constitutional rights (or the *Miranda* rule) by negligent or even deliberate failures to provide the suspect with the full panoply of warnings prescribed by *Miranda*. Potential violations occur, if at all, only upon the admission of unwarned statements into evidence at trial. And at this point, 'the exclusions of unwarned statements ... is a complete and sufficient remedy' for any perceived *Miranda* violation."

In the final issue, the exclusionary rule, the Court reiterated that the exclusionary rule was created to control police conduct. The court noted that the *Miranda* rule is not aimed at police conduct, and police do not violate the Constitution by mere failure to warn. "Thus, unlike unreasonable searches under the Fourth Amendment or actual violation of the Due Process clause or the Self-Incrimination Clause, there is, with respect to mere failures to warn, nothing to deter. There is therefore no reason to apply the 'fruit of the poisonous tree' doctrine of *Wong Sun* [*v. United States*], 371 U.S., at 488."

CASE SIGNIFICANCE: This case involved the suppression of physical, not testimonial, evidence obtained without the suspect being given the *Miranda* warnings. It did not involve the admissibility of statements or confessions obtained without the *Miranda* warnings (as is the issue in most *Miranda* cases); instead, it focused on the admissibility of the pistol that was obtained without the suspect being given the *Miranda* warnings and after he had asserted that he knew his rights. The Court held that the physical evidence obtained was admissible on the grounds that it did not violate the constitutional guarantee against self-incrimination because the evidence involved was physical, not testimonial (spoken). Neither was there any need to apply the "fruit of the poisonous tree" doctrine (which holds that evidence obtained from other evidence illegally obtained is not admissible in court) because the "fruit of the poisonous tree" doctrine involves a violation of the Fourth Amendment protection against unreasonable searches and seizures and is unrelated to the *Miranda* rule, which was the issue in this case.

BERGHUIS V. THOMPKINS
560 U.S. 370 (2010)

CAPSULE: After being read the *Miranda* warnings, a suspect must make an unambiguous invocation of the right to remain silent; otherwise, statements made will be considered voluntary and a waiver of the right.

FACTS: Police interviewed Thompkins concerning a shooting in which one person was killed and another injured. Officers presented Thompkins with a form that listed the elements of *Miranda*. The officer asked Thompkins to read the statement that he could decide at any time during questioning to remain silent or ask for an attorney, and the officer read the rest of the form. Thompkins refused to sign the form, and there was conflicting testimony about whether the officer asked Thompkins if he understood his rights. About 2 hours and 45 minutes into the interrogation, one officer asked Thompkins, "Do you believe in God?" Thompkins made eye contact with the officer and said a tearful "Yes." The officer then asked, "Do you pray to God?" to which Thompkins said "Yes." The officer then asked, "Do you pray to God to forgive you for shooting that boy down?" Thompkins answered "Yes" and looked away. Thompkins refused to make a written confession, and the interrogation ended about 15 minutes later. At trial, Thompkins contended he had not waived his right to remain silent, and that his statements were involuntary.

ISSUE: Does a suspect's silence after being read the *Miranda* warnings, combined with statements made during an interview, represent a valid waiver of the right to remain silent? YES.

SUPREME COURT DECISION: "Thompkins did not say that he wanted to remain silent or that he did not want to talk with the police. Had he made either of these simple, unambiguous statements, he would have invoked his 'right to cut off questioning.' [Internal citations omitted.] Here he did neither, so he did not invoke his right to remain silent."

REASON: In this case, Thompkins argued he invoked his right to remain silent by not speaking for an extended period of time during the interview.

The Court rejected this argument, relying on the decision in *Davis v. United States*, 512 U.S. 452 (1994) that a suspect must make an "unambiguous" request for an attorney, and that "if an accused makes a statement concerning the right to counsel 'that is ambiguous or equivocal' or makes no statement, the police are not required to end the interrogation, *ibid.*, or ask questions to clarify whether the accused wants to invoke his or her *Miranda* rights." The Court further concluded "[t]he Court has not yet stated whether an invocation of the right to remain silent can be ambiguous or equivocal, but there is no principled reason to adopt different standards for determining when an accused has invoked the *Miranda* right to remain silent and the *Miranda* right to counsel at issue in *Davis*." A corollary issue was, in addition to not invoking his rights, whether Thompkins waived his rights without an explicit oral or written waiver. This was an issue because of the statement from *Miranda* that "a valid waiver will not be presumed simply from the silence of the accused after warnings are given or simply from the fact that a confession was in fact eventually obtained." Drawing on *North Carolina v. Butler*, 441 U.S. 369 (1979), the Court stated that "a waiver of *Miranda* rights may be implied through 'the defendant's silence, coupled with an understanding of his rights and a course of conduct indicating waiver.'" The prosecution's showing that *Miranda* warnings were given and that Thompkins made several uncoerced statements established an implied waiver of the right to remain silent, as long as the prosecution made the additional showing that Thompkins understood these rights since he made no verbal or written indication that he did. Here the Court argued "there was more than enough evidence in the record to conclude that Thompkins understood his *Miranda* rights. Thompkins received a written copy of the *Miranda* warnings; [the officer] determined that Thompkins could read and understand English; and Thompkins was given time to read the warnings. Thompkins, furthermore, read aloud the fifth warning." Based on these findings, the Court ruled the statement was valid.

CASE SIGNIFICANCE: This case continues to clarify several issues for police related to *Miranda* warnings and confessions. Here, "all concede that the warning given in this case was in full compliance with these requirements. The dispute centers on the response—or nonresponse—from the suspect." To this, the Court stated, "There is good reason to require an accused who wants to invoke his or her right to remain silent to do so unambiguously. A requirement of an unambiguous invocation of *Miranda* rights results in an objective inquiry that 'avoid[s] difficulties of proof and … provide[s] guidance to officers' on how to proceed in the face of ambiguity. *Davis*, 512 U.S., at 458–459, 114 S. Ct. 2350. If an ambiguous act, omission, or statement could require police to end the interrogation, police would be required to make difficult decisions about an accused's unclear intent and face the consequence of suppression 'if they guess wrong.' *Id.*, at 461, 114 S. Ct. 2350." So police officers can rely on the fact that a suspect must make an unambiguous request to remain silent. Of course, the suspect can simply remain silent for the duration of the interview; but if the suspect does speak after being given the *Miranda* warnings (and there is evidence to believe the suspect understood the rights), it is considered a valid waiver of the rights and a voluntary statement.

SALINAS V. TEXAS
570 U.S. 178 (2013)

CAPSULE: A suspect in an interrogation must expressly invoke the privilege against self-incrimination. It is not enough to simply remain silent in response to officers' questions.

FACTS: Two brothers were shot and killed in their home. There were no witnesses to the murders, but a neighbor who heard gunshots saw someone run out of the house and speed away in a dark-colored car. Police recovered six shotgun shell casings at the scene. The investigation led police to Salinas, who was a guest at a party the victims hosted the night before they were killed. Police went to Salinas' home, where they saw a dark blue car in the driveway. Salinas agreed to hand over his shotgun for ballistics testing and to accompany police to the station for questioning. At the police station, all agreed the interview was non-custodial, and Salinas did not receive *Miranda* warnings. He voluntarily answered some of an officer's questions about the murder, but was silent when asked whether ballistics testing would match his shotgun to shell casings found at the scene of the crime. Salinas did not testify at trial, and, over his objection, the prosecution used Salinas' failure to answer the question as evidence of guilt.

ISSUE: Does a suspect in an interview invoke the privilege against self-incrimination by not answering the questions of an officer? NO.

SUPREME COURT DECISION: "Petitioner's Fifth Amendment claim fails because he did not expressly invoke the privilege against self-incrimination in response to the officer's question. It has long been settled that the privilege 'generally is not self-executing' and that a witness who desires its protection 'must claim it.'"

REASON: The foundation of this decision is the Court's statement that "[t]o prevent the privilege against self-incrimination from shielding information not properly within its scope, a witness who 'desires the protection of the privilege … must claim it' at the time he relies on it." The Court reasoned that, "[a]lthough 'no ritualistic formula is necessary in order to invoke the privilege,' a witness does not do so by simply standing mute." The Court concluded that "[s]o long as police do not deprive a witness of the ability to voluntarily invoke the privilege, there is no Fifth Amendment violation."

CASE SIGNIFICANCE: This case represents another element in the line of cases beginning with *Davis v. United States* and continuing through *Berghuis v. Thompkins.* It is mostly about prosecution and the ability of a defendant's silence during questioning to be used in court. But it is also instructive for law enforcement in that it reinforces the fact that a suspect in an interrogation must expressly invoke his or her Fifth Amendment privilege. Of course, a person can decline to answer questions of officers in the interrogation; but, based on this case, doing so might be used against him or her at trial.

Lineups and Other Pretrial Identification Procedures

20

INTRODUCTION

The police generally use three methods in witness identification of suspects: lineups, showups, and photographic identifications. In a lineup, a victim or a witness to a crime is shown several possible suspects at the police station for identification. In a showup, only one suspect is shown to the witness or victim. This usually takes place at the scene of the crime immediately following the arrest of the suspect. In photographic identification, the police show photographs of possible suspects to victims or witnesses.

These three methods raise questions concerning the constitutional rights of suspects involved in identification proceedings. Do they have any rights at all? The answer is yes, but they are limited. The four constitutional rights usually invoked by suspects in identification proceedings are the privilege against self-incrimination, the right to a lawyer, the right to due process, and the protection against unreasonable searches and seizures. Of these constitutional rights, only two have been held by the Supreme Court to apply in pretrial identification procedures. These are the right to counsel and the right to due process. The Court has held that an accused who has been formally charged with a crime has the right to have a lawyer present during a lineup. In contrast, there is no right to counsel if the suspect has not been formally charged with a crime. As for due process rights, the Court has held that lineups that are so suggestive that the resulting identification is inevitable violates a suspect's constitutional rights. In a subsequent case, the Court concluded that the admission of testimony concerning a suggestive and unnecessary identification procedure does not violate due process as long as the identification is reliable.

Lineups, showups, and photographic identification procedures are helpful police practices for suspect identification. The police must be careful, however, not to violate the suspect's rights to counsel and due process. The cases in this chapter help determine (in addition to department rules and regulations) what the police can and cannot do.

The leading cases briefed in this chapter on lineups and other pretrial identification procedures are *United States v. Wade* and *Kirby v. Illinois.*

UNITED STATES V. WADE
388 U.S. 218 (1967)

CAPSULE: An accused who has been formally charged with a crime has the right to have a lawyer present during a police lineup.

FACTS: A man with a small piece of tape on each side of his face entered a bank, pointed a pistol at a cashier and the vice president of the bank, and forced them to fill a pillow case with the bank's money. The man then drove away with an accomplice. An indictment was returned against Wade and others involved in the robbery. Wade was arrested and counsel was appointed. Fifteen days later, without notice to his counsel, Wade was placed in a lineup to be viewed by the bank personnel. Both employees identified Wade as the robber; but in court they admitted seeing Wade in the custody of officials prior to the lineup. At trial, the bank personnel re-identified Wade as the robber and the prior lineup identifications were admitted as evidence.

ISSUE: Should the courtroom identification of an accused be excluded as evidence because the accused was exhibited to the witness before trial at a post-indictment lineup conducted for identification purposes and without notice to and in the absence of the accused's appointed lawyer? YES.

SUPREME COURT DECISION: A police lineup or other "face-to-face" confrontation after the accused has been formally charged with a crime is considered a "critical stage of the proceedings"; therefore, the accused has the right to have counsel present. The absence of counsel during such proceedings renders the evidence obtained inadmissible.

REASON: "Since it appears that there is grave potential for prejudice, intentional or not, in the pretrial lineup, which may not be capable of reconstruction at trial, and since presence of counsel itself can often avert prejudice and assure a meaningful confrontation at trial, there can be little doubt that for Wade the post-indictment lineup was a critical stage of the prosecution at which he was 'as much entitled to such aid [of counsel] … as at the trial itself.' Thus both Wade and his counsel should have been notified of the impending lineup, and counsel's presence should have been requisite to conduct of the lineup, absent an 'intelligent waiver.'"

CASE SIGNIFICANCE: The *Wade* case settled the issue of whether an accused has a right to counsel after the filing of formal charges. The standard used by the Court was whether identification was part of the "critical stage of the proceedings." The Court, however, did not indicate exactly what this phrase meant; hence, lower courts did not know where to draw the line. In a subsequent case, *Kirby v. Illinois* (see below), the Court held that any pretrial identification prior to the filing of a formal charge was not part of a "critical stage of the proceedings," therefore no counsel was required. The Wade case did not authoritatively state what is meant by "formal charge" either, so that phrase has also been subject to varying interpretations, depending on state law or practice.

FOSTER V. CALIFORNIA
394 U.S. 440 (1969)

CAPSULE: Lineups that are so suggestive as to make the resulting identification virtually inevitable violate a suspect's constitutional right to due process.

FACTS: The day after a robbery, one of the robbers, Foster, surrendered to the police and implicated the other two people involved. Foster was placed in a lineup with two other men and was viewed by the only witness to the robbery. Foster was wearing a jacket similar to the one worn by the robber and was several inches taller than either of the two men. The witness could not positively identify Foster as the robber and asked to speak with him. Foster was brought into an office alone and was seated at a table with the witness; still the witness could not positively identify Foster as the robber. A week to ten days later, the witness viewed a second lineup of Foster and four completely different men. This time the witness positively identified Foster as the robber. The witness testified to the identification of Foster in the lineups and repeated the identification in court.

ISSUE: Do lineups conducted by the police that may bias a witness' identification of a suspect violate his or her constitutional rights? YES.

SUPREME COURT DECISION: Lineups that are so suggestive as to make the resulting identifications virtually inevitable violate a suspect's constitutional right to due process.

REASON: "This case presents a compelling example of unfair lineup procedures. In the first lineup arranged by the police, petitioner stood out from the other two men by the contrast of his height and by the fact that he was wearing a leather jacket similar to that worn by the robber. When this did not lead to positive identification, the police permitted a one-to-one confrontation between petitioner and the witness .... Even after this the witness' identification of petitioner was tentative. So some days later another lineup was arranged. Petitioner was the only person in this lineup who had also participated in the first lineup .... This finally produced a definitive identification .... The suggestive elements in this identification procedure made it all but inevitable that [the witness] would identify petitioner whether or not he was in fact 'the man.' In effect, the police repeatedly said to the witness, 'This is the man.' This procedure so undermined the reliability of the eyewitness identification as to violate due process."

CASE SIGNIFICANCE: This case tells the police how not to conduct a lineup. Lineups are important to the accused as well as to the police and, therefore, must be conducted properly. Any lineup that practically identifies the suspect for the witness is unfair to the suspect and violates due process. The procedure followed by the police in this case practically ensured the suspect's identification by the witness. Lineups must be fair to the suspect; otherwise, the due process rights of the suspect are violated. A fair lineup is one that guarantees no bias against the suspect.

KIRBY V. ILLINOIS
406 U.S. 682 (1972)

CAPSULE: There is no right to counsel at police lineups or identification procedures if the suspect has not been formally charged with a crime.

FACTS: A man reported that two men robbed him of a wallet containing traveler's checks and a social security card. The following day, police officers stopped Kirby and a companion unrelated to the robbery. When asked for identification, Kirby produced a wallet that contained three traveler's checks and the social security card bearing the name of the robbery victim. The officers took Kirby and his companion to the police station. Only after arriving at the police station and checking police records did the officers learn of the robbery. The victim was then brought to the police station. Immediately upon entering the room in the police station where Kirby and his companion were seated, the man positively identified them as the men who had robbed him. No lawyer was present in the room and neither Kirby nor his companion asked for legal assistance, nor were they advised by the police of any right to the presence of counsel.

ISSUE: Is a suspect entitled to the presence and advice of a lawyer during an identification procedure conducted before filing of formal charges? NO.

SUPREME COURT DECISION: There is no right to counsel at police lineups or identification procedures prior to the time the suspect is formally charged with the crime.

REASON: "The initiation of judicial criminal proceedings is far from mere formalism. It is the starting point of our whole adversarial system of criminal justice. For it is only then that the government has committed itself to prosecute, and only then that the adverse positions of government and defendant have solidified. It is then that a defendant finds himself faced with the prosecutorial forces of organized society, and immersed in the intricacies of substantive and procedural criminal law. It is this point, therefore, that marks the commencement of the 'criminal prosecutions' to which alone the explicit guarantees of the Sixth Amendment are applicable."

CASE SIGNIFICANCE: *Kirby* was decided five years after *United States v. Wade*. It clarified an issue that was not directly resolved in *Wade*: whether the ruling in Wade applied to cases in which the lineup or pretrial identification takes place prior to the filing of formal charges. The court answered this question in the negative, reasoning that what happened in *Kirby* was a matter of routine police investigation, hence not considered a "critical stage of the proceedings." The Court held that a post-indictment lineup is a "critical stage" whereas a pre-indictment lineup is not.

MANSON V. BRATHWAITE
432 U.S. 98 (1977)

CAPSULE: The admission of testimony concerning a suggestive and unnecessary identification procedure does not violate due process as long as the identification possesses sufficient aspects of reliability.

FACTS: Glover (an undercover police officer) and an informant (Brown) went to an apartment building to buy narcotics from a known drug dealer (it was later determined that the officer and informant did not make the drug purchase from the intended person). As they stood at the door, the area was illuminated by natural light from a window in the hallway. Glover knocked on the door, and a man opened the door 12 to 18 inches. Brown identified himself, and Glover asked for "two things" of narcotics and then gave the man $20. The man closed the door and later returned and gave Glover two glassine bags. While the door was open, Glover stood within two feet of the man and observed his face. At headquarters, immediately after the sale, Glover described the seller to two other officers; however, at that time, Glover did not know the identity of the seller. He described the seller as "a colored man, approximately five feet eleven inches tall, dark complexion, black hair, short Afro style, and having high cheekbones, and of heavy build. He was wearing at the time blue pants and a plaid shirt." One of the officers suspected who the seller was, obtained a picture of Brathwaite from the Records Division, and left it in Glover's office. Glover identified the person as the man who sold him narcotics two days before. Brathwaite was arrested in the same apartment building where the narcotics sale had occurred. At his trial, the photograph from which Glover had identified Brathwaite was admitted into evidence. Although Glover had not seen Brathwaite in eight months, "there [was] no doubt whatsoever" in his mind that the person shown in the picture was Brathwaite. Glover also made a positive in-court identification of Brathwaite. Brathwaite testified that, on the day of the alleged sale, he had been ill at his apartment, and at no time on that particular day had he been at the place of the drug deal.

His wife, after Brathwaite had refreshed her memory, also testified that he was home all day.

ISSUE: Should pretrial identification evidence obtained by a police examination of a single photograph be excluded as evidence under the due process clause if it was thought to be suggestive and unnecessary, regardless of whether it was reliable? NO.

SUPREME COURT DECISION: "The admission of testimony concerning a suggestive and unnecessary identification procedure does not violate due process so long as the identification possesses sufficient aspects of reliability."

REASON: Using a previous case, *Stovall v. Denno*, 388 U.S. 293 (1967), the Supreme Court concluded that reliability is the "linchpin in determining the admissibility of identification testimony." The factors for the court to consider for reliability were stated in *Neil v. Biggers*, 409 U.S. 188 (1972). The factors are:

1. the opportunity for the witness to view the criminal at the time of the crime
2. the witness' degree of attention
3. the accuracy of any prior description of the criminal
4. the level of certainty demonstrated at the identification procedure, and
5. the time between the crime and the identification procedure.

The Court then took the facts of this case and applied the five-factor analysis. Glover had a substantial opportunity to view Brathwaite as he stood within two feet of Brathwaite for two to three minutes while the man twice stood with the door open. Also, there was natural light entering a window in the hallway aiding the view. Furthermore, Glover was not a casual observer; and, being of the same race as respondent, it was unlikely he would perceive only general features. Glover then provided a very detailed description of respondent to the other officer immediately after the sale and identified him from a picture two days later. Glover was also very positive in his identification of Brathwaite as he testified: "there is no question whatsoever." The time between the crime and the identification procedure was very short, as Glover gave his description to the officer immediately after the crime and positively identified Brathwaite only two days later by the photograph. The Court concluded: "[t]hese indicators of Glover's ability to make an accurate identification are hardly outweighed by the corrupting effect of the challenged identification itself."

CASE SIGNIFICANCE: The Supreme Court concluded that the five factors set forth in *Biggers* should be used to test the reliability of the identification. The opportunity to view asks whether the witness was at a distance adequate to examine the suspect and whether the witness had a sufficient amount of time to examine him or her, while also considering the environmental factors, such as daylight. The degree of attention refers to the amount of attention the witness placed on examining the suspect. This could be revealed in the accuracy of the description: did the witness provide a very detailed description of the suspect, such as Glover's, or an undetailed description? The witness' level of certainty describes how certain the officer was of his identification of the suspect after the alleged incident or crime occurred. Finally, the time between the crime and the confrontation or identification of the suspect is important because long periods of time between the crime and identification produce a greater likelihood of the witness forgetting the details of the suspect, thus making the witness' identification less reliable.

UNITED STATES V. CREWS
445 U.S. 463 (1980)

CAPSULE: A pretrial identification is illegal if the arrest is illegal; however, an in-court identification is admissible if the victim's recollections are independent of the police misconduct.

FACTS: Immediately after being assaulted and robbed at gunpoint, the victim notified the police and gave them a full description of her assailant. Several days later, a man matching the description was seen by police near the scene of the crime. After an attempt to photograph him failed, he was taken to the police station, questioned briefly, photographed, and released. The victim identified the photograph as that of her assailant. Crews was then taken into custody and identified by the victim in a lineup. On a pretrial motion to suppress, the court ruled that the initial detention constituted an arrest without probable cause and that the photographs and lineup identifications were not admissible. The court, however, ruled that the courtroom identification by the victim was admissible.

ISSUE: Is the in-court identification of a suspect by a witness, when the identification is the result of a prior illegal arrest, admissible as evidence? YES.

SUPREME COURT DECISION: The pretrial identification of the suspect in a photograph and lineup are not admissible as evidence due to the illegal arrest. The in-court identification, however, is admissible because the victim's recollections were independent of the police misconduct.

REASON: The courtroom identification by the victim was wholly independent of any police misconduct. Aside from the fact that Crews was present in the courtroom, partially as the result of the illegal arrest, the prosecutor's case was established from the courtroom identification by the victim, which had nothing to do with the arrest. The conviction, independently established, was legal.

CASE SIGNIFICANCE: This case introduced the doctrine of "independent untainted source," an exception to the exclusionary rule. Under this exception, the police may use evidence related to an illegal search or seizure as long as it is not connected to the illegality. The Court concluded that the initial illegality (in this case the illegal detention of the suspect) could not deprive prosecutors of the opportunity to prove the defendant's guilt through the introduction of evidence wholly untainted by police misconduct. For example, a 14-year-old girl was found in the defendant's apartment during an illegal search. The girl's testimony that the defendant had sex with her was admissible because she was an independent source that predated the search of the apartment. Prior to the search, the girl's parents had reported her missing, and a police informant had already located her in the defendant's apartment (*State v. O'Bremski*, 70 Wash. 2d 425 [1967]). Note, however, that if the evidence has been tainted by police misconduct, such evidence cannot be admitted in court (see *Wong Sun v. United States* in Chapter 2).

Right to Counsel Related to Policing

21

INTRODUCTION

The right to counsel in criminal prosecutions is guaranteed by the Sixth Amendment, which states that "in all criminal prosecutions, the accused shall enjoy the right ... to have the Assistance of Counsel for his defense." Although generally associated with trial, the right to counsel has been interpreted to apply to "every critical stage" of the criminal proceeding. Some encounters with the police are considered a critical stage of an investigation and therefore require the presence of a lawyer if the evidence obtained is to be admissible in court.

The seminal case on the right to counsel is *Powell v. Alabama*, in which the Court held that the trial for a capital offense without a defense attorney in state court violated the right to due process. The Court held that "[w]ithout counsel, though he [the defendant] may not be guilty, he faces the danger of conviction because he does not know how to establish his innocence."

The first major right to counsel case involving the police was *Escobedo v. Illinois*, in which the Court held that the suspect in a serious offense is entitled to a lawyer during interrogation at a police station. *Escobedo* is credited with "having brought the right to counsel out into the police station" instead of being confined to the courtroom. Two years later, in *Miranda v. Arizona*, the Court extended the right to counsel and the privilege against self-incrimination when it held that those rights apply whenever there is "custodial interrogation," even if the interrogation took place outside a police station. *Miranda*, then, brought the right to counsel out into the streets.

The cases briefed in this chapter establish that the right to counsel is a basic right that must be observed by the police if the contact can be characterized as a critical stage. On the other hand, questioning during stops or while issuing traffic citations does not trigger the right to counsel because those are not critical stages in a criminal prosecution.

The important cases briefed in this chapter on the right to counsel related to policing are *Massiah v. United States* and *United States v. Henry*.

POWELL V. ALABAMA
287 U.S. 45 (1932)

CAPSULE: The trial in state court for a capital offense without a defense attorney violates the right to due process.

FACTS: Nine black youths were charged with the rape of two white girls while on a train in Alabama. All were illiterate. The atmosphere in the town was such that the boys had to be held in a different town under military guard during the proceedings. The judge appointed "all members of the bar" to assist the boys during the proceedings; however, they were not represented by any attorney by name until the day of the trial. Each of the trials lasted only a day and resulted in a conviction. The youths were given the death penalty.

ISSUE: Must defendants in capital punishment cases be given the rights to counsel and due process? YES.

SUPREME COURT DECISION: "In a capital case, where the defendant is unable to employ counsel, and is incapable adequately of making his own defense because of ignorance, feeblemindedness, illiteracy, or the like, it is the duty of the court, whether requested or not, to assign counsel for him as a necessary requisite of due process of law; and that duty is not discharged by an assignment at such a time or under such circumstances as to preclude the giving of effective aid in the preparation and trial of the case."

REASON: "Even the intelligent and educated layman has small and sometimes no skill in the science of the law. Left without aid of counsel, he may be put on trial without proper charge, and convicted upon incompetent evidence irrelevant to the issue or otherwise against him. Without counsel, though he may not be guilty, he faces the danger of conviction because he does not know how to establish his innocence."

CASE SIGNIFICANCE: The Sixth Amendment to the Constitution provides that "in all criminal prosecutions, the accused shall enjoy the right ... to have the assistance of counsel for his defense." This case provides the often-quoted reason (penned by Justice Sutherland) for this constitutional provision. Without a lawyer, an accused may be convicted, not because he or she is guilty, but because "he does not know how to establish his innocence." The right to counsel is a basic and fundamental right under the Constitution and must be respected by the police. Note that, in this case, the Court used the due process clause of the Fourteenth Amendment rather than the Sixth Amendment right to counsel to overturn the convictions. This is because, in 1932, when the case was decided, the provisions of the Bill of Rights had not yet been extended to state proceedings. Were this case to be decided today, the Sixth Amendment right to counsel provision would have been used.

GIDEON V. WAINWRIGHT
372 U.S. 335 (1963)

CAPSULE: A lawyer must be appointed for an indigent who is charged with a felony offense in state court.

FACTS: Gideon was charged in a Florida state court with breaking and entering a poolroom with intent to commit a misdemeanor, an act classified as a felony offense under Florida law. Appearing in court without funds and without a lawyer, Gideon asked the court to appoint a lawyer for him. The court refused, saying that under Florida law the only time the court could appoint a lawyer to represent an accused was when the crime charged was a capital offense. Gideon conducted his own defense and was convicted.

ISSUE: Does the Constitution require appointment of counsel for an indigent person who is charged in a state court with a felony offense? YES.

SUPREME COURT DECISION: The Sixth Amendment requires that a person charged with a felony offense in a state court be appointed counsel if he or she cannot afford it.

REASON: "The right of one charged with crime to counsel may not be deemed fundamental and essential to fair trials in some countries, but it is in ours. From the very beginning, our state and national constitutions and laws have laid great emphasis on procedural and substantive safeguards designed to assure fair trials before impartial tribunals in which every defendant stands equal before the law. This noble ideal cannot be realized if the poor man charged with a crime has to face his accusers without a lawyer to assist him."

CASE SIGNIFICANCE: This case mandates that when an indigent person is charged with a felony in a state court, counsel must be provided. This settled a controversy among lower courts, which had inconsistent rulings on the type of offense an indigent had to be charged with to be entitled to a lawyer. An earlier decision (*Betts v. Brady*, 316 U.S. 455 [1942]), which held that the requirement that counsel be provided to all indigent defendants in federal felony trials, did not extend to the states. This was overruled in *Gideon* when the Supreme Court held that the rule applied to criminal proceedings in state courts as well. Since 1963, both federal and state felony defendants must be given court-appointed counsel if indigent. Note that the *Gideon* case required the appointment of counsel for indigents only in felony cases. This was later extended to misdemeanor cases in *Argersinger v. Hamlin* (407 U.S. 25, 1972). Although not a case directly involving the police, the *Gideon* case is included here because it is helpful for the police to know what types of indigent offenders are entitled to a court-appointed lawyer during trial and because it helps to lay the foundation for the ruling in *Miranda*.

ESCOBEDO V. ILLINOIS
378 U.S. 478 (1964)

CAPSULE: A suspect in a serious offense is entitled to a lawyer during interrogation at a police station.

FACTS: Escobedo was arrested without a warrant and interrogated in connection with a murder. En route to the police station, officers told Escobedo that he had been named as the murderer and that he should admit to the crime. Escobedo replied that he wished to speak to an attorney. Shortly after Escobedo arrived at the police station, his retained lawyer arrived and asked permission from various police officials to speak with his client. His request was repeatedly denied. Escobedo also asked several times during an interrogation to speak to his attorney and was told that the attorney did not want to see him. Escobedo subsequently admitted to some knowledge of the murder and implicated himself as the murderer.

ISSUE: Is a suspect entitled to a lawyer, if he or she requests one, during interrogation at a police station? YES.

SUPREME COURT DECISION: A suspect is entitled to a lawyer during interrogation at a police station. Denial of counsel in this case was a violation of the suspect's constitutional right to counsel because the investigation had focused on the suspect, he had been taken into custody, and he had requested and been denied an opportunity to consult with his lawyer.

REASON: "We hold, therefore, that where, as here, the investigation is no longer a general inquiry into unsolved crime but has begun to focus on a particular suspect, the suspect has been taken into police custody, the police carry out a process of interrogations that lends itself to eliciting incriminating statements, the suspect has requested and been denied an opportunity to consult with his lawyer, and the police have not effectively warned him of his absolute right to remain silent, the accused has been denied 'the Assistance of Counsel' in violation of the Sixth Amendment to the Constitution as 'made obligatory upon the States by the Fourteenth Amendment,' and that no statement elicited by the police during the interrogation may be used against him at a criminal trial."

CASE SIGNIFICANCE: This was an easy case for the Supreme Court to decide because the police had indeed grossly violated Escobedo's right to counsel. *Escobedo*, however, left two issues unsettled:

1. Is the right to counsel available only when the suspect is accused of a serious offense, when he or she is being questioned at the police station, and when he or she has asked to see a lawyer?

2. What did the Court mean when it said that the right to counsel could be invoked when the investigation had "begun to focus" on a particular suspect? Because of its peculiar facts, the *Escobedo* case raised more questions than it answered. Lower court decisions disagreed on the

meaning of *Escobedo*, leading to conflicting interpretations. Further guidance from the Supreme Court was necessary, which led to the decision in *Miranda v. Arizona* (see Chapter 17). Because of the *Miranda* decision, the impact of *Escobedo* has been lessened because *Escobedo* brought the right to counsel only to the police station, whereas *Miranda* took it out into the streets.

MASSIAH V. UNITED STATES
377 U.S. 201 (1964)

CAPSULE: Incriminating statements are not admissible in court if the defendant was questioned by a government informant without an attorney present after the defendant was formally charged with a crime and had obtained an attorney.

FACTS: Customs officials received information that Massiah was transporting drugs from South America aboard a ship on which he was a merchant seaman. Officials searched the ship and found 300 pounds of cocaine. Massiah was indicted for possession of narcotics aboard a United States vessel. While out on bail, officials enlisted the aid of one of Massiah's confederates. The informant allowed officials to install a transmitter under the front seat of his automobile and then engaged Massiah in a conversation that could be overheard by officials. These incriminating statements were admitted over Massiah's objection at trial, and he was convicted.

ISSUE: Are statements that are elicited after the filing of formal charges and in the absence of an attorney, a violation of the Sixth Amendment's right to counsel? YES.

SUPREME COURT DECISION: Evidence in the form of incriminating statements is not admissible in court if the defendant was questioned without an attorney by police agents after the defendant was charged and had obtained a lawyer. The evidence is inadmissible, not because there was a violation of the right against unreasonable searches and seizures, but because the right to counsel under the Sixth Amendment has been violated.

REASON: "We hold that the petitioner [Massiah] was denied the basic protections of the guarantee [of the Sixth Amendment] when there was used against him at his trial evidence of his own incriminating words, which federal agents had deliberately elicited from him after he had been indicted and in the absence of his counsel. It is true that in *Spano* [*v. New York*, 360 U.S. 315 (1959)], the defendant was interrogated in a police station while in this case the damaging testimony was elicited from the defendant without his knowledge while he was free on bail. But, as Judge Hays pointed out in his dissent in the Court of Appeals decision, 'if such a rule is to have any efficacy it must apply to indirect and surreptitious interrogations as well as those conducted in the jailhouse.' In this case, Massiah was more seriously imposed upon ... because he did not even know that he was under interrogation by a government agent."

CASE SIGNIFICANCE: This case, although involving electronic surveillance, is really a Sixth Amendment right to counsel case rather than a Fifth Amendment privilege against self-incrimination. The Court discussed the electronic surveillance issue only briefly. It reserved most of its discussion to the right to counsel issue, concluding that, while evidence was obtained validly with the use of radio equipment, it had to be excluded because the suspect's right to counsel was violated. It is important to note that here the suspect had been formally charged in court and had obtained an attorney. If these factors had not been present, the evidence would probably have been admissible.

UNITED STATES V. HENRY
447 U.S. 264 (1980)

CAPSULE: A defendant's right to counsel is violated if the police intentionally create a situation that is likely to elicit incriminating statements.

FACTS: Henry was indicted for armed robbery and incarcerated. While in jail, government agents contacted an informant who was a cellmate of Henry and instructed him to be alert to any statements made by Henry, but not to initiate any conversations regarding the robbery. After the informant had been released from jail, he was contacted by the agents and paid for information he provided them concerning incriminating statements Henry made to him in reference to the robbery. There was no indication that the informant would have been paid had he not provided such information. Henry was convicted of robbery, based partly on the testimony of the informant.

ISSUE: Is a defendant denied the right to counsel under the Sixth Amendment if the government uses a paid informant to create a situation likely to induce incriminating statements? YES.

SUPREME COURT DECISION: The government violates a defendant's Sixth Amendment right to counsel by intentionally creating a situation likely to elicit incriminating statements.

REASON: "The question here is whether under the facts of this case a Government agent 'deliberately elicited' incriminating statements from Henry. ... Three factors are important. First, Nichols [the informant] was acting under instructions as a paid informant for the Government; second, Nichols was ostensibly no more than a fellow inmate of Henry; and third, Henry was in custody under indictment at the time he was engaged in conversation with Nichols." "The Government argues that federal agents instructed Nichols not to question Henry about the robbery. Yet according to his own testimony, Nichols was not a passive listener; rather, he had 'some conversations with Mr. Henry' while he was in jail and Henry's incriminatory statements were 'the product of this conversation.'"

CASE SIGNIFICANCE: This is a Sixth Amendment right to counsel case rather than a Fifth Amendment privilege against self-incrimination case. The evidence obtained was excluded because what the government did violated the suspect's right to a lawyer, not because what the government did amounted to a form of interrogation. The Court reasoned that, here, the government created a situation likely to induce the suspect to make incriminating statements without the assistance of counsel. Some observers find it difficult to accept this logic, particularly because the informant was instructed to simply listen to incriminating statements Henry made and not to interrogate him at all. Nonetheless, the Court concluded that incriminating statements were "deliberately elicited" by the informant, which the police cannot do in the absence of a lawyer. Great weight was given by the Court to the fact that the informant was acting under government instruction and that Henry was in custody under indictment at the time the incriminating statements were made. Moreover, the informant in fact engaged Henry in conversations that produced the incriminating statements.

The police must be careful when interrogating a suspect who has retained a lawyer. In these cases, courts frown upon such interrogations, not because no *Miranda* warnings were given, but because a suspect has the right to have counsel present whenever he or she is questioned by the police. In sum, once a suspect has a lawyer, the police should leave the subject alone unless a lawyer is present.

PATTERSON V. ILLINOIS
487 U.S. 285 (1988)

CAPSULE: A valid waiver after the *Miranda* warnings constitutes a waiver of the right to counsel as well as the privilege against self-incrimination.

FACTS: After being informed by the police that he had been indicted for murder, Patterson, who was in police custody, twice indicated his willingness to discuss the crime with the authorities. He was interrogated twice, and on both occasions was read a form waiving his *Miranda* rights. He initialed each of the five specific warnings on the form and then signed it. He then gave incriminating statements to the police about his participation in the crime. He was tried and convicted of murder.

ISSUE: Is a waiver of rights after the *Miranda* warnings a waiver of the Sixth Amendment right to counsel as well as a waiver of the Fifth Amendment privilege against self-incrimination? YES.

SUPREME COURT DECISION: A defendant who has been given the *Miranda* warnings has been sufficiently made aware of the Sixth Amendment right to counsel so that any waiver of that right is valid if it is a knowing and intelligent waiver.

REASON: "This Court has never adopted petitioner's suggestion that the Sixth Amendment right to counsel is 'superior' to or 'more difficult' to waive than its Fifth Amendment counterpart. Rather, in Sixth Amendment cases, the court has defined the scope of the right to counsel by a pragmatic assessment of the usefulness of counsel to the accused at the particular stage of the proceedings in question, and the dangers to the accused of proceedings without counsel at that stage ... . *Miranda* warnings are sufficient for this purpose in post-indictment questioning context, because, at that stage, the role of counsel is relatively simple and limited, and the dangers and disadvantages of self-representation are less substantial and more obvious to an accused than they are at trial."

CASE SIGNIFICANCE: Many believe that *Miranda v. Arizona* is a right to counsel case. It is not. Instead, it is a right against self-incrimination case, meaning that the main reason *Miranda* warnings must be given by the police is because these warnings protect a suspect's right against self-incrimination. The statement that "you have the right to a lawyer" is given primarily because a lawyer can help protect a suspect's self-incrimination privilege. In this case, Patterson conceded that he validly waived his Fifth Amendment right when he signed the waiver, but asserted that such waiver did not mean a waiver of his Sixth Amendment right to counsel, a right given the accused after charges are filed, as they were in this case. In essence, Patterson maintained that he ought to have been specifically informed of his right to counsel (apart from the *Miranda* warnings) and that there must be a separate waiver for that right. The Court disagreed, reasoning that the *Miranda* warnings were sufficient to inform Patterson of both rights and that his statements were, therefore, admissible in evidence.

KANSAS V. VENTRIS
556 U.S. 586 (2009)

CAPSULE: An informant's testimony is admissible to impeach a defendant's statements, even if elicited in violation of the Sixth Amendment right to counsel.

FACTS: Ventris and Rhonda Theel were linked to a robbery-murder by a person who transported them to the victim's home. Murder charges against Theel were dropped in exchange for an agreement to identify Ventris as the shooter at trial. Prior to trial, police placed an informant in Ventris' jail cell with instructions to listen for incriminating statements. According to the informant, in response to his statement that Ventris appeared to have "something more serious weighing in on his mind," Ventris admitted to shooting and robbing the victim. At trial, Ventris took the stand and placed full blame for the robbery-murder on Theel. The prosecution sought to call the informant to testify to Ventris' contradictory statements. Over Ventris' objection, the court allowed the testimony, admitting it was probably a violation of Ventris' Sixth Amendment rights but arguing it was admissible for impeachment purposes. Ventris was acquitted on murder but convicted of aggravated robbery and burglary.

ISSUE: Is a defendant's incriminating statement to an informant, elicited in violation of the Sixth Amendment, admissible at trial to impeach the defendant's conflicting statement? YES.

SUPREME COURT DECISION: "We hold that the informant's testimony, concededly elicited in violation of the Sixth Amendment, was admissible to challenge Ventris' inconsistent testimony at trial."

REASON: The Court stated in this case that "whether otherwise excluded evidence can be admitted for purposes of impeachment depends upon the nature of the constitutional guarantee that is violated." It stated that the Fifth Amendment "is violated whenever a truly coerced confession is introduced at trial, whether by way of impeachment or otherwise"; but Fourth Amendment "exclusion comes by way of deterrent sanction rather than to avoid violation of the substantive guarantee." The Court argued that the right to counsel is a trial right, but that it "covers pretrial interrogations to ensure that police manipulation does not render counsel entirely impotent—depriving the defendant of 'effective representation by counsel at the only stage when legal aid and advice would help him.' *Massiah* [citations omitted]." The Court argued the right to be free of uncounseled interrogation is infringed at the time of the interrogation, not when it is admitted into evidence. "The interests safeguarded by such exclusion [of tainted evidence] are 'outweighed by the need to prevent perjury and to assure the integrity of the trial process.' *Stone v. Powell*, 428 U.S. 465, 488 (1976)." "Once the defendant testifies inconsistently, denying the prosecution 'the traditional truth-testing devices of the adversary process,' *Harris* [*v. New York*, 401 U.S. 222], *supra*, at 225, is a high price to pay for vindicating the right to counsel at the prior stage." "On the other side of the scale, preventing impeachment by use of statements taken in violation of *Massiah* would add little appreciable deterrence." "We have held in every other context that tainted evidence—evidence whose very introduction does not constitute the constitutional violation, but whose obtaining was constitutionally invalid—is admissible for impeachment. We see no distinction that would alter the balance here [citations omitted]."

CASE SIGNIFICANCE: It has been established by the Supreme Court that police may not elicit statements from suspects after they have obtained a lawyer (see *Massiah v. United States* and *United States v. Henry* above). The Court made a distinction in this case because the prosecution was using the informant and information to impeach Ventris' statements, not to convict him. Had the information been a part of the prosecution's main case, the Court would have rejected the statements.

MICHIGAN V. BRYANT
562 U.S. 344 (2011)

CAPSULE: Statements made to police in the context of an ongoing emergency may be admitted into court even when there is no possibility to cross-examine a witness.

FACTS: Officers dispatched to a gas station found a victim in a shooting. Before he died, he told police he had been shot by Bryant through the back door at Bryant's house and had driven to the gas station. Officers went to Bryant's house, where they found blood, a bullet casing, and a bullet hole in the back door. They also found the victim's wallet and identification outside the house. Officers testified to the victim's statements at trial and Bryant was convicted of murder.

ISSUE: Does the confrontation clause of the Sixth Amendment bar statements made to police during an emergency situation from being admitted in court if the defense does not have ability to cross-examine the witness? NO.

SUPREME COURT DECISION: "We hold that the circumstances of the interaction between [the victim] and the police objectively indicate that the 'primary purpose of the interrogation' was 'to enable police assistance to meet an ongoing emergency.' *Davis*, 547 U.S., at 822. Therefore, [the victim's] identification and description of the shooter and the location of the shooting were not testimonial statements, and their admission at Bryant's trial did not violate the Confrontation Clause."

REASON: After examining several previous cases leading up to this one, the Court confirmed, "We thus made clear in *Davis* that not all those questioned by the police are witnesses and not all 'interrogations by law enforcement officers,' *Crawford*, 541 U.S., at 53, are subject to the Confrontation Clause." The Court drew from *Davis v. Washington*, 547 U.S. 813 (2006) to explain their meaning of *testimonial*, reasoning that "Statements are nontestimonial when made in the course of police interrogation under circumstances objectively indicating that the primary purpose of the interrogation is to enable police assistance to meet an ongoing emergency. They are testimonial when the circumstances objectively indicate that there is no such ongoing emergency, and that the primary purpose of the interrogation is to establish or prove past events potentially relevant to later criminal prosecution. *Davis*, 547 U.S., at 822." The Court then stated the determination of the primary purpose of an interrogation would be based on the circumstances in which the encounter occurred. In addressing an "ongoing emergency," the court concluded "The existence of an ongoing emergency is relevant to determining the primary purpose of the interrogation because an emergency focuses the participants on something other than 'prov[ing] past events potentially relevant to later criminal prosecution.' *Davis*, 547 U.S., at 822. Rather, it focuses them on 'end[ing] a threatening situation.' *Id.*, at 832. Implicit in *Davis* is the idea that because the prospect of fabrication in statements given for the primary purpose of resolving that emergency is presumably significantly diminished, the Confrontation Clause does not require such statements to be subject to the crucible of cross-examination."

CASE SIGNIFICANCE: In *Crawford v. Washington*, 541 U.S. 36 (2004), the Court had ruled that, for testimonial evidence to be admissible in court, the Confrontation Clause of the Sixth Amendment (essentially, the ability to cross-examine the witness) was a requirement. In *Davis*, the Court clarified where police interrogations fit in this framework. Here, the Court made a distinction between interrogations aimed at criminal prosecution and those seeking to end an emergency situation. This was in recognition of the dual role of police as first responders and as criminal investigators. The Court in *Bryant* ruled that, when officers are acting in their first responder role and attempting to resolve an emergency situation (e.g., a domestic dispute), statements made by those involved may be considered nontestimonial for the purposes of the Sixth Amendment Confrontation Clause. As such, there is no requirement for cross-examination of the witness; and police notes, interview recordings, and the officers' memory may be admissible in court.

Entrapment

22

INTRODUCTION

Entrapment is a defense that questions the propriety of police action. It is defined as the actions of government officials with the goal of criminal prosecution to induce a person to commit a crime that was not contemplated by the person. A person entrapped is not guilty of a criminal offense because of the presumption that the legislators did not intend to allow government agents to lure otherwise innocent persons into committing a crime so they can be prosecuted. Entrapment is a valid defense in a criminal case, but the act by the police of merely providing an opportunity for a person to commit a crime is not. That line, however, is sometimes difficult to draw and becomes a matter of proof during trial.

Entrapment tests may be divided into two general categories: the subjective test and the objective test. These are somewhat contradictory rules, and states may adopt either rule. It is important to know, therefore, which rule a particular court is likely to use. The subjective test (*United States v. Russell* and *Hampton v. United States*) focuses on a defendant's predisposition, and holds that entrapment exists only if the accused had no predisposition to commit the offense but did so because of inducement by the government agent. If the accused was predisposed to commit the offense charged, there is no entrapment because the accused is an "unwary criminal," and not an "unwary innocent." Under this test, a known prostitute cannot successfully claim entrapment, regardless of police conduct, because she or he had the predisposition. In contrast, the objective test (established in *Sorrells v. United States*) focuses on the conduct of the government agent by asking whether the activities of the government agent were so instigative that they could have induced an innocent person to commit the crime. Under this test, the accused's past conduct is irrelevant; what is relevant is the conduct of the government agent. Under the objective test, a known prostitute can successfully claim entrapment if the conduct of the government agent induced him or her to commit the offense charged.

The entrapment test that courts use is typically determined by the criminal code. The two tests are not mutually exclusive. Some jurisdictions combine an element of both, as in laws providing that the predisposition of a defendant defeats an entrapment defense, except in cases in which the conduct of the government agent is outrageous—in which case even a predisposed defendant can successfully claim the entrapment defense.

The leading cases briefed in this chapter on entrapment are *Sherman v. United States*, *United States v. Russell*, and *Jacobson v. United States*.

SHERMAN V. UNITED STATES
356 U.S. 369 (1958)

CAPSULE: Entrapment occurs when the government induces a person to commit a crime that he or she would not have otherwise committed or had no predisposition to commit.

FACTS: A government informant met Sherman in a doctor's office, where both were being treated for drug addiction. On several subsequent chance meetings, the informant asked Sherman if he knew a source of drugs. Sherman avoided the issue, but after several requests, Sherman offered to supply narcotics. Several times thereafter, Sherman supplied the informant with drugs for cost plus expenses. The informant notified FBI agents of the transactions and set up narcotics deals on three more occasions, which agents observed.

ISSUE: Were the actions of the government informant such that they induced Sherman to commit crimes that he would have otherwise been unwilling to commit, resulting in entrapment? YES.

SUPREME COURT DECISION: There is entrapment when the government induces an individual to commit a crime that he or she otherwise would not have attempted.

REASON: "The case at bar illustrates an evil which the defense of entrapment is designed to overcome. The government informer entices someone attempting to avoid narcotics not only into carrying out an illegal sale but also returning to the habit of use. Selecting the proper time, the informer then tells the government agent. The setup is accepted by the agent without even a question as to the manner in which the informer encountered the seller. Thus the government plays on the weakness of an innocent party and beguiles him into committing crimes which he otherwise would not have attempted. Law enforcement does not require methods such as this."

CASE SIGNIFICANCE: This case sets a current test used by many courts for entrapment: that there is entrapment if the government induces an individual to commit a crime that he or she otherwise would not have committed. In this case, the informant asked Sherman if he knew a drug supplier and then whether Sherman himself would provide the narcotics. Sherman first avoided the issue, but then gave in after repeated requests. The Court reasoned in this case that Sherman would not have committed the crime had the government officials not, effectively, forced him to do so. This case also held that the accused bears the burden of proving entrapment and that the factual issue of whether the defendant was actually entrapped is a question of fact, not a question of law, and is, therefore, for the jury to decide.

UNITED STATES V. RUSSELL
411 U.S. 423 (1973)

CAPSULE: Supplying one of the necessary ingredients for the manufacture of a prohibited drug does not constitute entrapment.

FACTS: Russell and two others were indicted and convicted of illegally manufacturing and selling methamphetamine. Shapiro, a federal law enforcement agent, met earlier with the three and told them that he represented a group desiring to obtain control of the manufacture and distribution of the drug. Shapiro offered to supply them with a chemical required to manufacture methamphetamine. In return, Shapiro wanted to receive one-half of the speed made with the ingredient supplied. Shapiro later received his share and also bought some of the remainder from Russell. There was testimony at the trial that the chemical was generally difficult to obtain because, at the request of the government, some chemical supply firms had voluntarily ceased selling the chemical. On appeal, Russell conceded that the jury could have found him predisposed to commit the offenses with which he was charged, but argued that he was entrapped as a matter of law.

ISSUE: Did the act by the undercover government agent of providing an essential chemical for the manufacture of a prohibited drug constitute entrapment? NO.

SUPREME COURT DECISION: The act by a government agent of supplying one of the necessary ingredients for the manufacture of a prohibited drug does not constitute entrapment. That conduct stops short of being a violation of "fundamental fairness" that would shock "the universal sense of justice." This is a case of an accused who was an "unwary criminal" and not an "unwary innocent."

REASON: "While we may some day be presented with a situation in which the conduct of law enforcement agents is so outrageous that due process principles would absolutely bar the government from invoking judicial processes to obtain conviction, the instant case is distinctly not of that breed. Shapiro's contribution of propanone to the criminal enterprise already in process was scarcely objectionable. The chemical is, by itself, a harmless substance and its possession is legal. While the government may have been seeking to make it more difficult for drug rings, such as that of which respondent was a member, to obtain the chemical, the evidence described above shows that it nonetheless was obtainable. The law enforcement conduct here stops short of violating that 'fundamental fairness, shocking to the universal sense of justice,' mandated by the due process clause of the Fifth Amendment."

CASE SIGNIFICANCE: The *Russell* case focused on the predisposition of the defendant to commit the alleged act, rather than on an analysis of the conduct of the government. Under this view, the entrapment defense applies only if the accused has no predisposition to commit the crime, but does so because of inducement by a government agent. The Court minimized the importance of Shapiro's supplying the accused with an essential ingredient for the manufacture of the prohibited drug, concluding that the chemical was a harmless substance and its possession was legal. Besides, although it was difficult to obtain the chemical, the evidence showed that it was, nonetheless, obtainable; therefore, the conduct of the government agent stopped short of violating the "fundamental fairness" mandated by the due process clause of the Fifth Amendment. In using this language, the Court implies that, even under this "subjective" test, there may be conduct by the government that may entrap a person who is predisposed to commit a crime. The Court, however, did not give any example of that type of prohibited government conduct.

HAMPTON V. UNITED STATES
425 U.S. 484 (1976)

CAPSULE: There is no entrapment when a government informant supplies heroin to a suspect who is predisposed to commit the crime.

FACTS: Hampton was convicted of two counts of distributing heroin in violation of federal law. The conviction arose from two sales of heroin by Hampton to agents of the Drug Enforcement Administration (DEA). The sales were arranged by an acquaintance of Hampton, who was also a DEA informant. Hampton claimed entrapment, stating that he neither intended to sell, nor knew that he was dealing in, heroin and that all of the drugs he sold were supplied by the acquaintance who was also a government informant.

ISSUE: Is there entrapment when a government informant supplies heroin to a suspect, who then sells it to government agents? NO.

SUPREME COURT DECISION: There was no entrapment here because the government informant supplied heroin to a suspect who had the predisposition to commit the crime. The entrapment defense applies only if the accused had no predisposition to commit the crime but was induced to do so by government agents who implanted that disposition in the accused's mind for the purposes of prosecution.

REASON: "Here ... the police, the government informant, and the defendant acted in concert with one another. If the result of the governmental activity is to 'implant in the mind of an innocent person the disposition to commit the alleged offense and induce its commission,' the defendant is protected by the defense of entrapment. If the police engaged in illegal activity in concert with a defendant beyond the scope of their duties, the remedy lies not in freeing the equally culpable defendant but in prosecuting the police under the applicable provisions of state or federal law."

CASE SIGNIFICANCE: To civil libertarians, this decision is shocking, that there is no entrapment even when a government informant supplies an illegal substance to an accused who then sells it to government agents. This case expanded the ruling in *United States v. Russell.* In the *Russell* case, the government informant provided the defendant with a difficult-to-obtain but legal item. In this case, however, the item provided was heroin, an illegal drug.

There are two views on the entrapment defense. The *Hampton* case reiterates the subjective view, which focuses on the conduct of the defendant, rather than on the conduct of the government agents. Under this test, if the defendant is predisposed to commit the crime, there is no entrapment, regardless of the conduct of the government agents. Using this test, there was no entrapment in this case although the conduct of the government informant in providing the accused with heroin was extreme. In contrast, the objective view rejects the predisposition test and focuses solely on the conduct of the government. If the conduct of the government is outrageous, the accused is entitled to the entrapment defense even if he or she is predisposed to commit the crime. Under this view, Hampton could have successfully claimed entrapment because the conduct of the government was outrageous. The Court, however, rejected this view (as it did in the *Russell* case) and took into account Hampton's predisposition.

JACOBSON V. UNITED STATES
503 U.S. 540 (1992)

CAPSULE: Government entrapment exists if government agents originate a criminal design, implant in an innocent person's mind the disposition to commit a criminal act, and then induce the commission of the crime so that the government can prosecute.

FACTS: In 1984, Jacobson ordered two magazines from an adult bookstore that contained photographs of nude preteen and teenage boys. The boys in the magazines were not engaged in sexual activity, and Jacobson's purchase was not illegal at that time. Subsequently, the Child Protection Act of 1984 was passed, which criminalized the receipt through the mail of a "visual depiction [that] involves the use of a minor engaging in sexually explicit conduct." In 1985, the month that the law became effective, a postal inspector found Jacobson's name on a mailing list from the bookstore and sent him a letter and application for membership from a fictitious organization espousing the rights of people to "read what we desire ... discuss similar interests with those who share our philosophy, and ... to seek pleasure without restrictions being placed on us by outdated puritan morality." Jacobson enrolled in the organization and returned a questionnaire, responding in part that he "enjoyed" preteen sexual materials but that he was opposed to pedophilia. Over the next 26 months, different government agencies re-contacted Jacobson through five fictitious organizations and a bogus pen pal (a postal inspector). In one of these contacts, the Customs Service sent Jacobson a brochure advertising photographs of young boys engaging in sex. Jacobson placed an order through this organization, but the order was never filled. In May of 1987, the Postal Service sent Jacobson a brochure from a fictitious Canadian company with the opportunity to order a catalogue of pornographic materials. Jacobson responded to the brochure and a catalogue was sent. From the catalogue, Jacobson ordered the magazine *Boys Who Love Boys*. The magazine was delivered and Jacobson was arrested. In Jacobson's home, government agents found only the two original magazines and the materials sent from the various fictitious organizations. Jacobson was convicted of receiving child pornography through the mail.

ISSUE: Did the government operations, lasting over two years, in which a person was repeatedly contacted in relation to criminal activities, offer enough inducement to cause the "unwary innocent" to commit a crime, such that it constituted entrapment? YES.

SUPREME COURT DECISION: "In their zeal to enforce the law, ... Government agents may not originate a criminal design, implant in an innocent person's mind the disposition to commit a criminal act, and then induce commission of the crime so that the government may prosecute."

REASON: "Had the agents in this case simply offered petitioner the opportunity to order child pornography through the mails, and the petitioner—who must be presumed to know the law—had promptly availed himself of the criminal opportunity, it is unlikely that his entrapment defense would have warranted a jury instruction. But this was not what happened here. By the time petitioner finally placed his order, he had already been the target of 26 months of repeated mailings and communications from Government agents and fictitious organizations. Therefore, although he had become predisposed to break the law by May 1987, it is our view that the Government did not prove that this predisposition was independent and not the product of the attention that the Government had directed at the petitioner since January 1985." (Citations omitted.)

CASE SIGNIFICANCE: The importance of this case to law enforcement lies in the Court's view of the concept of entrapment. The Court reversed the defendant's conviction in this case on the grounds that the "prosecution failed, as a matter of law, to adduce evidence to support the jury verdict that Jacobson was predisposed, independent of the Government's acts and beyond a reasonable doubt, to violate the law by receiving child pornography through the mails." Implicit in the decision is the requirement that, in entrapment cases, the government has the burden of proving "beyond a reasonable doubt" defendant's predisposition to commit the offense independent of the government's acts.

In this case, there were repeated efforts by two government agencies, spanning a period of two and one-half years and using five fictitious organizations and a bogus pen pal, to probe into the defendant's willingness to break the law by ordering sexually explicit photographs of children through the mail. The Court concluded that this was tantamount to implanting in the defendant's mind the desire to commit a criminal act. Such presumption could have been rebutted had the government established beyond a reasonable doubt that the defendant was predisposed to commit the act, but the government failed to prove that. It must be noted, however, that there is a big difference between implanting in defendant's mind the desire to commit a criminal act and merely affording opportunities or facilities for the commission of the act. The first leads to a valid entrapment defense, the second does not.

Legal Liabilities

23

INTRODUCTION

Being sued is an occupational hazard in policing. American society is litigious, and the police are an attractive target because they wield power and are public employees. Most lawsuits against the police do not succeed, but some are high-profile cases that generate media attention and result in large damage awards being made to the plaintiffs. It does not come as a surprise, then, that there is hardly any major law enforcement agency in the United States that has not been sued.

The police may be liable under state law and under federal law. These two types of liabilities may be subclassified into three general categories: civil liabilities, criminal liabilities, and administrative liabilities. Plaintiffs usually prefer civil liability cases because they are easier to win than criminal cases, they result in a monetary award, and they do not need the intervention of the prosecutor's office to file the case.

The Supreme Court has addressed a number of issues involving police liability. The issues include who can be sued, who can be held liable and under what circumstances, for what specific acts officers may be held liable, what defenses are available in police liability cases, and what level of negligence is required for police administrators and their employers to be held liable. The cases briefed in this chapter represent the more significant cases decided by the Supreme Court on police civil liability. Among these decisions are:

1. Police officers enjoy absolute immunity from civil liability when testifying, even if the testimony is perjured.
2. Inadequate police training can lead to liability under federal law, but only if it amounts to deliberate indifference.
3. Neither the state nor state officials acting in their official capacity may be sued under federal law in state court.
4. State officials sued in their individual capacity are liable for civil rights violations.
5. A municipality may not be held liable for a sheriff's single negligent decision to hire an officer unless the hiring constitutes deliberate indifference,

interpreted to mean that what happened was the plainly obvious consequence of the decision to hire the officer.

There are no indications that the number of lawsuits against the police will abate soon. The law and case law on police liability are complex and constantly evolving. The following briefs should be considered introductory, albeit leading, cases on the subject of police liability. Many more issues on police liability have been decided by lower courts, and even more issues remain to be decided.

The leading cases briefed in this chapter on legal liabilities are *City of Canton v. Harris*, *Board of the County Commissioners of Bryan County, Oklahoma v. Brown*, and *County of Sacramento v. Lewis*.

OWEN V. CITY OF INDEPENDENCE
445 U.S. 622 (1980)

CAPSULE: A municipality may be held liable in a Section 1983 lawsuit and cannot claim the good faith defense.

FACTS: The City Council of Independence, Missouri, decided that reports of an investigation of the police department should be released to the news media and turned over to the prosecutor for presentation to the grand jury, and that the city manager take appropriate action against the persons involved in the wrongful activities. Acting on this, the city manager dismissed the chief of police. No reason was given for the dismissal. The chief of police received only a written notice stating that the dismissal was made in accordance with a specified provision of the city charter. The chief of police filed a Title 42 U.S.C. § 1983 lawsuit against the city manager and members of the city council, alleging that he was discharged without notice of reasons and without a hearing, thereby violating his constitutional rights to procedural and substantive due process.

ISSUE: Are municipalities and municipal officials entitled to the "good faith" defense if a right is violated while officials are following the provisions of a city policy or custom? NO.

SUPREME COURT DECISION: A municipality has no immunity to liability under Section 1983 flowing from violations of an individual's constitutional rights, and may not assert the "good faith" defense that is available to police officers.

REASON: "We believe that today's decision, together with prior precedents in this area, properly allocates these costs among the three principals in the scenario of the Section 1983 cause of action: the victim of the constitutional deprivation; the officer whose conduct caused the injury; and the public, as represented by the municipal entity. The innocent individual who is harmed by an abuse of governmental authority is assured that he will be compensated for his injury. The offending official, so long as he conducts himself in good faith, may go about his business secure in the knowledge that a qualified immunity will protect him from personal liability for damages that are more appropriately chargeable to the populace as a whole. And the public will be forced to bear only the costs of injury inflicted by the 'execution of a government's policy or custom, whether made by its lawmakers or by those whose edicts or acts may fairly be said to represent official policy.'"

CASE SIGNIFICANCE: The *Owen* case makes clear that the municipality may be liable if a person's constitutional right is violated (in this case the right to due process prior to dismissal) by public officials who are acting in accordance with agency policy. Because they were acting in accordance with the provisions of the city charter, the city manager and members of the city council enjoyed a "good faith" defense, but the city did not. The implication is that municipalities must make sure that their policy does not violate individual rights. The fact that something is official policy does not mean that it is automatically valid. The Court ruled that individual blameworthiness is no longer the acid test of liability, substituting in its place the principle of "equitable loss-spreading," in addition to fault, as a fact in distributing the costs of official misconduct.

BRISCOE V. LAHUE
460 U.S. 325 (1983)

CAPSULE: In a Section 1983 civil action, police officers are entitled to absolute immunity from civil liability when testifying, even if the testimony is perjured.

FACTS: Briscoe was convicted in a state court of burglary. He then filed a Section 1983 suit in the District Court alleging that LaHue, a police officer, had violated his right to due process by committing perjury in the criminal proceeding leading to his conviction.

ISSUE: May a police officer be liable in a Section 1983 case for giving perjured testimony? NO.

SUPREME COURT DECISION: Police officers enjoy absolute immunity from civil liability when testifying, even if the testimony is perjured.

REASON: "The common law provided absolute immunity from subsequent damages liability for all persons—governmental or otherwise—who are integral parts of the judicial process .... When a police officer appears as a witness, he may reasonably be viewed as acting like any witness sworn to tell the truth, in which event he can make a strong claim to witness immunity. Alternatively, he may be regarded as an official performing a critical role in the judicial process, in which even he may seek the benefit afforded to other governmental participants in the same proceeding. Nothing in Section 1983 language suggests that a police officer witness belongs in a narrow, special category lacking protection against damages suits."

CASE SIGNIFICANCE: This decision assures police officers that they cannot be held liable under Section 1983 (the usual type of civil liability cases filed against government officials) for giving false testimony against a defendant in a criminal trial. The Court gives two reasons for this absolute immunity. First, the officer is just like any other witness who is sworn to tell the truth, and therefore enjoys witness immunity. Second, the officer is a public official performing a critical role in the judicial process. The decision does not mean, however, that officers have complete freedom to tell falsehoods in court. The officer who does so may be held liable under the state penal code, usually for perjury. Note that only when testifying in court does an officer enjoy absolute immunity. In all other aspects of police work, an officer enjoys only qualified (good faith) immunity.

MALLEY V. BRIGGS
475 U.S. 335 (1986)

CAPSULE: In a Section 1983 civil action, police officers are entitled only to qualified immunity, not to absolute immunity, when acting in an objectively reasonable manner in obtaining a search warrant that is ultimately found defective.

FACTS: On the basis of two monitored telephone calls pursuant to a court-authorized wiretap, Malley prepared felony complaints charging Briggs and others with possession of marijuana. The complaints were given to a state judge, together with arrest warrants and supporting affidavits. The judge signed the warrants, and the defendants were arrested. The charges, however, were subsequently dropped when the grand jury refused to return an indictment. The defendants then brought an action under 42 U.S.C. § 1983, alleging that Malley, in applying for the arrest warrants, had violated their rights against unreasonable searches and seizures.

ISSUE: Is absolute immunity afforded a police officer in Section 1983 actions when it is alleged that the officer caused the plaintiffs to be unconstitutionally arrested by presenting a judge with a complaint and a supporting affidavit that failed to establish probable cause? NO.

SUPREME COURT DECISION: A police officer is not entitled to absolute immunity, but only qualified immunity to liability for damages in Section 1983 cases.

REASON: "Although we have previously held that police officers sued under Section 1983 for false arrest are qualifiedly immune, petitioner urges that he should be absolutely immune because his function in seeking an arrest warrant was similar to that of a complaining witness. The difficulty with this submission is that complaining witnesses were not absolutely immune at common law. In 1871, the generally accepted rule was that one who procured the issuance of an arrest warrant by submitting a complaint could be held liable if the complaint was made maliciously and without probable cause. Given malice and the lack of probable cause, the complainant enjoyed no immunity. The common law thus affords no support for the petitioner."

CASE SIGNIFICANCE: Officer Malley argued that he be given absolute immunity because his function in seeking an arrest warrant was similar to that of a complaining witness. The Court held that complaining witnesses were not absolutely immune at common law. If malice and lack of probable cause are proved, the officer enjoys no immunity at all. The Court also rejected the officer's argument that policy considerations require absolute immunity for the officer applying for a warrant, reasoning that, as the qualified immunity defense has evolved, it provides ample protection to all but the plainly incompetent or those who knowingly violate the law. The Court considered this protection sufficient because, under current standards, the officer is not liable anyway if he or she acted in an objectively reasonable manner. The *Malley* case, therefore, makes clear that, under no circumstances will the Court extend the "absolute immunity" defense (available to judges, prosecutors, and legislators) to police officers. The only exception is when an officer is testifying in a criminal trial. This means that officers enjoy only qualified immunity, but that they will not be liable if they act in an objectively reasonable manner.

CITY OF CANTON V. HARRIS
489 U.S. 378 (1989)

CAPSULE: Inadequate police training may serve as the basis for municipal liability under Section 1983, but only if it amounts to "deliberate indifference."

FACTS: Harris was arrested and taken to the police station in a patrol wagon. Upon arrival at the station, Harris was found sitting on the floor of the wagon. When asked if she needed medical help, her reply was incoherent. Harris fell twice more during her stay at the station. She was ultimately left lying on the floor to prevent her from falling again. The officers did not offer medical assistance. When she was released an hour later, she was taken by an ambulance provided by her family to a hospital where she was diagnosed as having several emotional ailments and was hospitalized. Harris filed a Section 1983 lawsuit against the city for failure to provide her with adequate medical care while in police custody.

ISSUE: Can a municipality be held liable in a Section 1983 suit for constitutional violations resulting from a failure to properly train municipal employees? YES.

SUPREME COURT DECISION: Inadequate police training may serve as the basis for municipal liability under Section 1983, but only if the failure to train amounts to deliberate indifference to the rights of persons with whom the police come into contact and the deficiency in the training program is closely related to the injury suffered. Note that the Court stated it was unlikely Harris' circumstances would meet the standard set forth in this case, but the Court remanded the case for a new trial consistent with this decision.

REASON: "Only where a failure to train reflects a 'deliberate' or 'conscious' choice by the municipality can the failure be properly thought of as actionable city 'policy.' ... [T]he focus must be on whether the program is adequate to the tasks the particular employees must perform, and if it is not, on whether such inadequate training can justifiably be said to represent 'city policy.' Moreover, the identified deficiency in the training program must be closely related to the ultimate injury. Thus, respondent still must prove that the deficiency in training actually caused the police officers' indifference to her medical needs. To adopt lesser standards of fault and causation would open municipalities to unprecedented liability under Section 1983; would result in de facto respondent superior liability, a result rejected in *Monell* [*v. New York City Department of Social Services*, 436 U.S. 658 (1978)]; would engage federal courts in an endless exercise of second-guessing municipal employee training programs, a task that they are ill-suited to undertake; and would implicate serious questions of federalism."

CASE SIGNIFICANCE: This case settled an issue that had long bothered lower courts: "can a municipality be held liable for failure to train?" The Court in this case answered "yes," but subject to strict requirements:

1. the failure to adequately train reflects a "deliberate" or "conscious" choice by the municipality
2. such inadequate training represents city policy
3. the identified deficiency in the training program must be closely related to the ultimate injury.

What this means is that not every injury caused by police officers leads to municipal liability for failure to train. It is only when the three requirements above are met that municipal liability ensues. These three requirements are usually difficult for plaintiffs in Section 1983 cases to establish, hence discouraging the "deep pockets" approach (in which the municipality is involved in the lawsuit because of a greater ability to pay than the police officer) often used in civil rights liability cases. No liability on the part of the municipality for failure to train does not mean that the officer cannot be held liable. There are instances in which an officer may be liable even if the municipality is not liable for failure to train.

WILL V. MICHIGAN DEPARTMENT OF STATE POLICE
491 U.S. 58 (1989)

CAPSULE: Neither the state nor state officials, acting in their official capacity, may be sued under Section 1983 in state court.

FACTS: Will filed a Section 1983 lawsuit alleging that he was denied a promotion, in violation of his constitutional rights, because his brother had been a student activist and the subject of a "red squad" file maintained by the department. He named as defendants the Michigan Department of State Police and the Director of the State Police in his official capacity.

ISSUE: May state officials, acting in their official capacity, be sued under Title 42 § 1983 in a state court? NO.

SUPREME COURT DECISION: Neither the state nor state officials acting in their official capacity may be sued under Section 1983 in a state court. A suit against state officials in their official capacity is a suit against the state itself and, therefore, will not succeed because a state cannot be sued under Section 1983.

REASON: "Section 1983 provides a federal forum to remedy many deprivations of civil liabilities. The Eleventh Amendment bars such suits unless the State has waived its immunity ... . Given that a principal purpose behind the enactment of Section 1983 was to provide a federal forum for civil rights claims, and that Congress did not provide such a federal forum for civil rights claims against States, we cannot accept petitioner's argument that Congress intended nevertheless to create a cause of action against States to be brought in State courts, which are precisely the courts Congress sought to allow civil rights claimants to avoid through Section 1983."

CASE SIGNIFICANCE: This decision has limited significance because it applies only to state law enforcement officials, not local police. Public officials can be sued either in their public or private capacity. If sued in their public capacity, the agency will most likely pay if the officer is held liable, as long as the officer acted within the scope of his or her authority. If sued in their private capacity, liability is personal with the officer so the agency may refuse to pay. Plaintiffs prefer to sue officials in their public (official) capacity because of the "deep pockets" theory. The *Will* case held that state officials cannot be sued under Section 1983 in their official capacity because the Eleventh Amendment exempts states from liability in such lawsuits, unless the liability is waived by the state. This decision extends state immunity to state public officials when sued in their official capacity on the grounds that such lawsuits are, in fact, lawsuits against the state. The following points need to be emphasized, however, in connection with this decision:

1. Although state officials cannot be sued in their official capacity in a Section 1983 lawsuit, they can be sued in their personal capacity, although that approach is less attractive to plaintiffs.
2. State officials can be sued in their official or personal capacity in a state tort case because the *Will* case applies only to Section 1983 cases.
3. The *Will* case applies only to state public officials. Most law enforcement officers are municipal or county officials and, therefore, may be sued in state court in either their public or private capacity under Section 1983. This is because the Eleventh Amendment grants immunity to states, not local government.
4. State officials have immunity from Section 1983 cases in federal courts. The *Will* case held they now have immunity in Section 1983 cases filed in state courts. The problem, however, is that many states have waived sovereign immunity and, therefore, expose state officials to possible liability.

HAFER V. MELO
502 U.S. 21 (1991)

CAPSULE: State officials sued in their individual capacity are liable for civil rights violations.

FACTS: Hafer was elected to the post of Auditor General of Pennsylvania. As a part of her campaign platform, she promised to fire 21 employees of the Auditor General's office who allegedly secured their jobs through payments to a former employee of the office. After Hafer took office she did fire 18 people, including Melo. Melo and the others filed suit under 42 U.S.C. § 1983, seeking monetary damages. The District Court dismissed all claims, holding that such claims were barred under *Will v. Michigan Department of State Police*, which held that state officials acting in their official capacity are outside the class of "persons" subject to Section 1983 claims. The Court of Appeals reversed the ruling of the District Court, holding that *Will* did not apply in this case because Hafer had acted under the color of law in firing the employees, but was being sued in her personal capacity.

ISSUE: Can state officials be held personally liable for damages under Title 42 U.S.C. § 1983 based on actions taken in their official capacity? YES.

SUPREME COURT DECISION: State officials sued in their individual capacities are "persons" within the meaning of Section 1983, and therefore may be held liable for civil rights violations.

REASON: "State officers sued for damages in their official capacity are not 'persons' for the purposes of the suit because they assume the identity of the government that employs them. By contrast, officers sued in their personal capacity come to court as individuals … . [T]he phrase 'acting under official capacities' is best understood as a reference to the capacity in which the state officer is sued, not the capacity in which the officer inflicts the alleged injury."

CASE SIGNIFICANCE: In an earlier case, *Will*, the Court held that neither the state nor state officials acting in their official capacities may be sued under Section 1983 because a suit against state officials in their official capacity is, in fact, a suit against the state itself. *Will*, however, only held that state officials cannot be sued in their official capacity in a Section 1983 suit filed in a state court. This case held that state officials could be sued in their personal capacity in a federal court.

In this case, the auditor general who fired the plaintiffs and was subsequently sued, maintained that she was acting within her official capacity and therefore could not be sued under Section 1983 because such action fell within the authority of her office. The Court rejected that defense, reasoning that this lawsuit was filed by plaintiffs who sought to hold the defendant liable in her personal capacity and not in her official capacity. The fact that she was acting within her official capacity when she fired the plaintiffs did not make any difference because she was not sued for having acted in that capacity but instead as an individual whose actions allegedly violated the due process rights of the plaintiffs. Thus, although public officials acting in their public capacity may be protected from lawsuits under Section 1983, they can be sued as private individuals who can be held personally responsible for what they do.

COLLINS V. CITY OF HARKER HEIGHTS
503 U.S. 115 (1992)

CAPSULE: A city's failure to warn or train its employees about known hazards in the workplace does not violate the due process clause of the Fourteenth Amendment.

FACTS: Collins, a sanitation department employee of Harker Heights, died of asphyxia after entering a manhole to unstop a sewer line. His widow brought suit against the city under 42 U.S.C. § 1983, alleging that Collins had a right under the Fourteenth Amendment due process clause to be "free from unreasonable risks of harm," and that the city had violated that right by not training its employees about the dangers of working in sewers and not providing safety equipment and training.

ISSUE: Did the city's alleged failure to warn or train its employees about known hazards in the workplace violate the due process clause of the Fourteenth Amendment? NO.

SUPREME COURT DECISION: The due process clause of the Fourteenth Amendment does not impose a federal obligation upon municipalities to provide minimum levels of safety and security in the workplace. Because the city's alleged failure to warn or train its employees about known hazards in the workplace did not violate the due process clause of the Constitution, it could not be the basis of a Section 1983 lawsuit.

REASON: "Petitioner's submission that the city violated a federal constitutional obligation to provide its employees with certain minimal levels of safety and security is unprecedented. It is quite different from the constitutional claim advanced by plaintiffs in several of our prior cases who argued that the State owes a duty to take care of those who have already been deprived of their liberty .... Neither the text nor the history of the Due Process Clause supports petitioner's claim that the governmental employer's duty to provide its employees with a safe working environment is a substantive component of the Due Process Clause."

CASE SIGNIFICANCE: One of the elements of a Section 1983 case is that there must have been a violation of a constitutional or federally protected right (the other being that the offending person must have been acting under color of law). Plaintiffs in this case alleged that failure on the part of the city to train and warn them about the dangers of the workplace constituted a violation of their right to due process and therefore could be the basis for a lawsuit against the city. The Court rejected that claim, holding that the due process clause did not impose an independent substantive duty on the city to provide certain levels of safety and security in the workplace. Moreover, the municipality's failure to train its employees or to warn them about known dangers was not so arbitrary or conscience-shocking as to be a violation of a constitutional right. Had the Court's decision been otherwise, cities and municipalities would have been open to lawsuits stemming from failure to warn or train employees about the hazards of the workplace. This would have had a significant impact on the obligation of local government to train and to warn, as in policing. Under this case, such failure to warn or train about workplace hazards could still be the basis for a lawsuit as violating due process rights, but only if such omission is "arbitrary or conscience-shocking."

BOARD OF THE COUNTY COMMISSIONERS OF BRYAN COUNTY, OKLAHOMA V. BROWN
520 U.S. 397 (1997)

CAPSULE: A county cannot be held liable under Section 1983 for a single hiring decision made by a county official.

FACTS: In the early hours of the morning, Brown and her husband approached a police checkpoint and then turned around to avoid it. Two deputies pursued the vehicle for more than four miles at speeds in excess of 100 miles per hour. When the Browns stopped, one deputy pointed his gun at the truck and ordered them to raise their hands. The other deputy, who was unarmed, went to the passenger side of the truck and ordered Brown out of the vehicle. When Brown did not respond after the second request, the deputy pulled Brown from the truck by the arm and swung her to the ground. The fall caused severe injuries to Brown's knees, possibly requiring knee replacement. Brown sued the deputy, the Sheriff, and the county for her injuries under Section 1983, claiming that the Sheriff had failed to adequately review the deputy's background because he had a history of misdemeanor offenses, including assault and battery, resisting arrest, driving while intoxicated, and public drunkenness.

ISSUE: Can a county be held liable in a Section 1983 case involving excessive use of force for a single hiring decision made by a county official? NO.

SUPREME COURT DECISION: County liability for a sheriff's decision to hire does not "depend on the mere probability that any officer inadequately screened will inflict any constitutional injury. Rather, it must depend on a finding that this officer was highly likely to inflict the particular injury suffered by the plaintiff."

REASON: "Where a claim of municipal liability rests on a single decision, not itself representing a violation of federal law and not directing such a violation, the danger that a municipality will be held liable without fault is high. Because the decision necessarily governs a single case, there can be no notice to the municipal decision maker, based on previous violations of federally protected rights, that his approach is inadequate. Nor will it be readily apparent that the municipality's action caused the injury in question because the plaintiff can point to no other incident tending to make it more likely that the plaintiff's own injury flows from the municipality's action, rather than from some other intervening cause." "Where a plaintiff presents a Section 1983 claim premised upon the inadequacy of an official's review of a prospective applicant's record, however, there is a particular danger that a municipality will be held liable for an injury not directly caused by a deliberate action attributable to the municipality itself."

CASE SIGNIFICANCE: This case relieves some pressure from counties for liability when hiring police officers. In *City of Canton v. Harris*, the Court ruled that Section 1983 liability could be incurred from a single act of an officer if there was a finding of failure to adequately train the officer. The plaintiff in this case attempted to extend that theory to a single hiring decision made by the Sheriff.

The Court ruled, however, that hiring is different from training. In training, there is "policy or custom" involved in how the municipality views effective training of officers. That view can also be traced directly to any possible constitutional injury. Hiring decisions are different. Failure to adequately screen an applicant may represent poor judgment on the part of the municipal official, but it does not rise to the level of "deliberate indifference" required for liability to arise. Municipalities and municipal officials can be assured, then, that as long as a hiring decision does not rise to the level of deliberate indifference that can be traced directly to the officer's future actions involving a constitutional violation, the municipality is free from liability.

COUNTY OF SACRAMENTO V. LEWIS
523 U.S. 833 (1998)

CAPSULE: In high-speed vehicle pursuit cases, liability in Section 1983 cases ensues only if the conduct of the officer "shocks the conscience." The lower standard of "deliberate indifference" does not apply.

FACTS: Deputy Smith and another officer responded to a disturbance call. Upon returning to their vehicles, the other officer observed a motorcycle (not related to the disturbance call) traveling at a high rate of speed. The officer attempted to stop the motorcycle by turning on his blue lights, shouting at the driver, and moving his patrol car closer to Smith's. The driver of the motorcycle did not stop, swerved between the two patrol cars and sped off. Smith then switched on his blue lights and began to pursue the motorcycle. The pursuit lasted for approximately 75 seconds as the two traveled a little more than a mile through a residential area at speeds in excess of 100 mph. The pursuit ended when the motorcycle overturned while attempting to make a sharp left turn. The driver of the motorcycle and Lewis, a passenger, were thrown from the motorcycle. Smith had been traveling at about 100 feet from the motorcycle and was unable to stop before hitting Lewis, knocking him about 70 feet down the road and inflicting massive injuries. Lewis was pronounced dead at the scene. Lewis' family filed suit under 42 U.S.C. § 1983, alleging a deprivation of Lewis' Fourteenth Amendment substantive due process right to life.

ISSUE: Does a police officer violate the Fourteenth Amendment's guarantee of substantive due process by causing death through deliberate or reckless indifference to life in a high-speed automobile chase aimed at apprehending a suspected offender? NO.

SUPREME COURT DECISION: Only "conduct that shocks the conscience" leads to liability under Section 1983 in high-speed pursuit cases. "Only a purpose to cause harm unrelated to the legitimate object of arrest will satisfy the element of arbitrary conduct shocking to the conscience, necessary for a due process violation." "[H]igh-speed chases with no intent to harm suspects physically or to worsen their legal plight do not give rise to liability under the Fourteenth Amendment, redressible by an action under Section 1983."

REASON: "The Fourth Amendment covers only 'searches and seizures,' U.S. Const., Amdt. 4, neither of which took place here. No one suggests that there was a search, and our cases foreclose finding a seizure." "Our cases dealing with abusive executive action have repeatedly emphasized that only the most egregious official conduct can be said to [rise to a Constitutionally objectionable standard]." "To this end, for half a century now we have spoken of the cognizable level of executive abuse of power as that which shocks the conscience."

CASE SIGNIFICANCE: This case fills a void by clarifying the issue of a Fourth Amendment seizure versus a Fourteenth Amendment substantive due process violation when the police pursue a person suspected of a crime. Through the years, the Court has held that deadly force issues generally involve a "seizure" of the person; thus making these kinds of cases Fourth Amendment issues (see *Tennessee v. Garner*, 471 U.S. 1 [1985] and *Brower v. County of Inyo*, 489 U.S. 593 [1989]). But what is the prevailing constitutional issue prior to the police "seizing" the person? In *California v. Hodari D.*, 499 U.S. 621 (1991), the Court ruled that a person was not "seized" unless some physical force was applied (also relying on a statement from *Brower* that there must be "a termination of freedom of movement through means intentionally applied"). There was dissension in the lower courts, however, concerning what represented "seizure" in instances of police automobile pursuits, and the proper standard to be applied for possible liability in these cases. This case settled both of those issues and set forth a flexible standard that, when a police pursuit in which no physical force or "means intentionally applied" occurs, there is not a "seizure"; and if no seizure occurs to bring the action to the level of a Fourth Amendment issue, then the Fourteenth Amendment standard applies, which is a standard of conduct shocking to the conscience. This set a high standard to be met by persons bringing Section 1983 cases based on high-speed police pursuits that result in fatal injuries. With this decision, it is not enough that the officers may have acted recklessly or with indifference for life, the plaintiffs must prove that the officer acted with "a purpose to cause harm unrelated to the legitimate object of arrest." See also, *Plumhoff v. Rickard* in Chapter 16 and *Brower v. County of Inyo* in Chapter 4 for a discussion of pursuit cases.

SAUCIER V. KATZ
533 U.S. 194 (2001)

CAPSULE: A ruling on qualified immunity is not intertwined with a ruling on the violation of a constitutional right and should be made early in the proceedings so that, if established, the cost and expense of trial are avoided.

FACTS: The Vice President was to speak at a military base. Katz was concerned that a hospital at the base would be used for conducting experiments on animals, and planned to protest the speech. Katz brought a 4 × 3 foot sign to the speech and kept it concealed under his coat because he was aware that persons had been asked to leave the base in the past for certain behaviors, such as distributing handbills. Katz sat in the front row, next to a waist-high fence that separated the seating area from the stage. As the Vice President began to speak, Katz began to unfold the banner and walked toward the fence. Two military police officers, who had been specifically warned about Katz, intercepted him and rushed him out of the area (partially dragging him). Katz argued that they then shoved him into a police van, causing him to fall. Katz was taken to a police station and then released. Katz brought suit claiming excessive use of force. The District Court held that "in the Fourth Amendment context, the qualified immunity inquiry is the same as the inquiry made on the merits," and, thus, is a decision to be made during the trial.

ISSUE: Is an officer's qualified immunity defense an issue that is to be decided separately from the issue of an actual violation of a constitutional right? YES.

SUPREME COURT DECISION: A ruling on the qualified immunity defense is not intertwined with a ruling on an actual constitutional violation (in this case the use of excessive force) and should be made early in the proceedings so that the cost and expense of trial are avoided.

REASON: "In a suit against an officer for an alleged violation of a constitutional right, the requisites of a qualified immunity defense must be considered in the proper sequence. Where the defendant seeks qualified immunity, a ruling on that issue should be made early in the proceedings so that the costs and expenses of trial are avoided where the defense is dispositive. Qualified immunity is 'an entitlement not to stand trial or to face the other burdens of litigation.' *Mitchell v. Forsyth*, 472 U.S. 511, 536 (1985). The privilege is 'an immunity from suit rather than a mere defense to liability; and like an absolute immunity, it is effectively lost if a case is erroneously permitted to go to trial.' *Ibid.* As a result, 'we repeatedly have stressed the importance of resolving immunity questions at the earliest possible stage in litigation *Hunter v. Bryant*, 502 U.S. 224, 227' (1991)."

CASE SIGNIFICANCE: This decision favors police officers who are sued in federal court under federal law (Section 1983) for alleged violations of constitutional rights. A common defense in these cases is that the officer enjoys qualified immunity and therefore cannot be held liable. Qualified immunity under federal law provides that the officer is not held liable unless he or she violated a clearly established constitutional rule of which a reasonable person would have known. The Court in this case held that, if qualified immunity is established early in the proceedings, then the case should be dismissed and the officer does not have to go through trial. The Ninth Circuit, from where this case was appealed, held that the issue of qualified immunity and the actual violation of a constitutional right were so intertwined that a dismissal of the case after a finding of qualified immunity was not proper. This would have prolonged the case. The Court disagreed, ruling that these two issues are different and that, if qualified immunity is established by the officer early, then the case should be dismissed and the trial avoided. Thus qualified immunity, once established, immunizes the officer from trial and civil liability under Section 1983. This ruling is significant because it spares officers the burden of having to go through the whole trial once qualified immunity is established early in the case, usually in a motion to dismiss.

TOWN OF CASTLE ROCK V. GONZALES
545 U.S. 748 (2005)

CAPSULE: The wrongful failure by the police to arrest a husband who violated a restraining order does not amount to a violation of a constitutional due process right under the Fourteenth Amendment and therefore does not result in civil liability under federal law (Section 1983).

FACTS: Pending a divorce, Gonzales obtained a restraining order against her estranged husband that required him to stay 100 yards away from the house where she lived with their three children, except for specified visitation. The order commanded all law enforcement officials to "use every reasonable means to enforce this restraining order," and either to arrest or to seek an arrest warrant when there was "information amounting to probable cause that the restrained person has violated or attempted to violate any provision of this order." Three weeks after the order was issued, the husband took his daughters from the front yard of their house without Gonzales' awareness or permission. When Gonzales noticed the girls were missing she called the Castle Rock Police Department, which dispatched two officers. She showed them the restraining order, but the officers stated that there was nothing they could do about the order, and that she should call the police department again if her children had not been returned by that evening. Gonzales called her husband who said the children were at an amusement park with him. Gonzales called the police department again and asked that they have someone check for her husband's truck at the amusement park, or "put out an [all points bulletin]" for him. She was again told to wait until that evening to see if the girls were returned. Gonzales called the police department again at 10:00 P.M. and was told to call back at midnight. She called at midnight from her husband's apartment and was told to wait for an officer to arrive. No officer arrived, and at 12:50 A.M. she went to the police department and filed an incident report. The officer receiving the report took no action. At 3:20 A.M., the husband went to the police station, opened fire with a pistol purchased that evening, and was killed when police shot back. Police found in the husband's truck the bodies of his three daughters, who he had previously killed. Gonzales filed a Section 1983 suit against the city for failure to protect her children and to take action on the restraining order.

ISSUE: Is a town civilly liable under federal law (Section 1983) for having a custom or policy that tolerates non-enforcement by its police department of court restraining orders? NO.

SUPREME COURT DECISION: A town cannot be held civilly liable under federal law (Section 1983) for wrongfully and intentionally having a custom or policy that tolerates non-enforcement of court restraining orders. Such practice does not amount to a violation of due process rights and therefore does not result in civil liability.

REASON: The Court in this case relied on previous Supreme Court decisions. Such cases applied the due process clause of the Fourteenth Amendment through Section 1983 to determine what interests were protected in particular cases. The Court noted that the due process clause protects "property," so Gonzales was required to have a property interest in the enforcement of the restraining order for the due process clause to be applicable. Such property interests are enforced by federal law under the due process clause, but are created by state law. The Court of Appeals found in this case that Colorado had created such a property interest for persons like Gonzales by using the language "shall arrest or ... [shall] seek a warrant for the arrest of the restrained person" on the order. The Supreme Court rejected this logic because police officers traditionally had discretion not to enforce even "mandatory enforcement" laws. If the interest is one that government officials may grant or deny at their discretion, then under previous cases it is not a property interest. The Colorado statute had not specifically given or attempted to give Gonzales a property right; but even if it had, it would have been an indirect benefit. The due process clause protects property rights in "direct benefits" such as money from Medicaid, but not an "indirect benefit" such as enforcement of standards of care in a nursing home. The Court concluded that because it had not found any property interest that could be protected by the due process clause, it did not have to evaluate whether the actions of police in this case constituted a custom or policy of the town of Castle Rock.

CASE SIGNIFICANCE: This case is significant because it further clarifies when a government agency might be held civilly liable under federal law (Section 1983). Gonzales filed this case as a violation of the due process clause. The Court ruled that, to have a claim under the due process clause, a person must have a true property interest, not simply "an abstract need or desire," and the person must have "more than a unilateral expectation of it." The Court pointed out that "the Due Process Clause does not protect everything that might be described as a benefit." In determining whether this case represented a benefit, the Court ruled that "our cases recognize that a benefit is not a protected entitlement if government officials may grant or deny it in their discretion." In examining the law in this case, the Court held that it did not appear that the state law made enforcement of court restraining orders mandatory. Because of these circumstances, Gonzales did not have a Section 1983 claim because her rights under the due process clause were not violated.

MESSERSCHMIDT V. MILLENDER
565 U.S. 535 (2012)

CAPSULE: "Where the alleged Fourth Amendment violation involves a search or seizure pursuant to a warrant, the fact that a neutral magistrate has issued a warrant is the clearest indication that the officers acted in an objectively reasonable manner."

FACTS: A woman was attacked by her boyfriend and shot at with a sawed-off shotgun as she tried to leave. The woman later met with Detective Messerschmidt to discuss the incident. She described the attack in detail, indicated that her boyfriend had ties to a gang, and that he might be staying at the home of his former foster mother, Millender. Following this conversation, Messerschmidt conducted an investigation, confirming the story told by the woman. Based on this investigation, Messerschmidt drafted an application for a warrant authorizing a search of Millender's home for all firearms and ammunition, as well as evidence indicating gang membership. The application was submitted to a magistrate, who issued a search warrant. The ensuing search uncovered a shotgun, a California Social Services letter addressed to the boyfriend, and a box of .45-caliber ammunition. The Millenders filed an action under 42 U.S.C. § 1983 against Messerschmidt and his supervisor, alleging that the officers had subjected them to an unreasonable search in violation of the Fourth Amendment. The District Court granted summary judgment to the Millenders, concluding that the firearm and gang-material aspects of the search warrant were overbroad and that the officers were not entitled to qualified immunity from damages.

ISSUE: Are officers entitled to qualified immunity where they rely on a search warrant issued by a magistrate where "[n]o reasonable officer would have presumed that such a warrant was valid"? YES

SUPREME COURT DECISION: "Whether any of these facts, standing alone or taken together, actually establish probable cause is a question we need not decide. Qualified immunity 'gives government officials breathing room to make reasonable but mistaken judgments.' [*Ashcroft v.*] *al-Kidd*, 563 U.S., at ___ (slip op., at 12). The officers' judgment that the scope of the warrant was supported by probable cause may have been mistaken, but it was not 'plainly incompetent.' *Malley* [*v. Briggs*], 475 U.S. [1986], at 341."

REASON: "The doctrine of qualified immunity protects government officials 'from liability for civil damages insofar as their conduct does not violate clearly established statutory or constitutional rights of which a reasonable person would have known.'" *Pearson v. Callahan*, 555 U.S. 223, 231 (2009). "The question in this case is not whether the magistrate erred in believing there was sufficient probable cause to support the scope of the warrant he issued. It is instead whether the magistrate so obviously erred that any reasonable officer would have recognized the error." "Even if the warrant in this case were invalid, it was not so obviously lacking in probable cause that the officers can be considered 'plainly incompetent' for concluding otherwise." "Where the alleged Fourth Amendment violation involves a search or seizure pursuant to a warrant, the fact that a neutral magistrate has issued a warrant is the clearest indication that the officers acted in an objectively reasonable manner." "Nonetheless, under our precedents, the fact that a neutral magistrate has issued a warrant authorizing the allegedly unconstitutional search or seizure does not end the inquiry into objective reasonableness. Rather, we have recognized an exception allowing suit when 'it is obvious that no reasonably competent officer would have concluded that a warrant should issue.' *Malley*, 475 U.S., at 341. The 'shield of immunity' otherwise conferred by the warrant, *id.*, at 345, will be lost, for example, where the warrant was 'based on an affidavit so lacking in indicia of probable cause as to render official belief in its existence entirely unreasonable.' [*United States v.*] *Leon*, 468 U.S., at 923." "It goes without saying that where a magistrate acts mistakenly in issuing a warrant but within the range of professional competence of a magistrate, the officer who requested the warrant cannot be held liable."

CASE SIGNIFICANCE: This case gives some clarification to *Malley v. Briggs.* The basic rule to be taken from this case is that an officer is entitled to qualified immunity for actions taken pursuant to a warrant authorized by a magistrate. According to *Malley*, however, an officer would not necessarily be entitled to qualified immunity if he or she should have known the warrant application was so flawed it was unlikely a magistrate would sign it. But, as ruled in this case, an officer does not have to second-guess the competence of a magistrate; and only the clearly flawed would be a disqualifier for immunity.

Index